CHILDREN AND FAMILIES
IN THE SOCIAL ENVIRONMENT

Second Edition

MODERN APPLICATIONS OF SOCIAL WORK

An Aldine de Gruyter Series of Texts and Monographs

SERIES EDITOR

James K. Whittaker

Ralph E. Anderson and Irl Carter, **Human Behavior in the Social Environment: A Social Systems Approach** (fourth edition)

Richard P. Barth and Marianne Berry, **Adoption and Disruption: Rates, Risks, and Responses**

Richard P. Barth, Mark Courtney, Jill Duerr Berrick, and Vicky Albert, **From Child Abuse to Permanency Planning: Child Welfare Services Pathways and Placements**

Kathleen Ell and Helen Northen, **Families and Health Care: Psychosocial Practice**

Marian Fatout, **Models for Change in Social Group Work**

Mark W. Fraser, Peter J. Pecora, and David A. Haapala, **Families in Crisis: The Impact of Intensive Family Preservation Services**

James Garbarino, **Children and Families in the Social Environment** (second edition)

James Garbarino, Patrick E. Brookhouser, Karen J. Authier, and Associates, **Special Children—Special Risks: The Maltreatment of Children with Disabilities**

James Garbarino, Cynthia J. Schellenbach, Janet Sebes, and Associates, **Troubled Youth, Troubled Families: Understanding Families At-Risk for Adolescent Maltreatment**

Roberta R. Greene, **Social Work with the Aged and Their Families**

Roberta R. Greene, **Human Behavior Theory: A Diversity Framework**

Roberta R. Greene and Paul H. Ephross, **Human Behavior Theory and Social Work Practice**

André Ivanoff, Betty J. Blythe, and Tony Tripodi, **Involuntary Clients in Social Work Practice: A Research-Based Approach**

Paul K. H. Kim (ed.), **Serving the Elderly: Skills for Practice**

Jill Kinney, David A. Haapala, and Charlotte Booth, **Keeping Families Together: The Homebuilders Model**

Robert M. Moroney, **Shared Responsibility: Families and Social Policy**

Robert M. Moroney, **Social Policy and Social Work: Critical Essays on the Welfare State**

Peter J. Pecora, Mark W. Fraser, Kristine Nelson, Jacqueline McCroskey, and William Meezan, **Evaluating Family-Based Services**

Peter J. Pecora, James K. Whittaker, Anthony N. Maluccio, Richard P. Barth, and Robert D. Plotnick, **The Child Welfare Challenge: Policy, Practice, and Research**

Norman A. Polansky, **Integrated Ego Psychology** (second edition)

John R. Shuerman, Tina L. Rzepnicki, and Julia H. Littell, **Putting Families First: An Experiment in Family Preservation**

Betsy S. Vourlekis and Roberta R. Greene (eds). **Social Work Case Management**

Heather B. Weiss and Francine H. Jacobs (eds.), **Evaluating Family Programs**

James K. Whittaker, Jill Kinney, Elizabeth M. Tracy, and Charlotte Booth (eds.), **Reaching High-Risk Families: Intensive Family Preservation in Human Services**

James K. Whittaker and Elizabeth M. Tracy, **Social Treatment, 2nd Edition: An Introduction to Interpersonal Helping in Social Work Practice**

CHILDREN AND FAMILIES IN THE SOCIAL ENVIRONMENT

Second Edition

James Garbarino

with

Robert H. Abramowitz
Joanne L. Benn
Mario Thomas Gaboury
Nancy L. Galambos
Anne C. Garbarino
Kathleen Kostelny
Florence N. Long
Margaret C. Plantz

ALDINE DE GRUYTER

New York

About the Author

James Garbarino is President, Erikson Institute for Advanced Study in Child Development, Chicago.

Before joining Erikson Institute in September, 1985, Dr. Garbarino served on the faculty of the College of Human Development at Pennsylvania State University. Previously, he was a Fellow at the Center for the Study of Youth Development, Boys Town. He earned his B.A. from St. Lawrence University in 1968, and his Ph.D. in Human Development and Family Studies from Cornell University in 1973.

ALDINE DE GRUYTER
A division of Walter de Gruyter, Inc.
200 Saw Mill River Road
Hawthorne, New York 10532

The paper used in this publication meets the minimum requirements of American National Standard for Information Sciences—Permanence of Paper Printed Library Materials, ANSI Z39.48-1984.
∞

Library of Congress Cataloging-in-Publication Data

Garbarino, James.
    Children and families in the social environment / James Garbarino
  with Robert H. Abramowitz . . . [et al.]. — 2nd ed.
      p. cm. — (Modern applications of social work)
    Includes bibliographical references and indexes.
    ISBN 0-202-36080-6 (cloth). — ISBN 0-202-36079-2 (pbk.)
    1. Children. 2. Child development. 3. Family. 4. Human ecology.
  5. Child welfare. 6. Social policy. I. Title. II. Series.
HQ767.9.G38 1992
305.23—dc20   91-44558
                                                         CIP

Manufactured in the United States of America

10 9 8 7 6 5 4 3

To our families—past, present, and future

Contents

7 Cultural Diversity and Identity Formation
James Garbarino and Kathleen Kostelny

8 The Territory of Childhood
James Garbarino, Nancy L. Galambos,
Margaret C. Plantz, and Kathleen Kostelny

9 Developmental Issues in the Human Services
      James Garbarino and Florence N. Long

10 Social Policy, Children, and Their Families
       *James Garbarino, Mario T. Gaboury and
       Margaret C. Plantz*

11 In Conclusion: The Issues is Human Quality
       James Garbarino and Anne C. Garbarino

Foreword

Garbarino and his colleagues have done the social welfare field a service. Painting in broad brushstrokes, they provide a useful and integrative schema for understanding child development in context. As with the first edition, the writing is straightforward and clear. Practice examples abound at both micro and macro levels. New material on cultural diversity, neighborhood and community factors, and public policy make this volume an even more attractive option for courses in human behavior and social environment.

In examining the "risks" and "opportunities" present in the various environments that both affect and are influenced by the developing child, the authors cause us to frame the problems that beset children— abuse and neglect, for example, and family violence—in new and different ways. This approach in turn forces us to consider novel solutions at the level of the individual family, neighborhood, and community, and ultimately at the level of society itself. For Garbarino and his colleagues, the link between the proximate and distal environments of childhood is apparent, as is the connection between case intervention and broad-scale policy reform. Such an integrative approach is particularly welcome at a time when the human services field struggles with the question of balancing social treatment and social reform.

Urie Bronfenbrenner's seminal ideas on the ecology of human development are everywhere apparent in this volume. Garbarino and his colleagues have extended and deepened our understanding of the meaning of that construct for practice. Students, instructors, and human services practitioners will find much of value here. As noted in the earlier edition, the present authors have extended to the world of human services the ecological perspective articulated by Lewin and elaborated by Bronfenbrenner. As practical theorists of their own day, Garbarino and his colleagues have succeeded in providing a benchmark volume in human behavior and social environment for all those who provide care, treatment, and nurture for children and families.

James K. Whittaker
Seattle, Washington

Preface

"No man is an island" is a message that we need to hear repeated over and over again in this individualistic culture of ours. We Americans need to understand that our successes and our failures come to us as much by the efforts of others as they do by our own actions. The people close to us on a day-to-day basis play a large role in how well we channel our impulses into constructive activity, as well as in how we define ourselves. Likewise, people we may not know or even ever see exert significant influence over our lives through their institutional power and authority. This lesson on interdependence is vital to learn if we are to meet the environmental and political challenges of the twenty-first century.

Our success as *parents* depends in large measure on the character and quality of the social environment in which we bear and raise our children. Likewise, as professional helpers we need to understand how the social environment works for children and families, and why it sometimes fails to work on their behalf. We need an appreciation for how the practitioner and the policymaker can cooperate with and enhance social support systems in the family's environment. This book sets out to relate basic knowledge about human development to the problems of social risk and opportunity in a manner that is accessible and useful to the professional helper or the student in training for a professional role.

In writing the first edition of this book, I assembled a group of talented professionals, all graduate students at The Pennsylvania State University where I served as a faculty member. Each student shared special responsibility with me for at least one chapter, and all contributed to the overall writing of the book. Thus, this book reflects a collective orientation in form and process as well as content. The book is organic to the group, and its success is a credit to its collective wisdom and knowledge. As senior member of the group, I assumed responsibility for its faults. No book can be all things and in every way complete, so I assumed responsibility for deciding what we would not say as well as much of what we would.

The Afterword was a very personal statement on my part.

Since 1985, I have been President of Erikson Institute for Advanced Study in Child Development. In this capacity I have expanded my understanding of child development in several ways that motivated and guided the preparation of this revised edition of the book.

Coupled with the new research available during the 1980s and the changes in American society in the past 10 years, this growth on my part led to the current version of our book. Some of the original authors were unavailable to participate in the second edition. Those who did participate included Joanne Benn, Mario Gaboury, Anne Garbarino, and Margaret Plantz. In addition, a colleague from Erikson Institute, Kathleen Kostelny, joined us to prepare the revised manuscript.

Our goal in the second edition has been to update each chapter—new research, historical changes, and stylistic improvements—and to include a greater emphasis on ethnic, cultural, and racial issues in a new chapter. In doing so, we have responded to suggestions made by readers and users of the book over the past decade.

We have tried to speak clearly, without jargon. As teachers all, we have sought to present ideas, principles, and human lessons first, and recite facts only second, as necessary to illustrate and validate our view of the issues. Each chapter contains research and practice capsules, questions for exploration, and annotated suggestions for further reading. We hope these will aid the student reader to make good use of the book.

They say an army travels on its stomach. It is fair to say that a book travels on its typing. We have been fortunate to be on the receiving end of some excellent help in preparing the successive drafts of this manuscript. We tip our hats to Alice Saxion and Kathie Hooven who provided the principal secretarial support for the first edition. Norma Richman served this function for the second edition.

A number of people read the first draft of the manuscript and their comments and suggestions helped us to improve it. Our thanks to Susan Bates, Laura Dittmann, Eileen Furgeson, Marian Petroski, Stephen Smith, Karen Stierman, and Mary Ellen Yonushonis.

I also offer my thanks to Jim Whittaker, who first "incited" this project and who has offered advice and counsel along the way.

James Garbarino
Chicago, Illinois

1

An Introduction

James Garbarino and Mario T. Gaboury

Beginning at the End, or Ending at the Beginning?

Where does one start in seeking an understanding of children and families in the social environment? With the processes of development that characterize the individual child as a biological organism? With the family as a social entity? With the environment as a network of social institutions and events? Where is the beginning of this chain of relationships that binds together child, parents, aunts, uncles, grandparents, friends, neighbors, communities, and professional helpers? And where is the end? It would be easy to cast aside the many interconnections and pretend that there is *just* the developing child, or *just* the family as a social unit, or *just* the community power structure, or *just* the professional delivering human services. It would be easy, but we believe it would not be enough. Rather, we seek to capture the whole tangled mass of relationships connecting child, family, and social environment.

Much of what makes us human beings is bound up in the social dimensions that shape and are shaped by our biology. As human beings we are social creatures: we need society and society needs each of us to function. The ancient Greek philosopher, Aristotle put it this way:

> He who is unable to live in society or who has no need because he is sufficient for himself, must be either a beast or a god.
>
> (*Politics*)

We are all neither beasts nor gods. Therefore, we must understand ourselves in a social context, in a society where we must sink or swim. In this book we consider how we swim, and why we sometimes sink.

An Overview of Themes

The focus of this book is the development of competence—defined as the ability to succeed in life's major challenges. What are these challenges? Although different cultures have different emphases and themes, there are some common elements. Among these are the ability to master the roles of worker, citizen, lover, and parent.

Competence is thus more than a generalized abstract quality. It is defined and measured in terms of specific situations or contexts. Intelligence—broadly defined—is certainly important. We use "intelligence" here in the sense developed by Robert Sternberg (1985). In his book *Beyond IQ* Sternberg refers to three kinds of intelligence. The first consists of the ability to process information quickly and accurately—"componential" intelligence. This is the kind of intelligence measured by most IQ tests. A person needs at least an average amount of this form of intelligence to succeed in most situations (only a few specialized settings require high levels of this sort of intelligence).

Beyond componential intelligence is creative intelligence—the ability to recombine elements in new ways to solve novel problems, to see new patterns in experience and data. Suppose you were given a stopwatch and told to figure out the height of a building? How many different strategies could you come up with? This would be one measure of creative intelligence.

A third kind of intelligence is social. How effective are you at reading people and influencing their behavior? Just as componential intelligence tends to involve analyzing and manipulating symbols (e.g., solve for X where $2X + 42 = 16X - 23$), social intelligence tends to involve analyzing and manipulating people and social situations (e.g., how can you persuade the manager of a building to show you the building's blueprints so that you can discover its height?).

Of course, intelligence, or general "adaptivity" as psychologists often call it, plays a large part in determining whether or not one will handle situations competently. But there is more (McClelland, 1973). *Communication skills* are vitally important. One must be able to communicate accurately in word, look, or gesture. One must send and receive messages accurately. *Patience* is also important. Delaying one's response to a stimulus as long as it takes to respond effectively is a skill relevant to success in many situations. Likewise, it helps to have a reservoir of self-esteem and self-confidence to go along with social and intellectual abilities. We can call this generally positive orientation toward oneself and toward one's ability to master the world—"*ego development.*"

Where does competence come from? How do people get it? By and large, they develop it in childhood, and their families and communities play a large role in the process. Furthermore, within some general guidelines that we will consider as we go along, many different strategies and tactics lead to developing competence. Many alternate social arrangements are developmentally sound; they are different but genuinely equal. Therefore, we are led to a commitment to *pluralism*, to letting families and communities utilize and pursue their different strategies and tactics for producing competent children within some common agreement on basic principles such as the need for love, affection, and acceptance. We respect diversity, but want to search for ways to ensure that where there really are general standards, all families and communities can and do meet those standards. Pluralism implies diversity within fundamental consensus or agreement on basic principles. Throughout this book we seek pluralist models of human development as a guide for professional helpers. As our society becomes more ethnically and racially diverse, this becomes ever more important.

To do justice to our central themes—the development of competence and pluralism—we need to find some way to pull apart and then reassemble the complex interconnections among child, family, and social environment. We have found an intellectual tool for accomplishing this ambitious task. It is an ecological model of human development elaborated by human developmentalist Urie Bronfenbrenner. Bronfenbrenner's approach suits us well because:

1. It focuses on the developing child in the real world.
2. It pays a lot of attention to the social environment in its many diverse forms.
3. It recognizes the essentially active role of the individual—shaping as well as being shaped by social contexts.
4. It sees the social environment as a grand human experiment, and thus invites our efforts to improve it, to make it better.

An Overview of Topics

With all this in mind, our book begins with a discussion of Bronfenbrenner's ecological model in Chapter 2. In Chapter 3 we expand upon the model to analyze the issue of social risk and opportunity for children. Chapter 4 looks at the family as the primary environment for children. In Chapters 5 and 6 we examine two fundamental topics: the child as a biological organism, and childbearing and child rearing. Chapter 7 explores the fundamental issues of identity and ethnicity. Chapter 8 addresses the child's community and neighborhood. In Chapters 9 and 10 we outline how human services and social policy work with regard to children. Chapter 11 concludes the book by setting the issues of children, family, and social environment in the broader perspective of our society's history and future. Having reached the end, let's begin again with a more detailed introduction to these chapters and then proceed to greater depth.

The Ecology of Human Development

Chapter 2 discusses several factors that influence developing individuals. Each of these can be tied to one or more situations or "contexts" within which people develop. *Contexts* of development are those regularly occurring environmental settings that can affect development by presenting risks or opportunities. Some of the relevant developmental contexts are family, friendship groups, neighborhoods, schools, communities, states, and nations. We can arrange them on a scale from smallest (microsystems) to largest (macrosystems). Events that take place at each of these contextual levels have effects on children and their families.

Subsequent chapters concentrate on the various contexts more specifically. These more detailed analyses, however, should not detract from our explicit premise that the subsystems of the overall ecological system are inextricably interrelated, one with the other. We hope to demonstrate throughout this text the *interconnectedness* of the various actors and activities in the human ecology of the child. The degree of cooperation among these interconnected systems is a vital issue for those concerned with the quality or "habitability" of the social environment.

Contexts can be positive or negative influences on development—or both at one time or another. Depending on the balance of the multiple factors (ranging from individual biological endowments to environmental forces), individuals or families are exposed to many types of developmental risk and opportunity. We introduce this notion of *sociocultural risk* and *opportunity* in Chapter 2. Later in Chapter 3, we elaborate on it in greater detail.

Sociocultural Risk and Opportunity

Chapter 3 lays out more specifically the theme of sociocultural risk and opportunity. Disruption of the sociocultural systems that surround individual development results in the disruption of people's lives. This relationship is a basic equation in human development. Chapter 3 concentrates on relating the aspects of risk and opportunity to the social dimensions of the ecological system—from micro- to macro. For example, it considers the impact of smaller households in the United States, styles of raising children, emotional climates in the family, density of communities, local employment levels, conditions in the work place, national economic and political attitudes, and war, all as important contributors to or detractors from child and family development.

We undertake a discussion of pluralism in Chapter 3. Considered as a macrosystem issue, pluralism leads us to recognize that our culture is comprised of a diversity of traditions, each with its own strengths and weaknesses relative to any particular environmental condition. Our approach recognizes and respects the diversity of Americans. Pluralism stresses the importance of fostering the strengths in a people's special heritage. A pluralistic perspective helps us avoid imposing one cultural view upon another. It promotes tolerance and enhances the creative approaches available to human services workers and researchers. However, pluralism has its own set of challenges. Most important is gaining respect for diversity culture-wide, and divesting dominant groups of some decision-making power. Many of us tend to view "different" as meaning "less good," with the underlying danger that dominant beliefs, habits, and attitudes can be foisted unjustifiably on those with fewer numbers and less political clout. A concern for "empowerment" at all levels flows naturally from our ecological perspective.

The Family as a Social System

The discussion of both risk and opportunity on the one hand and pluralism on the other leads us to the family. In Chapter 4 we move from bigger levels of analysis (cultures and societies) to inquire into a smaller level, the family—its various types and functions within our social system. Utilizing sociohistorical, cross-cultural, and family systems perspectives to understand the variety of views regarding families, we review some interesting patterns: First, we draw a distinction between the abstract notion of "family" (what families *should be* based on dominant views) versus the particular types of families that exist (the different ways families actually *are*). Crucial to an understanding of pluralism and environmental influences is appreciation of the conflicts that often result from the imposition of the abstract "ideal" family on specific "real" families.

Are families important? The simple fact that humans have created family units in various forms throughout history and across cultures suggests the answer to this question. Chapter 4 makes the case that families are the mediators between individuals and their society. The various forms families take are related to their adaptiveness to contextual constraints. As well, many changes in the sociocultural environment are responses to the collective force of families. Interplay between social systems is the key here.

We explore family systems in detail in this chapter, emphasizing models that consider relationships between families and their settings in terms of stages of family development. Families change both in size and structure. Therefore, it is inappropriate to view them as static entities. How do families work? This becomes a central question in light of the almost overwhelming and complicated array of pressures involved. Forces within families (e.g., family goals, drives, and structure), and forces outside families (e.g., links to society, community/neighborhood make-up) are topics that we must consider.

The Developing Child

In Chapter 5 we descend our analytical ladder still further to consider the developing organism—the child. Children have been viewed quite differently throughout history. Differing perceptions of children's abilities and developmental agendas have resulted in wholly different descriptions of and proscriptions for proper and healthy growth. Is the child basically innocent and to be taught, or inherently wicked and to be punished? Many questions like these pervade the history of childhood and contemporary issues such as child abuse.

At the individual level of analysis, the biological or physiological aspects of development assume a prominent position. The focus here is on the intricate interrelationship between individual make-up and environmental forces. Chapter 5 broadly reviews the stages of development from conception through prenatal–perinatal development, early, middle, and late childhood. At each level, we discuss developmental landmarks (e.g., key changes and infant reactiveness, early language development, gender identity, as well as thinking ability and adolescent maturation). We introduce questions about the relative contribution of heredity and environment, and explore the relationships among biological, psychological, and social influences.

Childbearing and Child Rearing

Individual development represents our basic unit of analysis. However, individual development is intertwined with the other, broader levels. Having suspended our primarily social concerns in Chapter 5, we return to them in Chapter 6. Chapter 6 begins our journey back up through the ecological system, with the eventual goal being a discussion of society in its largest sense. We revisit the family and investigate more specifically the most important family functions, the bearing and rearing of children.

In every culture, having a child is an important event celebrated in traditional folkways and institutionalized rituals. Also, the culturally defined correct manner of raising one's children is generally specified for parents and other caregivers. Indeed, the lack of clear messages for parents on how to rear children is one of the stressful things American parents face. In this chapter, we are primarily concerned with the dynamics of parent–child relationships. Chapter 5 supplies the child development foundation necessary for understanding parent–child interactions, and Chapter 6 relates this information about individual development to the child's first and primary context, the family.

Childbearing is the first topic we consider in this chapter. There are many influences on this miraculous event. Most births in the United States take place in a hospital, and this setting, with its related practices, exerts influence over the possibilities and probabilities of early experiences between parents and their children. However, not all hospitals are alike, and various forms of childbirth practices—some old, some new— are available. Each can have an impact on the childbearing experience. This variety of possible practices involves changes in the physical setting (e.g., home-like hospital rooms and dimly lit delivery rooms), the psychological atmosphere (e.g., supportive versus insensitive) and the range of participants at each stage (e.g., dad's presence in the delivery room). The context of this birthing experience then is linked to early parent–child interaction, and to later parent–child relationships.

The child rearing section of this chapter picks up from the point of early experience to explore changes in parent–child interaction throughout the family's life span. We discuss the emotional climate within a family, rearing styles, the roles of various participants, and other adult– child relationships in terms of their impact on the intellectual development and competencies of children and the various patterns of parent– child relationships that ensue. Again, we view the family as the basic unit of human experience embedded within a series of environmental contexts. We consider cultural and institutional constraints on the family to be quite important, and we recognize them as professional issues, for the family is the mediator of sociocultural risks and opportunities for children and parents.

Identity and Ethnicity

American society is undergoing a rebirth of ethnic consciousness. The growing demographic and political influence of "people of color" has forced this on a society reluctant to make a commitment to multi-culturism. In Chapter 7 we explore the relationships between ethnicity and personal identity. How do we interpret and approach cultural differences? What do they mean for child development?

The Territory of Childhood

Chapters 5 and 6 offer a grounding in individual and interpersonal development, and thus provide a turning point in our analysis. We turn back to the task of understanding the social environment *around* families, having examined the social environment *within* families. Chapter 8 begins this process by focusing on the neighborhood and community levels of the ecology. Here we deal with the first wave of influence outside the family. As children are developing within families so families develop within neighborhoods and communities. Various attributes of these contexts affect the quality of a neighborhood as an environment for families. How densely populated is the area? What type of context for child development results from the design, amount, and level of maintenance of local housing? How active are family-supporting networks in the neighborhoods?

American communities are not static in nature. They change, in response to their internal dynamics and in response to broader social forces. Changes have occurred in response to historical events like mass immigration and world wars. Local business and industry managers, politicians, and other "social influentials" make decisions that also result in changes. Communities respond to changing levels of ethnic influence, and many are experiencing increasing diversity and decreasing homogeneity. Communities are urban, suburban, and rural. They are old, new, and in between. Most of all, neighborhoods and communities are contexts within which families and children behave, grow, and develop. As we demonstrate, what goes on at this level of the social ecology has much to do with the positive or negative course that individual development takes.

Developmental Issues in Human Services

Human service agencies and systems form an important link between families and neighborhoods, on the one hand, and state and national agendas for service delivery, on the other. Chapter 9 deals with many issues in the delivery of human services as they relate to the themes and concerns derived from our ecological analysis of developmental risk and opportunity. We delve into several issues in an effort to suggest some alternatives to conventional service practice. What is the proper role of the human service provider? What is the correct timing for intervention? What should be the scope of intervention? Where should a family's inalienable right to privacy begin, and is this threshold always the same? How are the costs of service delivery weighed against the benefits?

A brief historical background provides a perspective for discussing the present day politics of providing human services. These political, even philosophical, trends of thought have a great impact on the sort of practices and services that society and individual professionals see as legitimate. The nature of social supports, like many notions discussed in this book, is not a uniform and unchanging entity. Indeed, changes in attitudes result in changes in practices. Should we be "hands off" regarding our families, or rush in at the earliest sign of difficulty? What are the criteria for such decisions, and who is the proper decision-maker? What are the goals of the human services?

Families have the largest share of responsibility for producing competent members of society. Services provided to children and families by the state imply society's responsibility to compensate for forces in the family or beyond the family's control that by nature are detrimental to development. The interdependence issue arises again as we note the mutual obligations of family and state to improve and maintain healthy human development. We discuss new models for facilitating healthy development. Based in notions of shared responsibility, interdependence, and the strengths of people, we recommend a mix of formal and informal support and suggest various programmatic models.

Social Policy, Children, and Their Families

Chapter 10 brings us to the point of discussing how the mechanics of human services and the conditions of risk and opportunity are rooted in social policy. Here we discuss the many problems of families and children as they relate to social policy at the broader levels of the social ecology and different institutions and agencies within it. New perspectives on contexts of development come into focus so that we include transportation authorities, big business, and government as actors in the family's life together. The decisions made in these contexts reverberate through communities, the workplace, and service agencies, eventually taking their toll on or providing support for children and their families.

After a description of the policy scene, we make some suggestions about how to influence policy makers. How does someone who has embraced an innovative approach go about encouraging its implementation? Although there is no single method to influencing policy, and, of course, nothing is guaranteed, there are some basic approaches. One is the systematic documentation of the problem. Following initial identification is the gathering of information about who is being affected, who makes the important decisions, and so on. The chapter concludes with a discussion of the most important aspect of policy intervention: personal commitment to improving the lives of children and their families.

In Conclusion: The Issue Is Human Quality

Chapter 11 seeks to place our professional concern for the social environment of children and families in its broadest cultural and historical context. Where are we going as a society? Are we heading toward economic, political, and environmental disaster? Or, are we on the verge of cultural breakthroughs that will lead to a more humane, sane, and ecologically sustainable society? Is the current scene the precursor of an ugly future in which we turn our backs on children in favor of conspicuous materialistic consumption? Or, can we see the dawn of a brighter day? We think society's treatment of families will go a long way toward answering these questions. Chapter 11 explains our thinking.

Afterword: What Does It Mean to Be Human?

Throughout this book we speak of human development. But what does it mean to be human? What is this humanness we are seeking to protect, to conserve, to nurture, and to enhance in our efforts as professionals? Although it takes us far beyond the day-to-day confines of social science and professional services, we cannot end without considering this biggest of questions. Therefore, we have included an afterword to briefly raise and discuss the question of humanness. We think the answer lies somewhere in our ability and obligation to wrestle with the issue of good and evil. We believe this discussion is a fitting conclusion to our book.

Conclusion

Having mapped out our path through the complex tangle of human development in social context we are ready to begin our journey. The first step leads to our ecological perspective on human development in Chapter 2.

2

The Ecology of Human Development

James Garbarino and Robert H. Abramowitz

> Was ist das Schwerste von allem?
> Was dir das Leichste dunket,
>   mit den Augen Zu sehen,
> Was vor den Augen dir liegt.
>   Goethe, *Xenien aus dem Nachlass #45*
> (What is the most difficult of all?
> That which seems to you the easiest,
> To see with one's eyes
> what is lying before them.)

What makes a person? This simple question lies before our eyes, but the answer is hard to see. Chapter 2 explores the ecology of human development, those forces in the person's environment that affect and influence development. This ecological approach includes not only the immediate family and home environment, but also the wider social and cultural world as it affects the child and family. Urie Bronfenbrenner's model of the human ecosystem guides our discussion, making connections between children in families and in communities and the larger society that surrounds them. The human ecosystem model is much like the study of the natural ecology, focusing on the interactions between subjects at various levels of the environment as they affect each other. It differs in its emphasis on the active role of the human being in creating and recreating its environment.

Human Beings as Social Animals

By virtue of their helplessness in the first few years of life, human beings depend on others for their very survival. The developing infant's basic reality lies in the relationship he or she has to primary care givers—particularly the mother, in most families in most societies. It is impossible for individuals to exist independently of the influence of other people. Indeed, that which makes us human is our relatedness—linguistic, intellectual, economic, political, and religious. Aristotle correctly called us social animals.

This interdependence is part of a social systems perspective. A systems approach derives from the idea that all living entities share some common features.

All systems (from the simplest bacterium to the most complex people or groups) run on *energy.* They draw energy from the environment beyond their *boundaries* (as when a person eats food) or generate it from resources they contain (as when a person burns fat stored in the body).

The nature of these boundaries determines whether a system is closed (impenetrable boundaries) or open (permeable boundaries). Of course, no system in real life is likely to be either totally closed or totally open.

Systems seek *equilibrium* as conditions inside and outside their boundaries change. They *adapt* in ways designed to restore equilibrium. And systems are connected—the action of one influences the status of others. This is called *feedback.* Put all this together and we see the human being in the midst of an ebbing and flowing network of systems.

We believe that any discussion of human development must consider the contexts or settings in which development occurs. Like the biologist who must study an animal in context by learning about the animal's habitat, sources of food, predators, and social practices, the complete study of people involves examining how people live and grow in the social wild. The term "environment" here includes everything outside the organism. The developing child's setting includes family, friends, neighborhood, and school, as well as less immediate forces such as laws, social attitudes, and institutions that directly or indirectly affect the child. The result of these forces acting on the individual is called "environmental press."

"Environmental press" is the combined influence of forces working in a setting to shape the behavior and development of people in that setting. Environmental press arises from the circumstances confronting and surrounding an individual that generate psychosocial momentum and tend to guide that individual in a particular direction. We shape our environments and then those environments shape us. Rudolph Moss (1979) called this the principle of "progressive conformity."

As we shall see, the child's environment has specific physical dimensions, but it has multiple cultural facets and multiple social levels and is a complex network of forces. Our orientation to context and the interaction between organism and environment defines an ecological perspective, and like all fields using an ecological framework, we look beyond the individual organism to the organism's environment for questions and explanations about the organism's behavior and development. We do so from a tradition exemplified by developmentalist Urie Bronfenbrenner.

Experiments by Nature and Design

Bronfenbrenner represents a compelling "fourth force" for students of human development and social service practitioners (with the first three "forces" having behaviorist, psychodynamic, and humanistic perspectives).

Until recently, it could hardly be said that the experimental ecology of human development was a systematic theoretical conception. Indeed, it did not aspire to the status of a theory as we use the term in speaking of Freud's psychoanalytic theory, Rogers' humanistic theory, Piaget's cognitive theory, or Skinner's reinforcement theory. Rather, it was an emerging critique of conventional developmental psychology; a critique of what it studied and how it studied it. It then became an effort to define a field of inquiry, and its principal use has been as a framework for organizing knowledge, generating research questions and evaluating social policy (e.g., in the areas of child maltreatment, child care, and handicapped children). We will use it in this way throughout this text.

From efforts to understand issues of social policy and professional practice arose a set of propositions about the study of human development. These propositions and the rationale for them constitute the core of Bronfenbrenner's book *The Ecology of Human Development* (1979). This view sees the process of development as one that enlarges the child's conception of the world and the child's ability to act on that world. We need not go very far in summarizing this view here (but will do so later), except to say that it incorporates different levels of related social systems around the developing child in which what happens outside the immediate experiences of a child (i.e., outside a child's "microsystem") affects what goes on inside those experiences as much as if not more than do the internal forces of the child (biology and psychology). The frustrating thing about all this (and the source of its creative analytic power) is that almost everything in the content of development is variable, almost nothing is fixed, and the answer to most questions of the sort "Does X cause Y?" is "it depends."

What contributions has this perspective on the ecology of human development made? There are at least four that deserve attention.

1. Provoking a serious response from "conventional" developmental psychology.
2. Enhancing the common ground for collaboration and dialogue between European and American students of human development.
3. Providing a vehicle for serious interchange between sociologists and developmental psychologists.
4. Developing a model for defining issues, formulating questions, and approaching social policy problems.

The first contribution has been to provoke a response from more "conventional" or "establishment" developmental psychologists. The ecological critique, although initially resisted by some, has permeated American developmental psychology since the late 1970's. Major figures feel compelled to respond to the criticism with words—if not always with deeds. And although this is only a necessary beginning to genuine reform, it is significant. For thought to proceed, an adequate conceptual language is imperative. One contribution of *The Ecology of Human Development* has been to provide such a policy- and practice-oriented conceptual language with which to analyze the validity of research and theory in developmental psychology, and thus contribute to a dialogue on the process of this "science" of ours.

A second contribution has been to increase the basis for European-American dialogue. The ecology of human development contains three themes that link it to characteristically European approaches to human development. First, it emphasizes the "critical mode." Second, it emphasizes the subjective side of experience (phenomenology), a major theme in European work. This is no coincidence, since one of the formative influences of Bronfenbrenner's work was Kurt Lewin, a German psychologist of the first order. In seeking to integrate American interest in the "objective" with European concern for the "subjective," a more valid conception of "meaning" is emerging. Third, the ecology of human development stresses the role of political economy in shaping human development. This emphasis is undoubtedly strong (many would say too strong) in European work. It naturally leads to cross-cultural research, which permits us to observe, document, and analyze the effects of macrosystem variation.

In a similar vein, the ecology of human development has contributed to—and is in part a result of—serious dialogue between sociologists and developmental psychologists. In the United States such collaboration is rare, and rarely has it been as productive as Bronfenbrenner's association with Devereux, Brim, Kohn, Clausen, and Elder, for example. Indeed, some would say the ecology of human development is the result of a deliberate sociological "conspiracy" to co-opt developmental psychology. The ecology of human development is more than sociology, however, for two reasons. First, it places the *developing* organism at center stage, as an *active* force shaping social experience. Second, it envisions experimentation at *all* levels of environmental systems and does not accept the static or deterministic thrust of sociology. The subtitle of Bronfenbrenner's book, *Experiments by Nature and Design*, is significant and leads naturally to a concern for policy.

The final area in which a significant contribution has been made is in the development of a model or "paradigm." In this, the results of a positive conspiracy with sociologists are also evident. In addition to the theoretical propositions being developed, research is being generated. Moreover, researchers are being trained to have an appreciation for the ecology of human development. And now, students can have access to texts based on the model. A full paradigm requires all these elements.

The experimental ecology of human development is *not* a theory as the term is used here. Rather, it is a point of view or definition of a field of inquiry that aids in question formulation. Its content is that of other disciplines. Indeed, each of the systems (and levels of systems) proposed in the scheme has its own attendant discipline or disciplines. Sociology, anthropology, political science, philosophy, and economics tend to deal with macrosystem issues. Biology, psychobiology, and cognitive psychology deal with the organism as a system. Social psychology seeks to explain behavior in the microsystems of groups.

Bronfenbrenner's ecology of human development is different from traditional human ecology (cf. Hawley, 1950) and ecological psychology (cf. Barker & Schoggen, 1973). One of these is a substantive discipline and the other a substantive theory. The experimental ecology of human development is not really either a discipline or a substantive theory. Its principal virtue is its potential for eclecticism. In fact, it requires such an eclecticism—or "interdisciplinary focus"—because it focuses on intersystem relationships. This characteristic is a valuable one in the present intellectual epoch when narrow specialization (and *intra*system analysis) is so prevalent, and indeed is embedded in the dominant paradigms.

The experimental ecology of human development basically takes a critical stance. It is an "imagination machine": It generates questions (good questions) in response to the statement of policy issues, substantive interpretations of research findings, sociohistorical events, and intervention strategies. This is the sense in which we join Bronfenbrenner in embracing Kurt Lewin's maxim that "There is nothing so practical as a good theory." In this way the ecology of human development is "limited" in its scope and purpose to improving the *quality* of our knowledge (something the human service field so desperately needs). If we recognize that qualitative issues outweigh quantitative ones, the significance of this becomes even more apparent. But it goes further to embrace Dearborn's Dictum: "If you want to understand something, try to change it." Bronfenbrenner has tried this with his view of child development and its relation to social policy and practice, e.g., in his activist/scholar role in the development of the National Head Start Program. We can make good use of the progress that has been made.

The Interaction between Person and Environment

Within an ecological framework, the balance of environmental forces is not the sole determinant of outcomes for an organism. The character of the individual organism also figures significantly. Those who study people from an ecological perspective view individuals and their environments as mutually shaping systems, each changing over time, each adapting in response to changes in the other. Therefore, while environmental press is the environment's contribution to individual—environment transactions, the individual brings to the situation a unique arrangement of personal resources, a particular level of development, and other attributes, including temperament. Different people thus react differently to the same environment (just as different environments react differently to the same person).

This *interaction* between individual and environment forms the basis of an ecological approach to human development. This view sees the process of development as the expansion of the child's conception of the world and the child's ability to act on that world. An individual organism and the environment engage in reciprocal interaction: each influences the other in an ever-changing interplay of biology and society—with intelligence and emotion as the mediators, and identity and competence as the outcomes.

The relationship between parent and child, for example, changes and becomes more complex over time as each continually learns from and responds to the other. Neither can be viewed as a constant causing the other to develop; rather *the relationship itself* is a cause of change in both parents and children. One of the reasons brothers and sisters often have different experiences with the same parents is that the process of rearing one child makes the parents treat a later child in a different fashion. We must add to these differences the temperament of the child and changes in the community.

A major contribution of an ecological approach is the way it focuses our attention on the relation of development to both the immediate and the more distant cultural environment. Parents raising a child respond to this cultural environment, which is a complex web of activities, beliefs, and values. The ecology of human development is really the study of how a whole society functions to raise the children who will eventually take their place within that society. Children are the bridge between past and future, and society is always in a state of "becoming." A child's emergent identity is thus a snapshot of culture and society.

All over the world societies have different value systems, norms of behavior, and forms of social relations—different cultures. Yet some basic human needs are the same everywhere: food, shelter, affection, and continuity (Mead, 1966). In our society, as in most others, development varies greatly from person to person and group to group due to factors ranging from the different ways we go about meeting individual needs to the diversity of individuals themselves. The opportunities or risks for development that each individual faces depend on a particular mental and physical make-up and the type of environment inhabited. "Ecological niche" is the joining of both.

By "opportunities for development" we mean a person–environment relation in which the developing child is offered material, emotional, and social encouragement compatible with the needs and capacities of the child at a given time. The best fit between child and environment must be worked out by experience for each child within some very broad guidelines. Chapter 3 considers some of these guidelines, including the role of ethnicity and culture.

Risks to development can come from both direct threats and the absence of opportunities for development. Besides such obvious biological risks as malnutrition or injury, there are sociocultural risks that threaten development. Sociocultural risk refers to the impoverishment in the child's world of essential experiences and relationships. Chapter 3 considers these risks in detail and tackles the complex and difficult issue of culture as a source of risk.

We know that biology and society (or nature and nurture as we often refer to these forces) can work to enhance or impede development. Nature and nurture can work together or in opposition. The extent of risk and damage, opportunity and benefit experienced by a specific individual depends on the interplay of these two forces. In extreme cases, facts of nature can all but overwhelm environmental differences. For example, severe genetic or prenatal deficits can bring about severe mental retardation; an exceptionally gifted organism can triumph over serious adversity. Likewise, environmental conditions can be so powerful as to override all but the most powerful and extreme conditions of biology.

For example, an extremely toxic environment can produce sickness and impaired development in most children who encounter it. To make the point in the extreme, consider that individual variations in lung capacity would be trivial for people left unprotected on the surface of the moon: all would perish in moments due to the inhospitable environment.

In all but the most extreme cases of either nature or nurture, optimal conditions of the one can do much to ameliorate developmental risk or negative influences arising from the other. This is one of the keys to successful human services: help where you can overcome what you cannot change.

Understanding the interaction between nature and nurture in development is no easy matter. In fact, it is so difficult that most researchers do not even try to handle both parts of the equation at once. Rather, they tend to hold one side constant while letting the other side vary—as in studying genetically identical twins (nature constant) reared apart (nurture varied) to learn about the role of nature and nurture in intelligence, or as in seeing how different newborns (nature varied) respond to the same stimulus (nurture constant) such as a smiling face. Or, they systematically vary one while letting the other vary randomly—as in presenting children of different ages in a school with three different teaching styles and studying the overall effect of each. Thus, a researcher is rarely able to really look at the interplay of nature and nurture in development.

Because of this complexity, we rarely know what the real limits, potentials, and costs are in human development. Where risk is concerned, this is extremely unfortunate because the inevitable issues of policy making and service delivery *need* a science of the possibilities, along with the costs and benefits, of alternative experiences to the individual and to the society. In computing these costs and benefits, we have much to learn from the ways in which history fits into individual and cultural development. Understanding what has come before can illuminate the questions we ask today.

In a sense, our interest in development is really an interest in biography. We must discover how the lives of individuals and the lives of societies are interdependent. Events taking place at the level of nations—the big picture—often reverberate right down into the day-to-day life of the individual family—the little picture—such as was the case in the 1990–1991 Gulf War. Military mobilization led to widespread parent–child separation. Conversely, millions of individual decisions can add up to major social changes, such as when millions of women individually decide to delay childbearing so that they can pursue careers. This interplay of biography and history is at the heart of our interest in human development. Although easy enough to convey in generalities, this ecological conception of development is very difficult to apply in practice.

In using the word "ecological" here we mean to convey an interest in the way the organism and its immediate environment (the "ecological niche") respond to each other. It means that we cannot account for or understand the intimate relationships between the child and the parents without understanding how the conditions surrounding the family affect interaction between child and parent and define each family's particular experience, with culture and ethnicity being one of the connecting bridges.

The most important thing about this ecological perspective is that it reveals connections that might otherwise go unnoticed and helps us look beyond the immediate and the obvious to see where the most significant influences lie. Trying to understand many important developmental phenomena is like a shell game. You think you are sure where the pea is, only to find it is really somewhere else. Let us consider a specific example.

The Great Depression as a Source of Risk

What was the effect of the Great Depression of the 1930s on families? This question is actually like the one that asks, "What is more important, nature or nurture?" The answer is, "it depends." Few events— even things such as economic depressions that may seem obviously and totally bad—have a guaranteed, universal, and inevitable significance. Most derive their importance from the context in which they occur. In the case of the Great Depression, we have more than just speculation on which to go.

Economic deprivation is generally recognized as one of the principal sources of sociocultural risk to children. Major analyses of family life conducted by blue-ribbon panels of experts repeatedly conclude that poverty remains a critical threat to family life. The National Academy of Sciences (1976) and the Carnegie Foundation (Keniston, 1977) both cited inadequate economic resources as the central villain in undermining the adequacy of families as contexts for child development.

Inadequate family income translates into developmental risk for children in several ways. First, it cuts the child off from many important opportunities—for high quality health care and education in many cases. Second, it reflects parental inability to succeed in the economic life of the community. This failure may derive from incompetence, lack of credentials, discrimination, an inadequate supply of adequate jobs, or some combination of all four. For whatever reason, poverty is associated with poor child outcomes across the board. Inadequate income is not the only source of troubles for families, of course.

Rich people have family troubles, too. But anyone who looks at the data on the connection between poverty and family life must agree with Sophie Tucker when she said, "I've been rich and I've been poor, and rich is better."

It is exciting, therefore, to see a good study of the consequences of economic deprivation on human development. Conducted by sociologist Glen Elder (1974; Elder & Rockwell, 1977), this study permits us to look at the impact of the Great Depression of the 1930s on the children of that era. Two longitudinal studies of child development had been launched by an earlier generation of investigators in the period of 1929–1932 in Northern California, one in Oakland, the other in Berkeley. The first dealt with children born in 1920–1921 and the second with children born in 1928–1929. Both studies included middle-class and working-class families. A wide range of information was obtained about the children and their parents. The data was collected for more than forty years. When Elder came to the project in 1962, he saw a unique opportunity to explore the impact of the Great Depression on the life course of the children in these two studies. The data permitted him to look at how the Depression affected children as a function of the following:

1. Age: The Berkeley children were just entering school at the worst of the Depression, whereas the Oakland children were teenagers by that time.
2. Social class: Both middle-class and blue-collar families were included.
3. Level of economic deprivation: Some families were relatively unaffected, whereas others lost more than 35% of their income.
4. Sex: Both males and females were included.
5. Pre-Depression quality of family life: Both strong and weak marriages had been identified.
6. Self-concept and subjective analysis of personal experience.

Would you expect that the Depression affected all these subgroups equally and in the same areas? No. Does X cause Y? It depends. Elder found a very complex pattern of results. These findings are worth noting here because they demonstrate just how complicated this matter of sociocultural risk really is and just why we need the ecological framework to make sense of the data.

In families where the husband lost his job or much of his income and the marital relationship was weak, the mother often led the way in blaming the father for "his" economic failure. When this happened, girls were encouraged by the dominant performance of their mothers and boys were disillusioned by their father's failure, with the result that girls had less personality and emotional problems than boys in this case.

Remember that in the 1930s it was customary for men to be the bread-winners. Thus, economic "failure" meant a severe loss of status.

All these factors were intensified if the sons and daughters were young children when the economic deprivation occurred, because they were then more dependent on their parents and were exposed to the new situation for a longer period of time in the home. On the other hand, a strong marital bond was strengthened under the pressures of economic loss as families banded together in crisis. The effects were greatest for middle-class families—the positive effects on teenagers from homes with strong marital bonds and the negative effects on young children from homes with a weak marital relationship. Perhaps blue-collar families are more accustomed to dealing with unemployment and income loss. Expectations shape outcomes.

These findings all refer to the long-term effects of economic deprivation. The short-term effects were somewhat different. Some of the groups showing the worst long-term prognosis showed few short-term problems, and vice versa. We should note that all these findings come from families with a pre-Depression record of relative stability—parents were married and had an adequate work history. These were not the "hard-core" unemployed, nor were they single-parent households. For them, the experience of economic deprivation was an *event*, not a permanent condition. That is a significant part of the story and cautions against simple generalizations about other groups—such as the single-parent or chronic welfare case, the "underclass" about whom much has been written in recent years.

As if all this complexity were not enough, we must remember that the Great Depression was followed by the economic "boom" of World War II and the 1950s. Military service and later job opportunities beckoned. Teenage male "victims" of that era were ready to benefit from that opportunity while the child "victims" were not.

What is more, one response to events of the Depression itself was the creation and expansion of our whole social welfare system—unemployment insurance, Social Security, and the like. Ironically, some now consider this very system to be part of today's problems, saying that it stimulates and reinforces dependency. Also, Depression families were much more likely to see their economic deprivation as being their own fault, as opposed to families today with their greater appreciation for the influence of impersonal economic forces in arbitrarily imposing financial hardship on individual workers (Terkel, 1963). All these things add to the already large number of variables that we must take into account.

To be a child during a time of economic or social disaster adds an element of potential risk that is not present in less troubled times. However, whether the impact of those troubled times damages a child depends on how those forces are experienced by the child's family and community, and how they are transmitted to the child. Elder's study makes this clear. Families who were not directly hit with income loss did not show the effects that deprived families did; some occupations were more affected than were others; some communities suffered more than others.

What is more, we must keep in mind that the individual is not a passive participant. While Elder's account stresses the average effects of economic change and development, there was, of course, substantial individual variation. Some individuals were more affected than others; some capitalized on opportunities whereas others did not. It is precisely the characteristics of each individual, in concert with social factors, that make the ecological approach a valid model of the real world. Rarely is risk absolute; nor is it static. The child's vulnerability changes. Risk can be overcome or "disarmed." This comes through in Elder's study. However, the more impoverished the child's world is, the more likely the child is to fail when hurt by social, economic, or psychological stress. Risk accumulates in the child's life like a poison.

A Model of Developmental Risk

Before we go further in examining the social origins of risk, it is important to say something more about our model of risk in the life of a child. We start with the recognition that few children escape risk completely—life is like that. Most children have to contend with risk—a parent dies, the family experiences unemployment or poverty, a parent is mentally or physically incapacitated, the child incurs a physical disability, etc.

Research by Rutter, Sameroff, and others tells us that most children can cope with one or two risk factors. It is the *accumulation* of such risks that jeopardizes development—particularly where there are no compensatory forces at work. Consider, for example, the following figure (Figure 2.1) and how it illustrates this principle (Sameroff et al., 1987). It shows that mental retardation is a likely result when the number of risk factors in the child's life exceeds two. It seems most children can cope with one or two of these factors (which in this study included maternal mental illness, early negative parent–child interaction, poverty, low maternal education, single parent households, large family size, lack of family support, parental rigidity, and maternal anxiety).

We must bear this in mind as we explore our ecological model of risk.

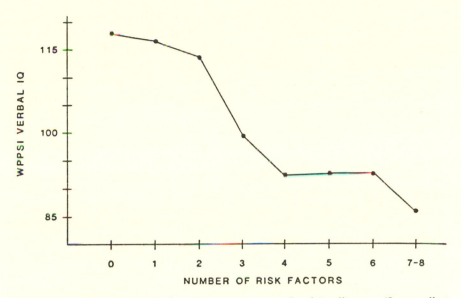

Figure 2.1. Effects of multiple risk scores on preschool intelligence (Sameroff et al., 1987)

In particular, it tells us that even when we confront a child or family facing one or two significant risks we can approach the job of helping with the hope that we can prevent the further accumulation of risk and thus the precipitation of developmental damage.

A Systems Approach to Sociocultural Risk

The framework proposed by Urie Bronfenbrenner (1979) provides a useful approach to the ecology of human development. It offers some tools to sort out the phenomena, highlight the issues, and formulate the questions we need to ask and answer about sociocultural risk. Like most frameworks, it relies on some special terms, and we need to define them before we can use them. We need them to proceed with the scientific study of how the individual develops interactively with the intermediate social environment and how aspects of the larger social context affect what goes on in the individual's immediate settings.

The child plays an active role in an ever widening world. The newborn shapes the feeding behavior of its mother but is largely confined to a crib or a lap and has limited means of communicating its needs and wants. The 10-year-old, on the other hand, influences many adults and other children located in many different settings and has many ways of communicating. The world of adolescents is still larger and more diverse, as is their ability to influence it. The child and the environment negotiate their relationship over time through a process of reciprocity— neither is constant, *each* depends on the other. One cannot reliably predict the future of one without knowing something about the other. Does economic deprivation harm development? It depends on how old one is when it hits, what sex one is, how society defines family roles, what the future brings in the way of vocational opportunity, what the quality of family life was in the past, what one's economic expectations and assumptions are, and whether one looks at it in the short or the long term. In other words, it depends.

Bronfenbrenner sees the individual's experience "as a set of nested structures, each inside the next, like a set of Russian dolls" (Bronfenbrenner, 1979, p. 22). In asking and answering questions about developmental risk and opportunity, we can and should always be ready to look at the next level "beyond" and "within" to find the questions and the answers. If we see husbands and wives in conflict over lost income, we need to look *beyond* to the economy that puts the husbands out of work and now may welcome the wives into the labor force, as well as to the culture that defines a person's personal worth in monetary terms and that blames the victims of economic dislocation for their losses. But we must also look *within* to the parent–child relationships that are affected by the changing roles and status of the parents. In addition, we must also look *across* to see how the several systems involved (family, workplace, and economy) adjust to new conditions over time. These social forces are the keys to ecological analyses, namely interlocking social systems. Bronfenbrenner (1979) offers a language to express these concerns in a systematic way that permits scientific study.

Microsystem

The level most immediate to the developing individual is the "*microsystem*," the psychological realities of the actual settings in which the individual experiences and creates day-to-day reality. For children, microsystems are the places they inhabit, the people who live there with them, and the things they do together. At first, for most children, the microsystem is quite small. It is the home, involving interaction with only one or perhaps two people at a time ("dyadic or triadic interaction") doing relatively simple activities such as feeding, bathing, and cuddling. As the child develops, complexity normally increases: the child does more, with more people, in more places. Indeed, in Bronfenbrenner's view, *the expanding capacity to do more is the very essence of development.* Love is at the heart of it. Play figures prominently in this process from the early months of life, and eventually is joined by productive labor (work). Playing, working, and loving (what Freud called the essence of normal human existence) are the principal classes of activities that characterize the child's microsystem. However, how much one does of those activities and how complex they are differs from person to person.

One of the most important aspects of the microsystem as a force in development is the existence of relationships that go beyond simple dyads (two people). For a child, to be able to observe and learn from being exposed to other dyads (such as his mother and father) enhances development. Development is enhanced when the child is able to observe differences in his or her own dyadic experience because a third party is present. Indeed, one of the most important aspects of a child's microsystem is the influence of other people—e.g., the effect of a father on a mother's relationship with their child.

So long as increased numbers in a child's microsystem mean more enduring reciprocal relationships, larger and more complex microsystems as a function of the child's age mean enhanced development (Bronfenbrenner, 1979). We measure the social riches of a child by enduring, reciprocal, multifaceted relationships that emphasize playing, working, and loving. We will return to this idea later, in Chapter 3, when we look more directly at risk and opportunity in the microsystem. First, however, we should examine the next level of systems, what Bronfenbrenner calls "mesosystems."

Mesosystems

Mesosystems are relationships *between* contexts or microsystems in which the developing person experiences reality. We measure the richness of mesosystems for the child by the number and quality of connections. Bronfenbrenner used as an example of a small mesosystem the child who goes to school on the first day unaccompanied. This means there is only a single link between home and school—the child's participation in both. Were this minimal "linkage" to persist, it would place the child at risk, particularly if there is little agreement and overlap between home and school in terms of values, experiences, objects, and behavioral style. Homes that do not value schooling, do not have formally educated people or books, do not involve reading and other basic academic skills, and do not use the formal language used for instructional purposes put the child at a disadvantage in school. In contrast, where all these links are strong, the odds favor the development of academic competence (Garbarino, 1981b). Where the actual participation of people other than the child in both settings bolsters the similarity between the two settings, academic success is still more likely. Thus, it is an important start for the parents to visit the school, and even for teachers to visit the home.

The central principle here is that the stronger and more complementary the links between settings, the more powerful the resulting mesosystem will be as an influence on the child's development. A rich range of mesosystems is both a product and a cause of development. A well-connected child's competence increases, and increases her or his ability to form further connections. A poor set of mesosystems both derives from and produces impaired development—particularly when home and school are involved. What determines the quality of the child's mesosystems? The initiatives of the child and his or her parents play a role, of course. But it is events in those systems where the child does not participate—but where things happen that have a direct bearing on the parents and other adults who do interact with the child—that play the largest role. Bronfenbrenner calls these settings "exosystems."

Exosystems

Exosystems are situations having a bearing on a child's development but in which the developing child does not actually play a direct role. The child's exosystems are those settings that have power over her or his life, yet in which the child does not participate. They include the workplace of the parents (for most children, since they are not participants there) and those centers of power (such as school boards and planning commissions) that make decisions affecting the child's day-to-day life.

In exosystem terms, risk comes about in two ways. The first is when the child's parents or other significant adults in the child's life suffer in a way that impoverishes their behavior in the child's microsystems: home, school, or peer group. For example, Melvin Kohn (1977) has found that when parents work in settings that demand conformity rather than self-direction, they reflect this orientation in their childrearing. The result is inflexible, rigid childrearing. Other examples include elements of the parent's working experience that result in an impoverishment of family life—such as long or inflexible hours, traveling, stress, or inadequate income.

The second way risk flows from the exosystem is when decisions made in those settings adversely affect the child or treat him or her unfairly. For example, when the school board suspends extracurricular programs in the child's school or the planning commission runs a highway through the child's neighborhood, they jeopardize the child's development. Thus, exosystem risk occurs when the child lacks effective advocates in decision-making bodies. Psychologist George Albee (1980) has gone so far as to identify powerlessness as *the* primary factor leading to impaired development and psychopathology. It certainly plays a large role in determining the fate of groups of children, and may even be very important when considering individual cases—such as whether or not a youth's parents have the "pull" to get him a "second chance" when he gets into trouble at school or with the police. Risk at the exosystem level is largely a political matter because "who gets what" is the basic political issue.

Macrosystems

Meso- and exosystems are set within the broad ideological and institutional patterns of a particular culture or subculture. These are the *macrosystems*. Thus, macrosystems are the "blueprints" for the ecology of human development. These blueprints reflect a people's shared assumptions about "how things should be done." To identify a macrosystem is to do more than simply name a group—Israeli, Palestinian, Swiss, American, Latino, African, Anglo, Native American—and is more like labeling a cultural system such as Judeo-Christian, Communist, or Democratic. We must compare these groups systematically on some common scales of measurement, such as "collective versus individual orientation" or "schooled versus unschooled." This analysis asks for variables rather than simple labels.

Macrosystem refers to the general organization of the world as it is *and as it might be*. The existence of historical change demonstrates that the "might be" is quite real, and occurs through evolution (many individual decisions guided by a common perception of reality) and through revolution introduced by a small cadre of decision makers. The suburbanization of America in the post-World War II era happened because of an intricate set of individual decisions, technological developments, and corporate and governmental initiatives. All together, they reshaped the experience of a great many children in families and schools (Wynne, 1977). The dramatic dismantling of the Berlin Wall in 1989 and the subsequent reunification of Germany in 1991 changed the ideological landscape for a generation of youth and their families. The eventual ramifications will be far reaching. We can assume that these changes have reverberated through Germany's schools and homes.

What are risk and opportunity when it comes to macrosystems? Risk is an ideology or cultural alignment that threatens to impoverish children's microsystems, mesosystems, and exosystem relations; opportunity promises to enrich development. It is a national economic policy that tolerates or even encourages economic dislocations and poverty for families with young children, versus one that gives special economic priority to families with young children. It is institutionalized support for high levels of community instability that disrupts neighborhood and school connections, versus action to promote stability. It is a pattern of nonsupport for parents, tolerating or even condoning intense conflicts between the role of worker and parent, versus parent-oriented policies and practices. It is a pattern of racist or sexist values that demeans some parents and thus raises the level of stress for their children, versus a pluralistic ideology that welcomes diversity and increases self-worth. In general, macrosystem risk is any social pattern or societal event that impoverishes the ability and willingness of adults to care for children and children to learn from adults, while opportunity is a social pattern or event that encourages and supports parents and children. It is an essential aspect of the human ecology.

An Ecological Map

In sum then, the ecological perspective on human development offers a kind of map for steering a course of study and intervention. With that in mind, examine the picture presented in Figure 2.2. It gives some visual approximation of Bronfenbrenner's framework.

Systems at each level have distinctive characteristics that are relevant to a child's development, and therefore different criteria are appropriate for assessing the impact of each level on the child. Furthermore, these effects may be either positive or negative—either opportunities or risks. And, while the family microsystem is usually the system of most immediate importance for a child, the overall impact of the environment emerges from the dynamic balance among all influences over time. DeLone (1979) did a good job of expressing the importance of interactions among the various environmental systems.

> To the large developmental contexts of class and caste one must add more intimate ones of which school, neighborhood, and family are clearly among the most important. For young children, especially, it is through these intimate contexts that contact with the broader dimensions of class, race, and the social and economic order is made. (deLone, 1979, pp. 158–159)

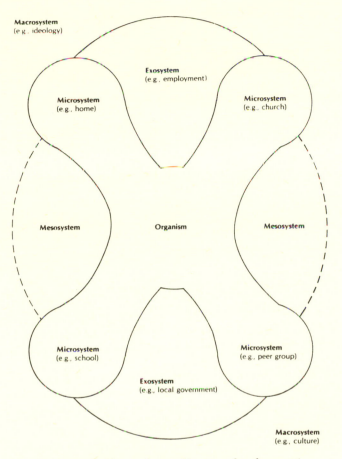

Figure 2.2. The ecology of human development.

In the following chapter, we will take a closer look at specific examples of risk and opportunity at each of the four "levels" of the child's ecology. In so doing, we will be using the diagram presented in Figure 2.2 to help train our ability to see where the sociocultural threats to children are, to come up with some ideas on how to deal with those threats once we do recognize them, and to appreciate and encourage opportunities for development. In that way, we can fill in more detail in our picture of sociocultural risk and opportunity, making it an accurate picture that is both socially and scientifically useful, one that can help the human service professional operate successfully on behalf of children and families. Table 2.1 summarizes the issues we will face.

Table 2.1. A Summary of the Ecology of Sociocultural Risk and Opportunity

Ecological Level	Definition	Examples	Issues Affecting Children
Microsystem	Situations in which the child has face-to-face contact with influential others	Family, school, peer group, church	Is the child regarded positively? Is the child accepted? Is the child reinforced for competent behavior? Is the child exposed to enough diversity in roles and relationships? Is the child given an active role in reciprocal relationships?
Mesosystem	Relationships between microsystems; the connections between situations	Home–school, home–church, school–neighborhood	Do settings respect each other? Do settings present basic consistency in values?
Exosystem	Settings in which the child does not participate but in which significant decisions are made affecting the child or adults who do interact directly with the child.	Parent's place of employment, school board, local government, parents' peer group	Are decisions made with the interests of parents and children in mind? How well do supports for families balance stresses for parents?
Macrosystem	"Blueprints" for defining and organizing the institutional life of the society	Ideology, social policy, shared assumptions about human nature, the "social contract"	Are some groups valued at the expense of others (e.g., sexism, racism)? Is there an individualistic or a collectivistic orientation? Is violence a norm?

RESEARCH CAPSULE

Rubin, L. (1976). *Worlds of pain: Life in the working-class family.* New York: Basic Books.

The ecology of human development is an approach to human life emphasizing the interplay of person and social influences. The complexity of family, social, and cultural forces affecting individuals with their own unique strengths and weaknesses is awesome; the study of lives as they are experienced is left to the artist and the most sensitive of social scientists. One such scientist is Lillian Rubin.

Worlds of Pain is a depiction of working class life. The interviews she conducted with young adult men and women center on the problems and pride in their lives, painting a portrait of a certain type of American. Their distinctiveness is palpable; working class values and attitudes make them what they are. The problems of making ends meet, raising children, coping with rigid sex roles, and striving for meaning, dignity, and control in their lives makes the experience of living in this type of life challenging. All four levels of the ecosystem can be seen as they come together to describe and delimit the voices of the subjects.

Research of this kind relies on long interviews, usually with just one person interviewed at a time. It is important to win the trust of subjects and to make them feel sufficiently at ease so that personal feelings and experiences may be shared. *Qualitative* research methods rely not on statistical analysis but on the richness and uniqueness of data gathered. Such data can lead to theories and hypotheses that may then be tested empirically. For this reason, qualitative research is important to contribute to our understanding of human development.

PRACTICE CAPSULE

The Prenatal/Early Infancy Project (PEIP) in western New York State demonstrates ways that an ecological model of human development can be translated into the design of comprehensive intervention for infants and families. The project was designed with the premise that while regular health care is a requisite for optimal fetal and infant development, more critical factors affecting early health and development are embedded in the environment in which the child is born and reared (Olds, 1986). Serving a population of mothers at risk for bearing and rearing children with developmental difficulties (e.g., the poor, adolescents, unwed mothers), the pilot project tests the effectiveness of providing various forms of support to parents in both the home and community in order to create opportunities for the healthy growth of the child.

Participants in the project were randomly assigned to one of four treatment groups. One received only transportation for healthcare, a second that plus early screening of infant development. In two other groups, the basic screening and transportation were supplemented with two years of bi-weekly visits from a nurse-home visitor in one group beginning prenatally, in the other starting after birth. The home visitation program was designed to prepare mothers for a healthy labor and delivery, to teach about infant growth and development, and to link the pregnant woman to supportive friends and family as well as health and social services in the community. It also reminds us that programs reach some families more easily than others (in this case, first time, young mothers vs. second time, older mothers).

Results from the project (Olds et al., 1986) indicate that those young, unmarried mothers involved with nurse visitors who began their relationship prenatally did better than other groups of mothers in the study. They did better in pregnancy—less prematurity, less smoking, better health, and greater participation in childbirth education programs. They also did better in the first 2 years of the child's life—less child abuse, fewer accidents, fewer premature second pregnancies, less spanking in the first year of life, and a more positive view of the child generally.

This project demonstrates the value of using a multimethod approach to early intervention. It suggests ways that a single program can be designed to meet the developmental needs of individuals and of the family as a unit.

FOR FURTHER READING

Bronfenbrenner, U. (1979). *The ecology of human development: Experiments by nature and design.* Cambridge, MA: Harvard University Press, 330 pp.

This important book lays out Bronfenbrenner's framework of the human ecosystem. Bronfenbrenner argues that child development is best studied in the context in which it occurs; that is, within the layers of the ecosystem. As well, any attempt to intervene and enhance development must take into account the ongoing relations between organisms and environment. Bronfenbrenner in this book challenges the child development field to approach development in context; the questions and probabilities he raises cannot be ignored.

Elder, G. H. (1974). *Children of the great depression.* Chicago: University of Chicago Press, 400 pp.

This book, summarized in this chapter, is a classic in the sociology of the life course. It is one of the richest and most exciting examples of longitudinal studies attempting to understand the processes of human change over time. The concepts of cohort (people born in the same period who experience historical events at the same age), and linkage (the connections between social events in the macrosystem and personality development in microsystems) guide Elder's analysis. This is not an easy book, but one in which students at every level can find something of interest.

Kohn, M. L. (1977). *Class and conformity: A study in values* (2nd ed.). Chicago: University of Chicago Press, 315 pp.

Kohn here demonstrates the ecological approach to development with an important study which investigates the links between social class and family values that affect children. Kohn's study establishes that class as an exosystem affects children by the kind of goals parents set for their children. Working class parents who are subject to discipline and submissiveness instill the same in their children; middle-class occupations require flexibility and independence which is extended to middle-class children. It is an interestingly written study with a clear explanation of research methods and analysis.

Theodorson, G. A. (1961). *Studies in human ecology.* Evanston, IL: Harper & Row, 625 pp.

This edited volume contains many important works in the tradition of human ecology. Begun in the 1920s with Park and Burgess' *Human Ecology,* it was at first an attempt to view human communities in the same light in which natural ecosystems are understood. Concepts such as competition and symbiosis were seen as *biological,* applying to human as well as plant and animal ecology.

The field evolved in the 1950s to encompass human culture as an intervening variable between the physical environment and the human community. Thus, politics, values, and traditions play a part in determining the organization of human society in a more complex way than in the natural ecosystem.

The present state of human ecology has become increasingly more sophisticated. This volume chronicles the evolving field of human ecology from its inception as it laid the groundwork for contemporary thinking on the ecology of human development.

QUESTIONS FOR THOUGHT

1. An extreme proponent of a "nature" or heredity stance on development would argue that biological factors overwhelm environmental factors in their effect on people, while an extreme "nurture" or environment position would take the opposite view. What are the implications for human services and social problems in general of an extreme "nature" or "nurture" position on human development? What are the practical benefits of a nurture vs. a nature position? What are the political implications?

2. Consider the concept of environmental press as it applies to differences between people, e.g., racial, social class, ethnic, age. Are *people* different? Is it their environment that is different? Or both? What are some examples of environmental press at all four levels of the human ecosystem? Consider your own life.

3. Elder's (1974) study of the Depression is one example of the interplay between history and personality development. What are some other historical events in your lifetime that have had major impact on the lives of children and families, and what were some of the effects?

4. Elder found that girls in the Depression were strengthened by their family's hard times. Do you think that similar patterns would be found in unemployed families today? Why?

5. Review the four levels of the human ecosystem. Thinking of a child you know, or going back to your own childhood, what are some concrete examples of how each systemic level influences the boy or girl being considered?

6. Explain how the neighborhood can be involved with all four systemic levels. Give an example illustrating each level of the ecosystem. How does taking an ecological perspective enhance our understanding of the influences of neighborhoods on children and families? What are some other examples of social institutions that exist in multiple levels? How can these institutions influence the success of human service professionals?

7. The chapter talks about the ecological perspective as an "imagination machine." How could you use it to think about some particularly interesting questions about human development? Try it on some issue that fascinates you (possible examples: teenage pregnancy, the "generation gap," impact of the 1991 Gulf War).

3

Sociocultural Risk and Opportunity

James Garbarino and Robert H. Abramowitz

Who is on my side? Who?

II Kings, 9:32

Some children have everything going for them. Others face a hostile
world alone. Under optimal conditions, the child grows up in a loving and
supportive family and a stable, supporting community. Chapter 3 enlarges
on the human ecosystem framework set out in the previous chapter by
exploring risks and opportunities that affect development at each level of
the human environment. We describe the benefits and dangers that can
come to the child from family, community, political and economic decisions, and finally from the culture as a whole. Given our professional
interests, we give special attention to recent patterns affecting children
and families.

The ecological perspective not only seeks to describe and explain the
effect of ecosystems on the individual, but also to help make the world a
better place for children and families. Therefore, it takes a stand on the
positive or negative impact of the social environment. This combination of
moral and scientific elements is a powerful tool for the social scientist,
service worker, or policymaker.

The Meaning of Risk: Case Studies

Sociocultural risk refers to the impoverishing of the child's world so
that the child lacks the basic social and psychological necessities of life.
Children who grow up wanting for food, for affection, for caring teachers, for good medical care, and for values consistent with intellectual
progress and social competence grow up less well than those children

35

who do not lack these things. Their absence places a child "at risk" for impaired development.

This simple truth is the beginning of our story: Children need loving care if they are to grow and develop normally. The sad fact is that some children are deprived of these basic necessities. They are starved physically and psychologically. Why? How do we make sense of a world that places children in jeopardy? It is not easy to understand the complicated chain of events that results in a child's basic needs not being met.

To see just how complicated this task is, let us take a look at some children at risk:

> Carlton is eighteen months old. He lives with his mother and father, both of whom are twenty years old. To put it bluntly, both parents feel Carlton was a "mistake." Both parents feel resentful over being tied down. They can't afford to get out on weekends. Carlton's father works long hours at a gas station and wants nothing more than to eat dinner and watch television when he comes home. He ignores Carlton except to yell at him. Carlton's mother feels trapped and depressed. She has no friends, and sees little prospect of making any in the apartment building where they live. She blames Carlton and his father. She belittles Carlton when he "causes trouble" and ignores him the rest of the time.

> Ella's family is large and a bit chaotic. At five, she has three sisters (two older) and two brothers (one younger). Her mother was married once before her present boyfriend, who is not Ella's father. Her mother tries her best. She works (at low paying jobs) and rents a little house in a run-down neighborhood. When her mother is at work, Ella is left at home on her own with her brothers and sisters and sometimes her mother's boyfriend. They have to stay inside the house because there are some "creepy" people on the street. Ella's family has lived in this house for seven months but still haven't really met the neighbors. Ella's mother is friendly, but she got such a cold reception when she spoke to the woman next door that she hasn't tried again since. There's a vacant house on the other side of the street that kids used to play in—breaking windows, writing on the walls, and so on. Drug dealers now use it to sell crack cocaine.

> Anita is twelve—the oldest of six kids. She hates to go to school because she doesn't fit in. She is having trouble learning to read and do arithmetic. Her favorite class is home economics, but she only has that two days a week, so she skips school as often as she can on the other days. At home she helps her mother, who came from Mexico when she was fifteen and now at twenty-nine speaks only broken English. No one in Anita's family reads except her father's sister, but even she would rather watch television. Anita's junior high school has 1500 students and she feels lost there. There are a couple of nice teachers—like the woman who teaches home economics—but they're all so busy keeping order and doing the daily assignments that there's not time for much personal attention. Anita figures she'll stop going to school altogether when she's sixteen so she can stay at home and help her mother take care of the other children. Last month her 16-year-old cousin was killed in a gang shoot out.

Three-year-old Juan's life came crashing down this past year. Things were pretty good before that. His mother stayed home to take care of him and his older brother while his father worked on the assembly line at the truck factory in town. But eleven months ago, the plant laid off 300 employees because of declining sales, and Juan's father was one of the people who got a pink slip. His father couldn't find another job, became depressed, and started drinking heavily. His mother found a job as a waitress and insisted that Juan's father take over the household and child care. He refused, saying that was her job. They argued and fought until finally he left to go live with his brother in Kansas City. Now his mother has filed for divorce. Juan has started wetting the bed at night, and he doesn't talk much. He's a sad boy.

All of these children are at risk. Their normal growth and development is threatened. Each story has its distinctive elements, however. Carlton is at risk because his parents reject him and, thereby, undermine his feelings of self-worth. Ella lives in a neighborhood that weakens her family's already marginal social existence. The unsupportive nature of her environment threatens her development. Anita needs all the help school can give her, but she gets lost in the shuffle at her large school and feels threatened by gang violence. She needs a lot of personal attention and encouragement if she is going to make it, but most likely, she will not get it. Juan's life has been terribly disrupted by an economic and social catastrophe not of his making and which even his parents do not really understand. When his parents separated, Juan was overwhelmed.

All these children are at risk, but the source of the problem is different in each case. For Carlton it lies in the poor quality of relationships within his family. He experiences rejection every day in every way. For Ella, the problem goes beyond her home to the neighborhood. Her family could make a go of it, and she would develop normally if the people nearby were a positive rather than a negative influence. Anita's problem is that she has trouble succeeding in one particular kind of situation, namely, school. She does fine at home, but her home life does little to prepare her for what is demanded of her at school. She could succeed in school if the school would encourage her, if she felt needed. But she doesn't, and that makes her give up trying. Juan's problem is related to the American economy. There is nothing really wrong with him, or even with his parents. The problem is that they live in a society undergoing economic disruption.

To deal with these children and their parents, we need to understand the sources of risk and opportunity in their social environments. We can profit from using the concepts of micro-, meso-, exo-, and macrosystems developed in Chapter 2.

Risk and Opportunity in the Microsystem

The microsystem is the immediate setting in which the child develops. It includes people, objects, and events that occur directly to and with the child. Look around you, and see where the children are. They are at home, in play groups, in the neighborhood, and in schools. Each of these "places" implies the existence of a set of enduring roles and relationships—parents and children, leaders and followers, teachers and students. The shared experiences that occur in each setting provide a record of the microsystem and offer some clues to its future, because microsystems evolve and develop much as the children themselves do from forces within and without.

The setting "school" is very different in June than it was in September for the "same" children, who, of course, are themselves not "the same" as they were at the beginning of the school year. The setting of the family, as experienced by the first-born child, is different from that experienced by subsequent children. Naturally, children themselves change and develop as do others in the setting. We must remember that the microsystem has a life of its own—it develops, too.

It is also important to remember that Bronfenbrenner's definition speaks of the microsystem as a pattern *experienced* by the developing person. The child influences and is influenced by the microsystem. By his or her participation, the child has a say in the character of the microsystem, while at the same time the setting provides the child with ongoing norms, regularities, and experiences that come to be known as "normal" to the child. One of the most important features of child development is the child's emerging account of his or her experience. These narrative accounts—what is my life about? who am I? what and who matters?—combine to form a map of the world, a cognitive map of the world from a child's perspective.

The cognitive maps we carry around in our heads are the reality we live by and act upon. Shakespeare said it well in *Hamlet* (II, ii, 259): "There is nothing good or bad, but thinking makes it so." Perhaps this idea was most clearly expressed by sociologist W. I. Thomas, who said: "If men define situations as real, they are real in their consequences" (Thomas & Thomas, 1928, p. 572). The individual child constructs the microsystem as much as he or she is shaped by it.

The child's microsystem becomes a source of developmental risk when it is socially impoverished. That is, the child's development suffers whenever the microsystem is stunted, be it because of too few participants, too little reciprocal interaction, psychologically destructive patterns of interaction, or some combination of the three. A stunted microsystem results in a warped image of the world.

A microsystem should be a gateway to the world, not a locked room. Bronfenbrenner recognizes this when he offers the following proposition about microsystems and individual development:

> The developmental status of the individual is reflected in the substantive variety and structural complexity of the . . . activities which he initiates and maintains in the absence of instigation or direction by others. (Bronfenbrenner, 1979, p. 55)

The "product" of a healthy microsystem is a child whose capacity for understanding and successfully dealing with ever wider spheres of reality increases. Such a child learns to have self-respect and self-confidence, to be socially and intellectually competent. Let us take a brief look at three types of socially impoverished microsystems—microsystems that are too small, too one-sided, and too negative—and how they work against competence and self-esteem.

Small vs. Large

The U.S. Census Bureau has predicted that almost one out of every two children born in the United States since 1980 will spend at least some part of his or her first 18 years in a single-parent household. Many children start out in one parent families; others "lose" a parent along the way. This represents the extension of a trend toward single-parent households that began after World War II, and has gained momentum ever since. Add to this the fact that the proportion of single parents who maintain separate households—rather than incorporating with another, usually related household—has doubled in recent decades (Bronfenbrenner, 1975), and you can begin to see why we worry about these households producing family microsystems that are "too small" to meet the child's developmental needs.

We must recognize that this analysis is not intended as a moral judgment or a plea for legal sanctions. It is a statement about what children and parents need to be successful. A mother can be "single" (in the sense that she is alone in her childrearing efforts) even if she is married (if her husband is absent, unsupportive, or hostile). An unmarried mother may have the full support of one or more "partners" who help her function well as a person and as a parent.

As *individuals*, single parents may be excellent caregivers. But as *microsystems*, their households may be insufficient, unless they are augmented from the outside to produce a fuller, richer range of roles, activities, and relationships for the child to *use* in his or her development. In this respect, the single-parent household is part of a larger trend toward an "emptying" of the family microsystem. Mothers are more likely to be working outside the home in the labor force (most do), kin are less likely to be involved in the child's day-to-day life because of geographic mobility and a trend toward privatism, age segregation in housing has increased (with old and young going their separate ways), and the many distractions of "modern life" pull parents away from the home and result in less time being spent in the kind of purposeful, cooperative activities that nurture child development (Garbarino, 1981c). A recent replication of a survey of youth done originally some 50 years ago found that adolescents now wish their mothers would spend more time with them, where once they seemed to take for granted that she would (Bahr, 1978). (They still wish that of their fathers, testimony to our continuing problems with the paternal role.) It is reasonable for us to worry about this "emptying" of the family microsystem because the available data suggest that it is linked to a variety of developmental difficulties (Bronfenbrenner, 1975). It is, thus, an aspect of sociocultural risk.

Conversely, microsystems made up of large numbers of relatives, neighbors, and friends provide an opportunity for rich and stimulating experiences. Children who have the benefit of growing up amidst a diverse set of relationships that span age groups, generations, and backgrounds enjoy a special social opportunity, whatever other risks may attend upon their situation. Thus, social risk and opportunity can exist side by side in the same environment. Indeed, as we noted in Chapter 2, the net result for a child's development depends in large measure on the accumulation of risk factors without compensatory forces at work.

Imbalanced vs. Balanced

One of the essential features of a healthy microsystem for the child is "reciprocity"—the give and take interaction that both respects and challenges the child, that stimulates and responds appropriately. When this essential reciprocity declines significantly, it jeopardizes the child's development. How does this happen?

It happens when the balance of power within the family microsystem breaks down. Typically, this means that the parent or parents seize complete control of the parent–child relationship and seek to dominate the child, thus thwarting his or her development. With an infant, this may mean taking a rigid stance with respect to feeding and other aspects of care giving. The "natural" and most developmentally enhancing way is for the infant to play an active role in shaping the parent's behavior, just as it is natural for the parent to influence the infant's behavior (Bell, 1968). This is a healthy family microsystem.

When the parent *refuses* to be influenced by the infant's tempo, rhythms, cycles, and spontaneous verbal and facial gestures, the essential principle of reciprocity is violated. Also dangerous is a parent who is psychologically unavailable to the child because of being incapacitated by drugs, alcohol, or psychiatric illness.

For the older child, the issue of reciprocity is found in the childrearing "style" adopted by the parent(s). Baumrind's studies (1979) of childrearing styles and their consequences for development provide an insightful look at how important the principle of reciprocity is to the family microsystem. She found that where reciprocity was maintained in day-to-day interaction—what she called an "authoritative" orientation—the child enjoys the greatest number of opportunities to develop social competence. Where the principle of reciprocity was systematically violated, the child's development suffered. An "authoritarian" style violated the principle of reciprocity by lodging excessive power in the hands of the parent and, thus, placed the child in a passive role. A "permissive" style inappropriately gave *carte blanche* to the child and his or her unformed drives and, thus, placed the parent in a passive role. Neither does justice to the child's developmental needs because both undermine the social richness of the family microsystem.

Consider an incident in which a 10-year-old child shows up at 6 o'clock when dinner was scheduled for 5 o'clock. The authoritarian parent might respond with, "You're late. Go to your room. There will be no supper for you!" When the child responds with, "But I . . . ," the parent interrupts with, "No but's. Go to your room." In contrast, the permissive parent might respond with, "Welcome home, dear, I'll cook your supper now." The authoritarian parent has not permitted the child to offer a response; the potentially useful process of bargaining and negotiating is short-circuited. The permissive parent, on the other hand, has not set the child's behavior against a standard and in that way has done him a disservice. Albeit for different reasons, the permissive style joins the authoritarian style in shutting off the developmentally enhancing process of negotiation, a quintessentially reciprocal process.

In contrast, the authoritative style emphasizes negotiation. The parent greets the child with" "It's 6 o'clock, and dinner was scheduled for 5 o'clock. You're an hour late. What's the story here?" When the child responds with, "But I was playing and lost track of time, then I had to help the other kids find the ball . . . ," the parent responds with, "I can see how you could lose track of time, but having dinner together is pretty important, and besides it makes more work when you're late. I suggest you find a way to keep track of time better, or you'll have to come straight home from school. Let's work on that. For tonight, your dinner is in the oven, I'll expect you to clean up your own dishes when you're done." When the family microsystem is working this way, the balance of power between parent and child and standards and impulses is appropriate and developmentally enhancing. When it is too one-sided, it places the child at risk.

One source of imbalance in a child's microsystem may be found in the life history of parents. Parents with a history of emotional deprivation or abuse may have great difficulty acting in the child's best interests because they may be driven by deeply rooted and unconscious forces that disrupt the needed balance within the family microsystems.

For example, Selma Fraiberg (1975) used the concept of "ghosts in the nursery" to refer to the fact that the parent's behavior may be in response to his or her own unresolved childhood issues more than a response to the child before them. These ghosts from childhood must be "exorcised" through therapy before the parent is free to act appropriately with the child and thus restore balance to the microsystem.

Negative vs. Positive

The child's experiences in the microsystem color his or her whole view of the world. Children incorporate these experiences into their emerging concepts of themselves, the world, and their place in that world. The microsystem problems of "too small" and "too one-sided" are important, but probably the single most important microsystem issue is "affective tone"—the emotional climate. A negative tone can be expressed in the full range of microsystem behaviors, including what is said (or not said), what is done (or not done). A positive climate produces a kind of "social momentum" in the child, while a negative climate produces "social deadweight." Positive climate contributes to success in the world because it gives the child a reservoir of self-confidence or "ego strength" that is an important foundation for competence (McClelland, 1975). Negative climate makes the child vulnerable to being easily discouraged by everyday problems and turns the child away from full and satisfying participation in the world.

Coopersmith (1967) demonstrated that the microsystem plays an extremely important role in determining whether children experience their world and themselves in positive or negative terms. A nurturant, involved, and actively contributing parent tends to produce high self-esteem, while a passive, neglecting, and uninvolved parent produces low self-esteem. Much as the slogan "you are what you eat" conveys the notion that we become what is offered to us, so the statement "you are what you are shown about yourself by others" conveys the notion that children construct an image of themselves based on the feedback from significant others. This view of personality is in the classic tradition of

George Herbert Mead (1934) and others who argue that by defining the role a person plays, we go far toward defining the person. To rob a child of positive self-regard, either by deliberately deprecating a child and his or her accomplishments or by conveying a sense of worthlessness by neglecting the child, is to place the child at developmental risk and may constitute psychological maltreatment (Garbarino, Guttmann, & Seeley, 1986).

To develop a positive sense of self, the child needs warm, responsive, and active "partners." The microsystem can fail the child in many ways, but the most serious threat comes from neglecting parents who starve the child of emotional sustenance. These parents are likely to exhibit what Polansky (1976) calls "the apathy–futility syndrome." The elements of this pattern are a kind of emotional deadness, an unwillingness to initiate or respond to actions of the child, a pervasive sense of ineffectiveness, and a general unresponsiveness to the initiative of the child. The developmental threat posed by adults who suffer from the apathy–futility syndrome is that they are unable or unwilling to provide the intense, responsive interaction necessary for the adequate development of competence and self-esteem in their children. Rather, these care givers project a world view of passivity, depression, and rejection. None of the active encouragement needed to develop a personal reservoir of self-esteem and positive regard exists.

Like all personality variables, the apathy–futility syndrome needs to be understood in terms of actual behaviors. Burgess and Conger (1978) provided such behavioral documentation. They observed families interacting in their homes, both in unstructured interaction and in pursuit of several tasks provided by the investigators. The principal conclusion of these studies was that parents who abuse and neglect their children characteristically ignore positive behavior in their children, have a low overall level of interaction, and emphasize negative behavior. This is certainly a "social engine" well-suited to the task of producing psychologically damaged human beings.

This psychological starvation is bad for children. It is part and parcel of a broader risk: rejection. Children who are rejected are in trouble. This is the conclusion of Ronald Rohner's wide-ranging studies of the problem. Rohner (1975) examined rejection, its antecedents and consequences, in cultures all over the world. He found that across cultures, rejection is a kind of emotional malignancy, a psychological cancer that eats away at the individual's capacity for self-esteem, social competence, and hope. Rohner concluded:

> that parental rejection in children, as well as adults who were rejected as children, leads to: hostility, aggression, passive aggression, or problems with the management of hostility and aggression; dependency; probably

emotional unresponsiveness and negative self-evaluation (negative self-esteem and negative self-adequacy); and probably, emotional instability as well as a negative world view. (Rohner, 1975, p. 168)

In support of the ecological perspective, Rohner also found that rejection increased when a child's care givers were isolated from the nurturance and feedback of interested others—kith and kin.

The environment of contemporary America contributes significantly to this problem. Drug and alcohol addiction incapacitates and isolates many family microsystems. Harsh conditions of life in many public housing projects—including the intersection of poverty and chronic violence—lead to widespread depression among mothers "left behind" to care for children (Kotlowitz, 1991). One study found that 50% of the mothers in one such setting were seriously depressed (Osofsky et al., 1991). This parallels findings from refugee camps in war zones (Garbarino, Kostelny, & Dubrow, 1991).

This is, of course, an issue that implicates the meso- and exosystems, and it is one we will consider shortly. At this point, suffice it to say that all three varieties of microsystem risk (too small, too imbalanced, and too negative) cannot be understood without looking at their antecedents and consequences in the meso-, exo-, and macrosystems. Just as parents guide and protect their children, the community is parent to all its families.

Risk and Opportunity in the Mesosystem

Mesosystems are the relationships between two or more settings in which the child is an active participant, such as school and home. The social richness of a child's mesosystem derives from the number and quality of these connections. At one extreme we have the case where the child is the only connection and the microsystems on both sides make incompatible demands; at the other, we have the case where there is total overlap between two or more settings and total agreement in their values. Mesosystem risk is defined first by the absence of connections and second by conflicts of values between one microsystem and another.

Weak vs. Strong Connections

A mesosystem is established at the point where a child first enters a new setting. This is what Bronfenbrenner calls an "ecological transition" (1979, p. 210). The two critical issues here are how this is done, and who is involved. If, for example, the ecological transition is defined as a very positive event by the child's parents, if the child is well prepared for the new setting, if the child is accompanied by the parents or other familiar persons are found there, and if the new setting receives the child with enthusiasm, the child is on his or her way to a strong and developmentally enhancing mesosystem. In such a positive case the whole (the mesosystem) will be greater than the sum of its parts (the microsystems).

Negative vs. Positive Connections

The stronger, more positive, and more diverse the links between settings, the more powerful and beneficial the resulting mesosystem will be as an influence on the child's development. A rich range of mesosystems is a developmental opportunity; a poor set of mesosystems engenders developmental risk. When the microsystems work in concert—a strong mesosystem—the child benefits. In general, when they work in isolation or in opposition, the child is at risk. Perhaps the major exception to this "rule" occurs when one microsystem is so negative or weak that the child requires compensatory treatment. Even here, however, the mesosystem issue concerns the match of microsystems from the child's perspective.

The School-Home Relationship as an Example

All this is easier to see when we look at the school–home mesosystem. For some children, this mesosystem is strongly positive: There are many connections, and there is mutual support between the two settings. The child's parents are interested and involved in the school. The home trains the child to be comfortable and competent in dealing with the school's basic activities: reading, writing, and arithmetic. The home conveys a positive regard for written materials and the use of language in formal, problem-solving, and systematic question and answer sessions, organized around the solution of problems involving objects, quantities, and relationships. Children raised with this pattern are more likely to work to the fullest of their potential at school. This pattern might be called the "academic culture" (Garbarino, 1981b), and it is composed of what J. W. Getzels (1974) calls "language codes" and "value codes."

> The language code gives the child the categories for structuring and communicating this experience. The value code tells him what in his experiences is important. For one child the codes learned in the family and those

required by the school may be continuous; for another they may be discontinuous.

Recent work on the culture of literacy (McLane & McNamee, 1990) highlights this. McLane and McNamee have explored the way children learn to value "the communication of meaning through point" as the key to literacy. Their in-depth investigations reveal that children look to parents and others in their microsystems for role models concerning literacy. Those who have those role models (models of both language codes and value codes) come to school with a framework of skills, attitudes, and motives that prime them for the academic agenda. The home–school mesosystem arises naturally for these children.

Some children come to school well equipped to be students, whereas others are aliens to the microsystem of the school and find its requirements alien to their own experience. In a world such as our own, where academic success is important, to be an alien to the academic culture is to be at developmental risk. Failure in school sets one up for a whole series of socially and personally "risky" experiences, e.g., conflicts over rules, economic penalties, threats to self-esteem, and further alienation from the mainstream of cultural and social experiences that the society has to offer. Trouble with school is a major contributor to juvenile delinquency (Gold, 1963).

Beyond this issue, there is the question of how well school and home work together to provide a healthy balance of objective and subjective responses to the child, how well they complement each other. Getzels (1974) has written persuasively that one measure of a healthy social environment is the balance between "universalism" and "particularism" in the child's experience. Universalism is based on treating everyone by the same standards, particularism looks at each person individually.

> In the particularistic relationship the important question is *who* is involved; in the universalistic relationship the important question is *what* is involved. (Getzels, 1974, p. 223)

While home and family tend to emphasize particularistic concerns, schools tend to emphasize universalistic ones. However, for a child to experience a healthy balance of particularistic and universalistic concerns, school and home must work in concert; they must complement each other. Neither should be so extreme as to place the role of the other in jeopardy. Also, some children may need the school to provide a compensatory "dose," either of particularistic or universalistic orientation, if the home is unable or unwilling to do so. This is clearly a mesosystem issue. Too much particularistic treatment will undermine the child's ability to deal with the abstract and the bureaucratic world. Too much universalistic treatment will impair the child's ability to deal with genuine intimacy. The implicit "danger" of the family is typically that it will go overboard on the particularistic end; the "danger" of the school is that it will overemphasize the universalistic. While there is no hard and fast rule to judge these matters, it does seem clear that large schools, because of their inherent tendency to overemphasize universalistic orientations, pose the danger of psychically starving students, particularly academically marginal students (Garbarino, 1980d). Like the small family, where there is a high ratio of adults to children (Lieberman, 1970), the small school provides more opportunities for the reciprocal interaction that enhances development (Barker & Gump, 1964).

The school–home mesosystem is one of the most important in the child's life. When it is strong and positive, it provides the child with the opportunity to develop intellectually and socially, to become a more complete human being. When it is weak and negative, it burdens the child with conflicts of values, style, and interest. So burdened, the child is held back from his fullest development. In recent decades, schools have become more isolated from neighborhoods and other community institutions, and the demands for academic success have increased, and the stresses on families magnified. The potential for developmental risk related to the school–home mesosystem seems to have increased (Garbarino, 1981b). However, studies of intervention programs aimed at strengthening this mesosystem have documented that this goal can be accomplished (Bronfenbrenner, 1975). Efforts to do so bring us naturally to the exosystem.

Risk and Opportunity in the Exosystem

An exosystem is a setting in which the child does not participate directly, but which has an effect on the child through the meso- or microsystems. As noted earlier, one source of exosystem risk is the world of work, such as when the child's parents are so stressed or discouraged by their jobs that they are not inclined to participate in a nurturant, responsive, and reciprocal manner in the family microsystem. A second is when people make decisions in their official capacities that adversely affect the child's day-to-day experience, as when the school board closes a small neighborhood school in favor of a large isolated school that requires a bus ride. Many of the most important exosystem risks to children fall within these two categories: a parent's diminished ability to participate productively in the child's microsystem, or people in institutional roles making decisions that adversely affect the child's microsystems.

One of the ground-breaking accomplishments of Bronfenbrenner's ecological approach is to highlight situations where the development of the child is significantly shaped by the actions of people with whom the child has no direct contact. Consider these two examples. First, because of fluctuations in the economy, a corporation board decides to shift operations from one plant to another, and hundreds of children are affected, either because their families are forced to move to a new location or because their parents lose their jobs. Second, parents who chronically abuse their children begin to attend Parents Anonymous group meetings and begin to be more nurturing to their children. Thus, discussions of exosystems involve both policy and program.

Stresses and Supports for Parents

Exosystems enhance development when they make life easier for parents, and undermine development when they make life harder for parents. Thus, exosystem opportunity lies in situations when there are forces at work outside the family on behalf of children and their parents. When child rearing "has friends in high places," the opportunities for children and parents increase.

At this point it is worth noting that the ecological perspective forces us to see risk beyond the narrow confines of individual personality and family dynamics (in the ecological approach, both are "causes" in the child's development and "reflections" of broader sociocultural causes). Recall the saying "if the only tool you have is a hammer, you tend to treat every problem as if it were a nail." If we only think about children at risk in terms of personality and interpersonal dynamics, we will never see the many other avenues of influence that might be open to us as helpers or that might be topics of study for us as scientists. Our goal here as always is to make use of the ecological perspective as an imagination machine to open our eyes to new approaches.

Anti-child vs. Pro-child Institutional Policies and Practices

Meso- and exosystem risk come together in contrasting the socially enriched with the socially impoverished neighborhood. It is fitting that we set the stage for our discussion of macrosystem risk by briefly examining how the multiple functions of neighborhoods—as microsystem, mesosystem, and exosystem—can exert a significant influence on children and their development. The neighborhood is the natural "ecological niche" of families, and it can serve as either a source of support or risk for the child.

Few concepts are so attractive and have so much feeling attached to them yet are so difficult to work with in a scientific way as is "neighborhood," and for this reason we will spend most of Chapter 8 examining its role in child development. The child acts as part of the neighborhood. Indeed, one definition of "neighborhood" is based on the walking range of a young child. It is thus a microsystem.

However, the complementarity of neighborhood and family is a mesosystem issue. The neighborhood is also a setting in which the parent participates independently of the child, and the quality of the support, encouragement, and feedback given by the neighborhood to the parent has an effect upon the child's development. The neighborhood, thus, also functions as an exosystem influence on development. A strong and healthy neighborhood enhances development by providing the kind of multiple connections and multiple situations for children that permit them to make the best use of their intellectual and social resources. Our point here is that the quality of the neighborhood depends in large part on how the community's economic and political institutions treat the neighborhood. Do they sustain it or undermine it?

All this has many important implications, two of which are worth noting here. First, it seems that many of the most important decisions people make that have an impact on child development are not *directly* about children. They are decisions about working, about residence, about budgets, about transportation, about housing, about civil liberties, about the whole range of things that shape the actual content and process of a child's microsystem. Second, these decisions reflect basic, cultural "blueprints" that describe what people understand to be "human nature" and "the way things are done," and they are heavily influenced by social history: by government stability and disruption, war and peace, and prosperity and economic collapse. This leads us to the macrosystem.

Risk and Opportunity in the Macrosystem

It should be clear by now that understanding the factors involved in producing sociocultural risk and in determining what its effects will be is no easy matter. It goes well beyond understanding individual personality, and even further than is implied in the notion of looking at the match of individual to situations. In fact, the issue of sociocultural risk goes directly to the heart of the culture and to the ideology of the society in which a given family, and therefore a child, is living.

Although we experience reality and construct it in the immediate settings in which interpersonal relationships take place (microsystems), and can extend our view to see the relevance of connections between settings (mesosystems) and the indirect influence of settings in which we do not ourselves participate (exosystems), many of the most important influences on our lives come from social, economic, and political changes that occur at the level of nations and whole societies. For example, World War I, World War II, and the Vietnam War exerted profound effects on the day-to-day lives of nearly all Americans. General George Patton reportedly said, "War dwarfs all other forms of human activity into insignificance." While we may hate that statement, it does contain much truth.

Patterns of migration brought Blacks out of the South and into the North in response to World War I. In both World War I and II, women entered the work force primarily in response to the needs of the war machine. Thousands of children experienced father absence, on a temporary or permanent basis. The economic face of the nation was permanently changed. Many men and women saw so many new worlds that they were motivated to reconstruct their own. The experience of African-Americans in World War II helped precipitate the civil rights movement of the 1960s. These macro-events produced myriad technological changes that have diffused into day-to-day life. All these changes and many more are the result of macrosystem effects.

Bronfenbrenner thinks of macrosystems as cultural blueprints that underlie the organization of institutions, the assumptions people make about social relations, and the workings of the political and economic system. Two aspects of this definition are particularly important for our purposes.

The first is that this treatment of culture goes beyond simple description. That is, in specifying culture as the blueprint for society, we leave open the possibility that the blueprints may be "in error." Bronfenbrenner offers us the possibility of criticizing culture and society on the grounds that they impede human development. While this may seem self-evident, it does represent something of a departure from the way many social scientists think of culture.

Using the term "cultural relativism," many social scientists argue that all cultures are equivalent, that one cannot and should not criticize cultures as being humanly wrong since all cultures arise as a specific adaptation to circumstances (cf. Tulkin, 1972). Translating culture into the concept of macrosystem, on the other hand, raises the possibility that such consistencies may not be in the best interests of children and their development. This, as we shall see, is an important point.

The second and related aspect of Bronfenbrenner's definition is found in his statement that macrosystem refers to consistencies "that *could exist*" (1979, p. 26). The ecological approach is intimately bound up with social policy, i.e., the decisions and principles guiding the behavior of public and private institutions. It necessitates a serious consideration of "social engineering" as a way of dealing with individual developmental problems. Naturally, this is of special relevance in the discussion of sociocultural risk, where the focus of attention is on problems in just those "consistencies in the form of lower-order systems" that do exist and have an adverse developmental effect on individuals. Thus, an ecological approach has a "moral imperative" attached to it; it both describes and prescribes. It tells us that to reduce risk at the most immediate level of the microsystem, we *should* consider changing things in the big picture. This means that the topic of sociocultural risk brings together the "helping" and "describing" traditions in human development. The meaning and implications of this moral and scientific approach to culture will emerge as we look at five examples of macrosystem issues implicated in understanding sociocultural risk.

Pluralistic vs. Totalitarian Societies

At the very start, we can look at the sociopolitical organization of the society in our efforts to seek the roots of sociocultural risk. The development of children, particularly their moral development, depends in part on the "political" structure of their experiences (cf., Almond & Verba, 1965). Children need a world that combines stability and diversity, consensus on basic principles coupled with alternative and competing expressions of those principles. Very young children need to form powerful attachments that provide the basis for prosocial motivation to develop. But once they have developed that basic prosocial motivation (to obey, to attend to rules, and to develop the rudiments of conscience), they need more, (Garbarino & Bronfenbrenner, 1976b). They need to be faced with moral dilemmas, but in a reasonably secure, nurturant, and supportive setting.

Two extremes, and therefore two dangers, are possible. On the one hand, there may be such a diversity of irreconcilable alternatives that the child cannot choose and at the same time avoid the hostility and alienation of those she chooses against. On an interpersonal level, Bateson (1972) has called such situations "double binds" ("damned if you do and damned if you don't") and linked them to schizophrenia. Children should be protected from these conflicts: They are unfair and developmentally threatening. On the other hand, where there is unanimity so complete that no choice is ever allowed and only a slavish obedience required, the child's moral development languishes.

One can imagine, for example, a society that irreconcilably pitted school and government against family. In such a situation, the child would be faced with an intense double bind. To remain loyal to the family would mean to estrange one's self from peers, from teachers, and in fact to place oneself in political jeopardy. To side with school and government would mean to make the intolerable choice of turning one's back on kin. Many totalitarian societies force this choice on children as a matter of course; Nazi Germany for one (Shirer, 1960). Democratic societies do not do so as a matter of policy, although such dilemmas may occur when there are irreconcilable differences between family and state. The situation is familiar to Native Americans, Latinos, and Blacks in the United States.

In contrast to the society in which there is irreconcilable conflict between family and state, there stands the society in which all social agents are unified in single-minded devotion. Here the developmental problem is not one of double binds but rather that the lack of diversity will impede higher order cognitive and moral development. For example, when church and state are under the same rulers (theocracy), such as occurred in Iran under the Ayatollah Khomeini, there is unchecked absolutism, and moral sensibility languishes. Where there is no diversity, the child can too easily satisfy society's demands. This too stands in contrast to the democratic society in which a measure of social diversity necessarily exists, where there are competing allegiances that the youngster must sort out and in so doing learn to develop higher order thinking and judgment (Garbarino, 1968). The child learns to live by principle in the democratic society.

The available data suggest that the greatest danger to children's moral development lies in the totalitarian society that commands total allegiance to the state. This is manifested in the authority of adults, such as teachers and youth group leaders. One study of these data (Garbarino & Bronfenbrenner, 1976b) looked at the moral judgments of youth (12 years old) in countries with varying degrees of social and political diversity. At issue was the degree to which the youths' moral judgments reflected a balance of adult and peer influences as a function of whether the society was totalitarian or democratic. The study used the term "pluralistic" to refer to the middle ground between irreconcilably intense conflict on the one hand and the extreme absence of conflict on the other. In a pluralistic society, there are completing allegiances that operate within a common framework: a consensus on basic principles, agreement to the rules of the game, and appreciation for the need to spare individuals impossible choices as much as possible. The results of the study indicated that across both communist and noncommunist societies, the less pluralism a society manifested, the less balanced were the moral judgments of the youth. The issue is one of totalitarian versus pluralistic societies, not necessarily one of political East versus political West—a distinction that has blurred in the 1990's.

What does this have to do with sociocultural risk? It tells us that when looking at macrosystem matters we should attend to whether or not the political culture of a society forces children and parents into intolerable dilemmas. It tells us that there are developmental grounds for supporting the "pluralistic society." Political freedom makes good sense developmentally. In fact, these developmental grounds have been illuminated in creative detail by White (1959).

White speculated that there is an inherent drive to master the environment and a natural "incongruity mechanism." That is, the human being thrives on "optimal discrepancy," a balance of the familiar and the different, of the known and the novel. Environments that provide the organism with this kind of optimal discrepancy serve to stimulate and enhance development. They provide the kind of richness human beings need. Thus, classic, philosophical traditions of democracy stand on firm scientific grounds. A democratic society—a pluralistic society—is in fact a healthy environment in which humans can grow. It offers them the greatest exercise of those characteristics (evaluating, deciding, and comparing) that are innately and particularly human. To deprive people of such a pluralistic environment is to damage their growth and development. Therefore, a nondemocratic social system—a macrosystem dominated by totalitarian influence—presents a sociocultural risk for those who live within it.

The developmentally enhancing character of a pluralistic ideology that values freedom of expression and guarantees human rights is evident vividly in the case of traumatized children and youth, particularly those growing up in war zones (Garbarino, Kostelny, & Dubrow, 1991). Such children and youth can travel one of two paths. The first is the path of "vendetta morality" and "the politics of revenge." Victims seek an explanation. Extremist ideologies offer an explanation and promise revenge (e.g., terrorism).

The second path is one of healing and a morality of forgiveness and caring. It comes when there is a political climate that encourages victims to "process" their experiences and seek positive and constructive expressions for their pain (e.g., by becoming a helper onself or by preventing future victimization).

The Economic System: Triumph of the Marketplace?

The economic system is one of the most powerful aspects of the macrosystem. It connects work, goods and services, and the social, biological, and physical environments that more than anything else define the kind of life we lead. The type of economic system—for example, laissez-faire capitalism or state-run socialism—and a person's place in the economy—rich or poor, working or unemployed, superior or subordinate—have an enormous effect on one's relation to one's family, community, country, and oneself.

The American economy grew out of the free-market assumptions first advanced by Adam Smith, tempered by twentieth-century innovations of government intervention. Laws and regulations, taxes and government programs attempt to "fine tune" the economy so it works better and ensures the survival and minimum well-being of all Americans. How well is the economic system working to support our nation's children and families?

At the heart of this question stands one of the great political, economic, and social debates of our time. As we said earlier, human needs are constant and basic; societies much more "primitive" than ours have had long and happy histories with little of the "creature comforts" or technology so basic to our way of life. We can all easily cite the benefits of our economy: unprecedented material wealth for many, social and geographic mobility, rising health and educational standards, to name but a few. At the same time, we must ask about the costs of our system to people and to the environment. One way to consider this is in terms of the underlying assumptions that determine "how things are done" in the economy (Garbarino, 1988a,b).

For example, our economy is based on the principle of permanent growth as a necessary condition for progress. Growth constantly requires new markets, resources, changing demands, and an emphasis on consumption. As a cultural blueprint, this idea seems obvious, even indisputable. Yet a small group of economists question the wisdom of continual growth (Daly, 1973). Starting from the idea that the Earth is a finite environment, they see the optimal economy as a steady-state system, with basically fixed levels of population and economic output. As technology advances, productivity and time, rather than increased production, would be gained. The economy would strive toward stable levels of consumption and economic activity and *maximum* durability and quality of goods, leaving people the means and freedom to fulfill their lives more independently of the economic system. One can imagine—at least as a vision—a combination of advanced technology and cottage industry, as people devote themselves to satisfying labor and minimize unpleasant work. Our ecological situation, of course, would be much improved by a system based on stability and the sustenance of all life, rather than constant growth and the exploitation that it requires.

Another aspect of the economic macrosystem is the use of the profit

motive as a basis for economic decisions. Rather than directly considering basic human needs of consumption, satisfying labor, and human
relatedness, our economy is based on the pursuit of profit. The distor-
tions we suffer in unemployment, poverty, worker alienation, pollution,
and stress, as well as the whole "malaise of affluence" (Lasch, 1978) are
by-products of our economic status quo. Although the riches we have
accumulated may be unparalleled, so are the problems and dangers
from which we suffer. We cannot take only the good; our economic tree
bears poisons along with its fruits—particularly for the poor.

Finally, the economic notion of "efficiency" as a basis for making
decisions is rarely examined. In a time of scarce energy and jobs, common sense would argue that a more labor-intensive approach to production would provide work for more people by using less non-human
energy. Yet the trend throughout the economy is toward increasing
mechanization and automation that puts people out of work and requires massive amounts of non-human energy. The agricultural sector,
for example, has "released" 25 million people from the farms of the
United States since 1940 by utilization of machinery (Berry, 1977). Yet,
agriculture has never been in a more precarious state than it is now, as
farmers are forced to farm larger acreage and go deeper and deeper into
debt to afford land and machines, while the topsoil which must sustain
us *forever* is being depleted at an alarming rate because of the necessity
of "mining the soil" to reap short-term yields. Moreover, food production is in the hands of fewer and fewer people, unemployment is a
permanent problem, especially for those at the bottom of the society
who need work most, and the quality of our food, if anything, is diminishing.

During the 1980s average income remained about the same for American families (after correcting for inflation). Conventional economic
thinking would have us believe that this means America's families were
holding their own. But that would be a serious distortion of reality.
Income increased for the top 40% of American families, but declined
significantly for the bottom 40%. Does that even out? Hardly. Every
additional dollar for affluent families means little or nothing in terms of
greater child well being. Each dollar subtracted from poor or financially
struggling families translates into heightened risk for children.

More broadly, we as a society continue to believe that everything is for
sale, that the bottom line is the only calculation that really matters.
Human economic life includes both the "monetarized" (where money
changes hands in the production and distribution of goods and services)
and the "nonmonetarized" (where no money changes hands). When we
move an activity from the nonmonetarized to the monetarized (such as
when child care becomes a business on a pay as you go basis) conven-

tional economic thinking defines this as "growth" (because Gross National Product increases). If we step out of this macrosystem we can see this more clearly as simply moving the transaction from one accounting system to another (with no guarantee of equal or higher quality). All this is true, and yet we proceed as if conventional economic thinking really made sense for children and families (Garbarino, 1992).

The fact that these basic assumptions are not questioned testifies to the extent to which they are ingrained as a macrosystem. Market payoffs, rather than human concerns, dictate what is to be the structure of our economy. We take it all for granted despite the fact that so much of what happens in the economic realm affects parents and children in critical ways. It is precisely the way we *think* of our involvement in the economy as workers, consumers, investors, and taxpayers that keeps the problems from getting solved.

Individualistic Competition vs. Interdependent Cooperation

One of the clearest ways to identify the operation of a macrosystem is to consider what people take for granted. Particularly when comparing macrosystems, one finds that what is taken for granted in one society is disputed in another. American culture views independence and autonomy as a norm, as a positive goal towards which individuals should strive. It assumes that individual competition and independence are part of "human nature." This belief is so firmly fixed in our macrosystem that many of us would find it hard to consider an alternative. Trainers who run group process workshops often report that when given a task—any task—Americans "automatically" define it as a competition, with winners and losers.

We see dependency as basically pathologic, or at least immature (Rotenberg, 1977). Our culture denigrates interdependence and sees it as a form of weakness. Just to present the issue this way is to raise the question: Is independence a self-evident good, or is it only good as defined within a particular culture, a culture subject to criticism on the grounds of its effect on development?

Few characteristics come without cost. We need to look at the social benefits and social risks of our culture. Our individualistic culture gives us a sense of personal responsibility, a rationale for achievement, and a justification for success. It provides a justification for our social system, differentiated as it is by economic and social levels. It provides justification for the winners (although it keeps a kind of Sword of Damocles of future failure always fixed above their heads). This narrowly individualistic culture of ours provides a kind of freedom, a fresh air of individuality that collective societies cannot match.

On the other hand, it clearly implies—and often makes painfully obvious—that if success is a matter of individual virtue, failure is a matter of individual deficiency. The other side of individualism is alienation, a sense of estrangement, of isolation, and of being perilously alone (Slater, 1970). Many social philosophers have argued that it is in the interdependencies and interconnections of one's social life that one finds enduring sources of what is meaningful. This basically philosophical position has received increasing scientific support as survey data and other investigations have shown that interpersonally well-connected people are the happiest and most satisfied with their day-to-day existence (Campbell, 1976).

The fact that social connectedness and enduring social relationships are what keeps us going in life suggests that our individualistic culture, and the competition and denigration of interdependency it implies, place us at sociocultural risk. Our culture tends to say "every man for himself" while our nature as human beings says "no man is an island." The use of "men" here is significant. Women are generally more attuned to interdependency, rapport, intimacy, and connection as a basis for social relations and individual identity (Gilligan, 1982).

There is a real, enduring, and intense conflict here. This conflict has been identified repeatedly in social and historical analyses of our society, analyses that go beyond gender. Sociologist David Riesman called it "the lonely crowd"; Philip Slater discussed it in his book, *The Pursuit of Loneliness*; James Webb, an historian, saw it throughout our history as "the parabola of individualism." It means that we—even of men more than women—value individual autonomy and privacy so much that we are always threatened with social isolation. Even if women do not subscribe fully to this culture, male dominance means they must contend with it.

We seem to say that everyone should be on his own and free, without recognizing that the price for such independence is the risk of alienation, a pervasive sense of dissatisfaction, and a heightened vulnerability to depression. Who bears this burden most acutely? Children do. They pay the price because this network of values leading to social isolation and alienation undermines responsible parenthood. It is one of the central issues facing our society (Garbarino, 1981c). Altogether, our excessive and unrealistic valuing of independence sets us up for unhappiness, and our children for impaired development. For example, depression often comes from social dislocation and produces neglectful childcare (Weissman & Paykel, 1974). This depression results in part from the macrosystem.

Just as is the case in moral development, where pluralism is the key, the matter of competition, individual responsibility, and interdependence requires a balanced, or middle road solution. Without a notion of

individual responsibility and accountability, it is unlikely that one can
develop sufficient "internal locus of control" (the belief that the individual himself rather than external forces determine the course of one's
own life) to keep our kind of society going. Indeed the very cornerstone
of our society is individual self-motivation and competition, with cooperation seen mainly as a means toward the goal of the individual's greater gain. On the other hand, without an appreciation for interdependence, and for the intrinsic worth of social connectedness, we are
constantly in jeopardy of alienation and depression. Both of these are
potentially serious social problems affecting parents, and therefore children. Dependency can make the individual unequipped to face the demands of our society, while extreme independence can make one unable
to share life's joys and hardships with others.

That this is a macrosystem effect is demonstrated by the fact that it
permeates all our institutional life. In schools we see it in the fact that
individual competition—primarily for grades—is a corrosive force undermining the self-esteem and development of the majority of students
who inevitably must be "losers" (Dreeben, 1968). Two sisters came home
from school, one with an "A" and one with a "C." The mother punishes
one. Which one? The sister with an "A." "If you're so smart," she says,
"why didn't you help your sister get a "B"? "Unamerican!" you say—
Yes, they're Hawaiian . . . they value cooperation above competition.

On a broader scale, we see the effects of it in our virtual inability to
restrain commercial exploitation of children and of their parents (Garbarino, 1981c), all of which goes forward under the banner of "individualism." Advertisers have an "individual right" to play to children,
while parents have an "individual responsibility" to counteract this advertising blitz that emphasizes materialistic gratification (and children
an "individual right" to choose products).

We saw it clearly when we once wrote to several airlines and government officials to complain that during a snow storm, parents with young
children (one woman was stranded with a five year old and an 18 month
old for 47 hours in the airport) were forced to "compete" on an equal
basis with adults without children for available flights and accommoda-
tions. When we wrote, we were told, "We can't give special advantage
to one group of our customers over another." Indeed!

An individualistic ideology tends to produce antichild, antifamily policies and practices. We see this ideology in policies that permit un-
restrained development of shopping centers, even where it is evident to
all parties—perhaps even the developers—that the net result will be
fragmentation of the community and its neighborhoods. All this is written in the American blueprint.

And all this represents sociocultural risk because it exposes the individual to values and experiences that undermine an important condition for healthy development, namely, social connectedness. One of the most bitter fruits of this "cultural poison" is violence, our next macrosystem issue.

Militarism

At any given time in the last three decades, millions of children have been growing up in war zones around the world (Garbarino, Kostelny, & Dubrow, 1991). According to UNICEF, most of the casualties in these wars are civilians—many of them children. These wars are often civil wars or wars of liberation. They usually employ antipersonnel weapons that kill indiscriminately.

Of course beyond the 40 or so small, chronic wars there are larger, more traditional conflicts. In the Gulf War of 1991 more than 100,000 Iraqi people were killed in a period of 8 weeks, and many tens of thousands more—many of them children—died in the months that followed due to war-induced disease and malnutrition. Allied forces—principally American war planes—systematically attacked the Iraqi infrastructure—sewage, water, electricity, bridges, etc.

What sustains war as a source of risk to children? One sustaining force is the macrosystem of militarism. Militarism is a set of beliefs and institutions that legitimatizes and profits from the use of armed forces to advance and protect national interests. The international armaments industry institutionalizes economic incentives to militarize public life and group conflict. Many countries divert a large proportion of their resources to military purposes. They then claim they cannot afford to meet basic human needs in the fields of medicine, housing, education, and nutrition. This must remain a shocking insult to those who seek to improve the well being of children. It is sociocultural risk at its worst.

"Normal" Violence and "Abusive" Violence

As we hope has become clear in this discussion of macrosystem issues, to speak of the macrosystem is to consider the meaning of "human nature." This is evident as well if we look at "normal" violence. Just as our culture sees individual competition as a fact of human nature, it tends to define violence as an inevitable and normal part of domestic relations (Goldstein, 1986). The use of violence and the approval of domestic violence is common in our society. The most recent and comprehensive study (Straus & Gelles, 1987) documents that among normal American families, domestic violence in some form is almost universal (involving at least some hitting in 90% of the families surveyed), and serious assault occurs in some 15% of our families.

The very fact that we define only the most damaging and extreme forms of physical punishment as "abuse," and permit the rest to be classified as only "normal discipline" is testimony to the acceptance that violence has in our culture. This, too, is a macrosystem issue because violence figures prominently in the blueprint of our domestic and institutional life (e.g., "the marriage license as a license to hit"). It is, in fact, a normal part of our experience. Educators, clergymen, and police all approve of the use of physical force and corporal punishment in punishing children and youth (Parke & Collmer, 1975).

Few parents can conceive of—let alone implement—alternatives to the use of physical force in social control and discipline (Garbarino, 1977a). The incredulous or hostile response given to calls for domestic *nonviolence* is testimony to this. When Sweden's legislature reaffirmed and strengthened its opposition to the use of corporal punishment by parents with their children, the American press treated the action as a ludicrous bit of nonsense, much the way a racist responds to civil rights legislation. The parallel is illuminating. When psychologist John Valusek issued a booklet under the title "People Are Not for Hitting," he found that most readers "naturally" assumed that he didn't include children in that message. He had to add "And Children Are People, Too" before the message was clear to many readers. Violence in general, but particularly domestic violence, is deeply embedded in our macrosystem.

At the same time, there are grounds for believing that the use of physical force is not inevitable, that it is a cultural phenomenon, and that alternatives can and do exist. The same investigators who found such widespread support for and use of domestic violence found that the level of such violence rises in direct proportion to a host of predisposing social stress factors such as economic inadequacy, marital conflict, and personal inadequacy. Rather than being an inevitable expression of human nature, the use of violence is a culturally conditioned expression of distress. Desmond Morris made the following observation about domestic violence based on his look at nonhuman species:

> The viciousness with which children . . . are subjected to persecution is a measure of the weight of dominant pressures imposed on their persecutors. (1970)

Cultural support for violence as a norm represents sociocultural risk because it presents and legitimatizes a dangerous outlet for stress. Some other cultures do not legitimize this outlet, and they have less domestic violence (Korbin, 1981). Some social stress is inevitable, and when we provide an outlet that can easily escalate into physically and psychically damaging behavior toward children, we place children in general at risk and the children of distressed families in special jeopardy. Where we condone the slapping of one child, we inevitably increase the likelihood that another will be punched. Where we accept husbands slapping wives on the grounds that it is a husband's right, we make it almost inevitable that women *and* children will be battered.

The insidious thing about macrosystem effects is that they send ripples throughout the human experience. In supporting the "rightness" of normal violence, we set in motion a chain of events that inevitably places substantial numbers of children at risk. On the other hand, insofar as we are able to start a countermomentum of nonviolence, we may serve to protect children who find themselves in stressful circumstances. Domestic violence is one of the most poignant and pressing areas of sociocultural risk with which our society must deal. Recent evidence suggests that a growing number of parents are hearing this message and are moving away from "normal" domestic violence (NCPCA, 1990; Straus & Gelles, 1990).

Sexism and Racism as Cultural Issues

One of the important principles guiding our efforts to enhance human development states that we should encourage the best possible match between individual characteristics and social settings. As we noted before, the ecological definition of development involves the idea that the more differentiated one's conception of reality and the greater one's skill in mastering reality, the greater the fulfillment of individual potential. This definition of development argues that ideologies or institutions which unnecessarily or unfairly limit the opportunities of individuals are a threat to development. Such factors unnecessarily and unduly restrict the experience, and hence the development, of those affected. Two such factors are sexism and racism, because they oppose the goal of individual development and are not linked to *necessary* group identities. They narrow the range of *social* contexts to which *individual* characteristics must be matched.

As an ideology, sexism asserts that there are rigid, inherent, and inevitable group differences between males and females that are and should be the basis for the differentiation of activities among individuals (Maccoby, 1966). In its best form, it is a "separate but equal" approach to development. In fact, according to research from a variety of sources, it contributes a "separate but unequal" macrosystem effect. It forces females (and males, for that matter) into unduly and unnecessarily narrow choices of activity and exerts a depressing effect on their competence. As recently as the mid-1960s, research on occupational development revealed that whereas young males name a very wide range of potential occupations—ranging from the close-to-home (policeman, doctor, and mailman) to the far-flung (spaceman, baseball star, and president)—young females, as early as four years of age, will restrict virtually all their choices to teacher, nurse, and mother (O'Hara, 1962). Things have changed somewhat since the 1980s, but sex-typing of activities and sexist discrimination remain strong. Clearly, this does an injustice to the diversity of interests and abilities that exist among females. Therefore, there are developmental grounds for seeing sexism as a source of sociocultural risk.

Sexism also forces males and females into roles and personality styles that may be difficult for them to maintain. It means that males who are temperamentally inclined to nurturant roles may assume such roles only with decreased self-esteem and a sense of failure. It means that females who are temperamentally inclined to adopt aggressive, athletic roles, for example, must cope with the role incongruity this implies—and perhaps social rejection. All of this flies in the face of the principle of matching individual characteristics to situations and is therefore developmentally threatening. Whatever *group* differences there may be (and there *are* grounds for believing that such average differences between the sexes do exist, Hutt, 1972) do not justify values and institutions that run roughshod over quite significant *individual* differences (Rosenberg & Sutton-Smith, 1972). For example, evidence from a variety of sources suggests that, on average, males and females routinely adopt different styles of communication in public and private settings; with males, using information is a competitive effort to establish dominance, whereas females talk more cooperatively to build connection (Tannen, 1990). Sexism would make this average into a fixed norm of conduct.

In the same manner, racism is a direct threat to development. By postulating racial differences in intelligence, moral character, and general competence, racism undermines the development of the children it defines as inferior—and even impoverishes the development of those judged superior (Tulkin, 1972). It places the "inferior" children at risk by creating a negative reality with which they must contend. It diminishes them. It has a demonstratively depressive effect on competence and contributes to a wide range of personality disturbances. Because it is a macrosystem effect, it permeates the institutional life of the society, and thus, forces its victims into extraordinary measures to cope. Even those who consciously reject it may find it lurking below the surface in their thoughts and feelings.

Attributing characteristics to individuals within a group presents a threat to the development of those individuals—particularly if they are cast in a negative light. There is almost always overlap between groups, whether the differences are due to actual genetic differences (such as the height of Chinese vs. Bantu people) or discriminatory testing (such as when Jews, immigrating to the United States in the early 1900s, were judged to be intellectually inferior on the basis of IQ tests administered to them in English, which they did not all speak).

Human development proceeds *through individuals,* although aggregate differences can and do exist. "Isms" that limit and define the range of possibilities for groups have an inevitably adverse effect on individuals by disrupting the natural process by which individual and environment are matched to facilitate development. Science and ethics merge in rejecting sexism and racism. These ideologies are not consistent with the process of fullest human development.

Reducing Sociocultural Risk: Support Systems

When a team of aeronautical engineers set themselves to the task of writing up a set of blueprints for a bumblebee, they found that by all their best judgments, a bumblebee shouldn't be able to fly. Coming this far in our discussion of sociocultural risk may create the impression that successful human development must be impossible, given the hostile forces aligned against the developing child. It might seem as though there is an overwhelming conspiracy at the micro-, meso-, exo-, and macrolevels to undermine and impair development. For some children this is exactly the situation, of course. The chronicling of risks to development is not the whole story, however.

The human being is notable for intelligence, resourcefulness, will, and adaptability. Intelligence and adaptability have served us well in adjusting to an incredible range of environments. Adaptability is our strength. It means that humans may live, if not thrive, in many environments that are purely and simply hostile. Children grew up in the concentration camps run by the Nazis in World War II. Amid chaos and despair, children grew and learned. In their report on these children and efforts to work with them, Freud and Dann (1951) report that the children clearly adapted to concentration camp life, even though it was an inhuman and inhumane situation. Their adaptation, which meant their survival and mental progress, is a testament to the strength of the human species. However, as Freud and Dann point out, that adaptation was not without cost. The children exhibited a variety of clinical symptoms of disturbed, if not warped, development. This point must be understood in looking at and evaluating sociocultural risk. The fact that humans *can* survive in the face of these risks should not be enough to excuse or rationalize the threats that those risks present. In looking at children who survive socially and culturally risky situations, we must always ask, "At what cost?" "What might they have been in a more nurturant and supportive environment?" and "What of those who did not survive?" Also, we must recognize that there is great individual variation in the response to sociocultural risk.

A generation of research on sources of coping and resilience among children exposed to developmental risks (poverty, impaired parents, stressful environments, disabilities, racism, etc.) has identified the following as critical to the child's success (Lösel & Bliesner, 1990):

- Actively trying to cope (rather than just reacting defensively) and temperamental characteristics that engender positive relationships with peers and adults (rather than passive withdrawal).
- Cognitive competence (at least an average level of intelligence—in the sense defined by Sternberg as "componential intelligence" in Chapter 1).
- Experiences of self-efficacy (being good at something builds a reservoir of confidence and self-esteem that can sustain the child in other areas of his or her life and over time).
- A stable emotional relationship with at least one person (who may not even be a parent, but who is committed to and attached to the child and who thus gives the child a model of what it means to care and be cared for).
- An open supportive educational climate (to engage the child in "processing" and interpreting experience and teach skills).
- Social support from persons outside the family (to connect the child positively to the community and thus help the child access its available resources).

We can reduce the risk posed by social and cultural factors that are inimical to optimal development; we have already done so in some areas. We can reduce risk by social action and by the individual characteristics of the child and those who care for the child. To understand how this happens and how to facilitate this process, we need to understand more about how families work and how children develop (Chapters 4–6). Once we have made progress in these basic areas, we can proceed to examine the social environment in which these basic structures and processes of life operate (Chapters 8–11). As a prelude to these discussions, however, we can examine two examples of sociocultural risk reduction.

There are at least two sources of sociocultural risk that run through the various micro-, meso-, exo-, and macrosystem problems discussed in this chapter. The first of these is "social impoverishment." Social impoverishment is the denuding of the child's environment of significant social resources. The second source of risk is "cultural impoverish-ment." Cultural impoverishment is a set of values or view of the world that undermines the characteristics on which competence is built. It may involve rationalizations for self-interest, values that benefit the indi-vidual at the expense of families, an ideology that is outdated and is no longer functional to meet the demands of a changed environment, a narrow and inaccurate view of child development, or values that other-wise seriously impair the child's ability to function in the required con-texts of social life outside the family. Both these forms of impoverish-ment find their most significant expression in the day-to-day content and structure of formal and informal support systems in a family's en-vironment.

A support system is a social arrangement that provides nurturance and feedback to individuals. One of the pioneering researchers and theorists in this field, Gerald Caplan, defines support systems as

> continuing social aggregates that provide individuals with opportunities for feedback about themselves and for validations for their expectations about others, which may offset deficiencies in these communications with-in the larger community context. They tell him (the individual) what is expected of him and guide him in what to do. They watch what he does and judge his performance. (Caplan, 1974, pp. 4–6)

Social and cultural impoverishment results when these support sys-tem functions are undermined, impaired, eroded, or destroyed. These destructive influences can come at the micro- meso-, exo-, or mac-rosystem levels. They can come because of attitudes or beliefs that cause people to isolate themselves from the community. They can come from institutional and social forces in the community that prevent these sup-portive relationships from forming and being maintained. They can come from a culture that poisons support systems by devaluing children and family life (Garbarino, 1981c). These support systems figure promi-nently, not simply in the day-to-day management of tasks and stress, but in the very creation of a meaningful existence. In his review of the data bearing on the "meaningfulness" of human experience, Campbell (1975) found over and over again that it is the *social* richness of indi-vidual experience that determines its meaningfulness—above and be-yond material resources. Naturally, economic deprivation is a serious threat to the human being. But it is the *social* deprivation that accom-panies economic poverty which is responsible for its truly devastating human consequences. Being poor is quite different from being im-poverished. The former may exist along with social affluence, while the latter implies a total denuding of the environment of the human neces-sities of life.

To speak of sociocultural risk as it applies to children is to look at how the essential functions of the parent are supported, encouraged, supplemented, and reviewed by people with a long-term investment in the welfare and well-being of the child. A truly poor child is one whose parents are left to their own devices, particularly when those devices are too limited for the difficult task of rearing a child. A poor child is one who is unprotected. A rich child is one whose life is full of diverse and enduring relationships and whose parents are similarly involved in an interlocking web of supportive, nurturant, and concerned relationships. The higher the personal risk of the child, the greater the importance of sociocultural resources. The principal task for the community is to know how socially well-fixed their families are and to proceed accordingly. The community needs to recognize positive forces where they exist naturally (and then leave them alone) and to learn how to generate and sustain them where they do not exist already. Community development is inseparable from reducing sociocultural risk in this sense. A prochild ideology is the foundation for a caring community.

Where are we to look for a macrosystem model for a caring community? One useful source is the UN Convention on the Rights of the Child. Adapted by the United Nations in 1989, after years of discussion, the Convention sets out the basis for an international pro-child ideology.

The Convention sets out a foundation for a caring community by specifying a child's rights to be cared for, nurtured, protected, and respected—in times of war and peace, among the rich and the poor. It also sets out a mechanism for assessing how well each society is doing in providing opportunities and reducing risks for children. Each country is to submit status reports to an international oversight committee. These reports should reveal areas of improvement and deterioration in efforts to guarantee the rights of children. For anyone concerned with the well being of children it is a marvelous accomplishment.

However, at the time of this writing, the United States remained one of only a handful of countries around the world (ironically, Iraq among them) that has refused to ratify the UN Convention on the Rights of the Child. The sticking points? One is that we as a society reserve the right to execute juveniles. More broadly, perhaps we do not care enough about children and meeting their needs as a matter of the highest national priority.

The ecological approach used to organize our discussion clearly directs our attention to many points at which intervention is possible. If we think of the task as one of weaving a strong social fabric around the child and parent, the task becomes more comprehensible. The pressing need is to establish an effective partnership between formal and informal support systems so that each child is protected and nurtured by both, directly as in the case of the small school, and indirectly as through the child's parents and primary care givers. The principal implication of our discussion of sociocultural risk is that this wondrous human child can and will become a competent person, if we only give it a chance. Against the many hostile forces chronicled in this discussion of sociocultural risk stands the child's own innate drive to master and succeed in the world, the parent's love and commitment to aid the child, and the community's motivation to care for all its children. The constant challenge to professionals and lay people alike is to help the constructive forces overcome the destructive ones.

RESEARCH CAPSULE

One clear and heartbreaking example of risk to development is child abuse and neglect. Scientists have looked at many different factors associated with child abuse in attempts to understand and prevent it, from the psychological attributes of the parents and child to the sociocultural home environment of the family.

One important study (Burgess, Anderson, & Schellenbach, 1980) examined the social interaction of abusive, neglectful, and control families. All families were drawn from similar social backgrounds: rural, poor, with parents averaging about ten years of education. By observing families performing simple tasks and engaging in discussions together, the researchers were able to score frequency of positive and negative communications and the types of sequences families engage in. The behaviors were scored by trained observers using a Datamyte 904 data collection system. This is a portable keyboard with number and four letter keys. Coded behaviors can be recorded and stored in computer format.

Observational research relies on accurate recording of phenomena as the basis of trying to understand it. Observations can be done in the laboratory or in naturalistic settings, and they can be done with or without the knowledge of the subject. The present study is an example of a structured naturalistic observation in which the researchers provided topics for interaction and then passively observed the families. The findings indicated that there is less interaction in abusive and neglectful families than in the control group. Both the abusive and neglectful families are less positive, more negative, and are more likely to reciprocate negative behavior than positive exchanges when compared to the control group.

The investigators also discuss demographic and family characteristics associated with patterns of abuse. Low socioeconomic status, single parenthood, large families, and particular child characteristics such as physical, intellectual, or behavior dysfunctions all are associated with high levels of abuse.

An intervention strategy aimed at increasing the positive interactions within abusive families is reported. The limited benefits suggest that while home-based skills training is possible, a more practical and effective strategy would involve the encouragement of natural helping networks to combat abuse and neglect among isolated, needy, and troubled families.

PRACTICE CAPSULE

Preschool education has been proposed as an effective and practical method for enhancing the development of young children. Public-funded preschools attempt to provide less advantaged youngsters with opportunities that are available to middle-class children at private nursery schools. Often preschool programs try to involve parents in their child's activities, both by inviting parents to the preschool and by making home visits. This is in the hope of establishing a strong home–school mesosystem from the beginning, making parents more aware and disposed toward helping their children to learn.

Varying approaches to preschool education exist; a central problem is the evaluation of the effectiveness of these programs. An example of one preschool program which has been thoroughly evaluated is the Perry Preschool Project. Based in a Ypsilanti (Michigan) neighborhood, the study followed 123 children who were three years old in the early 1960s. All of the subjects were Blacks from low SES families who had scored below average on the Stanford–Binet Intelligence Test. Fifty-eight children attended preschool for two years, 65 did not. The two groups were matched on personal, family, and demographic characteristics.

The curriculum at the Perry Preschool emphasized the child's cognitive developments and the strength of the family–school mesosystem. The student–teacher ratio was 6 to 1, and there was a weekly home visit in which parents were encouraged to aid in their children's development. The student's progress in school was evaluated and compared annually. By the end of the fifth grade, the two groups differed significantly on academic achievement. The students who had attended the preschool scored over a full grade level above the non-preschool children in reading, language, and arithmetic on the California Achievement Test. In fact, 49% of the preschool group scored at or above the fifth-grade level, versus only 17% of the children without the preschool experience. In addition, the preschool children had a lower rate of repeating a grade and a lower arrest record than the control group. The investigators estimate that in 1979 dollars, the one-year program cost $5,984 for each child and saved the public $14,819 for each child in reduced remedial education and social interventions.

Studies of preschool programs conclude that preschool succeeds in producing gains in academic, social, and health status for children and their families. Replications of this analysis throughout the 1980s continued to support this conclusion; early childhood education can exert a major positive influence. However, in the 1990s, as conditions have worsened for high-risk poor families, there is growing concern that this form of intervention is not sufficient to deal with the deeply rooted problems of the "underclass" (Halpern, 1991).

FOR FURTHER READING

Garbarino, J., & Gilliam, G. (1980). *Understanding abusive families*. Lexington, MA: Lexington Books, 263 pp.
    This book examines child maltreatment as a developmental and ecological issue. It begins with a discussion of the nature and definition of abuse and the

social context in which it is generally found. Family norms about childbirth and childrearing are then discussed with regard to risks and opportunities for bringing families closer together. Abuse is seen as an outgrowth of social isolation where parents lack the resources and support to effectively care for children. This book is an example of the applied work that can be done using the human ecosystem model.

Garbarino, J., Kostelny, K., & Dubrow, N. (1991). *No place to be a child: growing up in a war zone.* New York: Lexington Books, 177 pp.

This book explores the impact of war on children. It draws on field work in five war zones: Cambodia, Mozambique, Nicaragua, the Middle East, and inner city Chicago (where the gang wars put children in a combat zone). It examines the cultural and societal issues we face in seeking peace for these children within the framework of the UN Convention on the Rights of the Child.

Havighurst, R. J. (1962). *Growing up in River City.* New York: John Wiley, 189 pp.

An early classic in longitudinal studies of normal development, this book reports a 9-year study of adolescence and young adulthood. It was begun in 1951 when the subjects were in fifth grade and followed them until they were around 20 years old. The basic question the study asks is: What are the influences on these children's development, and how can we account for their success or failure as they embark on adult roles?

The children and their communities are studied together. The human ecosystem, from family to community agencies to social class difference are all considered together in their influence on the children. The book discusses the subjects' childhood, adolescence, and young adulthood, stressing the continuity of life patterns and the sociocultural influences on their development.

The book concludes with a review of the data and suggestions that this typical American town could enact to enhance the maturation of its children. These include more options and opportunities for the less successful and alienated students, increased possibilities for work experience, and preparation for the many girls who leave school for early marriage. *Growing Up in River City* is an easily readable and fascinating book, for its inside look at a time gone by and at the universal process of maturation in social context which produces human beings.

Kotlowitz, A. (1991). *There are no children here.* New York: Doubleday.

In this book Alex Kotlowitz presents the lives of two boys growing up in a crime-ridden public housing project in Chicago. The two boys—brothers—struggle to overcome the odds against them—poverty, violence, racism. It is a moving account.

Sale, K. (1980). *Human scale.* New York: Coward, McCann, & Geoghegan, 558 pp.

A review of society, politics, economics, and community from the perspective of scale. Sale's thesis is that any institution, from school to families to government, will function best at an optimal size. Person-to-person interaction and understandable levels of complexity are important for the effective functioning of organizations, and this book argues that many current social and interpersonal problems share the common root cause of inflexible, oversized, and exploitative institutions which fail to address human needs. Numerous ideas are put forth describing various institutions designed "to the human scale," meeting the needs of children and families and of society as a whole.

Tannen, D. (1990). *You just don't understand*. New York: Ballantine Books.

Tannen is a linguist. She presents an analysis of male/female communication differences as a matter of different cultures—masculine culture with its emphasis on competition, hierarchy, and independence; feminine culture with its emphasis on cooperation, intimacy, and connectedness. This book makes a good comparison for Carol Gilligan's classic *In a Different Voice* (Cambridge, MA: Harvard University Press, 1982), which is a "must" for those interested in gender and sexism.

QUESTIONS FOR THOUGHT

1.   In what ways can a family microsystem in which both parents work fulltime be a risk to a child's development? In what ways an opportunity?

2.   Negotiation is described in the chapter as a characteristic of authoritative parenting. Review how this differs from authoritarian and permissive styles of parenting and consider some risks to development in the latter two. Is the superiority of the authoritative style universal and absolute? Can situations require an authorization or permissive style?

3.   In this chapter we discovered the home–school relationship as one example of a mesosystem. What are some other important mesosystems for the child, and what are their risks and opportunities to development? What are some mesosystem problems that might arise? How might we avoid or prevent these problems?

4.   What are some ways to counteract the risks of the exosystem? Can families better serve themselves individually or by banding together in the community in the face of exosystem risk?

5.   The chapter discussed several examples of macrosystem risk. Think about some of their causes and the reasons they are so hard to overcome. What might be some ways of lessening their effect in our society?

6.   Consider the concept "support system." Describe support systems at each level of the human ecosystem. What are some of the important systems for children? for parents?

4

The Family as a Social System

James Garbarino and Robert H. Abramowitz

Social historian Colin Geer (1972) points out five common views on the
condition of "The American Family":

1. The family is decaying. In this view, the traditional family is falling
    apart, and the security of the nation is, as a result, in jeopardy.
2. The family is evolving. The adherents of this view say that the
    family, like any institution, must keep up with the times to do its
    job.
3. The family is not changing much at all. In this view, all the anxiety is
    misplaced—what is called the crisis of the family is simply a version
    of usual intergenerational conflict coupled with a dose of nostalgia.
4. There are changes in the family, but there is no need to worry about
    them. From this point of view, the institutional structure of society
    is always changing and family changes are simply a reflection of
    that.
5. The family is in retreat, defending itself against the power of the
    human-potential movement. In this perspective, the family is an
    oppressive agent of an oppressive social system that is being beaten
    back by the positive, progressive forces freed in a postindustrial
    society undergoing liberation.

Any discussion about the human ecosystem must deal with the family.
As the "headquarters for human development," families are the most
basic and enduring of social institutions. At the same time, families, like
all systems, are changing all the time in response to their members' needs
and the pressures of the society around them.

This chapter looks at the family in two ways: as a small group of people
sharing love, intimacy, and responsibility for children, and as a social
institution that serves and reflects the American macrosystem. All the
richness and diversity of the human species are present in families. We
view ethnic, cultural, historical, and personal variations as sources of po-

tential strength, as adaptations to specific conditions that provide different answers to the age-old question of how to achieve personal closeness and share rights, responsibilities, and participation in the wider society. But we also acknowledge that families can malfunction. Finally, the chapter addresses current family weaknesses and points of stress with an eye toward ways that helpers and policymakers can build family strengths and ameliorate family weaknesses.

What Is a Family?

Families are the thread that holds the human race together. Through our families we are connected to the past—the distant times and places of our ancestors—and to the future—the hope of our children's children. For most people, family means home, and home is where the heart is. In the words of Robert Frost: "Home is the place where/when you have to go there/they have to take you in" (from "The Death of the Hired Hand"). Family is a psychological rather than a physical place, but as we know from the plight of the homeless, having a place to be a family helps the system work for its members.

How can we go about studying and trying to help families? Families are the central microsystem, the "headquarters" for human development. Therefore, we must know the kinds of experiences families offer parents and children if we are to understand the ecology of human development. It is also possible to think of the family as a social institution and ask questions about family patterns throughout society. These viewpoints—individual families and "the" family—will be the two main approaches to families we use in this chapter. We will also discuss how we can understand and eventually strengthen and support families using the ecological approach to human development discussed in Chapters 2 and 3.

What is a family? Despite the fact that all over the world there are diverse cultures with widely differing family forms, three commonalities emerge in most analyses: marriage, childbearing, and kinship. According to Reiss, the universal essence of the family is "a small kinship-structured group with the key function of nurturant socialization" (Reiss, 1980, p. 29). "Kinship," however, is a matter of social definition, representing a consensus about the scope and limits of family membership. Generally it extends outward from the individual through linkages of blood and marriage. It can be based on genetic ties or social ties, and often implies economic rights and responsibilities. Within the family, parents contract with each other through marriage or at least through some enduring relationship to share the responsibilities of childrearing. Thus, the central elements of the family are kinship as seen by the family and others, marriage or its surrogate uniting parents, and dependent children cared for by family members. The family also serves a vital social function.

> The family means many things to many people, but in its essence it refers to those socially patterned ideals and practices concerned with biological and cultural survival of the species. (Keller, 1971, p. 1)

Contemporary social forms, most particularly the single-parent household, challenge traditional formulations of "family." Although single-parent families are certainly families, there is substantial debate about their inherent functionality. For purposes of rearing children, it seems clear that having a second adult in a family to support and complement the first in her (or his) relations with children makes abundant good sense. Must these two adults be married or even cohabiting to function this way? In principle, the answer is "no." In practice it seems much more likely they will cooperate on childrearing if they are members of the same household and—all other things being equal—are woman and man (if not wife and husband). Of course any discussion of family structures and forums is only a proxy for *processes* of interaction.

So although it seems clear that two parent families create a higher probability of success, a well-functioning one-parent family is better for children than a malfunctioning two-parent family—for example, one in which there is physical, sexual, or psychological abuse and neglect. (And, a well supported, well functioning step family *can* succeed better than a two parent family with both adults being the child's biological parents.)

So, we must admit single-parent families into our discussion without bias (albeit with the recognition that their success may hinge on finding other adults to complete the important micro- and mesosystem functions that require more than one adult).

So perhaps we need to base our discussion on a less restrictive criterion, namely, at least two people related by blood, marriage or adoption. Such a compromise seems better in tune with modern social realities. Our goal throughout this book is to respect diversity, and thus, we must adapt to changing norms. But we must do so without capitulating to the trends that produce them if we believe those trends to be harmful. Our goal is pluralism: diversity within a common framework of general principles.

Individuals are born into a family—called the family of origin—and eventually may start a family of their own—the family of procreation. Children, parents, and the lifelong bonds of kinship make up the basic family concept. The family of origin precedes the child, because he or she does not choose his or her family. Children are almost completely dependent for the first few years of life, and this basic biological fact necessitates social patterns that protect, nurture, and teach children. On children depend both the future of the families and the society into which they are born. Childhood is the one time when life really does "owe us living." In turn, children learn what they are expected to do to become members of society, what they must do to become a person (e.g., learning how to care for and socialize children). The family is a place for children to love and to be loved, to learn and to teach, to serve and to be served.

The family takes many different forms, both across cultures and within societies. The traditional norm for our culture is for a man and a woman to marry and then raise their children together. However, there are quite a few variations on that basic theme. Many children (18% at any one time) are raised by only one parent—almost half spend sometime in a single parent household during their first 18 years. Not all couples have children—perhaps 20% do not (Blake, 1979). Yet, the marital institution is, in many ways, the center of the family in culture and in practice. Theoretically, at least, it is a voluntary tie, one that offers certain benefits and responsibilities to a couple, and that makes possible the nurturance of children. Considering the families of origin and procreation, most people spend much of their lives in family units, and virtually all of their lives as part of an active kin system of some sort. We fulfill our needs for identity, relatedness, intimacy, and growth—our most deeply human qualities—through our lives in families. The family is the great humanizer. In the words of Margaret Mead:

> As in our bodies we share our humanity, so also through the family we have a common heritage . . . the task of each family is also the task of humanity. This is to cherish the living, remember those who have gone before, and prepare for those who are not yet born. (Mead, 1966, p. 11)

Many families evidence intergenerational themes—the same patterns are repeated across generations (e.g., themes of alcoholism, of early or late marriage or childbearing, of interest in the arts, or of marital conflict). For example, over three generations, Alexander Graham Bell's family evidenced an intense interest in problems in speaking and hearing. These family traditions seem to come to fruition in his invention of the telephone.

Families as Systems

Just as individuals develop within the family microsystem, families are situated within society. The relations between a family and the larger society are meso-, exo-, and macrosystem issues, as we defined these terms in Chapters 2 and 3. The mesosystems between families and such microsystems as schools, churches, and friendship networks are the most concrete expressions of the family–society relation. Exosystems of importance to the child include the parents' workplace and the local government. Finally, the overall cultural climate for families in society is an important influence on their well being. This is a macrosystem concern, and we will consider it again in Chapter 6 and then again in Chapters 10 and 11.

The family mediates between individual and society. Most children are prepared for membership in society through family socialization in social relationships. In this way the family can be seen as "society in miniature," localizing and concretizing societal values and practices in every household to a greater or lesser degree. The match between what the family models and teaches and what society wants and needs is not perfect, however. The family is not a "rubber stamp," automatically producing model citizens. The unique advantages and shortcomings of every family affect the future of our society in the form of our children, tomorrow's citizens. The macrosystem suggests blueprints, or models, for personal and social development; families respond based on their own inner workings, traditions, and values. The resulting dialogue between the individual, the family, and society is the stuff of history. Hagestad wrote: "It [the family] is an arena where lives are structured and interwoven, in which meanings are created in a blending of historical forces, family realities, and individual needs and resources" (Hagestad, 1981a, p. 11).

An excellent example of the kind of dynamics existing among individual, family, and society is Elder's (1974) study of the Great Depression summarized in Chapter 2. The intricate complexity of the connections may seem forbidding, but it does reflect the nature of these social realities. Family, individual, and society are inextricably intertwined; geneology, biography, and history are wedded. Extricating the thread of family from the fabric of human experience is no easy task, as the following account demonstrates.

The balance of power among the individual, the family, and society seems to differ across time and culture. This variety has been the topic of much speculation. In the 1940s Carle Zimmerman analyzed civilizations through history in terms of the relations among individual, family, and social power (Zimmerman, 1947). He saw three main family forms, each associated with a different phase of historical development, and each reflecting a particular constellation of social forces. His analysis tells us as much about him as it does about families, of course, and as much about his time and place as it does about the civilizations he studied.

In Zimmerman's view, the most primitive family type is the trustee family. Actually a clan or tribe, the trustee family tends to be the predominant force in "primitive" society. It is governed autocratically and parents rule by brute force. The individual is subservient, and there are few if any formal institutions apart from the clan. As Zimmerman saw it, the trustee family, based entirely on particularistic concerns, cannot exist outside of a primitive civilization. Of course, a more broadly based anthropological awareness tempers this view (Mead, 1935). Thus, we can see replicas of the trustee family in "modern" societies.

As Zimmerman saw it, the trustee family breaks down gradually. As individuals seek the freedom and diversity the clan does not offer, a more developed and elaborate community begins to evolve. A society emerges, with government, commerce, law, and literate culture. Individuals establish nuclear families ("the domestic family"), apart from the domination of the tribe, both as a cause and effect of socioeconomic development. An equilibrium is struck among the three levels (individual, family, and society), with each able to attain its goals. This phase of history, according to Zimmerman, constitutes a kind of Golden Age and has occurred in the prime of the Greek, Roman, and modern eras. Like most social commentators, however, Zimmerman saw his own era as a period of upheaval, and even dissolution, and "the decline of the family" was to blame. Ironically, Zimmerman's own era (the 1940s) is often cited by commentators in the 1980s as a Golden Era of family life.

The "atomistic family" is the third of Zimmerman's family forms, and it represents an excessive swing away from the trustee family. The balance achieved under the domestic family is threatened as society begins to usurp powers and functions from the family. As the family weakens, individualism grows to become the predominant cultural force. Family and social allegiances are minimized. The atomistic family is held together only by a private agreement, with the sacred tradition and the social pressure to maintain family institutions weakened. Sociobiologists see this as an "unnatural" family form because it deviates so markedly from our evolutionary history as a species (van den Berghe, 1979), and religious fundamentalists join them in this concern, albeit for quite different reasons. Zimmerman felt that the modern world was threatened with the fate suffered by the Greek and Roman eras, a downfall associated with the decline of the domestic family and the rise of atomism.

Many contemporary Americans share this concern about their own society, our society. Certainly one of the issues before us throughout this book is the analysis of the status of the modern family. Like Zimmerman, we may be seduced by the idea that our times are the worst of times, the times of decline. Therefore, we must be careful lest we impose unfounded biases on the phenomena and treat as "decline" and "deterioration" what may actually be simply adaptation—even healthy adaptation—to changed conditions. As the history of the term "cultural deficit" shows, this is a real and pressing danger for us (Tulkin, 1972). We are prone to see as deviation from societal norms what may actually be quite legitimate, equivalent differences in style. Certainly, we can see in Zimmerman's idealized domestic family a great deal that was in need of reform, particularly its patriarchical and authoritarian nature. Being a traditional male, Zimmerman was unable to see this as a problem.

Individual Families

As we said earlier, in some ways all families are alike, and in some ways each family is different. A family is a little society of its own, and in this sense every family has its own small-scale culture, government, language, foreign policy, and even its own myths. One way of understanding individual families is to describe the dimensions on which they vary.

Membership is the most basic dimension along which families vary. At a minimum, a family is two people related by blood or marriage, although such a small family is at one end of the membership continuum. These two can be a husband and wife, father and daughter, grandmother and grandson, or some other combination. An extended family, at the other extreme, is made up of a composite of nuclear families, with multigenerational ties. Cousins, aunts, and grandparents can join a couple and their young children to form a rich blend of ages and experiences. Homosexuals can join to create families.

A second important dimension along which families vary is their progress through various developmental stages. Several researchers have proposed models of these stages (e.g., Aldous & Hill, 1969). Duvall (1975) advanced one model of family life that focuses on the expansion and shifting of roles, both of individual family members and the family as a whole. The eight-stage model begins with marriage and traces the family through the growth of children and parents. Even in these most basic aspects, there is variation among families, however. Some families begin without marriage. U.S. Census data reveal a dramatic increase in the number of unmarried people cohabitating. These same data document a growing number of young women starting families without a permanent father in the family picture. At the same time, more families are existing as married couples without children, either temporarily (for 5 to 10 years) or permanently. Rather than jumping to the conclusion that these trends indicate social pathology because these families run against the model, we ought to first consider how well such patterns work for their participants and for the rest of society. This will allow us to see the "model" as an empirical standard rather than as a moral norm.

Stage 1. Beginning Families: when the couple is first married, before the birth of children. This represents creation of the microsystem. The principal ecological issue here is how macrostructural and other forces affect courtship and mating patterns. For example, wars tend to simultaneously speed up courtship and remove a major segment of the eligible bachelors. Both effects can influence who gets married and when. Also, until the last two decades it was common for marriage to follow pregnancy. One study estimates that 40% of first-born children in the 1940s and 1950s were premaritally conceived.

Stage 2. Childbearing Families: when the first child is born until it is 30 months of age (when a second child is in the works). Birth of a child radically alters the microsystem of the family. What is more, it makes relevant a whole new set of mesosystems (e.g., daycare–home) and exosystems (e.g., working conditions).

Stage 3. Families with Preschool Children: when the first child is between 2½ and 6 years old. Still additional mesosystems come into play (e.g., preschool–home), and the relevance of the neighborhood as a physical and social environment increases.

Stage 4. Families with School Age Children: first child between 6 and 13 years old. The school–home relationship is added to the list of relevant mesosystems, as is the relation between peer group and home.

Stage 5. Families with Teenagers: oldest child 13–20 years old. Again, the mesosystem potential (if not demand) increases, as does the influence of exosystems, as the child's world expands.

Stage 6. Families as Launching Centers: when the first child leaves until the last child leaves. Here the macrosystem becomes particularly important, because it has much to say about how ready the environment is to receive a specific youth.

Stage 7. Families in the Middle Years: from when all children are gone until breadwinner's retirement. Here the family depends on the children to establish themselves so that the parents may find support from them. This is a mesosystem issue (home$_1$–home$_2$).

Stage 8. Aging Families: from retirement until the death of one spouse. Here the progress of the family depends very heavily on all levels of the human ecology—the health of the organism, the functionality of the marital relationship, the support from outside the home and the socioeconomic blueprints that affect pensions and the status of the elderly in society.

These eight stages are organized around typical or normative events and do not apply to all families equally. However, they provide a general model that is useful for orienting ourselves to families and the relative importance of various social forces and institutions to them at different times. The differences we encounter across families, cultures, and communities are as important as the commonalities. In every case we must be ready to analyze these differences with an open mind and an eye on childrearing outcome. The professional helper should be prepared to deal positively with these differences as expressions of human coping until and unless proven differently.

A third dimension of families is actually external to the family itself, but exerts a powerful influence in determining a family's "personality." We refer to the cultural and historical context. Even within the United States, extensive variability exists among families, as we look across subcultures and over time. Family norms—commonly held ideas as to what should happen in families, and when—have a good deal of consistency *within* ethnic, religious, and socioeconomic subcultures (although even here there is substantial variability), at a given period of time, and a wide diversity *between* cultural and historical categories (although there are some generally common themes.)

A most fruitful focal point for our discussion of family differences is ethnicity. Ethnic differences in family norms embrace nearly all aspects of definition, structure, process, and outcome. They derive from historical experience—e.g., an agrarian, peasant tradition versus an urban, commercial tradition—and perhaps even from the evolutionary history of gene pools (Freedman, 1974). They touch family form and membership—e.g., nuclear vs. extended. They figure as both causes and mediators of demographic trends—e.g., marriage, fertility, and divorce—and social status—e.g., occupational and vocational aspirations and achievement. They incorporate norms about sex roles—e.g., who makes family decisions and who disciplines the children—and intergenerational relations—e.g., the authority of grandparents. They affect critical aspects of parent–child relations—e.g., the use of corporal punishment and expectations about independence and maturity demands. Although some ethnic differences have subsided in recent de-cades as the major pre-World War II European immigrant groups have been acculturated, strong differences remain, even among these groups. What is more, the very significant increase in Hispanic populations in much of the United States and the assertion of ethnic identity by Native Americans, African Americans, and Asians have meant a major up-swing in concern for ethnic variations. Assessing the meaning, signifi-cance, and service implications of ethnic and cultural differences for family relations is a major unmet challenge (Garbarino & Ebata, 1981; Cross, Bazron, Dennis, & Isaacs, 1989; Jenkins, 1981; Sue, 1981).

How Do Families Work?

Strong families find a way to produce competent children, to meet the emotional needs of the parents, and to serve a viable unit economically and socially. How do they do this? The National Commission on Chil-dren (1991) put it this way: there are several identifiable characteristics of strong families. Among the most important of these is clear, open, and frequent communication among family members. Similarly, strong fami-lies cultivate a sense of belonging to a warm, cohesive social unit, while at the same time nurturing the development of individual strengths and interests. In successful families, members provide one another mutual support, recognition, and respect, and they are willing to make sacri-fices if necessary to preserve the well-being of the family. A religious or spiritual orientation is an important characteristic of many strong fami-lies; so is the ability to adapt to and cope with stressful and potentially damaging events, as well as predictable life cycle changes. In part this adaptability relates to the family's social connectedness and the avail-ability of friends, extended family, neighbors, and community organiza-tions to lend a hand. Finally, in strong families, members tend to have clear, well-defined roles and responsibilities, and they enjoy spending time together. Although there are very few studies of minority families, one study suggests that among black families, a sense of racial pride or consciousness is an important indicator of strength. So, too, is a secure economic base, involving a steady source of income and a strong work orientation (pp. 254–255).

How does a family work? As a small group of individuals of different ages, sexes, and backgrounds, a family is a complicated, sometimes difficult, sometimes harmonious blending of different voices. Some fam-ily researchers have found it useful to consider three types of systems (Kantor & Lehr, 1975): the family unit, the interpersonal subsystems, and the personal subsystems. These systems divide the family into sections of decreasing size. The family unit is the family as a whole, the interaction of all members of a family. The interpersonal subsystem is the collection of smaller relationships within the family. A family of five people, for example, can be thought of as containing 10 different dyadic (two person) relationships (AB, AC, AD, AE, BC, BD, etc.). The personal subsystem is the total of individuals who come together to form a family and its interpersonal subsystems. Thus, a family of five members is five individuals in 10 possible dyads making up one family unit; a family of three individuals contains three dyads; a family of four contains six. Each member is an individual, a family member related to other family members, *and* a part of the whole family group.

The three family subsystems are helpful in understanding how families function. Family process—the give and take of daily life—depends on individual members, interpersonal relations, and the whole family group being able to come together and apart as needed. We can consider some important issues common to families to exemplify this point.

Family boundaries are the conceptual dividing lines among individuals, among the relationships between members, and between the family and the external world. Every family has its own ideas about where the rights and responsibilities of each member begin and leave off, vis-à-vis other members, the family as a whole, and the world at large. These ideas come mainly from the macrosystem's cultural blueprints, but may include idiosyncratic family traditions, personal histories, and ethnic aspects as well. Boundaries define how separate or connected the subsystems are, as well as the flexibility of movement between subsystems.

Boundaries define who is a stranger. A stranger entering a home can be made to feel welcome or intrusive, depending on the family's boundary to the external world. This can apply to members of the family, as in the case of a new baby, an adopted child, a stepchild, a child returning from foster care, or a stepparent. Adolescence is a trying time for many families because of the pressure to change family boundaries as the youth recedes from family authority and protection and enters intimate relationships outside the family that she or he may try to import into the family.

Internal organization is the pattern of interaction within a family. Communications, decision making, and family activities are some of the areas of internal organization. Family interaction establishes expectations for how members are to act toward each other. These are important to understanding what is considered "right" or "normal" in a family. In general, the nature of family life seems to generate norms about intimacy, frequency of contact, and power assertion (Burgess, 1980).

Family goals or themes are the priorities, values, and commitments the family sets for itself and for its members. These may be explicit or implicit and can range from very specific goals for children—e.g., attending college—to very general hopes—e.g., that the family will remain close over the years. Family goals often span the generations, acting as a cultural or genealogical legacy from the past that fosters continuity. Family goals are a key to the emotions and possible conflicts within families. Often such conflict is a result of mutually exclusive individual and family goals that reach crisis proportions in the hothouse of family interaction, as when one member wants to pursue personal fulfillment at the expense of the family business.

Virginia Satir, a noted family therapist, cited four areas that often present problems in troubled families (Satir, 1972): self-worth, communication, rules, and the link to society. Doubts about self-worth, the first problem, afflict the personal subsystem. Families can help or hinder an individual's positive self-regard, and when people suffer from basic doubts about their own worth and esteem, the family as a whole suffers. Rohner's work on rejection discussed in Chapter 3 reinforces this view, and we will expand on this in Chapter 6.

Communication problems are primarily problems of internal family organization. These can include a lack of dialogue, or a failure to get across each member's point of view. The classic complaint that teenagers and parents do not "speak the same language" is an example of this. Often more serious is the breakdown of communication between spouses. As noted in Chapter 3, gender differences in communication style (and goals) may contribute to communication problems between spouses. Linguist Deborah Tannen (1990) concludes from her research that often men and women really do not "speak the same language," and are as culturally different as any "mixed marriage" that combines ethnic differences (Anglo–Latin; Christian–Jewish, etc.).

In their study of abusive and neglectful families, Burgess and Conger (1978) reported that dysfunctional families were characterized by a relatively low level of overall interaction, and by couples with a tendency to ignore positive behaviors and respond to negative behaviors. Certainly any pattern that results in child abuse meets our criteria for being "at risk" rather than just different.

Family rules can be an interaction problem, or a problem associated with disagreement about attaining goals. These rules are often implicit and unstated, but they determine the ways in which members conduct their interaction. The rules become problems when they are ineffective in controlling behavior, when they do not facilitate the meeting of goals, or when members are no longer satisfied with them. A lack of flexibility is often part of the problem about rules (Baumrind, 1980). In this case, a family is not able to adjust to the pressures of inner or external forces smoothly, and members resist the normal transitions of life that produce role changes—e.g., the onset of adolescence or the wife going to work.

We can think of the family's link to society as a boundary issue. Family–society relations (meso-, exo-, and macrosystem issues) can be a problem when the walls are too high and rigid, as when a family distances itself from neighbors, institutions, and social supports (Gaudin and Polansky, 1985). Social isolation is a correlate of many family problems, such as child abuse (Garbarino, 1977a,b). The other extreme can also be a problem. If the family has no demarcation apart from society and is defenseless against outside influences, it may not provide adequate identity, support, and guidance for its members. At the extreme, it may cease to exist as a distinct entity.

As should be clear by now, scholars of the family are addicted to typologies, and the matter of boundaries is no exception. Kantor and Lehr (1975) have described three general types of contemporary families (not to be confused with Zimmerman's historical forms). Each has its own type of organization and method of attaining equilibrium among individuals, the family, and the outside world. Each views the family as a semipermeable system, with a constant stream of information and influence flowing in and through the family.

The first of Kantor and Lehr's family types is the "closed" family. Its limits are rigid, with clear and well-defined boundaries. Time is regular; the family functions on the basis of scheduled rhythms that supersede individual priorities or whim. Energy is steady, with family projects and concerns primary. The closed family is based on a "family comes first" philosophy, regulated by conformity to family goals, strict family events, family-defined reality, and an emphasis on stability. This family presents a challenge to us as helpers because it tends to resist the initiatives of human services and social policy, particularly when and if its members are having trouble. But there is usually strength and commitment to draw upon, if the professional can win over the family and gain its cooperation.

The second family type is "open." The open family is organized around flexibility. Its limits are variable, as members flow in and out of family realms easily. Scheduling of time is variable. Members try to regulate family events and the family tries to accommodate its members' concerns. There are family events, but they are flexible, based on the shifting needs of the members. Energy is flexible, with members free to involve themselves in both family and extrafamilial activities. Consensus is the usual operating procedure for decision-making in the family, and the family hangs together as the sum of individually and family-oriented members. It is strong, but inclined to be adaptive. It can make good use of external resources. It is the ideal form from the perspective of the human service provider and policy-maker. The danger, of course, is that the relative ease of serving this type of family will tend to make it the only family served.

The third family type is "random." The random family is marked by instability. Boundaries are unclear, shifting, and amorphous. Time is irregular, as members follow their own individual schedules. Any family event is more a coincidence than a planned commitment. Energy is fluctuating; members seek involvements in or out of the family with no limits or ongoing pattern upheld. The family as such barely exists, and is rather a collection of individuals sharing a household and engaging in interaction only when it happens to suit them. The random family is often the bane of existence for the provider of human services. It is difficult to get any social leverage on individual or dyadic problems through such families. It is like wrestling with jello. Unlike the closed family, it does not actively resist external forces, but often passively overcomes them. The challenge to the professional helper often seems overwhelming.

Building Strong Families

As we have said, each family is unique. Just as clearly, some families work better than others. How does one recognize which families are more successful? How can we encourage family strengths?

The crucial property of families, and of systems in general, is that the whole and its parts must both be able to meet their goals for both to continue. A family "works" when its members feel good about the family, when their needs are being met, and development and relationships flow smoothly. The whole functions best when the subsystems, in Kantor and Lehr's (1975) terms, recognize their responsibilities toward the family as a whole (the family unit), and when the family unit is flexible enough to encompass all its members as they pursue their individual goals. It is a very complex "All for one and one for all," along with a dose of "Each man for himself."

Stinnett, Chesser, and DeFrain (1979) studied a group of families suggested by community contacts as "strong families." Their interviews with them generated the following common characteristics:

Appreciation: The members regard each other warmly, positively, and give support to each other as individuals.
Spending time together: Strong families spend time together and enjoy it.
Good communication patterns: Family members are honest, open, and receptive toward each other.

Commitment: The family unit is important to its members, as are the interpersonal subsystems within the family. Much energy and time are directed inward toward the family rather than outward to other interests.

High degree of religious orientation: Strong families seem anchored in a sense of purpose that is often religiously based. A spiritual sense of life gives family members a common belief and promotes family values.

Ability to deal with crises in a positive manner: Strong families are able to deal with conflicts and band together in mutual support when bad times arise.

Lewis and his colleagues (1976) conducted a similar study based on urban Southern middle-class white intact families containing at least one adolescent child at home. Using rater observation scale, clinical interviews, and analysis of family communication, the investigators divided a small subsample of twelve families into six optimal and six adequately functioning families.

Based on 6 hours of clinical interview with each family, seven characteristics were found that distinguished the two groups and that correlated highly with the other two methods. The seven characteristics are as follows:

1. An affiliative, as opposed to an oppositional, attitude about people.
2. A respect for the subjective world view of self and others.
3. Openness in communication, as opposed to confusing or distancing communication.
4. A firm and solid parental coalition in dealing with children, as opposed to parental competition for the allegiance of the children.
5. Appreciation for complex human motivation, as opposed to a simple, controlling outlook.
6. Spontaneity, as opposed to a rigid or stereotyped approach to interaction.
7. The encouragement of unique and creative (as opposed to routine or bland) human characteristics and interests.

The individual members of the two groups also exhibited differences: Husbands from the optimal families were more interpersonally oriented, were supportive of their wives, and found vocational satisfaction important. Wives in the optimal group were more likely to have higher marital and family satisfaction than wives from the adequate group. Likewise, they suffered from symptoms of depression, psychopathology, and obesity less often. Of all family members, wives were the most vulnerable to family problems, being the first to show signs of distress.

It seemed that they absorbed the family's issues and carried its costs. There were no striking differences among the children in the two groups.

The researchers also found family organization to be an important and distinctive characteristic. Similar to Kantor and Lehr's (1975) three family types, the most dysfunctional families were those with a chaotic, disorganized structure. Adequate families had a rigid, conforming orientation, while the optimal families tended to exhibit a flexible structure balanced between individual and family needs, similar to Kantor and Lehr's open family.

The characteristics found in the two studies cited can be interpreted as being either causes of, or as results of, strong families. If it is the latter, it would not help to tell an unhappy, poorly functioning family to simply assume the characteristics of a strong family. But on the other hand, there are qualities associated with strong families that social service workers and all of society should recognize , respect, and encourage. The welfare of each individual member and of the family as a whole is an important characteristic of strong families. Stressing one at the expense of the other can be an invitation to trouble.

Learning to think in "family" terms, as opposed to "individual" terms, has led many people toward the growing field of family therapy. Unlike individual therapy, which treats a person outside their social environment, family therapy focuses on the troubled family as the unit of analysis for treatment. Often the family may join the "identified patient" in therapy—a child afraid to go to school, a rebellious, self-destructive teenager, or a feuding husband and wife. It is the family that is seen as a primary cause of members' problems or dysfunctions.

There are a number of different approaches to the family therapy movement, all attempting to help troubled individuals by intervening into patterns of family interaction. Some derive their approaches from psychoanalytic theory, others from behavioral modification theory, and still others from General Systems Theory. Family therapy holds out the hope of being an effective method of helping troubled families, as well as providing new insights into family process and dynamics.

Whither *The* Family?

Although there is probably no such thing as a "typical" family, we are interested in what families are like on the whole, and in how they change, particularly in how their structure and membership change. Demographic studies give us a sense of general family trends and allow us to speculate about the reasons for those trends. History is usually studied on a social level, but life is lived by individuals, and they are the real subject of attempts to understand the changing face of society. Rosa Luxemburg, the European socialist of the early twentieth century, said: "It is in the tiny domestic struggles of individual people, as they grope toward self-realization, that we can most truly discern the great movements of society." Sociologist C. Wright Mills echoed this theme:

> We have come to see that the biographies of men and women, the kinds of individuals they have become, cannot be understood without reference to the historical structures in which the milieux of their everyday life are organized. Historical transformations carry meanings not only for individual ways of life, but for the very character—the limits and possibilities—of the human being. (Mills, 1975)

Are Americans changing because American families are changing? The rate of divorce more than doubled from the 1960s to the 1980s (Reiss, 1980), so that now the Census Bureau estimates that between 40 and 50% of recent marriages will end in divorce (Spanier, 1980). Divorced parents are less likely than they were in the past to move in with a relative, and this separateness may produce both independence and vulnerability. One study reported that in 1900 one-half the households contained a nonparental adult (mainly boarders), while by 1970 less than 10% did (Bronfenbrenner, 1975). Demographers estimate that more than half the children born in this country will spend some of their first 18 years in single-parent homes. Research of the postdivorce experience of children reveals that 2 years after the breakup, only 53% of the children are seeing their noncustodial parent monthly. By 10 years after divorce, only 28% have monthly contact (Furstenberg et al., 1991). Thus, the number of adults in families living with children has declined.

The number of children per family has also fallen, from an average of over three children per woman born in the 1930s to an estimated rate below two children per woman born in the 1950s (Cherlin, 1981). This may partially offset the declining number of adults in American households, but it may present other challenges to family dynamics. Age at first marriage seems to be rising, with the median age now 24.4 for men and 22.8 for women, up almost 2 years for both sexes since the 1950s (U.S. Bureau of the Census, 1980a). Some of this is due to a decline in the likelihood for teens to marry as a *consequence* of pregnancy.

The proportion of all households in America that contain children declined from 1970 to 1990: from 45.3 to 36.2%. The proportion of households with married couples declined from 70.5 to 56% over that same period. Among households with married couples the proportion with children declined from 40.3 to 26.3%. Among all families, the proportion

with three or more children declined from 16.5% in 1970 to 7.0% in 1990.
As the average number of people per family was decreased (from 3.6 in
1970 to 3.2 in 1990), the number of people living alone has increased
(from 17.1 to 24.6%). Whereas most White, Asian, and Hispanic families
contain married couples (83, 82, and 70%) only half of African-American
families do (50%). In all cases, the 1990 figures reflect a significant decrease from 1970. Most of the single-parent families continue to be
female headed. Table 4.1 summarizes these changes.

One interpretation of these figures is that the lives of Americans are
becoming increasingly isolated. Because we are marrying later, divorcing more frequently, having fewer children, and living alone more often,
the number of people living together is declining. What effect does this
have on the family's social resources? When a child grows up in a household with "too few" people there is risk to development as discussed in
Chapter 3. We naturally wonder whether parents, too, are increasingly
deprived of intimacy and support, especially single parents who must
raise children alone.

Table 4.1.   Summary of Family Changes 1970–1990

Nature of Change	1970 number (%)	1980 number (%)	1990 number (%)
Married couple with children	25,532,000 (40.3)	24,961,000 (30.9)	24,537,000 (26.3)
Households with children	28,732,000 (45.3)	31,022,000 (38.4)	32,289,000 (34.6)
Households with married couple	44,728,000 (70.5)	49,112,000 (60.8)	52,317,000 (56.0)
Families with 3 or more children	10,440,000 (18.5)	7,109,000 (8.8)	6,496,000 (7.0)
Average number of people per family	3.6	3.3	3.2
Number of people living alone	10,851,000 (17.1)	18,296,000 (22.7)	22,999,000 (24.6)
Proportion of families with married couple			
White	41,029,000 (88.9)	44,751,000 (85.7)	46,981,000 (83.0)
Hispanic	1,615,000 (80.6)	2,282,000 (75.3)	3,395,000 (70.1)
African-American	3,317,000 (68.3)	3,433,000 (55.5)	3,750,000 (50.2)
Asian	(unavailable)	691,000 (84.5)	1,256,000 (82.0)

Source: U.S. Bureau of the Census (1991).

On the other hand, as Mary Jo Bane has shown in her book *Here to Stay* (1976) families are in no danger of extinction. The percentage of men and women who do marry eventually is quite high; by age 30 over 90% of men and women have been married at least once. Moreover, although many people delay childbearing, few forsake it completely. Though divorce is increasingly common, remarriage awaits 80% of currently divorced partners (Reiss, 1980)—one-half within 3 years. Fewer children per family may actually improve the quality of parent–child relations by allowing more time for each child and by reducing the risk of unwanted or unaffordable children (Blake, 1979). Research also shows that within social classes, children in smaller families score higher on intelligence tests than children in larger families (Claussen, 1966; Zajonc & Markus, 1975). We can expect that smaller families make it easier to operate in the "authoritative" style described by Baumrind (1979).

How do people feel about their families? A study published in 1976 on the quality of life in America found marriage and family life to be highly important to people (Campbell, Converse, & Rodger, 1976). Seventeen domains of life including standard of living, religion, family, work, and friends were assessed for their contribution to life satisfaction and their importance to the respondents. Health, marriage, and family life were cited most often as being "extremely important" factors, and marriage and family life were the domains that best predicted overall life satisfaction. Fifty-six percent of the women and 60% of the men were completely happy with their marriage, and 44% of the women and 43% of the men were completely happy with their family life in general. Only 6% of the men and 8% of the women rated the family as less than neutral in satisfaction. Perhaps the increasing acceptance of divorce in unsatisfactory marriages means that the "still married" include more satisfactory spousal relationships. These survey results suggest that family life is an integral part of people's lives and does much toward determining their overall life satisfaction.

It is interesting to note that satisfaction with marriage (an individual life-cycle variable) varies systematically over the family life cycle. Studies show that the transition to parenthood brings about a reduction in marital satisfaction, with the low point being the time when the children are teenagers. Once the children leave the parents at the "empty nest" stage, marital satisfaction may increase, even returning to the levels found in newlyweds (Rollins & Feldman, 1970; Rollins & Cannon, 1974; Campbell et al., 1976).[1]

---

1. Interestingly, this may be due in part to the most dissatisfied couples divorcing, leaving the more satisfied couples overrepresented in later years. A longitudinal design may be required to assess changes in marital satisfaction over time (Spanier, Lewis, & Cole, 1975).

What can account for the current trends in family life, and what can possibly help us understand the direction in which we are heading? One place to look is in the changes in fertility and mortality rates; the entrances and exits of individuals in families. The family is like a cross-country train. We may get on in Des Moines and get off in Denver, but the train started long ago in New York and will continue on without us until San Francisco. The actions of one generation have been influenced by the preceding generation and will have an effect on the next generations to come aboard. Hagestad writes:

> We have "ripple effects" because of the intimate interconnections of roles and lives. Marriage in one generation creates in-laws in another. Parenthood creates grandparenthood. Voluntary childlessness may create involuntary grandchildlessness. "Voluntary" divorce leaves children to be raised "involuntarily" in single-parent homes and creates "ex-relationships." (Hagestad, 1981a, p. 20)

Thus, the current trend toward small families will limit the possibility of large extended families in later years. The daughter of two only children will have no cousins because she will have no aunts or uncles. The increase in the life span will mean that potential intergenerational relations will increase. There will be more grandparents and great-grandparents, and they will be alive for more of the lives of their decendents. For the same reasons, people are spending proportionately fewer years of their lives with children at home, but they may paradoxically be financially responsible for them longer because of increased involvement in higher education (Garbarino, 1981b). The time spent in the "empty nest" stage of marriage may increase. Widowhood, too, is more probable because of the increasing gap in the life expectancy of men and women (Hagestad, 1981a). A family, then, changes along with the life pattern of its individual members.

Families and Social Change

Social, cultural, and technological change has also had a profound effect on families. In the midst of rapid technological and economic change, we expect social institutions and relations, especially the family, to continue in an unchanging, eternal pattern. Any change is generally considered to be a loss, a decline (Bane, 1976). "The good old days" is the often heard refrain regarding the family of yesterday. Yet the very nature of the ecology of human development tells us that family and society are connected. Families respond to rapid and significant changes felt in every aspect of contemporary public life. We must always examine our view of family life for projections of our own fears and hopes about the phenomena. Thus, we must be careful of defining change as "decline" or "deterioration," unless we can actually evaluate the direction of the change as negative Much of what we see as change is actually continuity; some of what we define as decline is actually healthy adaptation. Some things that we define as positive may be risk. And, even when we do observe real change, it may have no effect on children—one way or the other.

How have changes in society affected the family? The view of the family as a semipermeable system discussed earlier suggests an exchange between domestic and social forces, each influencing the other. Some say, however, that it is the family that has reacted to social change in this century, rather than the other way around. W. F. Ogburn, a sociologist writing in the early twentieth century, concluded "that the nuclear family was inappropriate and unstable in an urban industrial society" (Ogburn, 1922). The problem he saw and emphasized was the loss of family functions. On the farm or in a small family business all family members worked together. Modern society stripped the family of its productive and educational responsibilities. The family became an emotional and developmental center, rather than an economic entity. Women, especially, were limited by the nuclear family because it provided them neither personal outlet nor opportunity for contribution to the family's material needs. Other scholars (e.g., Aries, 1962) emphasize that even these deletions do not affect the nuclear family so much as the *addition* of functions previously handled by kin, elders, and church, or never performed in the first place.

The nuclear family may have reached a distinctive phase in the 1950s. Families in earlier generations were more frequently broken up by death, in later decades by divorce. The 1950s were an oasis of stability (Hagestad, 1981a). Cherlin (1981) points out that long-term trends were suddenly reversed after World War II: More people married; they married earlier and more permanently, had more children, had children earlier, and lived more in nuclear families than did people before or after that time. Thus, what we often see as the deviant 1960s and 1970s actually represent a return to long-term trends, while it is the 1950s that may have been deviant—albeit in a positive way from the viewpoint of those who appreciate the traditional male-dominated family with wife as full-time homemaker as in *Leave it to Beaver*.

Parsons and Bales' (1955) influential work on role specialization provided a theoretical perspective on nuclear families that was empirically well suited to the demography and ethos of 1950s. They found that small groups in laboratory studies contained "instrumental" and "expressive" leaders; the former were necessary to accomplish group goals, the latter, to keep the group's morale and feelings positive. Parsons and Bales saw men in the instrumental role, women in the expressive, despite the abundant evidence that both sexes perform both functions across different settings, to different degrees. This traditional ideology sees men as "naturally" extending their activities to instrumental spheres beyond the family (e.g., work), whereas women are primarily and "naturally" suited to the home or to limited involvements of an expressive nature beyond the home (e.g., nursing, teaching, volunteer work) (Parsons, 1949; Parsons, Bales, & Shils, 1955).

The theoretical serenity of the 1950s was not permanent, however. Family role differentiation theories were assailed as being both simplistic and inaccurate. Critics charged that men and women display both expressive and instrumental qualities in family life (Slater, 1961; Udry, 1974). Women, who were questioning the justice of being confined in rigid roles at home and denied choice, while their husbands had only to bring home a paycheck as fulfillment of familial responsibilities, were being heard publicly and in print in greater numbers.

Bernard (1981) calls this change the fall of the male "good provider" role. Under the growing market economy men had become identified and judged solely on the basis of their ability to provide for their families financially. Emotional and domestic responsibilities were secondary in the idealized middle-class home. The cooperation between men and women in providing for the families became a differentiated split. Separate? Surely. But equal? Each sex was identified in opposition to the other, unable to share in common tasks or concerns. Bernard describes the consequences of this role arrangement, and conveys the hostility and resentment some felt:

> As the pampered wife in an affluent household came often to be an economic parasite, so also the good provider was often, in a way, a kind of emotional parasite. (Bernard, 1981, p. 10)

In middle-class families the male provider role flourished as women were relegated to the home exclusively. Women have always been primarily responsible for childrearing, but only in the nineteenth and twentieth centuries has mothering been the full-time job for most middle-class women (Degler, 1980). The homemaker role makes sense only when there are many children for whom to care. It declines when fertility declines. The good provider role makes sense only in a family in which women are to be provided for. Bernard (1981) foresees this role diminishing as women more frequently both join the labor force and raise children alone. Some commentators now see the consequences of arbitrary sex roles, that idealize men working and women home with children, as destructive to men, women, and their children (Slater, 1970; Chodorow, 1978).

More egalitarian sex roles will require deep changes in our institutions and in our relationships. Children, work inside and outside the home, and the options men and women can choose from in general will have to be reexamined in order to accommodate and support families who want to decide for themselves how to balance the activities and responsibilities of their lives. The changing role of women is, thus, a challenge and an opportunity for families. Can families continue to provide for the needs of their members, while at the same time allowing them to become all they would like to be? All social arrangements have costs, as well as benefits. Can we decrease the former and increase the latter?

Alternative roles and careers for women make new and different demands on the men in their lives, as well as on the women themselves. Successful adaptation to those changes will depend on adaptations both within and beyond the family as all of society learns to cope with new family forms. Such innovations in business and industry as in-house day care, flexible work hours, part-time and split-time positions, maternal and paternal leaves, and a rethinking about just what is women's and men's work will help. However, available research shows that we have a long way to go in making these adjustments (Bronfenbrenner & Crouter, 1981). There is no doubt that maternal employment patterns have changed markedly; what is not clear is that society has responded well to these changes.

Work as an exosystem has traditionally been more an opponent than an ally of family relations. But as mothers employed outside the home become the rule rather than the exception, and as more fathers seek increasing involvement with their growing children, business and industry is adapting to workers' needs as parents. Job satisfaction and stability can be enhanced by creating a working atmosphere where workers do not feel cut off from their personal lives all day. A better integration of work and family responsibilities will, no doubt, improve the quality and satisfaction of both adult microsystems (Garbarino and Crouter, 1982).

Bruno Bettelheim, a child psychologist, singles out two other social innovations that have deeply affected the modern Western family: the rise in the standard of living and the availability of birth control (Bettelheim, 1980). The increased wealth made possible to the general public in modern society has tended to free the nuclear family from dependence on other families and family members. There is more mobility, both within and between families, as the economy expands. Young adults are able to move away from their parents, and older people are

more likely to be able to support themselves. Wealth has facilitated and
been accompanied by increased distance between family members. The
question is, will that distance be experienced mainly as freedom or as
isolation (Garbarino, 1977b)? And, as many families experience economic contraction in the 1990s, how will they respond?

Advances in contraception have made childbearing less the destiny
and more the choice of women. Clearly, sexual behavior, size of families,
women in the labor force, and the role of women in general are all
intimately affected by the ability to control pregnancy. Both affluence
and birth control make the family an institution created and maintained
more by choice and less by biological or economic necessity. The family
of today faces challenges precisely because the family is more voluntary.
What exactly are the challenges today's families face, and how can families be strengthened to stand a better chance of meeting them?

Families operate in the context of an ideological debate that has politicized microsystem and exosystem issues affecting parents and children. On one side stand adherents of "traditional families," who view
innovation as an enemy and personal fulfillment (especially women's
and children's) as a threat to the family. On the other side, many assail
the family as repressive and stultifying, a domestic straitjacket of conventional morality and guilt. The middle road between these two extreme positions sees an appreciation for individual development and
changing needs over the span of life, as well as for lifelong uncondi-
tional closeness and trust of family ties, with "family" defined loosely
enough to encompass more than just the traditional form. Is not the
ideal for people to have room to develop to their fullest, in the context of
the support and feedback of caring kin—and to do so in a way that
contributes to the vitality and stability of society?

Families are on their own. Family privacy, economic prosperity, and
mobility patterns all separate parents and children from traditional
sources of support and feedback, e.g., the church, elders, kin, and
neighbors. Isolation is contagious; we become estranged from each
other, and all families lose the social support of close and caring loved
ones. It is increasingly difficult for family values to compete with the
garish materialism and freedom of commercial society, and the ethic of
individualism works against the cooperation and mutual sacrifices necessary for stable families to operate.

Our level of expectation is very high. A kind of social inflation, born of
a rising tide of expectations, has made us acutely vulnerable to frustration and stress. The inevitable disappointments of life are magnified by
what are often unrealistic standards for self-fulfillment. On the economic scene, our expectation that everyone can and should live in a
single-family house, in the suburbs if possible, has led many families to

become financially overcommitted. The result is a high level of stress and disruption of family life. We experience well-being because of social rather than material conditions, as discussed earlier (Campbell et al., 1976). A biblical passage speaks to this point: "What profiteth it a man that he should gain the world if he should lose his soul?" The same goes for families.

A family is in a constant state of becoming. Parents meet and marry; children are born and grow and move on, possibly to start families of their own. At this time, we still know little about the strain placed on individuals and families at each of these normative life changes. Looking back to Duvall's (1975) family life cycle, every stage involves adjustments by members to changes in their own and other members' lives. More understanding and attention, aimed at helping families deal with change, would go a long way to strengthen families and prevent further and more serious problems.

There is and there will continue to be an increasing flexibility and innovation in human relations. Traditional family forms will not be replaced, but will instead exist alongside less long-lasting unions, single parents, groups of adults (related and unrelated, heterosexual and homosexual) living together and raising children, amidst a breakdown of gender roles in society. As customs and institutions, formerly required for economic survival, give way to more chosen and voluntary ties, we face an opportunity and a challenge to increase our capacity to meet people's needs for intimacy, love, and meaning, *and* to build social institutions that support these goals. The family will exist as long as we recognize and respond to our needs for close lifelong bonds.

We have begun to see how important family life is to human development through the entire span of life. Families are in crisis because of unsupportive social environments and cultural challenges. We need a sense of toleration to new and different family forms along with a commitment to the enduring needs of children and parents. The community, our institutions, and all of society must move carefully and respectfully around families, so as not to disturb the fragile and terribly important process going on within them—the building and sustenance of human beings.

RESEARCH CAPSULE

Of all the methods available in the study of families, none is more challenging or promising than naturalistic observation of families. Proponents of this method contend that family process can be best studied in the family's natural environment, where each family's unique dynamics are manifested.

The problems of naturalistic observation include the discomfort and anxiety of the families being observed and the great amount of time required to get a full and varied sampling of family life. Virtually any observational method will be faced with the problem of reactivity, of people acting differently because they are being observed. The advantage of natural observation as compared to laboratory or clinical studies is the fact that, in the home, the family is in their element and the subject of interaction will be the family's own concerns.

Two important examples of natural observation of families are Kantor and Lehr's *Inside the Family* (1975) and Jules Henry's *Pathways to Madness* (1973). Kantor and Lehr's work is described in the chapter and was used primarily to advance theoretical systems of family dynamics. Henry's work is essentially anthropological; each family is entered as if it were a foreign culture. He entered and spent a week (approximately 100 hours) in five different families, each containing a psychotic institutionalized member. During the week he lived with the family, participating as a guest or visiting relative might have. His account of his observations is a fascinating and rich description of the personalities and family dynamics of each of the families observed. Naturalistic observations can uncover family norms and patterns, the "social reality" of each family, and in the case of these families, their destructive nature. Such research offers an experiential base from which theory and understanding can readily spring.

PRACTICE CAPSULE

The idea of family impact analysis arose in the late 1970s as a way of evaluating the effect of government policy on families. In some ways analogous to environmental impact studies routinely done on the projected effect of development on the local ecosystem, family impact analysis determines how existing or proposed government programs and policies affect or could affect the nation's families.

Formed in 1977, the Consortium of Family Organizations (COFO) is composed of five national organizations working together to promote a family focus in public policy and social programs. Member organizations of COFO are the American Association for Marriage and Family Therapy, the American Home Economics Association, Family Resource Coalition, Family Service America, and the National Council on Family Relations.

COFO has developed a tool to serve as the basic framework for evaluating the impact or potential impact of public policies. The tool is organized around six principles to guide policymaking.

1. *Family Support and Responsibilities.* Policies and programs should aim to support and supplement family functioning and provide substitute services only as a last resort.

2. *Family Membership and Stability.* Whenever possible, policies and programs should encourage and reinforce family, parental, and marital commitment and stability, especially when children are involved.

3. *Family Involvement and Interdependence.* Policies and programs must recognize the strength and persistence of family ties, even when they are problematic.

4. *Family Partnership and Empowerment.* Policies and programs must consider families as partners when providing services to individuals.

5. *Family Diversity.* Families come in many forms and configurations, and policies and programs must take into account their different effects on different types of families. Policies and programs must recognize the diversity of family life, neither discriminating against nor penalizing families solely for reasons of structure, roles, cultural values, or life stage.

6. *Targeting Vulnerable Families.* Families in greatest economic and social need and those judged to be most vulnerable to breakdown should have the first priority in government policies and programs.

FOR FURTHER READING

Hewlett, S. A. (1991). *When the bough breaks: The cost of neglecting our children.* New York: Basic Books.

Hewlett is an economist with an interest in social issues. This book presents data from many sources to document the thesis that America neglects its children. We do not have many of the supportive policies common to Western Europe, and our children suffer as a result, poor *and* rich.

Parker, B. (1972). *A mingled yarn.* New Haven: Yale University Press, 333 pp.

This account of a woman's family history, written by a psychologist, traces the forces which led to the dissolution of her family and one member's insanity. It reads like a good novel with a psychoanalytic flavor and offers a rare insight into a family's workings. Recommended for readers interested in the intergenerational transmission of values and problems.

Reiss, I. R. (1980). *Family systems in America* (3rd ed.). New York: Holt, Rinehart & Winston, 538 pp.

A leading text on the family, covering such topics as courtship, mate selection, marriage and childbearing, and cross-cultural and ethnic perspectives on the family. Reiss has a special interest in sexuality, and the book is particularly strong in that area. The section on family research methods is a welcome addition.

Satir, V. (1972). *People making.* Pala Alto, CA: Science and Behavior Books, 304 pp.

A wonderful book for and about families. It discusses common family problems and concerns in lay terms. There are many exercises and projects that families or groups can work on to facilitate communication, empathy, and family bonds. It is a very "up-beat" book with anecdotes and a "fun for all ages" appeal.

Stinnett, N., Chesser, B., & DeFrain, J. (Eds.). (1979). *Building family strength: Blueprints for action.* Lincoln, NE: University of Nebraska Press, 449 pp.

This book was the first of a series from the National Symposium on Building Family Strengths. Held at the University of Nebraska, this symposium is devoted to the advancement of "positive family life models." The volume contains articles on family strengths, approaches to family enrichment and counseling, effective parenting, children with special needs, and the family in later life. This book and the series that follows have proved successful in contributing to the growing literature on the strengthening and support of families.

QUESTIONS FOR THOUGHT

1.   Discuss the many types of families that occur in our society and around the world. Do they share any commonalities? How are they different?

2.   What are some of the risks and opportunities families face in times of rapid social change? Think about such factors as mobility, changes in the labor force, sex roles, and generation gaps.

3.   How are ethnic differences important for the person who works with children and families?

4.   Duvall (1975) described eight developmental stages of families. Discuss some of the different challenges and problems families face at each stage of the family life cycle. What examples of families can you think of that do not fit this general pattern? What implications do those differences have for the development of these families? Are the same supports available to them as to the families that are "typical?" Does it matter if families take these steps "out of order"— e.g., having a child before getting married?

5.   Satir (1972) regards self-worth, rules, communication, and links to society as four key areas with a potential for problems for the family. Review and discuss how each can become a source of family problems, and make suggestions on how to improve conditions for families with such problems.

6.   What are problems you would expect to be typically associated with each of Kantor and Lehr's (1975) three family types?

7.   Many families are currently adopting more egalitarian sex roles in childrearing, housework, decision-making, and work outside the home. What implications does this change in roles have for adults in the family? for children?

8.   Considering the evidence of recent demographic trends, would you conclude that the family is in trouble, or merely adapting? Consider some of the family typologies described in the chapter (e.g., Zimmerman, Kantor & Lehr) to defend your point of view. Are new family functions replacing old ones no longer performed by the family?

5

The Developing Child in a Changing Environment

Joanne L. Benn and James Garbarino

Children provide the building blocks of human society. Bronfenbrenner (1970) reminds us that one important clue to understanding the values and robustness of a society is to look at how it does by its children. When children are suffering we are seeing a society in trouble.

In this chapter we explore the basic developmental processes that transform the human organism into the person, the fertilized egg into the child. We begin prenatally and chart the child's progress through adolescence. Although we are interested in the forces that give a common shape to early development, we are more concerned with the ways developmental blueprints are modified within contrasting social environments.

Most of all, we are fascinated by the complexities in the developmental process, complexities that flow through and from the way thinking, acting, feeling individuals help construct their own environment.

What Is a Child?

The answer to this question should be simple but it is not. Over time, terms like "child," "baby," "girl," and "boy" have conveyed several different meanings.

Typically, the terms are used to provide information about age or maturity. Even then the message is not a simple one. At what age does childhood begin: at conception, viability, birth, or the end of infancy? Is its end marked by physical signs, individual accomplishments, elaborate rites of passage, or the attainment of an arbitrary legal age?

Sometimes, "child" has been used to give information about special relationships. Regardless of how old we become, we will always be our parents' children. Those of us who are the last born will always be "the baby of the family," regardless of our age, accomplishments, or physical attributes. In the distant past, these terms also were used to connote economic dependence or servitude. Then, it was an accepted practice to refer to a worker as "child" or "knave." Today, we cringe when an insensitive employer says, "I'll have my girl type it," or describes an African-American adult as "A hard-working boy."

For other insights into our ideas about childhood, we can consider what is meant by the description "child-like" and "childish." For some of us, "child-like" conveys an adult who has the simple directness and wonder of a child. But "childish" means cute, innocent, playful, or untrained.

Debates about the nature of childhood are not new. During the Middle Ages, children were thought to be inherently sinful and parents were encouraged to punish them often (some fundamentalist Christians still believe this). By the eighteenth century, attentive childrearing was encouraged to safeguard the child's innocence.

The philosopher John Locke likened the mind of the newborn to a blank slate that provides form but not content to the individual—"tabula rasa." Environment, then, would shape the child's development. His contemporary, Jean-Jacques Rousseau argued for the need to protect the "natural goodness" of children from corruption by the influences of society.

Certainly, the way that we think and feel about the term "child" depends on our experiences with individual children, our understanding of current "cultural wisdom" about what is best for children, and our own personal experience as a child. What we know and care about children is revealed in the actions we take to help ensure their development.

What Is Development?

To understand the meaning of development, it is useful to distinguish development from growth. Typically, early growth rates are characterized by steady increases during infancy, plateaus during the preschool years, and noticeable spurts that seem to signal school entry and the onset of puberty. Under normal conditions growth tends to follow a path described by heredity—to be "canalized." As a result, slowed growth during periods of illness is often followed by dramatic spurts of "catch-up growth" on the child's recovery.

Although we reserve the term for an increase in the size or number of cells, "growth" is a word that is best reserved for simple physical changes such as adding pounds or inches. On a diet of hot fudge sundaes, we will *grow* fat but we will not be described as "well developed."

In contrast, development involves increasing differentiation, complexity of organization, or refinement of functioning in a selected developmental domain. During the early years, development often follows an orderly progression, with each accomplishment presenting new challenges that leads to still other developmental tasks.

Sometimes development in one domain seems to take precedence over others, such as when an infant's attentions alternate between the monumental tasks of learning to walk and talk. More often, achieving a developmental task in one domain also promotes development in another area of functioning. For example, the change in perspective when physical development allows infants to change from a "lie down to a sit-up world" is usually matched by advances in cognitive development. Later, achieving the ability to read brings a surge in self-confidence while concrete operational thought promotes shifts in moral reasoning. The physical changes of puberty raise questions of personal identity.

As we study the course of human development, our tasks are to describe developmental changes and explain how these changes occur (Baltes, Reese, & Nesselroade, 1979). When appropriate, we also can try to optimize the potential for positive change.

What is distinctly human in the development of children? It is not the process of learning. All organisms learn—albeit not with the eventual depth and complexity of human beings. What is most striking about human development is the complexity and depth of human *teaching*. Child development is intrinsically *social*; happening through and in the context of relationships. The Soviet psychologist Lev Vygotsky (1962) recognized this, and built his approach to child development on this recognition.

In Vygotsky's approach, the key is the difference between what a child can do alone and what that child can do in the company of a good teacher. This "teacher" can be anyone who interacts with the child and offers responses that move the child beyond where he or she is to where he or she could be. Vygotsky called this the zone of proximal development (ZPD) to reflect the fact that the optimal response to the child is neither too "close" nor too "far" from where the child is operating at any given moment. Optimal child development occurs when the child and the teacher operate in the child's ZPD.

Many child development manuals designed for parents and certain introductory textbooks for professionals are organized according to normative ages of acquisition, or the chronological age at which the "typical child" will accomplish individual developmental tasks.

This "age and stage approach" acknowledges the progression of developmental tasks that seem to unfold in a predictable fashion from
infancy through adolescence. It is true that biological influences play
such a prominent role during the early years that individual variability
in development is less striking than it will be during adulthood. For that
reason, knowing a child's chronological age frequently provides reliable
clues about a child's current developmental tasks. But memorizing developmental norms does not make a child development expert any more
than development is the simple act of completing a checklist of skills!

It is important to remember that the "typical child" of textbook fame is
the product of statistical calculations, not reality. The normative ages
that mark this mythical child's development are merely the age by which
50% of a sample of children achieved particular skills. For example,
parents often expect infants to take their first steps on the first birthday,
an expectation confirmed by norms on the Bayley Scales of Infant Development (Bayley, 1969). However, 5% of the 1262 children in Bayley's
standardization sample took at least three steps alone by 9 months; it
was not until 17 months that at least 95% of the children had walked
alone successfully. Does it matter much in the long run if a child is
"early" or "late"? In most cases, the answer is "no."

Adhering to expectations for the typical child, rather than appreciat-
ing the wide range of needs and abilities represented within a group,
can frustrate adults and hamper children's development. Recent trends
in kindergarten entrance have made this a pressing issue (cf. Bredekamp
& Shepard, 1989; National Association for the Education of Young Children, 1990).

Whereas some parents push for early kindergarten enrollment as an
answer to child care dilemmas, others practice so-called "redshirting,"
holding children out of kindergarten for an extra year in hopes of decreasing the problems of immature children, and in some cases even in
an effort to seek developmental advantage over their peers. The effects
of these practices are heightened by institutional policies such as preschool readiness testing—which deems some children "not ready" to
begin school—and kindergarten retention—which indicates that either
the child or the educational institution has failed the kindergarten experience. As a result of these trends, the chronological range in any kindergarten classroom might be more than 3 years, and the developmental
age even greater! To offer a program designed for a textbook norm or
even the average child in the class is sure to sour many children on their
introduction to school.

When working with groups of children, then, it is usually preferable
to consider the age *range* in which normal children tend to accomplish a
certain developmental task and the variability within a specific group

across a number of different tasks. The Position Statement on Developmentally Appropriate Practices in Early Childhood Programs (Bredekamp, 1987) issued by the National Association for the Education of Young Children suggests ways that teachers and caregivers can provide educational programs that reflect the developmental diversity likely to be represented in classrooms for young children.

The guidelines define developmentally appropriate practices as those that are both age appropriate (reflecting the abilities and interests typical of a particular age group) and individually appropriate (sensitive to the different skills, styles, and needs brought by individuals in the group). Adopting an ecological approach to early education, the guidelines also call for ongoing exchanges between teachers and family members, plus cooperation among families and all participating agencies during times of transition. As many early childhood programs nationwide have implemented the guidelines for preschoolers and those in the primary grades, child advocates have urged extending the basic principles to programs for older children and adolescents.

To understand how adults can help create the best circumstances for early development, it is important to consider the many factors that influence the developmental course.

The Genetic Code: A Developmental Blueprint

A developing child is a miracle. From a microscopic speck containing the genetic blueprint of the species comes an organism complete with individual variety. Sometimes that variety is an asset, such as beautiful eyes or an extraordinary talent. At other times, the genetic or chromosomal structure alters the body and brain in such a way that it creates additional challenges for the developmental agenda. Down's syndrome is one example.

We can begin to appreciate the vast potential for human variation by thinking of the number of different codes transmitted. The moment of conception is the union of 46 chromosomes; 23 from each parent. Those chromosomes contain 100,000 genes, which in turn contain three to six billion chemical subunits that contain the genetic code. Because conception can result in any possible combination of sperm and ova; it has been estimated that the world's population represents the potential for as many as 70 million different genetic blueprints (Hetherington & Parke, 1979).

To date, genetic scientists have identified more than 3000 hereditary diseases resulting from a single defective gene, some of which are extremely rare. In fact, it has been estimated that fewer than 8% of all congenital malformations result from the action of single genes and another 6% are associated with chromosomal abnormalities (Kalter & Warkany, 1983). The effects of some of these conditions are so severe that they arrest prenatal development; more than 50% of all spontaneous abortions have been linked to genetic causes. Despite the many recent advances in the field, geneticists will labor well into the next century to identify the complex gene combinations and genetic–environmental interactions associated with a host of additional conditions.

Some genetic or chromosomal anomalies result from simple mutation, a quirk in transmission. Others reflect maternal history: For example, both radiation exposure and the age of the ova are linked to chromosome damage. More often, however, the faulty codes are inherited, or transmitted within a family line.

Some groups are prone to certain genetic anomalies because their common history has pooled the tendency to inherit certain characteristics. Thus, for example, people descended from areas in which serious malaria outbreaks occur (e.g., Central Africa and the Mediterranean region) are more likely to have red blood cells that are sickled, deviating from the characteristic round shape. Because the sickled cell structure offers protection from the malarial parasite, those with the sickle cell gene seem to have inherited an adaptive advantage for survival in specific geographic areas. They survive and pass on *both* the protection from malaria and the risk of sickle cell anemia.

This advantage does not extend to other locales, however. Although generally healthy, those who are heterozygous for the sickle cell trait, including about 8 to 10% of African-Americans, run the risk of severe oxygen deprivation under extreme conditions, such as physical exertion in high altitudes. When two parents with the sickle cell trait pass their recessive genes to an offspring, the result is sickle cell anemia, a sometimes fatal condition associated with chemical alterations of hemoglobin molecules and painful damage to vital organs.

The concentration of inherited characteristics depends on the exclusiveness of mating. For example, hemophilia once ravaged the royal houses of Europe because of marriage restrictions tied to title and lineage. The deleterious genetic code for Tay-Sachs Disease, a lethal condition that produces mental and physical deterioration, remains strong today because of in-group marriage ("homogamy") among Eastern European Jews. One in every 25 Jews carries the gene for Tay-Sachs disease, compared to a rate of 1 in 300 for most other Caucasians.

Each of us has some faulty genes. Fortunately, most of them are rare. Most are also recessive, meaning that both parents must possess the deleterious gene for it to be harmful to an offspring. In recent years, a number of techniques have been developed to help couples prepare for the likelihood of a child born with a genetic anomaly. Potential parents can visit genetic counseling centers, affiliated with most teaching hospitals, to discuss family histories, undergo chromosomal analyses, and assess the odds of producing a child with a given genetic condition. Analysis of blood and skin samples currently can identify carriers of such disorders as sickle cell trait, thalassemia, Tay-Sachs disease, and cystic fibrosis, the most common genetic disease among Caucasians. One recent advance uses a computer scan of adult handprints to detect the risk of producing offspring with one of 10 hereditary conditions, including Down's syndrome, one of the most common causes of mental retardation.

During any pregnancy, several of the techniques available to assess prenatal development can provide information about the fetal genetic blueprint. The most commonly used diagnostic procedure, the sonogram, uses ultrasound imaging to reveal information about developmental progress and structural integrity. In the ninth week of pregnancy, the sonogram can be used to guide a catheter through the cervix to extract cells from the outside of the chorion, or gestational sac. This procedure, known as chorionic villus sampling (CVS), currently allows the earliest possible analysis for obvious chromosomal aberrations such as Down's syndrome. However, the decision to undergo this relatively new procedure must be weighed against the associated risks of miscarriage, maternal infection, or fetal damage, currently estimated at 1 to 3 cases per 100 tests.

By week 14 of pregnancy, a simple analysis of maternal blood can reveal the presence of α-fetoprotein, a substance excreted by the fetal liver and spilled into the mother's bloodstream. The α-fetoprotein test provides some of the information about suspected chromosomal disorders offered by CVS with significantly less risk to the fetus. More importantly, the test screens for defects of the neural tube, including the brain, spinal cord, and vertebral column. Neural tube defects, including anencephaly (the absence of a complete brain), spina bifida (incomplete closure of the vertebral column), and hydrocephaly (brain swelling caused by an accumulation of cerebrospinal fluid), currently occur in about 1.2 of every 1000 births in the United States. Multifactorial inheritance resulting from complex gene interaction or gene–environment interaction is suspected in these disorders.

Increasingly, women with elevated AFP levels, those with questionable CVS results, and women over age 35 who are at increased risk for chromosomal abnormalities are encouraged to undergo analysis of fetal cells that have been sloughed off into the amniotic fluid—"amniocentesis." Performed during weeks 15–17 of pregnancy, the sonogram-aided procedure uses a hollow needle inserted through the abdomen to extract a small amount of amniotic fluid. Fetal cells in the fluid are cultured for about 2 weeks, then analyzed for the presence of deleterious conditions.

Some medical ethicists argue that the risk of miscarriage or fetal damage from amniocentesis, currently estimated at between 0.3 and 1%, is sufficiently great that their use should be restricted to those expectant parents who would consider terminating the pregnancy. Others are concerned that the lateness of the procedure and the length of time necessary to complete the analysis bring any decision to abort perilously close to viability, the point at which an aborted infant could survive life outside the womb. Still others maintain that tests like amniocentesis can serve as a valuable early warning system, helping parents prepare for the arrival of a child at risk for medical complications or special developmental challenges.

Unfortunately, the ability to identify genetic disorders prenatally has advanced much more rapidly than available treatment. Despite dramatic advances in the last decade, the ability to use genetic information to prevent or provide *in utero* treatment of potential problems still is limited to a small but important number of cases. For example, erythroblastosis, the often deadly effects of maternal–fetal incompatibility in Rh blood type, has been drastically reduced by a medication that prevents mothers from developing antibodies to fetal blood. The incidence of spina bifida has been reduced simply by providing mothers with multiple vitamins before and during pregnancy. Fetal thyroid disease has been treated by injecting medication directly into the amniotic sac. The most dramatic interventions to date, however, have involved fetal surgery, including intrauterine operations to treat urinary tract obstructions and hydrocephaly.

Successful experiments with animals suggest that the technology to correct human genetic defects before they have an opportunity to hamper development might soon be available. It is unlikely, however, that widespread gene therapy in humans will be implemented without heated debates about the ethical implications of genetic engineering.

There are thousands of separate genetic codes that determine individual appearance, behavior, and potential. Some are explicit, providing precise specifications within a limited range of variability. Others, however, are merely guidelines that suggest direction and set parameters, known as the range of reaction (Gottesman, 1963). The way that these genetic guidelines (the genotype) are translated into an observable characteristic (the phenotype) depends on the environment.

The crucial role played by socialization in shaping an individual's gender identity has been underscored by the work of John Money and his colleagues at Johns Hopkins University. The researchers followed the development of several children who, because of ambiguous genitalia at birth, were given a gender label that contradicted their chromosomal blueprint for maleness or femaleness. Following the mistake of gender assignment, they were exposed to the sexual tradition-bound socialization, or canalization, for the "wrong" sex. The researchers found that the child's core gender identity, or the definition of self as male or female, was so firmly established during the second year of life that it defied change. By puberty, when secondary-sex characteristics began to appear, it was easier to perform a sex change operation in order to bring the body into accordance with the gender identity than to attempt to change the psychological sense of being male or female. It was concluded that most of the stereotyped distinctions between the sexes are derived from the interaction of biologically based average trends and differences with culturally reinforced differences in roles (Money & Ehrhardt, 1972). Therefore, although biology determines basic physiological differences between the sexes, the combined effects of such powerful influences as parents, peers, schools, and the media determine just how traditionally feminine or masculine a child will be.

Clearly, the process of socialization for both children and their parents involves influences outside the individual and family contexts.

Environmental Influences on Development

The Womb as the First Environment

The romantic image of the womb as a totally protective environment is shattered by the reality of numerous prenatal assaults that can be experienced by otherwise healthy fetuses. Each year, an estimated 1 in 10 American children is born with some kind of congenital anomaly. By some estimates, up to 90% of all serious intellectual and neurological outcomes are linked to prenatal events (Hagberg, 1975).

Although some of these conditions result from genetic causes alone, others stem from assaults experienced *in utero*. The placenta was once thought of as a protective barrier that ensured safe prenatal development. Today, however, it is viewed as a faulty filter that can dispense harmful substances directly into the fetal environment. Those who study birth defects focus on the identification of teratogens, or agents that cause malformation or deviations in fetal growth. The word *teratogen* is derived from the Greek word teras, meaning "monster" or "marvel." Although there are scores of known teratogens, most can be grouped into three general categories: microorganisms, physical agents, and chemicals.

Health providers use the acronym "TORCH" to identify those microorganisms that pose the most serious threats to the developing embryo and fetus. The first letter of the acronym represents toxoplasmosis, a parasitic disease transmitted by eating undercooked meat or handling cat feces. The symptoms of the disease in adults are so mild that most expectant women might dismiss them as general fatigue or a slight cold. Its effects on the baby, however, include deformities, miscarriage, premature delivery, or stillbirth. The "r" in the acronym stands for rubella, or German measles. During a major rubella epidemic in 1965, 20,000 babies were born deaf, blind, or mentally retarded as a result of the disease. At least 11,000 additional unborn and newborn babies died. Unfortunately, an estimated 10–20% of women of childbearing age are not immunized for this readily controlled disease. The last two letters stand for cytomegalovirus, the most common prenatal infection, and genital herpes, both of which cause neurological damage. The letter "o" stands for "other," a full range of infectious diseases that can affect prenatal development. These include syphillus, gonorrhea, mumps, and most recently HIV, the virus associated with acquired immunodeficiency syndrome (AIDS).

A recent study of births in 38 states (Gwinn et al., 1991) reported that in 1989, 15 of every 10,000 women giving birth in the United States were infected with the HIV virus. Assuming a rather conservative perinatal transmission rate of 30%, the researchers predicted that 1800 newborns will acquire HIV directly from their mothers each year. Others can be exposed to the virus postpartally through their mothers' milk. AIDS-infected babies tend to be afflicted with bacterial diseases, experience developmental delays, and suffer neurological abnormalities. Our concerns for children exposed to the HIV virus must extend past the direct assault of the virus on early development, however. We also must be concerned with who will be available to care for these children if one or both of their parents are in engaged in risk factors associated with transmission of the virus (such as intravenous drug use) or is suffering from an HIV-related condition.

Some microorganisms affect the fetus directly by crossing the placenta. Others influence development through maternal symptoms such as high fevers. Excessive heat, a physical agent, can threaten organogenesis, or the development of organ systems, during the first trimester of pregnancy. Hyperthermia between the eighteenth and thirtieth days of pregnancy has been implicated in some types of neural tube defects, including anencephaly. Although moderate exercise during pregnancy is encouraged, strenuous activities that cause overheating or oxygen deprivation are believed to be harmful to the developing fetus.

Another physical agent that threatens fetal development is radiation. Whether it is derived from natural sources or through X rays, large doses of radiation can alter organ development or predispose the child to some forms of cancer. X Rays are just one example of a form of medical treatment that can cause serious complications during pregnancy.

Many drugs designed to treat maternal disorders also threaten fetal development. Both anticonvulsants prescribed for the treatment of seizure disorders and antidepressants can cause cleft lip and cleft palate. Tetracycline, an antibiotic, discolors the child's permanent teeth and affects bone growth; sulfa drugs can cause liver damage. Anticoagulants can produce mental retardation and eye and heart defects. Certainly, the potential benefits of prescribing any drug during pregnancy must be balanced against any potential harm to the baby. In general, limited use of prescription and over-the-counter drugs is recommended for any women who could be pregnant. If possible, all medications should be avoided during the first 14 weeks of pregnancy.

In the last several years, some chemical agents prescribed to assist pregnancies have been implicated in fetal damage. Diethylstilbestrol (DES), a drug once believed to prevent spontaneous abortions, was given to thousands of pregnant women from the late 1940s to 1977. As the seemingly healthy offspring reached adulthood, their doctors began to report previously undetected damage to their reproductive organs. Females experienced adenocarcinoma, a rare cancer of the cervix, infertility, and problems carrying infants to term. Their male counterparts have suffered cancer of the testes. Thalidomide, a sedative given to women in Europe and Great Britain during the 1960s, was responsible for the births of children with malformed limbs. More recently, Benedictin, a drug widely prescribed to relieve so-called "morning sickness," the nausea and vomiting of early pregnancy, was withdrawn from the market because of a spate of law suits claiming complications including brain damage, musculoskeletal deformities, and defects of the respiratory, gastrointestinal, and cardiovascular systems.

The risks associated with other chemical agents are increased by their ready access and widespread use. Caffeine, found in coffee, tea, cola drinks, and cocoa, readily passes the placenta, causing drug-like effects that are magnified in a tiny, developing body. Some herbal teas, selected to avoid caffeine, can cause allergic reactions or induce miscarriages.

Maternal cigarette smoking, especially during the second half of pregnancy, has been associated consistently with preterm delivery, low birth weight, and poor Apgar scores at delivery. During infancy, children of smokers are prone to experience cardiovascular and respiratory problems and run an elevated risk of Sudden Infant Death Syndrome (SIDS). Recently, it has been shown that even inhaling air-borne smoke from others's cigarettes ("passive smoking") while pregnant can result in later cognitive deficits in the child.

One of the most tragic examples of teratogenic effects from a readily available chemical is Fetal Alcohol Syndrome (FAS). The most apparent signs of FAS are growth deficiencies with no catch-up growth and characteristic facial features including flattened midface and nasal bridge, upturned nose, thin upper lip, and growth-retarded jaw. The most serious effects, however, are revealed in dysfunctions of the central nervous system, including microcephaly, mental retardation, infant irritability, and poor motor coordination and learning deficits in childhood (Eckardt et al., 1981). Damage to various organ systems includes cardiac defects, scoliosis, limited joint movement, and urogenital defects. Although some research has suggested that the most serious prenatal effects are experienced by women with heightened sensitivity to alcohol, it should be remembered that *no study has established a safe level of alcohol consumption for pregnant women.*

Cocaine, another so-called recreational drug, has been associated with infants born prematurely or small for gestational age. Unusually hard and fast labor is not uncommon, leading to anoxia and signs of fetal distress (Lifschitz et al., 1986). Maternal and fetal blood pressure can rise dramatically after administration of the drug, resulting in premature separation of the placenta, fetal stroke, or intracranial hemorrhage. Drug effects are reflected in neonatal performance: cocaine-exposed newborns show tremulousness, frequent state changes, an inability to engage visually, and poor consolability (Chasnoff et al., 1985).

Tragically, research on the effects of illicit drugs has been hampered by the number of chemicals abused. Tobacco, alcohol, and caffeine use— together with poor maternal nutrition—often accompany use of illegal drugs. In a study of maternal health habits conducted at Boston City Hospital, 32% of the women used two or more recreational drugs during pregnancy. Of those, 84% of the women used alcohol and cocaine, 79% used marijuana and alcohol, and 67% combined marijuana and cocaine (Zuckerman, 1986).

The threat from other familiar chemical agents is often ignored by pregnant women. These include household cleaning agents, decorating products, hobby supplies, lawn and garden products, food additives, and even some beauty products. Indeed, the birth defect claims by Vietnam veterans sprayed with the chemical defoliant Agent Orange suggests that both men and women of childbearing age might be affected by chemical agents in the home or work environment.

The type, timing, and amount of an environmental assault are important determinants of its effects. The potential harm from each environmental risk depends on its method of invasion and the specific developmental process that it interrupts. Thus, X rays and most infectious diseases pose the greatest threat during the first trimester, during the time when basic systems are forming. Maternal malnutrition, in contrast, endangers fetal growth and brain development during the last trimester. Unlike most other infectious diseases, herpes affects only those babies who come into contact with active lesions during a vaginal delivery. Unfortunately, cocaine use at any time during pregnancy puts both mother and child at risk.

The variety of potential assaults, both genetic and environmental and the time lag between a risk event and observation of its effects make prenatal risks particularly difficult to identify and prevent (Kopp & Krakow, 1983). In general, however, the earliest risks carry the greatest threat of serious effects (Kopp & Krakow, 1983). The potential for harmful effects is not uniform: the physiological status of the mother and maternal and fetal genotypes can influence vulnerability to prenatal risks.

Too often, some of the same risks confronted *in utero* continue to threaten the developing child after delivery.

The Developing Child in the Physical Environment

Imagine fetal life within the watery environment of the womb: the constant temperature, the darkness and muffled sounds, the snug but elastic fit. What changes await the newborn in the extrauterine environment!

Of all the possible threats from the physical environment, one of the simplest and most pervasive is lead. Currently, an estimated 12 million children in this country are at risk of lead poisoning (National Commission on Children, 1991), including half of all children in inner cities (Waldman, 1991).

Lead can be found in household dust, the drinking water of homes and schools, the sand of outdoor play areas, and in vegetables grown in backyard gardens. Its greatest source, however, is lead paint, which can be found in an estimated 75% of American homes built before 1980 (Waldman, 1991). As old paint chips off, leaches through layers of new paint, or is removed by concerned parents, fine lead dust fills the child's environment.

Despite popular myth, children do not have to eat chips of paint to become lead poisoned. This metal is so toxic that poisoning can occur gradually during normal activity. For many children, the first exposure to lead often occurs *in utero*, as parents' initiate home improvements to prepare for the expected arrival. Infants are exposed to lead as they crawl across carpeting saturated with invisible particles or put a painted toy in their mouth. Indoors, older children might be fascinated by the feel of chipping or peeling paint; outdoors, they might inhale lead from exterior paint, auto emissions, or industrial smokestacks.

A number of factors make children especially vulnerable to environmental toxins, including lead. These include functionally immature organs and body systems engaged in rapid growth, larger body surface, higher metabolic rate, and greater oxygen consumption in relation to body weight, and special energy and fluid requirements (World Health Organization, 1986).

The Centers for Disease Control report that 6 million children currently have blood lead levels high enough to cause permanent physical, neurological, and cognitive damage (*The Boston Globe*, 1990). In fact, lead poisoning is the most common pediatric environmental disease suffered by children in the United States (Needleman, 1991).

Although many children show no physical signs of lead poisoning, others exhibit fatigue, headaches, constipation, or loss of appetite. Some extreme physical symptoms include convulsions, coma, and death. Most often, however, the effects of lead poisoning reveal themselves in behavioral problems and cognitive performance.

Landmark research by Needleman and his colleagues (cf. Needleman, 1991) has demonstrated the long-term effects of even low doses of lead. Babies born with lead in their umbilical cord blood at extremely low levels showed IQ deficits 2 years later. A longitudinal study of children with elevated lead levels in their baby teeth demonstrated poor overall functioning in second grade, including lowered IQ scores, poor speech and language performance, impaired attention, and poor organization. By fifth grade, earlier exposure was associated with lower IQ scores, special needs services, and grade retention. These effects persisted into adolescence, with reading disabilities, poor vocabulary, slow reaction time, and academic difficulties that resulted in absenteeism or elevated drop-out rates.

The U.S. Department of Health and Human Services has developed a strategic plan outlining prevention, screening, and treatment procedures to deal with this pervasive environmental threat. However, the current federal budget has allocated less than $50 million dollars of the estimated $1 to $10 billion dollars necessary to tackle this problem.

Lead poisoning does not discriminate by social class: children living in lovingly restored historical homes and elegant condominium conversions may be exposed to as much lead as those in the ghetto. However, the threat of long-term damage becomes greater for those children whose bodies are weakened by poor health and nutrition or lack of adequate medical care. Many poor children suffer from iron deficiency anemia, a condition that heightens their susceptibility to lead poisoning.

One in four infants born in the United States today starts life in poverty. Overall, about 20% of all American children currently live in poverty, a figure that rises to at least 40% for Latino children and more than 50% for African-Americans. Not surprisingly, the risk of being poor increases dramatically in families with only one potential earner (Baer, Farnam, & Mauer, 1990).

Poverty means more than parental unemployment. In fact, 72% of American families in poverty work at least part time, but do not earn enough money to rise above the poverty level, currently $12,675 for a family of four (U.S. Department of Health and Human Services, 1990). Rather, poverty might result from failure to enforce child support decrees. It might mean cuts in child welfare and job opportunity programs or unemployment compensation programs that have run dry. To young children, however, poverty means gaps in care, obstacles to development, and missed opportunities.

For many poor children, poverty translates into malnutrition. Worldwide, as many as 150 million children under the age of 5 suffer from malnutrition, including between 2 and 5.5 million children in our own country (National Commission on Children, 1991). Although malnutrition is a problem for any child, its consequences are especially severe prenatally and during infancy. An estimated 250,000 babies are born seriously underweight each year. Some of those tiny babies arrive prematurely, others have been born to malnourished mothers. During infancy, adequate nutrition and sufficient caloric intake are vital for brain growth. Malnutrition has been associated with decreased number of brain cells, chemical changes in the brain, and faulty transmission of neural impulses resulting from disrupted myelination.

Children who are poor and hungry are also more likely than their advantaged peers to be sick. Each year, an estimated 40,000 American children die from largely preventable diseases. In 1990, only half of all inner-city toddlers were immunized against the childhood infections of measles, mumps, and rubella (National Commission on Children, 1991). Is it any wonder, then, that in the same year there were 26,000 cases of measles in this country, nearly 100 of which resulted in deaths?

It has been estimated that 13% of all children under 18 and 9% of pregnant women currently lack any health insurance protection (National Commission on Children, 1991). Ironically, although this nation ensures health care coverage to most Americans over age 65—regardless of income—there are no similar assurances for America's children.

Lead, food, innoculations: Each of these is tangible, physical. But do these physical entities act alone to promote or impede children's health? Probably not.

Viewing development from an ecological perspective allows us to consider the complex ways that developmental risks are imposed on a child. Why is the child malnourished or chronically ill? Do these conditions result from an inborn, constitutional weakness? Are they necessarily a sign of parental neglect? What are the responsibilities of health care providers, the media, or others in the community? Should the government play a role in ensuring that the next generation will be healthy, or would that be an intrusion on parental rights? These are complex issues that reside in the social environment, issues to which we will return, particularly in Chapters 10 and 11.

Development in the Expanding Social Environment

Certainly, many of the neonate's first encounters with the environment will be physical, from the chill and bright lights of the delivery room to the experiences of basic feeding, burping, and changing. During those encounters with the physical world most infants also seem primed for social interaction.

Although their vision is limited, newborns are capable of focusing on the pattern of the human face placed 10–15 inches from their own. The neonate also is responsive to sounds, often becoming alert by high-pitched female voices and being calmed by low voices and monotones. Smelling ("olfaction") is well developed, with 5-day-old infants demonstrating the ability to discriminate the smell of their mother's milk from that of other lactating women (MacFarlane, 1977). As newborns make their first forays into the social world they demonstrate individual differences in response to stimuli, cuddliness, alertness, and soothability to their caregivers (Brazelton, 1973).

Beyond ensuring basic physical integrity, we are concerned that infants learn to know and trust the immediate environment (Erikson, 1963). A social relationship is built and strengthened as caregivers meet the infant's physical needs sensitively and lovingly and infants respond to their efforts.

A look of alert attention, crying, and smiling are all forms of communication used by the neonate. The fact that mothers tend to respond to cries of pain more consistently than any other form of cry attests to the communicative power of the infant cry. The course of emotional development will continue to be characterized by differentiation and elaboration of gross reactions (pain, pleasure, and interest) into the full range of human emotions (Ricciuti, 1974).

Beginning with the work of John Bowlby and Mary Ainsworth, a growing body of research has focused attention on development of attachment, the first important bonds with significant others.

The attachment relationship results from the initial behaviors both mother and child bring to the relationship and emerges through their recurrent interactions. Although initially all infants become attached in some manner to their caregivers regardless of how they are treated by them, the quality of the attachment relationship differs according to the quality of care the infant receives. A secure attachment relationship results when the child knows that his or her caregiver is accepting, sensitive, available, and responsive. When the child does not have a strong feeling of security and confidence in his or her caretaker, an anxious or ambivalent attachment relationship results.

Furthermore, the attachment relationship is a potent determinant of the child's social, emotional, and cognitive development (Garmezy & Rutter, 1983). If the attachment relationship is supportive, stable, and affectionate, then development most likely will proceed along a normal path. A child is part of a dyadic relationship—the parent's response is crucial to the child's development and mental health.

Regardless of the quality of children's relationships with their parents, it is important that they have opportunities to interact with others. Trust in the immediate environment and confidence in a secure attachment relationship as a "safe base" allow a child to begin to explore an expanding social environment.

Attachment is not limited to the basic caregiver. In a steady progression, the securely attached child is capable of forming attachment relations with parents, grandparents, and child care providers. The number of children who use stuffed animals and well-worn blankets as "transitional objects" suggests that feelings of attachment might not be restricted to animate objects.

From early relationships with caregiving adults, young children gradually expand into a play world populated by others who share their size, abilities, and interests. A longitudinal study of socially and emotionally at-risk mother–infant pairs (Erickson, Sroufe, & Egeland, 1985; Sroufe, 1983) has demonstrated how social development progresses from basic attachment to peer relationships. Compared to their peers, infants who were securely attached to their mothers at 1 year were judged to be more sociable at 18 months and more compliant with mothers at age 2. By preschool, they were characterized as independent and ego resilient. Their healthy self-esteem seemed to spill over to peer relations, with many distinguishing themselves by their empathy, social competence, and tendency to provide positive affect to classmates. Children who had been insecurely attached as infants, in contrast, were described as hostile, socially isolated, or disconnected in the preschool setting.

Although expressions such as "peer pressure" suggest that peers are a negative influence often leading children astray, there is mounting evidence that peers offer children learning opportunities that they can find nowhere else.

> Peer relationships provide children with the opportunity to interact with equals. In a peer group, a child has the chance to play a variety of roles that are not so readily available to him or her in interactions with adults. With agemates, a child experiences a greater opportunity to lead as well as follow, to contribute ideas and suggestions, to respond to others' ideas and suggestions, to negotiate, and to compromise. (Kemple, 1991, p. 48)

Peer relationships provide an important link between the family and the unfamiliar. When families fail to meet children's needs, the social skills necessary to reach out to other support figures can be a lifeline for a vulnerable child. Indeed, the failure to establish satisfactory peer relationships has been linked with adjustment difficulties in adolescence and adulthood. The child's life is played out in a dynamic relationship with the social environment. Thinking about this relationship itself has a history.

Development in Historical Context

In earlier chapters ways that the macrosystem, or dominant thinking of the larger group, can influence the policies and practices that shape the course of individual development have been discussed. This has been true since Aristotle and Plato began their efforts to conceptualize human development.

Plato struggled with the eternal issues of childrearing, particularly how to instill a sense of self-control without destroying individuality and initiative. He believed that most Athenian parents were imbued with the decadence of the society and therefore were unfit to raise their own children. Even those parents who gave every appearance of being capable were not prepared for the challenges of preparing citizens for some future ideal state. Because parenting techniques differed so widely, Plato feared that the separate influences would create a "medley of incongruities" in the character of developing citizens. Therefore, he urged that all children be separated from their parents early in life, allowing the state to control socialization and education. We see the same impulse at work today when people get frustrated and discouraged about parenting, particularly among groups different from their own, and argue for mass replacement of parents among the "offending" group.

Like Plato, Aristotle also was devoted to the concept of the "ideal society." He opposed state control of childrearing, however, on the grounds that it denied individual parental liberties. As he affirmed different parenting styles as a key to individuality, Aristotle also emphasized parents' ownership of their children, a concept that most observers today recognize as a cultural problem (cf. Garbarino, 1977b).

It is difficult to assess the extent to which these philosophical debates had an immediate or direct influence on the lives of children of the time. However, they set in motion traditions that continue to shape contemporary practices. To the present day, children often find themselves at the mercy of parental will or governmental dictate: always a possession, rarely a trust. For example, without governmental intervention many abused children will remain powerless victims. This is especially true in cases of incest, where informed consent is impossible because the judgment is outside of the child's level of reasoning and the power lies outside the child's control (Finkelhor, 1979). Yet many policymakers draw the line on intervention when it comes to providing quality child care or ensuring access to medical and nutritional services on the grounds that to do so would undermine the basic rights and responsibilities of families.

How is development influenced by changes in social attitudes or cultural practices across time? Those who study life-span human development typically categorize developmental influences as age-graded, history-graded, or nonnormative (Baltes, Reese, & Nesselroade, 1979). Age-graded influences, such as entering kindergarten, starting puberty, or going on a first date, are biological or environmental changes associated with one's chronological age. Age-graded events are described as normative because their occurrence can be anticipated for most of the population within a fairly narrow span of time.

Nonnormative events, in contrast, are those that are neither predictable nor typical. In this culture, children experience life-threatening illnesses, the death of a parent or sibling, major responsibility for the care of younger children, and long-term separations from the family as nonnormative. The potential impact of nonnormative life events on individual development depends on their timing, pattern, and duration (Baltes et al., 1979) plus the resources available to respond to the situation.

Between predictable chronological changes and unexpected events are history-graded influences. These include wars, epidemics, and dramatic economic or social changes that shape the experiences of a given time period. When the experience of a history-graded event varies for specific age groups, they are known as cohort effects.

Bronfenbrenner (1986) has suggested the term "chronosystem" to describe environmental influences on individual or family development over time. In their simplest form, chronosystem effects are normative or nonnormative events that are associated with individual life transitions. On a larger scale, however, the chronosystem is "the cumulative effects of an entire sequence of developmental transition(s)" over the life course.

An excellent example of the impact of history-graded influences or chronosystem effects on individual and family development is provided by Glen Elder's work, *Children of the Great Depression* (1974). As we saw in Chapters 2 and 3, for the most part, the effects of the depression were transmitted to children indirectly, through changes in family functioning and roles. The impact was greatest for families suffering severe deprivation and those experiencing the greatest change in status within the community.

Boundaries between childhood and adulthood were diminished, while sex-typing of children increased. If mothers went to work to help supplement family income, their daughters assumed greater household responsibilities. Sons took outside jobs, becoming less oriented to their families in the process. Girls from deprived families became worried, emotionally sensitive, and self-conscious; boys demonstrated their emotional sensitivity through anger and frustration.

Poor adaptation to family hardships predicted enduring problems in adulthood. Men who joined the job market early chose modest but secure jobs that offered them little satisfaction. Males who had reacted to their plight with emotional outbursts during adolescence were later involved in unstable marriages. Their female counterparts were likely to become ill-tempered parents.

The childhoods of those in Elder's study were dramatically different from those of children born during the relative peace and prosperity following World War II, the so-called Baby Boom generation. As the country turned its attention to the enjoyment of home and family, large numbers of American children exerted an influence that was both social and symbolic. This cohort had its childhood shaped by the relaxed child-rearing advice of Benjamin Spock, the emergence of suburbs, the introduction of television, and the pressures of the Soviet–United States "race for space." During adolescence, many Baby Boomers had their political and social consciousness shaped by the Civil Rights Movement, assassination of a president, and a Cold War that precipitated the war in Southeast Asia. Like the proverbial "favorite son," members of this populous generation continue to capture the attention of the media as they travel through the life course.

How will the current generation of children be viewed from the vantage point of the twenty-first century? A look at both popular and professional publications can give us a clue. A content analysis of two publications for parents from 1955 to 1984 (Young, 1990) revealed increasing emphasis on the quality of mother–infant interaction and the role of appropriate stimulation in children's perceptual–cognitive development over time. Although articles on working parents, child care options, and the father's role in child development reflected recent demographic change, the publications took an ambivalent stance on these issues.

Thumbing through the pages of current magazines or scanning the crowd at a children's event can give us some clues about the current generation of young Americans. Once again, however, we must be cautious in making assumptions about "typical" American children and their families. Today, American families are more likely than ever to be headed by an immigrant lacking legal resident status, a stepparent, or a single parent, often a teenager. Their children are more likely to be from minority groups and to be poor. Indeed, it is increasingly likely that the "typical middle-class American child" represents an average between two widening economic extremes.

At one extreme are the offspring of affluent, usually well-educated parents who have delayed parenthood until they can establish themselves professionally or create a comfortable economic base for their children. In a childrearing environment where parents' high expectations are often matched with self-doubts and guilt, the motto becomes "Only the best for my child." Too often, however, "the best" is measured in terms of amount of money spent—for designer clothes, high tech toys, or organized activities to fill the child's day. As these children have captured the attention of the media they have been dubbed "gourmet babies" (Zigler, 1986), "overscheduled children" (Powers, 1989), and "fast-lane kids" or "superbabies" (Shreve, 1988).

At the other end of the economic continuum, in contrast, are the "invisible children" known only as statistics. These children come from many different kinds of families, most of them poor. They include the children of single parents who receive no child support and have no access to adequate substitute care while their mothers work. They are children from homeless families who are denied health and educational services only because they have no permanent address. They are children who have been removed from dysfunctional homes only to be bounced from one foster placement or institutional setting to another until they are too old or too troubled to be "adoptable."

One social critic, economist Sylvia Ann Hewlett (1991), describes those at both ends of the continuum as children of neglect. The poor, she charges, suffer from governmental negligence while the more affluent suffer from a deficit of parental time. Many of her concerns echo Elkind's (1985) book, *The Hurried Child*, which decries the unrealistic and developmentally inappropriate pressures placed on children across all social strata. Together, the evidence presented by these authors seems to confirm LeShan's (1967) warnings of 25 years ago about a growing "conspiracy against childhood."

Some children's lives are overscheduled with "networking opportunities," or structured activities that leave them no free time to relax or reflect. Others are overburdened prematurely with the responsibilities of adulthood or stressed by family and societal changes that they are too young to comprehend. Many are alternately coddled or ignored. Either way, many American children are missing out on the simple joys—and basic developmental necessities—of childhood. Increasingly, we ask ourselves, "Do American children know how to play?" "Do they know how to be children?"

Many children are overwhelmed by unrealistic demands. Others have not been prepared to meet either basic responsibilities or environmental pressures. Too many have given up. Is it any wonder, then, that an estimated 7.5 million American children show signs of some form of psychological illness (Toufexis, 1990)? Or that some urban high schools have drop-out rates approaching 50%? Or that suicide rates among teenagers have tripled between 1960 and 1987 (Toufexis, 1990)? We must heed what these signs tell us about the typical American child.

Children's Contributions to Their Own Development

Thus far, much of our discussion has centered on external factors that influence a child's development. Certainly, myriad factors in the immediate environment and the larger social and historical context can and do shape development. However, it is important to realize that children also play an active role in determining their own development (Bell, 1968): Although it is customary to assume that families can influence or "cause" children's behavior, it is also important to examine possible reciprocal effects, cases in which children have an impact on their caretaking environments.

One team of researchers (Crnic & Greenberg, 1990), for example, found that "parenting hassles," including picking up children's messes and being nagged, whined at, or complained to, predicted family functioning. Parenting a young child with behavior problems or poor social competence was associated with both the frequency and intensity of parenting hassles. The level of intensity, in turn, was negatively associated with parenting satisfaction, life satisfaction, and two measures of family functioning.

We can derive a better understanding of the child's influence on the caregiving environment by studying temperament, a group of tendencies that helps define an individual's characteristic behavioral style. Although some researchers have narrowed their focus to a single temperamental attribute such as shyness (Kagan, 1991) or difficulty (Bates, 1980), most study a cluster of behavioral traits that reveals characteristic patterns of activity, reactions to unfamiliar stimuli, sociability, and mood (Goldsmith et al., 1987).

In the most extensive study to date, Thomas, Chess, and Birch (1968; Thomas & Chess, 1977) initiated a study of 3-month-old children in 1956 that has continued to the present (Lerner & Lerner, 1983). The researchers identified and tracked nine temperamental traits, including activity level, biological regularity, and general mood. Initial responses to stimuli were examined in terms of type of response (approach–withdrawal), threshold of responsiveness (the magnitude or duration of stimulation needed to elicit a response), and intensity of reaction. The categories of adaptability, distractibility, and attention span were used to rate behavioral changes and reactions to change. Ratings of each of these separate traits were used to derive global classifications of "easy," "difficult," or "slow to warm up."

Subsequent studies of temperament by other research teams have varied these categories (Goldsmith et al., 1987). Some, for example, focus on emotionality, activity, and attention (Derryberry & Rothbart, 1984), whereas others have restricted themselves to the behavioral expression of emotions (Goldsmith & Campos, 1986). Buss and Plomin (1975), who study distress, or the negative expression of emotions also include activity and sociability as key temperamental traits.

Despite the lack of consensus regarding a definition of temperament, most researchers agree that temperamental differences are evident at birth or soon after (Korner, 1971; Goldsmith et al., 1987). Some researchers maintain that temperamental traits have a strong genetic base (Goldsmith, 1983). Indeed, for generations, the variety in pregnant women's reports of fetal activity and response to extrauterine stimuli have suggested that individual differences emerge early in the developmental course. Today, twin research has provided evidence that characteristics such as activity level, sociability, and task orientation are heritable (Rutter, 1988).

Most attempts to demonstrate stability of specific temperamental traits over an extended period of time (Chess & Thomas, 1984; Maziade, Cote, Boudreault, Thivierge, & Boutine, 1986; Rutter, 1988) have been disappointing, however. This suggests that more than heredity is at work in the expression of temperament.

Thomas, Chess, and Birch have proposed the term "goodness of fit" to describe the interplay between a child's characteristic style and the caretaking environment. What do others expect of the child? Does the child's temperament match a parent's or teacher's behavioral style? What kind of a response does the child elicit from others?

Others have used the term "niche-picking" to describe our tendency to seek those environments that are most compatible with our biological predispositions (Lerner & Lerner, 1983). How do an individual's choices—from playtime activities to occupations—reflect genetically influenced temperamental traits? In what ways do children's behaviors reflect an attempt to create a match between their preferred level of stimulation and the mood of a particular setting?

Several researchers have demonstrated the far-reaching effects of a child's temperament on both individual development and family functioning. One study, for example, demonstrated that mothers are more likely to abandon plans to return to work after the birth of a difficult or fussy child (McBride & Belsky, 1985). Another project, which followed children from 1 year to age 8, found that children who had been rated as difficult and noncompliant as toddlers experienced lower levels of maternal involvement, a less positive emotional environment, and less optimal stimulation than their more pleasant and adaptable peers (Bathurst, Gottfried, Guerin, & Hobson, 1988a). Not surprisingly, children who were unsociable and persistently negative and noncompliant as toddlers showed trouble with socialization and daily living at age 8, whereas those who were fussy and difficult experienced communication difficulties (Bathurst, Gottfried, Hobson, & Nordquist, 1988b).

Other researchers have demonstrated that an understanding of the interactions between measures of temperament and family functioning during early childhood can help predict later difficulties. Research designed to examine the continuity of extreme temperamental ratings during middle childhood (Maziade et all, 1986) found that 7-year-old children who were rated as "extremely easy" in terms of initial response, adaptability, mood, intensity, and distractibility retained those ratings 5 years later. Ratings of "extremely difficult" temperament were less stable, however. Although more than half of the temperamentally difficult children remained extremely or moderately difficult at age 12, a few—all in well-functioning families—had become dramatically easier over time. Interestingly, those children who remained temperamentally difficult tended to be from lower SES families and families that functioned poorly in terms of clarity and consistency of rules.

Two additional studies using the original Thomas, Chess, and Birch sample have linked childhood temperament and associated family functioning with problems in adult life. Vicary & Lerner (1983) found a relationship between difficult temperament at age 5 plus weak, rejecting, or inconsistent parenting with heavy use of alcohol and drugs in adulthood. Steinberg's analysis of the same data set (1985) revealed an association between preschool temperament and Type A adult personality, the aggressive, hostile, and competitive personality type associated with coronary disease. Although poor adaptability and quality of mood were associated with later Type A behaviors across the study, the association between early activity level and adult personality differed for boys and girls. Steinberg speculated that parental responses to low activity in difficult boys and high activity in difficult girls were later reflected in Type A adult behavior.

Together, these findings demonstrate that it is not temperament alone that should interest researchers and practitioners. Rather, it is the reciprocal influences of transactions between children and their caregivers.

Sameroff and Chandler (1975) have proposed a model to explain the ways that children contribute to their own experience of the caretaking environment. According to the model, both parent and child continue to be influenced by their ongoing interactions, their "transactions."

This transactional model demonstrates how a single attribute, such as a congenital condition, can influence the developmental trajectory. Along the way, the condition itself will become far less important than its impact on family functioning and available resources. Does the family have the material and psychological resources necessary to meet the child's needs? Are formal or informal supports available to help parents meet extra challenges? Is the child loved and accepted or viewed as a punishment or a source of shame? How does the child's progress shape expectations for the future?

These examples begin to illustrate the complexities underlying a "continuum of caretaking causality" (Sameroff & Chandler, 1975).

Compounded Developmental Risk

Sameroff and his colleagues (Sameroff & Chandler, 1975; Sameroff, 1983) used the term "continuum of caretaking casualty" to describe the ways by which environmental conditions heighten or mitigate the vulnerability of children born at biological risk. They contend that whether they are physical, social, or historical, developmental risks rarely act alone. Instead, related categories of risks often act synergistically, with each compounding the other's effects.

One of the most tragic examples of compounded risk is homelessness. There are innumerable ways that a family can become homeless. Some reflect intergenerational patterns of poor education, teen pregnancy, restricted employment opportunities, or family dysfunction that seem to destine families to life in the "cycle of poverty." Other parents manage to achieve or maintain a measure of comfort and stability for their families only to be plunged into homelessness by a single misfortune (an accident or fire, an illness that extends beyond available health coverage or sick leave, a plant closing, a condominium conversion).

Most of the available research on homeless children has focused on those fortunate enough to receive the meager support services available at overburdened shelters (Whitman et al., 1990). Despite their relative advantage among the homeless, the parents in one shelter reported lengthy histories of disruption within their families of origin (Bassuk et al., 1986). The instability extended into their adult lives in the form of poor employment records, family violence, substance abuse, problems with physical and mental health, and the lack of supportive relationships. Indeed, the only support person some homeless mothers could name was their child!

Homeless children, in turn, are at least twice as likely as other children to suffer from untreated respiratory ailments, ear infections, heart problems, severe anemia, and neurological disorders (Bassuk et al., 1986). They also show serious developmental deficits (Bassuk et al., 1986), especially in the area of language (Bassuk et al., 1986; Whitman et al., 1990). Interestingly, the homeless children in at least one study (Whitman et al., 1990) showed patterns of developmental delay more characteristic of an abused and neglected population than those in a typical mentally retarded population.

Homeless preschoolers exhibit a number of behavior problems, including shyness, dependent behavior, aggression, and poor attention span. By the time children reached elementary school age, one-half of the girls and two-thirds of the boys required further psychiatric evaluation (Bassuk et al., 1986). Moreover, as teenagers those in homeless families are more likely than others to experience emotional problems, early pregnancy, and substance abuse (Bassuk et al., 1986).

Unfortunately, few of these children are able to use school or other child-oriented organizations to help them overcome their vulnerability. As homeless families make frequent moves to find shelter or avoid danger, the educational experiences of their children are characterized by sporadic attendance, delayed requests for special services, and frustrations associated with the changing demands of different settings. Often, the negative experiences are compounded by stereotyping from teachers and peers. As a result, "the school world is an additional stress rather than a haven" (Whitman et al., 1990, p. 519).

The compounded risks of life in a homeless shelter are portrayed in

Rachel and Her Children, Jonathan Kozol's (1988) account of the lives of homeless families in New York City:

> Those who do not fail to thrive in their first hours of life will be released from the obstetric wards to rooms devoid of light, fresh air, or educative opportunities in (the) early years. Play is a part of education too; they will not have much opportunity to play. Their front doors will give out upon a narrow corridor; their windows on a courtyard strewn with glass, or on the street, or on the wall of an adjacent wing of the hotel. . . . They are children who will often have no opportunity for Head Start. Many will wait for months before they are assigned to public school. Those who get into school may find themselves embarrassed by the stigma that attaches to the "dirty baby," as the children of the homeless are described by hospitals and sometimes perceived by their schoolteachers. Whether so perceived or not they will *feel* dirty. Many, because of overflowing sewage in their bathrooms, will be dirty and will bring the smell of destitution with them to class. (pp. 30–31)

As we think of the numerous physical and social factors that threaten early development it often is impossible to be certain about which single risk might set off a complicated chain of assaults. This poses real problems for those policymakers and practitioners bent on assigning blame and compartmentalizing solutions.

Do compounded risks necessarily *doom* a child to developmental delay, social dysfunction, or a life of disappointment? Fortunately, no. It is true that each risk poses a challenge to development and compounded risks heighten vulnerability to developmental problems. However, children seem to be able to use internal resources and external supports to overcome adversity to achieve happy and successful lives if we give them a chance.

Resilient Children: Overcoming the Obstacles

What have we learned about children who triumph over the negative circumstances of their lives? Some have labeled these "come-back kids" "invulnerable" (Sameroff & Chandler, 1975) or "stress-resistant" (Garmezy & Rutter, 1983). Emmy Werner (1988a,b) has describe them as "vulnerable but invincible."

In an ambitious and enlightening project, Werner and her colleagues (Werner, 1988; Werner & Smith, 1982) followed the development of 698 children born on the Hawaiian island of Kauai in 1955. Although most of the children were born into supportive homes after healthy pregnancies and uneventful deliveries, one in three was placed at risk by perinatal assaults or an impoverished or troubled home environment. Among the children in the high-risk group, 75% of those experiencing cumulative risk before age 2 developed serious learning or behavior problems by age 10 or had delinquency records, mental health problems, or pregnancies by age 18.

However, one of every four of these vulnerable children was able to overcome risk status to become "competent, confident, and caring young adults" (Werner, 1988a,b, p. 2). Werner labeled those who were able to marshall personal and environmental protection against stressful life events as "resilient children."

Some of these children benefited from simple demographic advantages. First-born boys fared well, along with children in families of four or fewer offspring spaced 2 or more years apart. All had the opportunity to establish a close bond with at least one caregiver. Most had enjoyed a great deal of positive attention during the first year of life; few had experienced prolonged separations from primary caregivers during that time.

They also were skilled at engaging others and recruiting support when necessary. As infants, resilient children tended to be described as active, affectionate, cuddly, good-natured, and easy. Physically, they experienced fewer eating and sleeping problems and quicker recuperation from illness than their less hearty peers. As toddlers, they distinguished themselves by their robustness, alertness, and responsiveness. Although determined, independent, and even aggressive, resilient toddlers also were described as cheerful, responsive, and self-confident.

Throughout childhood, resilient children were able to engage easily in social interactions. Often, they used these skills to recruit "substitute parenting"—care, support, and encouragement—from siblings, grandparents, neighbors, or teachers. Many assumed household responsibilities or outside jobs that not only helped their families but also gave them a sense of competence.

A follow-up study of 80% of the sample at age 30 (Werner, 1988b) revealed that those in the resilient group were highly achievement oriented. Most had pursued additional education and were engaged in satisfying full-time employment. Interestingly, 86% of the women but only 59% of the men were married and had children. Those who are parents list acquisition and personal competencies as primary goals for their children.

An unexpected finding of the most recent phase of the study was the number of those in the high-risk/nonresilient group who had overcome the problems of childhood and adolescence to lead happy and productive adult lives.

Life is not fair. Risk accumulates and compounds. Some children face an ecological conspiracy against them, often working in league with biological disability. But most children have a "self-righting" tendency; most adults try to help children overcome the dangers they face. Deficits can be overcome and negative events need not have long-term negative consequences. Many of those engaged in the practice known as human development intervention believe that environmental changes can overcome developmental risk and optimize potential outcomes. It is a sustaining belief. And that belief begins best in families and in parent–child relationships, the topic of Chapter 6.

RESEARCH CAPSULE

According to Newman et al. (1979), the history of cross-cultural research is not noteworthy for its contributions to the research on child development. While researchers have been able to use different cultures as settings for research into important issues of child development, cross-cultural research has, by and large, failed in its ambition to "increase the generality of psychological laws." In other words, researchers are often unable to investigate successfully a particular developmental concept across cultures. What are the reasons for this failure? It may be that cross-cultural research is simply an untrustworthy method for unraveling the knot of variables affecting growth of the individual. The average researcher might like to be able to investigate the manifestation of one factor, such as cognitive development, across cultures, but he or she should realize that this does not exist in a vacuum. Any variable under examination is affected by a pooling of social, cognitive, physical, and cultural factors. This is a fact that has escaped some researchers.

Cross-cultural research offers a great promise as well: We can simply learn more about child development and cultural differences by using a cross-cultural design as the mode for investigation of a particular child development issue. Perhaps it is useful to look at one such study as an application of the strengths and weaknesses inherent in this type of study.

Furby (1978) sought to answer the following questions: What are the bases across cultures of children's decisions about *sharing*? With whom do they share their personal possessions and why? What is the relationship of the developmental course to the sharing of one's possessions?

The researcher took two samples: a "developmental" sample and a "cross-cultural" sample. The developmental sample consisted of 30 American subjects at each of five age levels: 5–6 years, 7–8 years, 10–11 years, 16–17 years, and adults. The cross-cultural sample was introduced to investigate "the degree of variability that might be found in Western, industrialized societies with respect to the use of sharing of personal possessions." The comparison groups were American children at both the ages of 5–6 and 10–11 years, compared with groups of Israeli city dwellers and Israeli kibbutz dwellers at the same ages. The comparison envisioned was that of the industrialized, individualistic society (American) vs. the collective society (kibbutz residents) vs. a hybrid of the two (Israeli city dwellers) that might contribute to an understanding of the differences between the two groups at "extreme" ends of the spectrum. For each group, 30 subjects were chosen at each of the two age levels. In all groups, there was equal participation by both sexes.

Subjects were interviewed as to the issue of sharing of personal possessions. They were asked questions about the "morality" of sharing as well as other reasons for sharing. Each subject was interviewed in his or her own language. These interviews were then analyzed for their content.

In the developmental sample, it was found that 5–7 year olds shared largely with their own family or with those they thought friendly. The believed "sharing is good"—a belief shared by older children. They feared damage and destruction of their possessions, and this was also a consideration for older children. Seven- to eight-year-old children implied that they would not share with those who would not share with them. Ten to 11 year olds believed the evaluation of the person to be shared with was important. They also shared to foster well-being in the other person—to allow them to experience some activity or have something they did not already own. Sixteen to 17 year olds shared with those they believed honest and responsible. They also assessed their own need for the object and the use made of it by the borrower. Adults based sharing on the trustworthiness of the other and the happiness it gave them to share.

In the cross-cultural sample, the 5–6 year olds in the American and nonkibbutz Israeli samples used their families as the basis of evaluation for sharing. In the kibbutz, children are surrounded by a family of their peers. Therefore, it is with respect to their peers that they receive the greatest pressures to share. Decisions about sharing tend to be based on the standard of "If you won't share with me, I won't share with you." This rationale became equally as important for American children at the ages 10–11, since by then they were spending much of their time in school.

Determination was also made about the morality surrounding sharing. In the developmental sample, younger children tended to believe that to share was inherently good, while older children and adolescents saw sharing as a way of "helping thy neighbor." Adults tended to feel that sharing "inspired positive interpersonal interactions." In the cross-cultural sample, younger children of American culture and the Israeli kibbutz saw sharing as inherently good, but Israeli children also deemed that the owner has the right *not* to share. Older children across all groups were more concerned with doing a favor for another.

This study presents a sizable amount of information as to the bases of decision making about sharing across two cultures and across a large age range. What are the strengths of this study? It clearly provides information on the subjective notion of sharing, particularly in childhood and adolescence, and presents how these notions change and stay the same across ages and cultures. But several shortcomings can also be noted.

The study, as such, is cumbersome due to the fact that it separates age from other factors on one level (the developmental sample), and then combines age and culture effects on the other (cross-cultural sample). It might have made more sense to combine these factors in one population or to totally separate them. The age samples and culture samples are arbitrarily selected—it is not clear why Israel was considered as a comparison site rather than England, France, or Russia. There is, likewise, no rationale given for the age grouping.

Caution must also be taken in how the findings are interpreted. This is *not* a study of sharing *behaviors*, but a study of subjective *beliefs* about sharing. One cannot determine from this study how actual *patterns* of sharing change across ages or cultures.

Most importantly, this study again falls prey to the pitfall that Newman and his colleagues (1979) talk about: It is an attempt to isolate the effects of two variables upon sharing without an acknowledgment of other influences. Furby does not consider what the influence of socioeconomic status or intelligence upon beliefs surrounding sharing may be, but they *are* part of the overall picture. To be fair, to consider the effects that all possible factors have on one belief or behavior may be beyond the grasp of the average researcher. It is still important for the reader to carefully scrutinize the message any study tries to support.

PRACTICE CAPSULE

Health professionals are still learning how to improve the health and well-being of children. In the case of fetal development, they are particularly concerned about the possible effects of *teratogenic substances*, e.g., those substances that enter the mother's system (alcohol, drugs, etc.) and contribute to the creation of a less-than-optimum environment for the formation of the infant. One special problem that has arisen as the result of alcohol consumption during pregnancy is fetal alcohol syndrome (FAS).

When a pregnant woman drinks, she increases the risk of birth defects for her baby (Iber, 1980). The ingestion of alcoholic beverages interferes with pregnancy, and the effects on the fetus may be permanent. The strength of these effects is a result of the susceptibility to alcohol of both the mother and the fetus. It is clear, however, that alcohol consumption is the most prevalent single cause of mental impairment in infants in the Western world.

Fetal alcohol syndrome was first noted and described by Dr. David W. Smith at the University of Washington. He determined that drinking any amount of alcohol, in excess of the level at which the body will detoxify it, will put the fetus at risk. The mother who takes as little as one drink per day may be causing the risk of learning impairments in her child. Those who take two or three drinks a day may run the risk of spontaneous abortion.

Severe defects may result in those children whose mothers consume five or more drinks daily. The effects can be modified by good nutrition on the part of the mother and the natural resistance of the fetus to adverse influences. The most severe injuries include brain damage, deficiency in intellectual and neurological growth, low birth weight and size, small head size, abnormal facial features, near-sightedness, undersized teeth, cleft palate, and heart defects. None of these effects is reversible.

Twenty-three to 29 percent of children born to heavy drinkers demonstrate full-blown syndrome effects while 33% have minor congenital abnormalities. Two cases are reported for every 1,000 live births. This does not tell the whole story. A large number of cases still go undiagnosed, as not all doctors recognize the signs and symptoms of the syndrome as yet.

As much as reliable diagnosis techniques are needed, prevention campaigns aimed at reducing the occurrence of FAS are even more necessary. It is up to the health professional to recommend that the woman contemplating pregnancy avoid all alcohol from the time of conception until the child is born. If total avoidance of alcohol cannot be achieved, then at least vigilance and caution in alcohol intake should be insisted on. The woman should be educated to know the effects of alcohol on her own system and to monitor these. There are existing education/prevention programs in this area for mothers to be as well as movements to label the hazard on the bottles of alcoholic beverages themselves. In the final analysis, the responsibility for the safety of the fetus lays in the hands of the mother herself and her primary health care giver.

FOR FURTHER READING

Dorris, M. (1989). *The broken card*. New York: Harper & Row.

When Michael Dorris's application for single-parent adoption landed an offer of a 3-year-old Sioux child diagnosed as mentally retarded, he responded optimistically. Although Adam had been born 7 weeks prematurely to a woman who drank heavily, Dorris was confident that with the "positive impact of environment" the boy would soon overcome any developmental obstacles. He soon learned that even the best environments, together with a wide range of medical and educational services, have their limits. He learned, too, about the ravages of fetal alcohol syndrome and the effects of alcohol on the Native American population. This biographical account, which describes Dorris's life with Adam through age 18, is also an informative text on fetal alcohol syndrome.

Garbarino, J., Stott, F., and Faculty of the Erikson Institute. (1989). *What children can tell us*. San Francisco: Jossey-Bass, 373 pp.

This book is subtitled "eliciting, interpreting, and evaluating information from children." It is a primer on child development applied to the fundamental issue of communicating with children in order to obtain information about emotionally sensitive issues—such as child maltreatment, health care, psychological assessment, and child care arrangements.

Pence, A. R., Ed. (1988). *Ecological research with children and families: From concepts to methodology*. New York: Teachers College Press.

This collection demonstrates the value of using an ecological perspective in the design and evaluation of policies and practices affecting young children and their families. A foreword by Urie Bronfenbrenner calls for the design of community-centered human intervention programs that empower their clientele to become the principal agents of change.

Shames, S. (1991). *Outside the dream: Child poverty in America*. New York: Aperture/CDF.

By now, the statistic that more than 20% of America's children live in poverty is familiar to those who read the newspaper or watch television news. However, statistics do not have names and faces; to many in comfortable suburbs or protected college towns the children of poverty are invisible. Stephen Shame's stark black-and-white photographs make the reader confront those faces and helps the readers understand the meaning of poverty in America.

QUESTIONS FOR THOUGHT

1. Select a single developmental risk, such as fetal alcohol syndrome, lead poisoning, or poverty. Identify programs in your area designed to prevent or eliminate the risk factor before it can affect an infant or young child, help minimize or overcome the effects of the risk factor, or treat developmental problems that result from the risk situation.

2.   Consider the ways that the same developmental problem might manifest itself at several points from infancy through adolescence. List all the possible "causes" for the problem. Try to suggest several strategies to help the child minimize or overcome the problem. Address ways that parents and teachers can assist the child.

3.   List several developmental risks facing children during infancy, early and middle childhood, and adolescence. Discuss ways that the risks interrelate.

4.   Document changing ideas about child development and family life by conducting a content analysis of a popular parents' magazine or professional journal over a period of 10 years or more. Alternatively, you might want to trace the amount of time it takes for research findings reported at conferences or in professional journals to make their way into the popular media. How long does it take for research to begin to influence policy and practice? How do you explain that time lag?

5.   Imagine that it is the year 2020 and you have been asked to lend your expertise to a publication on Child Development in the Twentieth Century. What will you say about the experiences of your own generation? How would you describe the family patterns, childrearing beliefs, educational practices, and competing societal concerns that shaped your generation's experience of childhood? How was your experience different from those in other cultural groups in the same country? How do you think childhood experiences will influence later adult experiences of your cohort group?

6.   Research on resilient children suggests that their ability to cope depends on both personal attributes and the characteristics of the extrafamilial environment. Suggest ways that a child care center, school, recreational program, or youth organization can support the efforts of resilient children to overcome the developmental obstacles presented by a dysfunctional family. What other types of efforts might be necessary to help vulnerable children who are less adept at using outside supports?

6

The Ecology of Childbearing and Child Rearing

James Garbarino and Joanne L. Benn

> There are two lasting bequests
> we can give our children—
> one is roots, the other wings.
>
> Anonymous

The decision to accept the responsibilities of parenthood is a bold confrontation between dreams and doubts, between past and future. This chapter uses the ecological perspective to examine the social and psychological aspects of becoming and sustaining a healthy family. Beginning with childbirth as a critical life event, we explore the importance of active parent participation in decisions affecting child development and family life. Important variations in childbirth practices across cultural and historical contexts form the basis for discussing basic issues in parent–child relationships from childhood through adolescence. All those concerned with optimizing the potential of our youngest generation must appreciate the monumental task of maintaining the delicate balance of supports and challenges that give children both roots and wings.

Childbearing: Birth of the Parent–Child Relationship

A baby emerges from the protection of the mother's womb into a new environment. Without the buffering influence provided by the prenatal home, the newborn must adjust to bombardment by the sensations of light, sound, and temperature change. The baby's parents, too, are encountering profound changes. For the mother, the final stages of labor and delivery mark the culmination of more than 9 months of bodily changes to accommodate the growing fetus. For both parents, the delivery is another important phase in the psychological and social preparation for becoming a parent. Bronfenbrenner (1979) calls these life changes ecological transitions.

Defined as alterations in an individual's position in the environment resulting from a change in role or setting, ecological transitions are numerous during pregnancy and childbirth. Examples of transitional events experienced by most parents during the perinatal period include entering the birth setting, seeing and touching the newborn for the first time, and taking the neonate home. Together, this cluster of activities and associated role changes defines and gives meaning to the birth experience as a critical life event that can affect profoundly both newborn and parents for the remainder of their lives.

Examining the Microsystem of Childbirth

An ecological perspective encourages us to study the transactions *between* the members of the dyad. Because the ecological approach recognizes the dyad as the essential building block of the microsystem (Bronfenbrenner, 1979), it provides us with a framework for viewing the multiple dyadic relationships that come into play during the perinatal period. It goes beyond narrow approaches to bonding that simply focus on the feelings of one individual (the mother) toward another (the infant).

Naturally, we direct much of our concern with the ecology of childbearing toward the roles, relationships, and activities of the microsystem in the setting in which delivery takes place. Ironically, although the parents are the two individuals most responsible for the birth of the infant, their roles and status have the greatest variability across delivery settings. In a delivery using heavy anesthesia, for example, the mother may be unconscious or relegated to the role of passive observer, and the father is often excluded from the setting. In that case, the principal dyadic relationships within the microsystem are those of doctor–nurse, doctor–infant, and nurse–infant. In contrast, unmedicated delivery replaces the passive observer with an alert and active mother. The father, or a familiar support figure selected by the mother, is on hand to "coach" the delivery, share the experience with the mother, and "greet" the newborn. Here, then, the number of potential dyads increases tremendously to include mother–father, mother–infant, mother– or father–doctor, mother– or father–nurse, and father–infant. The focus has clearly shifted to include the parents as important participants in the labor and delivery and to increase the number of connections within the setting.

A number of trends in obstetrical and newborn care that have become popular in the past 25 years offer examples of ways that changes in policies and practices can affect the microsystem of childbirth. Prepared childbirth, sometimes called Lamaze delivery, or natural childbirth, is based on the use of physical and psychological exercises to help manage labor and delivery with little or no medication. A series of prenatal childbirth preparation classes offered to the pregnant woman and a selected support figure (usually the father) often include visits to the obstetrical unit, discussions about breastfeeding, and training in infant development. Key features of prepared childbirth are awareness, control by the mother, and participation of familiar support figures. In contrast, cesarean delivery, a surgical procedure removing the infant directly from the womb, necessarily lessens the degree of parental control offered in deliveries that are both prepared and unmedicated.

Recently, however, parents' rights organizations such as Cesarean-Support, Education, and Concern (C-SEC) have made important advances in bolstering the role of parents during a cesarean delivery, e.g., gaining admission for fathers to the delivery room to support their wives and hold the baby soon after birth. Together, these alternative delivery practices suggest ways that parental roles and activities can be expanded during a crucial period in the transition to parenthood.

Still other variations in the microsystem of delivery accompany differences in the physical features of the setting. For example, a growing number of couples have reacted to the stark atmosphere and emphasis on illness pervading many hospital settings by opting for delivery at home. Attended by a nurse–midwife, a physician, or a lay support person, home births match familiarity of surroundings with high levels of parental control. Unlike traditional delivery settings that separated mothers from familiar support figures, the setting for the home birth often includes friends, relatives, and even siblings.

When medical risk or personal preferences make home birth an unacceptable option, couples may select an alternative birth setting located in a hospital or a separate maternity center. Designed to offer the couple a comfortable, homelike setting, both offer birthing rooms that usually serve as a combined facility for labor, delivery, and aftercare.

Research on births to low-risk women delivering at 84 independent birth clinics nationwide showed a lower than average rate of complications, plus dramatic decreases in cesarean deliveries compared to existing statistics for hospital births (Rooks et al., 1989). Other advantages associated with alternative birthing settings are greater accessibility, lower cost, and a commitment to maximizing a couple's participation in the labor and delivery.

A third variation in the physical environment of the perinatal period is offered by the practice of "rooming in." Rather than confining infants to a newborn nursery for all but scheduled feeding periods, rooming-in offers an opportunity for neonates to remain in their mother's rooms for all or part of the hospital stay. Not only does rooming-in allow extended periods for mother–father–infant contact, it also provides opportunities for parents to gradually gain confidence in the role of caregiver prior to hospital discharge (Greenberg, Rosenberg, & Lind, 1973).

Each of these alternatives provides an illustration of ways that we can expand the microsystem of childbirth to accommodate the psychological and social needs of the family. Whether childbirth actually is a family-centered event and whether parents actually are actively involved across settings and activities, however, are issues grounded in the wider social and historical context.

The Family in the Medical Setting: The Mesosystem

The most obvious and pressing mesosystem issue surrounding child-birth is, of course, congruence between home and hospital. How well do roles assigned to parents in hospitals approximate their roles in the home and family? Are the same people involved in both? Is the child the only link? What are the relationships between those present for labor and delivery? One of the primary criticisms of hospital-based delivery has been that although parents have a high-status, active role in the home, they often assume a low-status, passive role in the hospital. Following an in-depth study of 13 couples and the medical personnel they encountered from early pregnancy through delivery, sociologist Sandra Danziger (1979a,b) concluded that asymmetrical relationships were a key feature in the situation (1979b), especially for fathers. Over-whelmingly preoccupied with minimizing their perceived intrusion in the medical setting, many fathers became passive observers. Those who took a more active stance, especially those who questioned medical procedures, were met with hostility. Capitalizing on their role as experts, doctors wielded control in determining the course of interactions with a patient. Patients, in turn, usually deferred to members of the medical staff, acting "like guests in someone else's home."

Danziger's findings are illustrated by another account of a particularly frustrating hospital delivery:

> I was truly well-behaved; I wasn't causing any trouble or crying out. I didn't feel as though I could ask the nurses any questions when they came

in. . . . They wheeled me into the delivery room and strapped my arms down. I asked, "Do you have to do that" and (a nurse) said "yes." You're supposed to have your arms free in natural childbirth. But I was never one to protest, and in that vulnerable position I could never cross anybody on anything. Because you feel totally helpless and I just wouldn't want to make anybody mad at me in that situation. (Harvey, 1977, p. 10)

Childbirth experiences can also hamper formation of the parent–child relationship, particularly when that relationship is jeopardized by other risk factors.

Benn (1987) has demonstrated how incongruities in childbirth can influence other aspects of the transition to parenthood. Women whose expectations for high personal control and low medical intervention were violated by the actual labor and delivery later expressed negative appraisals of childbirth. Violated expectations and negative perceptions of childbirth, in turn, undermined maternal confidence in caring for the newborn. Regardless of infant outcomes, perceptions of the child-birth experience were related to maternal adjustment at 4 months post-partum.

An earlier-than-expected delivery interrupts the usual psychological process by which parents prepare for a normal, fullterm delivery. As a result, parents may feel an intense sense of failure in their first task of parenting. Parents' feelings are marked by ambivalence. They grieve for the delivery experience they had anticipated, the perfect child they had dreamed about, and the lost opportunity to be a "normal parent" (Fleischman, 1986). At the same time, they are gripped by the fear that their real infant might die. Feelings of helplessness and loss of control are intensified as mother and infant are separated and others take over the caregiving functions usually assumed by parents (Fleischman, 1986; Seashore, 1981).

During the 1970s, clinicians and researchers paid considerable atten-tion to the role of parents during the first minutes and hours of life. In attempts to generalize from studies demonstrating a sensitive period for the development of mothering behavior among some animals, Marshall Klaus, John Kennell, and their associates investigated the effects of op-portunities for extended skin-to-skin contact with the newborn on the mother's tendency to "bond" or form strong attachments with her baby. In a much-cited study, the researchers compared the behaviors of two groups of mothers: one, experiencing the modest amount of contact with their newborns dictated by conventional hospital routine, the other, given opportunities for 16 hours of additional contact beginning at the time of delivery and continuing for extended visitations through-out the hospital stay (Klaus et al., 1972).

The researchers found that when presented with her nude baby, a mother in the extended contact group often displayed an "orderly prog-ression of behavior," massaging and examining the infant's body and engaging in *en face*, or face-to-face, interaction with the baby. When observed during a feeding situation with their infants 1 month later, this group of mothers showed significantly more soothing, fondling, and *en face* exchanges than the controls. At 1 year, mothers in the treatment group were still rated higher than the controls on two measures of maternal responsiveness: proximity to the infant during a physical ex-amination and tendency to soothe their babies when they cried (Kennell et al., 1974).

By providing a touching portrait of mother and child within a single time frame, this body of research has played a crucial role in heightening our awareness of the psychological components of the immediate postpartum period. In particular, it has expanded parental knowledge of infant capabilities and catalyzed research on the importance of early contact for individual and family development. In addition, it has led medical professionals to reconsider the advisability of routine separation of mother and infant following delivery (cf. AMA Recommendations on Parent and Newborn Interaction, 1977).

Unfortunately, the immediate and emotional response to initial inves-tigations of bonding also may have obscured the fact that a number of important questions remained unanswered: What are the specific ele-ments of early contact that translate into heightened maternal respon-siveness? Might observed differences in the extended contact group be attributed to effects of the research team or hospital staff (so-called "Hawthorne effects")? How do race, parity, age, or socioeconomic status relate to parental responsiveness (Seashore, 1981)? What are the links between early bonding of parent to child and later evidence of specific attachments of the infant to a caregiver (Matas, Arend, & Sroufe, 1978). Most importantly, what are the contributions of the infant, the father, and other family members to the bonding process, and how do their effects vary across social context and historical time?

Moreover, the inherent appeal of an opportunity to solve many prob-lems associated with early parent–child relationships by merely provid-ing for a few extra hours of mother–infant contact may have clouded our vision of important practice and policy issues. For example, if close contact during the immediate postpartum period enhances infant devel-opment, will the lack of contact necessarily have deleterious effects? How can we account for the generations of parent and offspring who successfully "made up for lost time," forming close, sensitive rela-tionships despite the lack of early contact? Will the popular emphasis on bonding actually undermine the early parent–child relationship by in-creasing parental anxiety or producing feelings of guilt among those who do not experience bonding (Hersh & Levin, 1978)? Clearly, relationships between developing individuals across the life span are more complex than the literature on bonding reveals. Although early contact within a supportive environment may serve as a rewarding component of early intervention, we still lack sufficient evidence that opportunities to bond, per se, can account for appreciable long-term differences in family outcomes.

To narrow one's perspective to the single act of bonding is to confine the conception of the perinatal period to a restricted number of actors and a limited time interval, or "sensitive period" (Hales et al., 1977). Specifically, it neglects the impact of a wide range of events and experiences on individual development and on the development of the family as a unit (Howells, 1972). Furthermore, viewing early family relationships through the bonding lens may well blind us to the far-reaching influences of sociocultural factors in shaping the developmentally formative events surrounding childbirth and the transition to parenthood.

As earlier discussions of the ecological approach have demonstrated, human development is not a single still photograph; it is an epic motion picture with a "cast of thousands" spanning numerous scenes and settings. Therefore, to understand the complexities of the period including delivery and the early weeks thereafter, we need to view childbirth as a social event in which the roles and status of family members influence their behavior and the outcomes—i.e., the child's healthy development and the quality of parent–child relations (Garbarino, 1980a; MacIntyre, 1977; Oakley, 1979). Using the ecological approach helps us present childbearing in broader scope, as a period in which there are multiple sources of variation on each "side" of the equation.

The stresses of premature parenthood, together with the confusing and poorly organized behaviors presented by the preterm infant, often undermine the synchrony of the early parent–infant relationship. Some parents may respond to this frustrating set of circumstances with physical or emotional withdrawal (Klaus & Kennel, 1976; Seashore, 1981). Others overcompensate with levels of stimulation that are beyond the infant's tolerance or ability to respond (Barnard, 1981). By the time their infants are developmentally ready to engage in meaningful interaction, earlier frustrations are reflected in lower social responsiveness and signs of "parental burn-out" (Barnard, 1981).

Fortunately, many parents can and do overcome these early deficits in their relationships with preterm infants. In fact, by age 2, parental attitudes and quality of caregiving are better predictors of infant outcome than the severity of the original biological risk (Cohen et al., 1986; Greenberg & Crnic, 1988).

The deficit is especially striking when the high physical vulnerability

of a premature infant is compounded by environmental factors undermining the parent's abilities to provide contact and care. As Seashore
(1981) notes, the mother of the hospitalized newborn "is prevented from
fulfilling her expected role as mother. It is a nurse, not she, who is caring
for her infant's physical and emotional needs—feeding, soothing, and
showing affection to the newborn" (1981, p. 76).

Often, hospital practices that undermine parental roles can have serious consequences for the family unit. Segal and Yahraes (1978) provide
an example in their moving account of the events surrounding the death
of a 3-month-old baby who had spent his entire life in the hospital:

> At no time had we considered the feelings of the parents who had visited
> every single day, standing at the observation window. When the baby
> died, the mother asked to hold him. Crying, she rocked him and explained
> this was the first time she had ever touched him. (p. 82)

While the couple in this example continued their vigil throughout the
period that their child was in the intensive care unit, others respond to
long-term separation by psychological abandonment. Prolonged separation of mothers and their premature infants has been linked to both
maternal detachment and an inability to engage in close, reciprocal exchanges with the infant (Klaus & Kennell, 1976; Seashore, 1981). Indeed,
in their follow-up study of 146 infants who had been placed in neonatal
intensive care, Kennell, Voos, and Klaus (1976) found that 23% of those
babies receiving less than three visits over a two week period, compared
to only 2% of those visited more frequently, subsequently experienced
serious problems in the early parent–child relationship including abuse,
abandonment, or failure-to-thrive. As these findings attest, one of the
strongest cases made for the developmental wisdom of family-centered
childbirth may be its potential for diminishing family dysfunction associated with child maltreatment (Garbarino, 1980a; Gray et al., 1977; Gurry, 1977).

Obviously, mothers play an essential biological role during pregnancy,
labor, and delivery. During the postpartum period, hormone levels
and milk production help maintain a physiological link to nurturance of
the newborn. Fathers, by contrast, have no direct physiological involvement after conception. Therefore, when obstetrical personnel have
viewed childbirth as merely a physiological, somewhat pathological
event (Haire, 1973) father involvement has been dismissed as an unnecessary hindrance. However, when conceptions of the childbearing experience have been expanded to include crucial social and psychological
factors, the father is seen as an integral part of the childbirth team (El
Sherif, McGrath, & Smyrski, 1979).

Within the past 20 years, a number of studies have begun to demonstrate the importance of active participation by fathers for the way that both men and women experience the transition to parenthood. For example, two studies by Block and her colleagues (Block & Block, 1975; Block et al., 1981) have demonstrated the father's role in determining a couple's successful use of prepared childbirth techniques. Prenatally, the likelihood that either of the marital partners would attend Lamaze childbirth preparation classes was determined largely by the husband's willingness to participate and his ability to coordinate class attendance with other time commitments. Men retained their "gatekeeping" roles throughout labor; active assistance from the husband was linked to a woman's ability to manage pain during contractions and her subsequent evaluation of the labor experience. Similarly, interviews conducted by Fein (1976) revealed the importance of husband presence during delivery in determining the evaluation of that experience by their wives. In addition, active participation in labor and delivery has been shown to have direct effects on early father attachment to the newborn (Gearing, 1978; Greenberg & Morris, 1974; Peterson, Mehl, & Leiderman, 1979) and on the ease of entrance to the paternal role (Fein, 1976).

An additional way to consider the mesosystem of childbirth is to look beyond the congruence of parental role and status across home and hospital to consider ways of strengthening the family's relation to both formal and informal support systems. Olds and his colleagues (1986), for example, created a project that matched nurse–home visitors with families during the prenatal period and who continued a relationship with family during the first 2 years of the child's life. In many cases, participation in the project helped increase family awareness of available community services. In addition, the home visitors encouraged families to identify valuable resources within their informal support networks and to seek out others with similar concerns and interests. As in the case of childbirth preparation classes, families brought together during the prenatal period to learn about labor and delivery techniques often formed strong support networks with activities ranging from reunions to child care cooperatives, support groups, and parent education classes.

Many observers have noted that new parents seem particularly receptive to sources of support from the "outside" while they are in the microsystem of the hospital (e.g., Gray et al., 1977; Klaus & Kennell, 1976). This openness raises the possibility of interventions aimed at strengthening the family's ties to social support systems. Linking a representative of a supportive service with the family during pregnancy or while the family is still in the hospital can help establish a strong home–health services mesosystem.

Boger and Kurnetz (1985), for example, helped new mothers form relationships with experienced parent volunteers while still in the hospital. Phone contacts and home visits during the first postpartal month were supplemented and later replaced by support groups with peers who had delivered at the same hospital. In another postpartal support program (Anisfield & Pincus, 1987), foster grandparents made home visits to socially isolated young women at risk for child abuse. This unique program offered advantages to all three generations involved.

The use of home visitors to provide postpartal support is a central feature of postpartal care in most of Western Europe (Miller, 1987). In the Netherlands, a nation noted for family-centered obstetrical services, new families are visited at home by a midwife or general practitioner and also receive infant care and housekeeping services from a specially trained maternity home helper available for up to 8 hours a day until the tenth day postpartum (Miller, 1987).

A review of the research (Gottlieb & Pancer, 1988) suggests that different types of support may be especially beneficial during various points of the transition to parenthood. The decision on when to become a parent, for example, depends on information that leads to confidence about a decision or action in terms of the larger social context—"coherence support." Coherence support related to the decision to start a family can be influenced by educational and career options, number of siblings the couple has, pressures and potential support from one's parents, and similar timing decisions made by friends and co-workers.

Two additional forms of support, "tangible aid" and "cognitive guidance," are important during the pregnancy. Expectant parents who are involved in a dense, interconnected social support system are likely to use the network for advice about pregnancy symptoms, prenatal care, and plans for childbirth.

Much of the research on support during childbirth has focused on the emotional support provided by the woman's partner. One exception, however (Sosa et al., 1980), showed that women who were offered the supportive companionship of an untrained layperson during labor experienced advantages in terms of both delivery complications and opportunities for contact with the newborn. Regrettably, little attention has been focused on the father's need for support during this important event (Gottlieb & Pancer, 1988).

New types of support are necessary for parents during the postpartal period. Some parents may need practical support such as child care or household help to help overcome fatigue and competing demands on their time. In addition, opportunities to share interests and concerns with social intimates can help reduce vulnerability to postpartal depression.

Gottlieb and Pancer point out that in some cases, intended support can actually create new stresses for parents. Unwanted advice, conflicting suggestions, and interference can work against adjustment. In the best situations, however, it can force parents to seek new affiliations to fill the gaps in their existing support system.

Others maintain that the specific intervention technique may be inconsequential, provided that efforts are made to support parents in their roles across home and hospital settings. As pediatrician and family advocate T. Berry Brazelton explains:

> In a violated system such as the one we provide presently around labor, delivery, and being in a hospital with a new baby, the effects of *any* positive intervention are magnified. Any experience that can be interpreted by the patient as positive or reinforcing for their feeling of self-value or importance to their new infant, becomes of enormous symbolic meaning as they search hungrily for support in such a non-reinforcing system in our present lying-in hospitals. To go on treating deliveries as if they were corrective surgery and patients as if they were ill, insensitive, or both, is patently destructive. Hence, any (prosocial) intervention . . . will be likely to produce surprisingly significant results in the light of the mother's (and father's) wish to feel individual, important, and adequate to that baby. (Brazelton, 1981, p. 121)

As Brazelton's message reveals, decisions about the way a family adds a new member are often bound up in practices and policies established outside the family. The support necessary to institute programs that can bridge settings often resides in exosystem issues.

The Institutional Context of Childbearing: Exosystem Issues

In the present case, the principal exosystem phenomena lie in the institutional policies and practices of the hospitals and medical establishments that have a bearing on the nature and construction of the microsystem of childbirth. As such, they also play a crucial role in shaping the mesosystem issues resulting from the relationships between settings. As in other areas of child and family development, action often results from scripts being written in administrative offices without input from the principal actors—the family members.

Over the span of several centuries, the medical community has radically altered the character of the microsystems of labor and delivery. During the Colonial period, childbirth was characterized by a comprehensive social orientation (Wertz & Wertz, 1977). Pregnant women rarely became involved with a health care delivery system. Rather, infants were delivered at home with the assistance of midwives and family members; mother and newborn had ready access to family and community supports. During the nineteenth century, the Industrial Revolution was accompanied by urban crowding and menacing health problems. Many women died in childbirth; those infants who survived delivery were likely to succumb to sepsis or infant diarrhea. But in response this era was also a period of great advances in medicine, public health, and education, as professionals and advocates sought to ameliorate the conditions faced by families.

The medical approach to childbirth was a by-product of these parallel developments (cf. Clark, 1979; Klaus & Kennell, 1976). Early hospital deliveries included moving patients from labor room to delivery room, issuing standing orders for anesthesia, delivery in the lethomony, or flat-on-back position, routine episiotomies, and separation of parents and newborn following delivery. With improvements in medical technology, these procedures, which had been designed for difficult or problem deliveries, soon became standard practice.

In recent years, hospital practices have expanded to include more elaborate forms of medical intervention in the delivery process. For example, expensive and often cumbersome electronic fetal monitoring (EFM) equipment is used routinely to measure changes in the fetal heart rate during uterine contractions. External monitoring, which uses a belt strapped around the mother's abdomen, necessitates confinement to bed during the time that monitoring is in progress. Significantly more invasive, internal monitoring uses a spiral electrode inserted into the vagina and attached to the presenting part of the fetus (usually the scalp).

Once heralded as an important advance in detecting fetal distress (Zuspan et al., 1979), EFM has proved to be generally ineffective. For example, in one study comparing the use of electronic fetal monitoring and periodic evaluation with a stethoscope in preterm deliveries, EFM was associated with significantly prolonged disruption of fetal heart patterns (Shy et al., 1990). Eighteen months later, the infants in the EFM group had a rate of cerebral palsy that was 2.9 times higher than for those monitored by traditional methods. They also had significantly lower scores on measures of infant development. In addition, none of the randomized trials using EFM in more than 17,000 full term births has demonstrated any long-term benefits from its use (Freeman, 1990). Despite these findings, many physicians trained during the last two decades continue to use EFM, a practice that can lead to escalating obstetrical costs and the likelihood of additional intervention.

Overzealous or untrained use of electronic fetal monitoring has been tied to an appreciably more invasive procedure, the cesarean delivery (Cohen, 1983). Despite advisories attempting to reduce surgical intervention in childbirth (Rosen, 1980), the cesarean delivery rate soared from 5.5% in 1970 to 23.8% by 1989 (Toffel et al., 1991). Fearful of both fetal injury and resulting malpractice suits, obstetricians are likely to resort to cesarean delivery as a response to fetal risk (Holt, 1988). The slight increases in fetal outcomes must be balanced against greater medical risks to the mothers, however (Pritchard et al., 1985). During the postpartal period, these risks are compounded by the physical challenges of parenting a newborn following major abdominal surgery and the psychological adjustments associated with often abrupt changes in the planned birth process (Grossman, Eichler, & Winickoff, 1980; Pederson, Zaslow, Cain, & Anderson, 1980).

A second form of intervention, induction, involves artificial stimulation of labor by the injection of synthetic hormones. The use of therapeutic inductions can greatly benefit both mother and fetus when the pregnancy is placed at risk by maternal hypertension or diabetes or in cases of placental insufficiency, postmaturity, or premature rupture of the membranes (Butnarescu, Tillotson, & Villarreal, 1980). Increasingly, however, induction has been used as an elective procedure, with the delivery scheduled to meet the social schedules of doctors or parents. Norwood (1980) has estimated that by the mid-1970s, many hospitals in England and the United States were inducing labor in 20 to 30% of their private patients despite growing evidence of multiple risks, including unusually strong and frequent contractions necessitating the use of anesthesia, increased use of forceps or surgical delivery, prematurity, and respiratory distress of the newborn.

Although many have heralded recent technological refinements in the delivery process, others argue that the original intention (intervention in high-risk pregnancies) has given way to the establishment of policies and practices designed for the convenience, legal protection, or economic benefit of medical personnel. Critics point out that despite the routine use of obstetrical technology—and perhaps because of the often unnecessary intrusions into the natural course of labor and delivery— the United States leads all developed countries in the rate of infant deaths associated with birth injury and respiratory distress. Of the fourteen countries with lower infant mortality rates, those with the lowest— Sweden, the Netherlands, Finland, and Japan—are more likely to use "natural" or family-centered childbirth techniques and are less likely to use any form of obstetrical intervention. Furthermore, critics contend that invasive delivery practices not only contribute to medical risks but may also undermine important social aspects of the perinatal period.

Indeed, a growing body of data has begun to demonstrate that decisions about childbirth must be viewed within a field of possible alternatives and a complex package of likely consequences. For example, maternal fears and tension during the last trimester of pregnancy have been linked to increased discomfort during labor (Yang, 1981). The administration of larger doses of pain relieving drugs to reduce the discomfort is associated with longer first-stage labor as well as with drug effects on the newborn that extend through the important first weeks of postpartum life (Brackbill, 1979). Conversely, adequate preparation for childbirth has been related to decreases in the use of chemical and surgical intervention, lower rates of fetal distress and postpartum infection (Hughey et al., 1978), and strong positive reactions to the baby and the birth experience (Doering & Entwisle, 1975).

It is also important to note that childbirth practices are sometimes associated with both mixed and unintended results. For example, two landmark studies of families with infants born by cesarean delivery found that although the delivery mode was associated with negative evaluations of the birth experience and constrained parent-infant interactions for mothers, it also resulted in heightened paternal concern for the infants and a greater caregiving role for fathers (Grossman, Winickoff, & Eichler, 1980; Pedersen et al., 1980).

Perhaps one of the most dramatic examples of exosystem effects is associated with teenage parenthood. Despite the commonly accepted assumption that a teenage pregnancy is inevitably and intrinsically a high-risk pregnancy, increasing evidence suggests that most adolescent pregnancies need be no more risky then others, if adequately supported by parents, peers, teachers, and medical personnel (Shelton & Gladstone, 1979). Because of its perceived social deviancy in our society, however, teenage pregnancy and parenthood often lack appropriate or sufficient social support. The risks associated with teenage parenthood are most pronounced when the mother is poor and unwed.

To understand the many exosystem issues associated with childbearing, it is important to recognize the policies instituted by hospitals, schools, and governmental bodies that can affect infants and their families both during the immediate postpartal period and beyond. The prominent role of the exosystem is also reflected in several pressing policy questions: Should public schools offer information on family planning or provide early training for parenting? Should a physician who blocks active parent participation in childbirth decisions be charged with malpractice? Will the federal government enact and enforce legislation regarding the assurance of both maternity and paternity leaves for American workers or the establishment of comprehensive child-care regulations? Will we have a comprehensive national health insurance system? The diversity of opinions on these topics helps underscore the interplay between the exosystem and the wider contextual sphere, the macrosystem.

Following a 2½ year study, the National Commission on Children (1991) recently called for guaranteed health care for pregnant women and all children under the age of 18. Their recommendation was accompanied by a strongly worded minority opinion focused on morality (unwed parenthood) rather than health. According to this group, "the sort of people who produce babies without first bothering to create a genuine family and home are rarely the sort of people who will take great pains to safeguard their physical health" (National Commission on Children, 1991, p. 162). We wonder where these same commissioners would stand on other issues related to infant mortality: sex education and complete access to family planning information.

The minority report—and the legislative debates that will follow the commission's recommendations—will highlight the range and magnitude of attitudinal barriers and policy restrictions that impinge on the development of young children.

Another exosystem issue that presents obstacles to new parents is the lack of a policy on parental leave to care for newborn or newly adopted children. Currently, fewer than half of all businesses in the United States have developed any kind of parental leave policy (National Commission on Children, 1991; Zigler, 1991). Interestingly, those with established policies most frequently offer mothers limited 6- to 8-week leaves, the same recuperative period granted to those recovering from heart attacks. In most cases, fathers and adoptive parents are excluded.

An underlying bias in this country against working mothers and a pervasive ambivalence toward children have been reflected in the obstacles facing attempts to establish national policies for medical and family leave. Most legislative proposals, offered annually since 1985, have included 4 months of unpaid leave with continued health coverage and job security for employees experiencing the birth or adoption of a child and those caring for a seriously ill child, parent, or spouse. Because the proposed law would protect only those employed for 1 year or longer at businesses with 50 or more employees, it covers less than 40% of the American work force.

Although generally modest in scope, these proposals have been opposed by business organizations who place their concerns about the cost of temporary replacement personnel above the physical and psychological well-being of a trained employee. Some, neglecting their own needs for well-trained and well-adjusted workers in generations to come, have declared that family responsibilities should be the concern of the individual workers, not their employers. A Family and Medical Leave Act passed by Congress in 1990 was vetoed by President Bush on the grounds that this type of legislation is bad for business and undermines the fabric of the American family.

Sweden, in contrast, offers a package of parental leave options to support the families of young children. Fathers are granted a ten-day fully paid leave to take care of the mother and newborn (Sidel, 1986). A national "parental insurance program" providing either parent up to 9 months parenting leave at 90% salary was so successful that the available leave time has been doubled. Until the child is 8, parents may opt to reduce their time at work to a 6-hour day, with a proportionate reduction in pay (Sidel, 1986).

The Swedish program might sound utopian, but it is not an isolated experiment. Currently, 75 countries—including several developing nations and every industrialized country except the United States—provide some form of maternity leave (Kammerman, Kahn, & Kingston, 1983; Sidel, 1986). These include an average of 4 or 5 months leave plus benefits of between 60 and 90% of a woman's salary (National Commission on Children, 1991; Zigler, 1991).

Two pressing issues underscore the importance of the exosystem in shaping the transition to parenthood. The first is this country's excessive infant mortality rate. Recent statistics put the number of deaths to American children under the age of 1 year at approximately 40,000, or 9.1 per 1000 live births (U.S. Department of Health and Human Services, 1990). In some urban centers, the death rate for minority children, especially African-American infants, is nearly three times greater. In fact, Boston, a city known as a center for medical advancements, carries the shame of a minority infant mortality rate that is greater than that of many third-world countries.

Citing low birthweight (less than 5.5 pounds) as the leading contributor to infant mortality in this country, a recent report from the National Commission on Children (1991) submits that low-birthweight babies are 40 times more likely to die in the first month of life than their more robust peers. Ironically, it is basic prenatal care, not advanced medical technology, that is needed to save many of these children. It has been estimated that one-quarter of this country's infant deaths could be prevented by basic care that monitors maternal health and nutrition and the growth of the fetus throughout the course of pregnancy (Robinson, 1991).

Currently, the United States and South Africa are the only industrialized nations that do not provide pregnant women and infants with guaranteed medical care. In 1990, Congress passed the Healthy Birth Act to improve and consolidate health care, social and nutritional services, and information and referral for pregnant women. Although the law remains on the books, to date no money has been appropriated for services.

The Macrosystem of Childbirth

Activities associated with the birth of a child vary widely with cultural setting and historical period. The macrosystem prescribes the context in which specific patterns of behavior take place and influences important social dimensions of the perinatal period. It defines what is normal for one time and place.

Often, childbirth practices within a subculture stand as a direct reflection of other life activities. Bing (1975), for example, has demonstrated the ways that the home-based activities of the Amish are particularly compatible with family-centered approaches to childbirth. Among other groups, such as the Navajo of North America and the Cuna of Panama, music is such an integral part of daily life that it is considered a requisite part of labor (Newton, 1979). Similarly, Mead (1955) reported that members of African tribes and certain groups of native Americans rejected modern hospital deliveries that would separate them from stimulating conversation during labor and from immediate postnatal support and care provided by family and friends.

Activity surrounding the addition of a new member to a group also reveals the tradition-bound values and beliefs of a culture. In sixteenth-century Europe, for example, the only men allowed at the site of a delivery were astrologers summoned to cast a precise horoscope. While the midwives attending the event lacked any medical training, they were licensed by the bishop of the church to provide impromptu baptismal services for failing neonates (Tucker, 1974). The ceremonial nature of childbirth is also reflected in the practices of several traditional African cultures, where the pregnant woman observes local dietary taboos, dons ceremonial garb, and spends the period of confinement at the home of a culturally mandated family member. Her husband, in turn, might observe the custom of *couvade*, a rite of paternal passage. Prenatally, he may indulge in a wide range of pregnancy symptoms. During the delivery and subsequent lying-in period he engages in a kind of ceremonial childbirth, including seclusion and abstention from normal work activities (Munroe & Munroe, 1975).

As these examples reveal, many cultures regard childbirth and the transition to parenthood as an important social event. In contrast, critics have argued that our own country has instituted childbirth practices that limit the vital physiological, psychological, and social roles played by parents. Haire (1973) has implicated these practices in what she calls "the cultural warping of childbirth." Furthermore, Rossi (1968) argues that the abruptness of the transition to parenthood, coupled with inadequate preparation for the responsibilities of the role, has been accompanied by a severe weakening of the web of supportive relationships available to new parents. Together, these factors undermine the ideological underpinnings of American parenthood.

Is it possible to change the macrosystem—to alter ideas and ideals woven into the very fabric of the culture? The best answer to that question is probably a qualified "yes." While certain beliefs and values are deeply ingrained, others have evolved in form or substance to accommodate the social and demographic characteristics of the times. As recently as 40 years ago, for example, the childbirth experience of most American couples was characterized by meager preparation. Most women were heavily medicated during labor and unconscious during delivery. Denied access to labor and delivery rooms, their husbands were usually left to pace in the hospital lounge.

> Parents approached the entire process of childbearing—pregnancy, childbirth and postpartum—unaware. . . . The mother did not question the use of obstetrical medication, did not know the value of breastfeeding, did not know that she might play an active role, have rights in, and assume responsibility in the birth of her baby. (Otto, 1978)

During that period, at the peak of the postwar Baby Boom, a "sellers market" existed in the field of obstetrics. Flooded by requests for services, doctors had no reason to change their practices. Within the last two decades, however, consumer action and the women's rights movement have made inroads into a number of institutional settings, including hospital maternity wards. Today, the birth rate has slowed. Fewer children are born, and among *adult* parents, they are more likely to be planned. A "buyer's market" exists, as hospitals with empty beds are forced to compete for services. With increases in the perceived value of parents as consumers in the medical marketplace, medical personnel are likely to be more receptive to the needs and demands of their patients (Garbarino, 1980a).

The ecological approach tells us that to understand the significance of changes in the microsystem of childbirth we must look to the mesosystem (the congruence between home and hospital), the exosystem (how decisions are made about childbirth in bureaucratic administrative and medical offices), and the macrosystem (how the broad social history of parenthood may increase the importance of family-centered childbirth as a way of compensating for socially impoverished support systems for families). The ecological framework has helped us demonstrate that to understand childbirth we must see the needs and potential benefits that alternative arrangements of the social events of childbirth might have for the individual development of child and parent as well as for the corporate development of the family. As the remainder of the chapter demonstrates, this perspective can also provide valuable clues to increase our understanding of the complexities of child rearing.

Becoming a Parent

What do we know about child rearing, about the nature of parent–child relations? For our purposes here, we can focus our attention on the basic issues and pitfalls in parent–child relations, the way the immediate social context of the family affects what happens between children and their parents, and how the broader society affects the content and meaning of parent–child relationships. Let us begin by examining the early development of the parent–child relationship.

Prenatally, parents engage in a special psychological acquaintance process with the fetus (Colman & Colman, 1971; Gloger-Tippelt, 1984). Particularly after fetal movements ("quickening") begin, expectant parents are likely to nickname the unborn child or make predictions about the infant's temperament or appearance from the amount of fetal activity or the mother's appearance. Birth accelerates the acquaintance process. Parents anxiously explore the physical and temperamental features of the newborn using a kind of mental checklist: Which family members does the infant resemble? Are there any features that are distinctively the infant's own? How does the infant compare to prenatal expectations? Is everything all right?

As parents discover the capabilities and distinctive characteristics of their babies, we can assume that these early, emotion-charged encounters begin to teach infants important lessons about the social environment. For example, in healthy social settings, infants learn that when they make social overtures and signal their need for caregiving, they will get a response from special others. They begin to trust themselves and those around them (Erikson, 1963). In time, they will use the relationship with specific attachment figures, usually the parents, as a secure base from which to discover the expanding horizons of the physical and social environment (Ainsworth, 1973). Throughout this period of active learning, the infant is also an effective teacher, communicating interests, preferences, and needs. Building on our discussion of attachment in Chapter 5, we can note Susan Goldberg's (1979) work with preterm infants and Selma Fraiberg's (1968, 1973) studies of the attachment behaviors of blind babies. These studies make it clear that one of the most important tasks of new parents is to learn to understand, or decode, infant communications and respond appropriately. It is an essential fact of development that starting from the very earliest social exchanges, socialization is a reciprocal process (Bell, 1968, 1974).

The mutuality of parent–child influences has been demonstrated by descriptions of the patterns of interactional behaviors used in the early social exchanges of mothers and infants. Examining videotapes of mother–infant social play, Stern (1971, 1973) described maneuvers used by mothers to capture and retain infant attention (i.e., high-pitch, sing-song speech, exaggerated facial expressions, and close-range body placement). Infants, in turn, use gazes, smiles, and changes in head and body position to initiate, respond to, or discontinue social exchanges. Stern found that a baby's attention seems to cycle toward and away from the mother. A related study by Brazelton, Koslowski, and Main (1974) complements Stern's research by showing that the most positive mother–infant interactions occur when the partners read each other's cues, negotiating synchronized cycles of attention and nonattention.

Both scholars and practitioners have recognized that parenthood, or the sense of oneself as a parent, unfolds gradually in series of stages corresponding to the demands of the role and the child's corresponding developmental tasks.

Bromwich and her colleagues (Bromwich et al., 1981) outlined a six-step progression of parenting behaviors that evolves as parents "grow with their infants" (p. 97). In the first three stages, enjoyment of the infant helps parents read behavioral cues and engage in mutually satisfying exchanges that establish an emotional base for the relationship that leads to attachment. Parents use this base to expand their awareness of developmentally appropriate activities as they learn to anticipate their child's increasing complex needs.

Similarly, Brazelton (1985) has used a four-step model to describe the development of parent–infant interaction from the newborn period until the fourth month postpartum. He sees the process as so essential to the developing parent–child relationship and the establishment of secure attachment that he uses the model to argue for mandatory 4-month maternal and 1-month paternal leaves during the transition to parenthood followed by a gradual return to work for parents employed outside the home. Once parents have returned to work, flexible work schedules and quality child care with no greater than a 1:3 adult–child ratio for infants can help support the dual-career family.

Viewing parenthood across a much broader time span, Galinsky (1987) has identified six stages of parenthood from pregnancy to the child's adulthood. She describes pregnancy as the Image-Making Stage, when parents define expectations for parenthood and prepare for the impending delivery. During the child's infancy, a stage dominated by nurturance, parents reconcile earlier expectations for parenthood with the realities of child care. As they give to their child and receive gratifying responses in return, parents become attached to the child. This "honeymoon" can end abruptly with a toddler's defiant "No!." During the third stage, then, both parents and children will have their first trials regarding issues of authority: Who sets the limits for behavior and what happens if the rules are broken?

The Interpretive Stage emerges when parents begin to prepare their child for an increasing number of experiences away from home. With the child's entrance to kindergarten, for example, parents often review their images of parenthood, asking how realistic they have been. They also confront questions about how to introduce their child to an expanding world outside the family home. The questions of authority first confronted when the child was two reemerge during adolescence. If resolved satisfactorily, parents and children can form a new relationship characterized by interdependence and mutual respect. The last stage in Galinsky's model, the Departure Stage, finds parents evaluating their successes and failures and preparing for a different type of relationship with an adult child.

Stage models of parenthood help demonstrate that becoming a parent is an ongoing process that coincides with the developmental tasks of children. However, reliance on a perspective that depends on an orderly, sequential progression also can obscure the complexities of adult development and family life (Shanock, 1990). To appreciate those complexities, imagine using Galinsky's model to explain the parental dilemmas facing the parent of three children, ranging in age from infant to adolescent. Now add the additional ecological constraints that could be imposed by marital discord or single parenthood, social isolation, demands of education or career, or insufficient housing.

Shanock (1990) suggests an alternative model, which treats the transition to parenthood as a "marker process" with special importance for adult development, rather than as a developmental stage. Based on the notion that intimacy and identity are the important organizational constructs of adult development, she distinguishes between the task of parenting a child and the process of becoming a parent. *Parenting* is an intense relationship based on the evolving needs of the developing child. Because of its ongoing demands and the potential for mutual satisfaction, parenting influences intimacy. *Parenthood*, in contrast, can be defined as a role or even a career. Because parenthood involves self-definition and the presentation of oneself in relation to family, friends, and others in the community, it influences adult identity. As parents refine their behaviors to meet children's changing needs and as they redefine themselves in relation to their parental responsibilities, they are engaged in the interlocking tasks of parenting and parenthood, the ongoing process of becoming parents.

Family relationships do not end when a young adult leaves home. The parent–child relationship continues to affect one's life long afterward and may even endure after the death of one of the members of the dyad (Hagestad, 1981b). Whatever else a developing individual becomes in life, that individual is always the child of his or her parents. Research on child abuse, for example, shows that the memory of one's parents lives on in one's own child rearing style, particularly when that style was harsh and punitive (Kempe & Kempe, 1978). Similarly, studies of adults whose parents were alcoholics reveal strong intergenerational issues and themes.

Just as the nature of the parent–child relationship shows variations with the capabilities and ages of the individual actors, a growing body of research suggests that still other variations may be associated with parents' gender-related roles. Especially during the periods of infancy and early childhood, mothers tend to assume the primary responsibility for child care. While the quantity of time devoted to father–child interaction usually increases with the age of the child (Lewis & Weinraub, 1976), the average amount of time fathers spend in direct contact with infants is often less than an hour per day (Pedersen & Robson, 1969; Rebelsky & Hanks, 1971). Of greater importance than the *quantity* of father–infant interaction, however, is the father's contribution to the *quality* of interactions within the family unit. Ross Parke (Parke, 1979; Parke & O'Leary, 1975; Parke & Sawin, 1976; Sawin & Parke, 1979), for example, conducted a series of observational studies during the perinatal period that show high levels of paternal interest and sensitivity to infant cues. Similarly, Michael Lamb (1976, 1977a,b, 1978) has demonstrated that although fathers provide less care giving and initiate fewer conventional games than mothers, they are more likely to engage infants in unique kinds of physically stimulating play.

Recently, studies have shown that fathers also exert powerful indirect influences on the quality of a child's experiences with the mother (Belsky, 1981). In the interest shown to the infant and the support given to his spouse as a mother and a wife, the father is able to mediate mothering behavior toward the infant (Lamb, 1978; Sawin & Parke, 1979). These influences, which Bronfenbrenner (1979) calls second-order effects, underscore the value of studying the parent–child relationship within the context of the family system (Feiring & Lewis, 1978).

Becoming a parent is especially challenging when it conflicts with the developmental tasks of adolescence. The demands of parenting can be trying for any new mother who lacks knowledge of child development, adequate experience with child care, or inadequate resources to meet the needs of an infant.

This is especially true for a teen parent who is thrust into the demands of adulthood before accomplishing the developmental tasks of adolescence (Musick, 1990; Osofsky, Osofsky, & Diamond, 1988). Certainly, some young mothers rise to the challenge of teen parenting. These tend to be young women who derive a sense of achievement, respect (Klerman, 1986), or purpose (Musick, 1990) from their new role and those able to marshall adequate support (Colletta, 1981; Stevens, 1988; Unger & Wandersman, 1988). For others, however, early parenthood is a major roadblock to meeting their developmental potential. For example, 40% of females who drop out of school list pregnancy or parenthood as the reason (Lewin, 1988). Unfortunately, some teens see parenthood as the only means of attaining a meaningful role in the adult world. Overall, poor teens are up to four times more likely to get pregnant than those from middle-class families; among the poor, those lacking basic skills are twice as likely to become teen parents (Perry, 1988).

Too often, the stress of adolescent parenthood is compounded by complications of pregnancy or childbirth, including preeclampsia, anemia, cephalopelvic disproportion, pregnancy-induced hypertension, and a range of complications associated with poor nutrition, substance abuse, and sexually transmitted diseases (Osofsky et al., 1988). As a result, infants of adolescent mothers—especially those lacking appropriate prenatal services—are more likely to experience developmental challenges including prematurity, neurological difficulties, small size for gestational age, and respiratory difficulties than those born to the population at large (Osofsky et al., 1988). These at-risk infants of at-risk parents require considerable resources to overcome the threat of developmental sequelae.

Although the number of births to adolescent parents has leveled off in recent years, 500,000 American teenagers—including 10,000 of those under age 15—have babies each year. Reversing previous trends, at least 95% opt to retain custody of the child.

Moreover, fewer mothers than ever before consider marriage a prerequisite to parenthood. Just 20 years ago, fewer than one-third of all teen mothers were unmarried (Lewin, 1988). Currently, one in four American infants is born to unwed mothers, many of whom begin parenting during adolescence. Among minorities, more than 50% of all infants are born out of wedlock.

Overall 50% of all African-American families, 33% of all Latino families, and 15% of white families are headed by females (Halpern, 1987). Unwed parenthood is just one demographic trend contributing to the dramatic rise in the number of families headed by a single parent. Another is a divorce rate that has quadrupled in 30 years. Today, the United States has the highest divorce rate in the world, with half of all marriages ending in divorce (National Commission on Children, 1991).

There is general agreement that marital hostility is a disturbing force that can affect children's emotional well-being and alter parent–child relationships. Many would argue, then, that where serious discord exists separation or divorce is in the best interest of all family members. Marital dissolution is not without its own consequences, however (Honig, 1986).

Children often react to divorce with feelings of anger, terror, or guilt. They grieve for the lost parent and fear further losses and catastrophes (Wallerstein, 1983). Helping children cope with dramatic changes in the family is an important task for the custodial parent. To this responsibility are added personal adjustment, shifts in family roles and household routines, and an overload in terms of economic burden.

Indeed, one of the most striking ways to measure the effects of single parenthood is in economic terms. The average income of single-parent families headed by women is only 40% of that for two-parent families. In 1989, young women heading households had a median income of $3005, far below the poverty level for a family of three. In fact, it has been estimated that 75% of children in single-parent families experience poverty, often for sustained periods, during their first 10 years of life (National Commission on Children, 1991). The number of mother-headed families is one of several reasons that for the first time in history, children are the poorest group in American society.

Single parenthood is just one of the challenges facing those who develop policies and programs designed to support the development of children and families. Other recent changes in the American family include the large number of children and unwanted infants left in the care of hospitals, older children in the custodial care of grandparents or foster families, and all those who experience the confusions of complex joint custody or irregular child care arrangements.

As always, we find that the challenges facing families rarely occur in a vacuum. Instead, each of the recent demographic changes in the American family is likely to bring other social, economic, and attitudinal challenges to the already difficult role of parent.

Current census data on the changing American family stand in stark contrast to the popular media image of the white, two-parent, suburban family typical of the post-World War II Baby Boom era. In fact, the supposedly typical family with working father and homemaker mother is representative of less than one-third of all American families. In fact, more than 25 million children spend their lives outside a traditional two-parent family, including 2 million who live with neither parent (Zill, 1991).

Without question, parent–child relations present us with some real intellectual, policy, and practice puzzles. On the one hand, we know that what parents do with their children makes a difference. As we saw in earlier chapters, virtually all social events are mediated by parents; very few touch children directly. The nature of a specific parent–child relationship is the single most important social factor in one's biography. And yet, we know—and research shows—that although differences in style and orientation make some difference, overall, most parents tend to do reasonably well by most children, most of the time. Despite the widespread assumption that each and every childhood event carries with it life-long consequences, we are learning that for each constancy there is a variable, that development is a continuing process in which contemporary events play a large role in shaping what we are (Brim & Kagan, 1980). We all know families where the parents' best laid plans for their children have gone awry or even have been actively thwarted by those same children. We recall a cartoon that appeared in the *New Yorker* magazine some years ago. It pictured two denim-clad, bead-laden hippies lamenting the "failure" of their parenting efforts—a boy dressed in suit and tie carrying a briefcase. It is clear that parents rarely are able to prescribe or orchestrate the details of their offspring's lives. Temperament, out-of-home experiences, and unintentional parental effects play a large role.

The Basic Tools of Healthy Development

What do children need? Perhaps a child's single most important psychological necessity is self-esteem, positive self-regard. Children can and do grow up to be adequate adults within a wide variety of disciplinary styles, intellectual climates, and levels of social interaction. But, when all is said and done, it appears that very few children can grow up adequately on a psychological diet of rejection (Garbarino et al., 1986; Rohner, 1975; Rohner & Neilson, 1978). Acceptance, then, seems to be a prerequisite for adequate human development. Perhaps the Beatles went too far when they sang, "All you need is love," but they were on the right track.

Chapter 3 posed rejection and neglect as underlying dangers of sociocultural risk, the most surely deadly poison that can contaminate parent–child relations. Rejection and neglect are general terms, of course, but we can identify some of their more specific behavioral expressions as the child moves from infancy to adolescence (cf., Garbarino et al., 1986).

In infancy, the dangers are twofold: First, we must be concerned about the rejection and neglect of positive, natural behaviors such as smiling, mobility, exploration, vocalization, and manipulation of objects. Research from a variety of contexts demonstrates that caregiver behavior can have a direct impact on the performance of these basic human skills (cf. Brackbill, 1958; Foss, 1965). There is an inherent drive for mastery or "effectance" (Goldberg, 1977; White, 1959). To punish or ignore this drive and its accompanying behaviors is a decided threat to the child's development of competence.

A second danger comes from parents thwarting the attachment relationship between themselves and the child. As we saw earlier in this chapter, caregiver–infant bonding and later attachment have emerged as important issues in child development (Klaus & Kennell, 1976). Disruptions of attachment have been linked to physical abuse (Kennell et al.,

1976), failure to thrive (Spitz, 1945), and a variety of competence deficits (Bronfenbrenner, 1970). Child rearing styles that consistently undermine attachment, therefore, pose a direct threat to adequate development. The infant is hungry for attachment. Deny it and the child starves psychologically.

Once the infant advances into childhood, the rejection issue—like the child—changes as a function of development and maturation. While attachment is no longer so simply and directly at stake, its natural product—a sense of self-worth—is. Self-esteem, one of the engines driving adequate development, is the positive valuing of one's characteristics, a positive identity. It rises and falls in response to the behavior of others, and it is linked to a variety of prosocial characteristics (Coopersmith, 1967). The unloved of any age must always suspect that they are unlovable. To discourage self-esteem is to attack a fundamental component of competent development. To reject or neglect developing children is to jeopardize their very view of their place in the world. For example, because alcohol addiction often incapacitates parents—making them emotionally unavailable—it often translates into rejection and neglect from the child's point of view.

What else do children need from their parents beyond a measure of acceptance? A child needs the experience of learning how to regulate impulses. Thus, matters of discipline and control emerge repeatedly in studies of parent–child relations, to complement the fundamental issue of acceptance–rejection. This discipline–control issue has found expression in many studies, under many names. Put in broad terms, however, the key is that parents should be flexible in providing enough in the way of limits and controls to offer adequate protection *for a particular child* and to model the necessary process of self-control. Although many theorists use different terms for this essential process, the underlying issue is the same: children need moral structure to their lives.

Of course, as Aristotle tells us from across the centuries, "In all things, moderation." Both too much and too little control threaten the optimal development of children. Of course, the optimal level varies from child to child, from setting to setting, and from one developmental phase to the next, but either extreme is dangerous for most children. How do caregivers decide the proper mix of freedom and control? The research suggests that most successful families accomplish a good balance by negotiation among members with both respect and dignity (Baumrind, 1980). Successful parents avoid the extreme of too little control ("I'm his mother, so I should do whatever he wants.") and too much control ("He's my child, so he should do whatever I want him to do."). Baumrind called this middle road the "authoritative" approach (in contrast to permissive or authoritarian styles), and concluded that it achieves an appropriate balance of control, maturity demands, communication, and nurturance (Baumrind & Block, 1967). Therefore, parents who are most successful in facilitating the development of socially competent and happy children are those who do not shortchange *any* of the child's basic psychological needs: for protection and reality testing, for encouragement to achieve and become competent, for rich verbal interaction, and for positive regard, openly expressed.

Parents and Children and the Wider Social Context

How do parents know how to provide all a child needs, on an ongoing basis, in a way that is appropriate for a specific child? Of course, it takes the motivation to give. Fortunately, nearly all parents have that motivation because of their personal investment in the child's character and well-being (Barash, 1977; Garbarino, 1981a). In part, parents' efforts come as a natural by-product of being socially competent and happy adults.

Parental incentives also come from being part of a parent–child relationship that is embedded in a network of social resources that provide feedback and nurturance (Belsky, Lerner, & Spanier, 1984). Valuable information from the support network consists of both regular feedback on parent–child relations and general knowledge of appropriate norms, expectations, and techniques concerning childrearing. It derives from regular day-to-day observation and discussion of parent–child relations, informal folk wisdom based on extensive historically validated first-hand experience, and formal, professional expertise. This is "parent education" in its broadest sense.

The need for information is a direct function of situational demands that are both internal and external to the parent–child relationship. The family that is adapting to separation or divorce provides a prime example. With more than one fourth of our children expected to spend some part of their first 18 years in a household where parental divorce or separation has occurred, parent–child relationships must often progress in a changing variety of family forms. Most children can and do cope with having only one parent, having divorcing or divorced parents, and having stepparents. For the most part, children can meet these challenges if their basic psychological necessities continue to be met—if they still receive nurturance, appropriate maturity demands, sufficient control, and clear communication.

Too often, however, family disruption and changes in form and composition of the family unit *tend* to undermine delivery of these basic psychological necessities. When family members are separated, for example, the noncustodial parent's role is often ambiguous and his or her involvement in the family's life declines to the point where the child feels abandoned and the custodial parent (the one in whose household the child is living) feels overwhelmed by responsibilities. Moreover, the child care and housekeeping responsibilities of the divorced woman are frequently compounded by economic stresses; divorce translates into poverty for many divorced mothers. Less than half of all divorced women receive alimony or child support. When they seek employment, they generally receive lower salaries than their male counterparts.

As demands on the family increase, so do the parents' needs for information. Formal institutions can become effective sources of information when they are actively linked to the family's social network. These linkages can act directly through the parent, or indirectly through relationships with others who, in turn, link the parent with formal institutions. Social isolation can be a serious threat to adequacy in the parent–child relationship because those indirect links to resources are lacking. Like their parents, children need the skills, support, and opportunities necessary to participate in the social environment.

While the process of child rearing begins as a dyad or triad with one child, it soon comes to include other children. If there are other children in the family, parents must consider how siblings affect childrearing and serve as an adjunct to their childrearing efforts. Eventually, the child's nonfamily peers come into the picture. The child may go to a babysitting group or a nursery school or begin to have contact with neighborhood children.

Peer-group relations are an important influence in development, particularly in their contribution to the socialization of both aggressive and prosocial behavior (Hartup, 1978). Throughout childhood, more and more peers in wider and wider circles become part of the child's life. At each step of the way, the parent's influence may remain strong—even prominent—in matters of basic values and in the acquisition of intimate behaviors. In matters of fashion, taste, and custom, however, the parent must be increasingly ready and able to recognize the existence of their child's peer reference group in family discussions. The 4-year-old child wants a Ninja Turtle because the other kids in his or her preschool have them. The 7-year-old child must watch the latest "in" show on television. The 13-year-old child will "die" if her or his haircut is wrong. The 17-year-old cannot come home before midnight because "no one is leaving that early!" The point is that every age responds to peer influences, but the central role of the parent–child relationship remains.

When parents reject the child's efforts to make a place in the world beyond the family, they deprive the child of one of the basic psychosocial necessities of life, and create what has been called the "World of

Abnormal Rearing" (Helfer, 1980). To create such a world and force the child to live in it is one of the principal threats to adequate child development.

Punishing interpersonal skills necessary for adequate performance in nonfamilial contexts, such as schools and peer groups, is another form of rejection or neglect with which we must be concerned. Burgess and Conger (1978) observe that abusive and neglectful parents do not provide positive reinforcement for key interpersonal behaviors. Others have noted that abusive parents typically discourage normal social relations among their children—e.g., the formation of friendships outside the home (cf. Friedman, 1976; Garbarino, 1977a,b; Parke & Collmer, 1975).

Few parent–child relationships will go seriously awry and stay that way if both parents and children are well connected or if they are part of a social network invested in their well-being. The social character of family relationships is a central aspect of the health and vitality of the child's life. Just as we can join with John Donne in asserting that "no man is an island," we know that no family can always stand alone. A positive orientation toward relationships beyond the family (beyond even the larger kinship network) is necessary to complement or even counteract the particularism of family patterns. Parenting is "intrinsically social" in the sense that it draws meaning and strength from the community.

This principle is underscored by examples provided by three prominent agents of socialization—supplemental caregivers, the schools, and television.

Child Care. Almost all cultures have developed arrangements that enable parents to provide for basic child care while maintaining other duties instrumental to family well-being. Among hunter–gatherer societies, for example, mothers carry their nursing infants in slings when they go on gathering expeditions. As the children grow older, they spend most of their time playing with a large group of age-mates under the watchful eyes of the entire social group (Konner, 1976). In contrast, Weisner and Gallimore (1977) demonstrated that in many traditional sedentary societies, as the mother engages in work away from the home, her youngest children are left in the care of a designated sibling.

Most child care arrangements may be seen as solutions offered for the support of the parents and the well-being of the child. As demonstrated by the examples of the child care centers of the Israeli kibbutzim, the Soviet Union, and China, however, supplemental child care also can be a strategy used to help a society meet its goals. In those systems, child care centers are viewed as a key to providing for full participation of adults in the social and economic life of the society, as well as for the socialization of children in a manner appropriate to societal goals (Robinson et al., 1979; Sidel, 1986).

In our own country, supports provided to parents in the provision of quality care for children lag far behind that of other industrial countries. The first significant piece of federal legislation to support child care for preschool and school-age children was not passed in the United States until 1990. Traditionally, child care in the United States has been viewed as the sole domain of the parents. Supplemental care, when necessary, was to be provided by close friends and relatives.

Although both parents share caregiving for about half of all young children, only 10% of all dual-earner couples have nonoverlapping schedules that permit them to care for their children without outside help. As a result, families have developed a "patchwork of arrangements" (Zigler & Lang, 1991) to meet child care needs. Today, about half of all children of working mothers are cared for by a relative (Hofferth, 1989).

Recently, changes in family mobility and employment patterns have led to increased reliance on care by nonrelatives. In 1965, 87% of children receiving mother-substitute care were looked after by relatives or babysitters in their own homes; this figure had dropped to 54% by 1987 (Hofferth, 1987). As of 1990, about 43% of preschool-aged children of employed mothers are looked after by relatives or babysitters (U.S. Bureau of the Census, 1990). This change has been matched by increased use of both family day care (a group of children cared for in someone's home) and center-based child care.

In a powerful essay underscoring gaps in American commitment to children's services, Hartman (1990) notes that in this country

> boundaries around a nuclear family are to be inviolate under almost any circumstances. These principles combine to create a society that is very reluctant to interfere with the family, that is deeply individualistic, and that expects parents to take total responsibility for and full care of their children. This reluctance to care is expressed in and rationalized by neglect. Somehow, Americans believe that a person's destiny is appropriately determined by the accident of birth—by the parents he or she is born to. There is no conviction that children belong to themselves, to the community, or to the future. (p. 484)

However, creation of a coherent child care policy also has been hampered by deep schisms within the child development community. Should we continue to push for federal interagency standards for day care, which were developed more than a decade ago but blocked from implementation by a wave of government deregulation? Or do federal guidelines undermine parental choice and hamper development of a rich variety of local options (Zigler & Lang, 1990)? Should we discourage infant care because some research studies suggest that it might lead to insecure attachment (Belsky & Benn, 1988) or improve the likelihood of secure attachment by helping parents find quality care (Howes, 1988)? Should we promote quality infant care because maternal employment can be psychologically beneficial for mothers who desire to work (Hock & De-Meis, 1990) or because working is an economic necessity for a growing number of mothers (Halpern, 1987)?

Currently, there is no shortage of suggestions for helping parents mesh their professional and economic needs with the developmental needs of their families. Suggestions for governmental support range from monetary subsidies for the poor and tax credits for working families to legislation such as the Act for Better Child Care, which requires states to enact minimum standards for care, expand available services, recruit and train child care providers, and provide parents with information and consumer protection (Public Policy Report, 1988).

Businesses have been urged to follow the lead of companies such as Merck Pharmaceuticals, which offers a generous parenting leave policy, Stride Rite Shoe company and Little Tyke Toys, which established on-site child care, or IBM in providing employees with a nationwide child care resource and referral network. Other options are flextime and job sharing, which allow parents to match work and family schedules, and parental leave policies that enable parents to care for newborns or sick children.

But of course most of these proposed solutions assume that parents are involved in stable, fulltime employment during "regular" daytime hours. What about the children of seasonal laborers, workers on "swing shifts," or those with a sporadic work history? What about the dilemmas faced by parents in small or nontraditional businesses, those who work "after hours," and those who must travel? The heart-rending child care dilemmas faced by reservists called to active duty during the war in the Persian Gulf underscored the problems faced when the demands of an employer conflict with family life.

The government-mandated extended maternity and paternity leaves of the Scandinavian countries and the social insurance that gives parents in Poland, Sweden, and Germany funds to cover the salary lost while caring for a sick youngster are largely unheard of in this country. In the U.S., legislation to provide *unpaid* leave for new parents has been vetoed on the grounds it is a threat to business. Neither are our children offered the national programs of state-supported preschool education and care found in France, Belgium, and Russia.

Whereas the growing number of dual-career families necessitates the need for a variety of supplements to parental care, child care still lacks widespread public and governmental support. Current efforts must contend with a history of ambivalence and hostility to "day care." In 1972, for example, Sibbison found that of the mothers she surveyed, 29% rejected the use of day-care services for other people's children under most conditions, while 44% rejected that option for their own children. Moreover, in a survey conducted in the early 1970s, one in five of the respondents felt that working women neglect their children (Rodes & Moore, 1973). Nowhere is our country's anti-day care sentiment more prevalent, however, than in the chronic failure of the federal government to legislate and enforce guidelines ensuring quality comprehensive care. Despite the realities of life for families today, some people still consider day care to be "un-American."

Just as much of the research on child care in the United States has failed to demonstrate appreciable long-term gains from supplemental care, detractors of child care also have not been successful in showing that adequate out-of-home care has any serious negative effects on young children (Peters, 1980). A growing body of research shows that child care practices based on the developmental needs of young children at various ages contribute to children's growth and learning. This research provides the foundation for guidelines for quality in early childhood programs (Bredekamp, 1987a,b). Similarly, developmental theory and research on school-age children, as well as evolving practice, have contributed to developmentally appropriate practice guidelines for school-age child care (Albrecht, 1991; Albrecht & Plantz, 1991).

Quality child care can supplement the direct childrearing functions of the family by serving as a source of nurturance, affection, instruction, and socialization (Peters & Benn, 1980). Although children's ties to their parents remain primary, the child care setting can offer rich opportunities for children to interact and form close relationships with other caregivers and their peers (Ricciuti, 1974, 1977). In addition, when parents and child care providers establish a partnership of care, a number of indirect functions can also be achieved (e.g., economic, self-actualization, and advocacy).

> the relationships among the day-care provider, the natural parent(s) and the children are seen as dynamic, multidimensional and developmental ones that have the potential of serving many of the functions formerly provided by the extended family. In this sense, they represent a social support for, rather than a replacement for, the responsibilities of the nuclear family in whatever form it is currently found. (Peters & Benn, 1980)

The Family and the Schools

In a modern society, school success is an important precursor to life success (Garbarino, 1981b). Thus, one of the major tasks in parent–child

relations is to facilitate academic achievement. After many years of research and efforts at intervention, we know that two aspects of the
parent–child relationship stand out on this score. First, we know that
parent–child relationships vary in their manifestation of the "academic
culture." To the extent that parents adopt a style of interaction that
emphasizes the use of conceptual language in solving problems, manipulation of symbols, and a hypothesis-oriented style of personal inquiry
(Garbarino, 1981b), they teach their children skills that are adaptive in
academic settings.

A second aspect of the parent–child relationship relevant to school
success is whether or not the parent communicates a positive regard for
schooling. Two primary indicators are a positive orientation toward written materials (e.g., reading and having books in the home) and efforts to
support and encourage the school's activities (e.g., by attending meetings or checking homework). These are keys to academic development
(Bronfenbrenner, 1974).

Of course, the parents' willingness and ability to convey positive attitudes about schools and the educational process are predicted by their
own academic histories. Joy and triumph or bitterness and defeat from
early school experiences are bound to color the way that parents perceive later educational opportunities for themselves and their children.
Those early feelings may also be magnified by the attitudes of teachers
and the policies of the schools. Does the school system recognize and
support the value of ethnic and racial diversity in its classrooms? Are the
family and the community acknowledged as rich sources of information? Do teachers and parents recognize learning as a life-long process
that is enhanced by cooperation and sharing?

If successful, schools do more than impart information. When they
help children ask questions and find answers, effective schools instill an
appreciation of life-long learning. By offering opportunities for children
to work and play with others, they provide a forum for the exploration
and exchange of ideas and a site for developing social relationships. For
better or worse, schools also are the first large institutions that most
children will have to navigate without their parents present.

Although most parents are not physically present in their children's
classrooms, they have a profound influence on the ways that their children view schools and learning. The extent to which the family at home
reflects key elements of the academic culture directly affects specific
types of school performance. Bradley, Caldwell, and Rock (1988), for
example, demonstrated a relationship between characteristics of the early home environment and school performance in the fourth grade. The
variety of appropriate play materils available to children as toddlers was
related to later reading achievement.

Similarly, parents who continued to involve their children in enriching cultural and social experiences, and who participated in developmentally stimulating experiences with their families, had children whose academic competence was reflected in both achievement test scores and task orientation in the classroom. Some positive classroom behaviors could be traced to the learning environments experienced when the children were only 6 months old: Appropriate parental responsiveness during infancy was related to considerate classroom behavior 10 years later, irrespective of the intervening environment.

Stevenson and Lee (1990) demonstrated ways that the home environments of elementary school children in three different cultures accounted for the high academic achievement of Asian children compared to their American counterparts. The Minneapolis mothers who composed the American sample were described as taking a "casual approach" to their children's school performance. More concerned with general cognitive development than academic achievement, they read to their children, provided them with emotional support, and encouraged their participation in an array of recreational and social extracurricular activities.

Two samples of Asian mothers (from Japan and Taiwan), in contrast, dedicated themselves to their children's school achievement. They were more likely to provide—sometimes at great sacrifice—a desk or other quiet space for their child to study, time for homework and other academic activities, and direct assistance with children's studies. Whereas their American counterparts believed that academic success was tied to innate abilities and tended to overestimate their children's achievements, Asian mothers held high expectations for academic achievement based on hard work.

The relative value of learning for its own sake versus "making the grade" in school can be debated. However, no one can deny the importance of a "can-do spirit," believing in oneself as a learner. In a study of highly competent third graders, Phillips (1987) found that children's achievement test performance was related to their perceived competence. That is, children who believed they were bright and capable matched that self-appraisal with higher achievement test scores than their less confident peers. Children with low perceived competence, in turn, found their current schoolwork more difficult and held lower expectations for future success than their more confident classmates. Which comes first, confidence or competence? Certainly they reinforce each other, but confidence is an important ingredient in the development of competence.

In Stevenson's study, the children's feelings of academic competence were more likely to be derived from parents' appraisals than by evidence of their objective experience of past classroom success. Children with low perceived competence felt greater parental pressure for academic achievement. However, they also perceived correctly that their parents estimated their abilities poorly and expected less of them in terms of academic performance.

Low parental expectations for a child can be a projection of a parent's own school experiences. Parents who experienced earlier difficulties in school might unwittingly discourage their children from full and meaningful participation in an academic environment. This is especially true for some low-income and minority families who feel alienated from the culture of predominantly white, middle-class schools (Harrison et al., 1990). In such situations, children may feel that to achieve school success is a betrayal of the family. The result is discipline problems that sabotage the classroom culture or deliberately poor performance aimed at winning family approval (Greenberg, 1989).

Especially for young children and those from ethnic minorities, the two worlds of home and classroom often can seem in conflict (Comer, 1988; Lightfoot, 1987; Harrison et al., 1990). Serious discontinuities between the family and school ecologies, in turn, can adversely affect school achievement and social adjustment (Harrison et al., 1990).

Parents can increase a child's comfort and ability to travel between the two settings greatly by communicating some measure of endorsement for the school and its practices (Greenberg, 1989). When parents demonstrate their endorsement by involving themselves in school activities, they can generate broader and more complex strategies for themselves in dealing with educational institutions. This sense of competence, in turn, is reflected in children's school performance (Stevenson & Baker, 1987).

Of course, to build a strong home–school mesosystem, it is essential for schools to meet families halfway. An essential first step is for classroom teachers and school administrators to identify the ways that the curriculum, along with school policies and practices, reinforce stereotypical notions about the "ideal" or "typical" family at the expense of the flesh and blood families they are supposed to serve.

How many families are excluded from participation in school events only because a teacher is unwilling to meet with them outside the narrow time frame prescribed by a contract? How many children are hurt or confused by classroom projects focused on making gifts "for your mother and father"? How can children learn to value school when they hear a principal describe their family as a "broken home" or their neighbors as "those people from the projects"?

Schools begin to communicate an appreciation for families when the curriculum is directly relevant to life outside the classroom. Classroom materials should reflect the ethnic composition of the community with an eye to helping children appreciate other cultures represented in the region. Moreover, as the work of Hale-Benson (1982) and Heath (1983) has demonstrated, teachers also must be aware of the ways that distinct, culturally based learning and teaching styles used in some families can influence a child's reactions to classroom experiences. For example, native Hawaiian children bring a very strong collective/cooperative orientation to school. Teaching and testing must accommodate this culture if they are to succeed with Hawaiian children.

Discussions about topics from holidays and foods to notions of fairness and loyalty should be conducted with sensitivity to the cultural differences represented in the classroom and the practices of individual families (Coleman, 1991). We cannot expect children to understand world geography if we fail to communicate an appreciation for their families, their communities, and the plurality that contributes to the richness of American society.

One of the most effective ways for schools to show that they value parents and others in the community is to arrange opportunities for meaningful participation in a range of support, partnership, and leadership roles (Coleman, 1991). As the evidence from Head Start and other innovative early childhood experiments demonstrates (Berreuta-Clement et al., 1984; Lally et al., 1988; Lazar et al., 1982), parent involvement in early education can be beneficial for both children and their families. Certainly, a key factor in building a strong home–school mesosystem is the degree to which parents are recognized as the first and most influential educators of their children.

Another way that schools can address the importance of parents as role models and teachers is to help families negotiate the stresses of daily life (Klugman & Benn, 1987). Schools that offer early childhood services, breakfast and lunch programs, before- and after-school care, support for children experiencing family crises, and recreational activities during school vacations express a willingness to help parents meet the complex needs of the whole child. When they help parents fulfill children's basic needs, schools help parents find time for more meaningful involvement in their children's lives.

Schools have an opportunity to play a unique role in promoting child development and facilitating family functioning. Unlike most other children's programs, schools are oriented toward primary prevention—the promotion of healthy development rather than attempts to fix existing problems (Klugman & Benn, 1987). Moreover, they offer universal services to children in a given locale and maintain daily contact with their "clients" for most of the year. Through children, schools can maintain contact with most of the young families in a community. They can and should be the great producers of strong mesosystems.

Television

At least one television set resides in more than 98% of all American homes. Parents and children alike are drawn to its appeal as an entertainer and "babysitter." Preschoolers watch on average nearly 28 hours per week (Nielsen Media Research, 1990). Once children begin elementary school, organized sports, and after school activities, viewing drops slightly—to 23.5 hours per week. In fact, most American children devote more time to watching television than to any other waking activity. Certainly any socializing agent that is that popular must also serve as a powerful educator.

The pervasiveness of television violence (Liebert, Neal, & Davidson, 1973) and the medium's presentation of stereotypic and often degrading portrayals of gender roles, ethnic characteristics, and age-related characteristics challenge many of the essential values of many parents.

In the 1980s, government deregulation allowed much commercial children's programming to degenerate into an extended series of commercials, many for undesirable products. In one study (Center for Science in the Public Interest, 1991), children who viewed a limited sample of 4 hours of Saturday morning television were exposed to more than 325 commercials, 200 of them for highly sugared "junk foods" such as sweetened cereals, candy, cookies, and fruit-flavored drinks. Advertising for highly sugared cereals outnumbered those for low-sugar types 17 to 1. In all, fewer than 10% of the food ads were for nutritious products.

In other cases, the programs themselves have become 30-minute commercials thinly disguised as cartoons. Toy manufacturers and others deliberately pitch their products directly to young consumers who are less discriminating than their parents. The methods used are tantalizing though mindless programs whose sole purpose is to promote spin-off products including toys, clothes, and fast-food promotional items. Too often, these commercially successful programs use violence to capture the attention of their young audiences (Carlsson-Paige & Levin, 1991). Turning on the television set for a child is an agreement to share child-rearing responsibilities with powerful outside forces. When parents relinquish their right and obligation to monitor and limit exposure to television, they are telling children implicitly that they approve of the messages presented by this powerfully persuasive electronic parent.

In some communities, parents have helped reduce their children's reliance on television by participating in TV-free weeks. As families take a pledge to forego television for a week, community schools, libraries, and recreational programs help children discover alternative ways to occupy their time.

Others, recognizing television's importance as a powerful teaching tool, have used a variety of methods to improve the quality of children's programming while reducing the amount of commercial advertising directed at young consumers. Probably the most influential has been Action for Children's Television (ACT), which had its start as a neighborhood discussion group made up of parents concerned about their children's television viewing.

ACT disbanded in 1992 after passing the Children's Television Act (1990), which requires both network and cable broadcasters to demonstrate how they are meeting the educational and informational needs of children in their viewing areas. Because station managers are required to keep a file of correspondence, feedback from parents, teachers, and others concerned with the selection or quality of programs, it can have a direct effect on the license renewal process. By and large, however, the institutions of our society have adopted an attitude of tolerance toward the economic exploitation of children, and have simply exhorted parents to monitor and resist these commercial onslaughts. Perhaps our society's inability or unwillingness to prevent or even seriously limit child pornography is but an extreme form of this tolerance for the "use" of children to serve adult commercial interests.

It seems we generally expect parents to go it alone in meeting their responsibilities as parents while contending with the institutional life of the society. This brings us to another general issue in parent–child relations, one so fundamental it deserves a special category: the economic and ideological value of parenthood.

The Political and Economic Value of Parenthood

Are we a child-centered society? Do we really want to be? When W. C. Fields said, "A man who hates children and dogs can't be all bad," he struck a responsive chord, one that resonates with some fundamental aspects of our culture. These feelings need close scrutiny, for as Edward Zigler (first Director of the federal government's Office for Child Development) has remarked: "The greatest single impediment to our improving the lives of America's children is the myth that we are a child-oriented society already doing all that needs to be done" (Zigler, 1976).

How can this be? Don't we make sacrifices daily so that our children can live well? Don't we work overtime so our kids will be well provided for? Don't we put our children first? We do all these things and yet Zigler's claim is well founded. In fact, the very nature of our *personal* sacrifices on behalf of *our* children is ironic testimony to the validity of Zigler's analysis. It is because our society is not child centered that we must struggle so much in our personal lives to give children their due.

Parents and others concerned with the well-being of children are swimming against the institutional and cultural tide, and that is what makes it so hard to do well by our children.

What do we say when children respond to the existence of Father's Day and Mother's Day with the perfectly plausible question, "When is Kid's Day?" We reply, with more or less annoyance depending upon our mood, "Every day is Kid's Day!" Is it really? In one sense, every day (or nearly ever day) *is* Kid's Day. Contemporary adults are preoccupied with their relationships with children—whether or not to have them, how many to have, how much time to spend with them, what will become of them. Indeed, one's relation to children has become a topic of intense speculation. It is a key social and personal issue. Elective parenthood has turned an assumption (one's relation to children) into a question. Adding to the issue raised by the biology of elective conception is the whole cultural paraphernalia of integrating the often discrepant roles of worker and parent.

The fact that the roles of worker and parent are so often at odds and that government does so little to help is now one of the principal challenges faced by individuals and institutions. Resolution of this issue will force us to put our money where our mouths are in relation to children and will test our cultural mettle. We see evidence of this all around us.

In a press release announcing his decision not to seek reelection, John Cavanaugh, a successful young Midwestern congressman remarked:

> While I consider participation in our political process a noble goal and the sacred duty of each citizen. . . . I am removing myself from consideration for further public service. . . . In order to serve the people I have asked my wife, Kate, to make more personal sacrifices than either the bonds of marriage or the boundless generosities of life entitle me. She has made them cheerfully, and we have greatly enjoyed our ten years together. But now I have other considerations as well. Four children under the age of seven years have a rightful claim to the attention and affection of their father. I have concluded that to continue to defer those claims "until after the next election" is an endless road traveled sadly by too many men too deeply captivated by public life. Simply stated, I want to pursue the opportunity of spending more time with my wife and children.

How many successful men and women would or do make this choice? How many could "afford" to do so? There's a genuine cultural conflict here. On one side stand children, hearth, and home; on the other stand adulthood, achievement, and personal autonomy. Men are increasingly troubled by the home side of the equation, while increasing numbers of women are now contending with the career side. Can one be a success and still follow the baby's progress on the potty? Is it possible to pursue an idea, a career, or any wordly goal and yet still take the necessary time off to stay home with a sick child, go to parent–teacher meetings, and give birthday parties? These issues are permanent features of human experience—at least in modern historical times. What makes them different for us now is the changed historical context. Now, both parts of the questions and issues apply to women and men alike.

The real test for our society, the measure of its child centeredness, will come in how well we do in responding to the circumstances. A host of cultural currents indicates that the matter is far from resolved, and the issue remains in doubt. As they arrange for substitute child care, many modern couples find themselves saying, "We wish we had a wife." Many child-service workers ironically are pulled away from *their* children to care for the children of *other* people. If Aristotle once posed the question, "Who guards the guardians?" We now ask, "Who cares for the caregiver's children?" It's an issue we all face as professionals serving children and families.

Clearly, the decision to bear and raise a child is a complex one with lifelong implications. Once one begins a child, one remains a parent. It seems too many people don't seem to realize that choosing to become the parent of a cute baby also implies becoming the parent of a teenager in the next decade. In this chapter, we have tried to show how the human ecology can help or impede parents gaining positive psychological momentum with their children. In the next chapter, we will examine how the community and the neighborhood work on that psychological momentum, how they support and nurture families, and why they sometimes do not.

RESEARCH CAPSULE

While divorce is a legal arrangement between the individuals in a marital dyad, E. Mavis Hetherington and her colleagues (Hetherington, Cox, & Cox, 1978) also define divorce as "a critical life event that affects the entire family system and the functioning and interactions of members within that system (1978, p. 149)."

To study the impact of divorce on family functioning and child development, the researchers completed a longitudinal study of 48 middle-class families during the 2-year period following divorce. Each of the families had at least one nursery school-age child placed in the custody of the mother. The divorced families were matched with intact families having a preschooler of the same sex, age, and birth order as the target child from the divorced family. Measures included personality scales, interviews, and diary records from the parents, observations of child behavior and parent–child interaction at home and in the nursery school, and peer and teacher ratings along with tests of sex-role typing, cognitive performance, and social development for each target child.

Individual adjustment, exchanges between the former spouses, and the nature of parent–child interactions changed drastically over the 2-year period. The two months following the divorce were a time of particularly intense emotions, coupled with often unsuccessful attempts to redefine family relationships. Exchanges between the former spouses were characterized by sustained attachment, ambivalence, and resentment. Sixty-six percent of all interactions between divorced couples involved conflict, including disagreements over finances, intimate relations with others, and childrearing. Showing an immediate reaction to separation from their children, divorced fathers maintained high levels of contact with their children. Indeed, one-fourth of the divorced fathers had more face-to-face contact with their children during this initial adjustment period than before the divorce. While divorced fathers were extremely permissive and indulgent with their children, the childrearing strategies of divorced women often included futile attempts to control children with greater restrictiveness and commands.

A peak period of family disorganization and conflict was reached one year following divorce. During that time, the formerly married were distinguished from those in intact relationships by higher levels of anxiety, depression, anger, and rejection. Feelings of competence plummeted; the divorced subjects felt that they had failed as parents and spouses and expressed doubts about their abilities to be successful in any future marriages. The stress was reflected in household disorganization, with divorced families reporting problems coping with routine household management and in maintaining family routines. This period was marked by maximum levels of negative behavior for children in divorced families and by troubled parent–child relations, particularly for mothers and sons.

Two years after divorce, families appeared to be engaged in a period of reduced conflict and reorganization. Divorced parents and their children seemed to develop new and better organized life patterns. Contact with fathers in divorced families had dropped significantly, with only nineteen of the fathers having contact with their children once a week or more. Although some parent–child interactions remained troubled, especially between divorced parents and sons, one-fourth of the fathers and one-half of the mothers reported that the relationship with their children had actually improved over those prior to divorce.

Family disruption was less extreme and restabilization was achieved earlier in those families where former spouses could establish a positive, mutually supportive relationship including continued father involvement and agreement about child discipline. The researchers concluded that although divorce is often accompanied by family distress and disrupted behavior, it can also be a positive solution to destructive family functioning.

In a follow-up study with an expanded sample when the focal children were 10 years old (Hetherington, 1988, 1989), the long-term effects of divorce varied dramatically with both gender of the child and the mother's current marital status.

Divorced mothers who did not remarry continued to experience difficult relationships with their sons but not their daughters. Although these mothers were physically and verbally affectionate with their children, they tended to "nag, natter, and complain" (Hetherington, 1989, p. 429) to their sons. More lonely, depressed, and anxious than the other mothers in the study, the divorced mothers who remained single felt less in control of their own fate. It is not surprising, then, that they were less able to control their angry sons, who engaged them in negative and coercive cycles of interaction. Mothers' psychological well-being and their sons' behavior often improved when mothers remarried. In fact, after a period of adjustment to remarriage, many sons established close relationships with their stepfathers.

Daughters in the divorced group, in contrast, experienced the greatest adjustment difficulties when their mothers remarried. Accustomed to having more power, more responsibility, and less supervision than children in nondivorced families, these girls had developed warm and mutually supportive relationships with their single mothers. When mothers remarried, these girls viewed their new stepfathers as intruders who were hostile, punitive, and unreasonable. The stepfather–stepdaughter tensions were greatest in the first 2 years after remarriage, despite stepfathers' attempts to be supportive, pleasant, and even ingratiating. After the initial period of adjustment, however, these girls continued to be more antagonistic and disruptive than girls in other family types, while their stepfathers grew more impatient with their behaviors. For both boys and girls, mothers' remarriages begun during a child's preadolescence were least successful.

During the initial period of adjustment following a divorce, a key factor in family adaptation was external support from family and friends and attempts to maintain some measure of stability within the nuclear family unit. Teachers, especially those with an authoritative style, played a buffering role in mediating family stress.

Over time, the families in the study followed several routes toward adaptation and reorganization. About a third of the divorced women remained single but developed new social contacts and strengthened ties with their families of origin. Most remarried, creating step- and blended families. Ten percent transferred custody to the father.

For most of those families in the study, active and consistent participation in childrearing, an authoritative parenting style, and spousal support in childrearing activities were associated with parental life satisfaction and more harmonious parent–child relationships.

This study underscores the complex consequences of family change. Its use of a multimethod approach provides a rich body of data on the effects of divorce on individuals, dyadic relationships, and the family as a unit. The longitudinal design highlights the many paths to adaptation and reorganization and the additional stresses that might lie ahead.

PRACTICE CAPSULE

Although the American family has experienced many transitions in recent years, parents of diverse situations and life-styles continue to share certain overriding experiences, needs, and concerns that define the role of parent. As Americans confront the challenges of family life, however, "they experience a double message in our society, one that claims a commitment to families and stresses the importance of raising bright, stable, productive citizens, yet remains so bound by an ideal of 'rugged individualism' that parents receive little support in their task" (Weissbourd & Grimm, 1981, p. 6).

Based on the premise that a parent's sense of confidence has a direct effect on the quality of the parent–child relationship, Chicago's Family Focus, Inc. offers parents the nurturance that they need to provide for their children.

The organization offers a variety of neighborhood-based programs designed to bolster parents' sense of self and promote the ability to master the myriad tasks associated with parenting a young child. Each of the program's six centers provides parents with social, educational, and recreational programs plus resources and support. While parents participate in program activities, their children are involved in an education-based child care program. Skilled social workers and early childhood educators model appropriate adult–child interaction and help identify children in need of special services.

Program founder Bernice Weissbourd, a former early childhood educator, views the quality of the environment in which the family lives and the family's ability to negotiate that environment as major factors in family development (Weissbourd & Grimm, 1981). The program serves as a family advocate, informing community agencies about the needs for child and family services and helping families gain access to appropriate services. It also encourages the development of self-help projects (e.g., carpools, babysitting and clothing exchanges) that evolve from informal contacts at the centers.

Acknowledging that all parents need support, regardless of family situation, the program addresses the specific needs of parents who reside in the neighborhoods served. For example, Our Place, the center neighboring an Evanston high school, serves as a drop-in center for teenagers. The center offers "Straight from the Heart," a curriculum for teens who are not yet parents and "Kids in Careers," a program based on academic and vocational goal setting. Adolescent mothers participate in a teen parent services network and a retreat program matching them with older women who had been teen mothers. Its Family Community Center, which serves as a focal point for family services in the area, also houses several related nonprofit organizations.

The West Lincoln Park center began with a mother visitor program staffed by trained neighborhood parents. Today, the center helps middle-income parents build ties to others with similar concerns and interests. A unique aspect of this center is its focus on the needs of dual-career families, including workshops on balancing work and family and selecting child care. It also offers programs for substitute caregivers who bring children to the center while parents are at work.

Other centers have focused on the special parenting concerns of Latino families who have recently immigrated to the area. These parents are confronting the demands of a new culture, including sometimes conflicting childrearing beliefs, without the traditional supports of their extended families. Program activities have included preparation for high school equivalency exams and a guild for mothers to make and sell crafts of their native countries.

After more than 15 years of success, the organization recently has broadened its scope to include specialized training programs for family support providers nationwide. Its public education and policy project (Kids PEPP), administered with the Ounce of Prevention Fund, has been a vocal advocate for improvements in early childhood education, welfare, and maternal and child health.

This organization demonstrates a willingness to help families by responding to parents' individual interests and abilities. As each center is tailored to meet the needs of groups of parents in various geographical settings, it acknowledges the powerful role of the community in the lives of developing families.

FOR FURTHER READING

Cochran, M., Larner, M., Riley, D., Gunnarsson, L., & Henderson, C. R. (1990). *Extending families: The social networks of parents and their children.* Cambridge, UK: Cambridge University Press.

This study documents the role of personal social networks in the lives of children and their families. The role of relatives, neighbors, friends, and others in the community during times of individual and family change are discussed in detail.

Comer, J. P. (1988). *Maggie's American dream: The life and times of a black family.* New York: Penguin.

James Comer, professor of child psychiatry at the Yale Child Study Center, presents a moving tribute to his mother and a positive example of an effective African-American family. An oral history by the 84-year-old mother is complemented by her son's analysis of the family's successes. Comer credits strong family ties, his mother's ability to reach out to the public schools, and the social skills necessary to negotiate conflicting environments for the academic achievements of Maggie's five children.

Hochschild, A. (1989). *The second shift.* New York: Viking.

This book presents the results of an 8-year study on the lives of dual-earner couples. It provides an in-depth look at the way that a small sample of American couples deal with the multiple demands of career, marriage, and parenthood. By focusing on the division of household labor, the author demonstrates the diversity of arrangements that couples develop to meet their daily responsibilities and underscores the substantial gap between their ideals and the realities of everyday life.

Powell, D. R. (1989). *Families and early childhood programs.* Washington, D.C.: National Association for the Education of Young Children.

The author surveys the empirical and theoretical evidence in support of parent involvement in early childhood programs. Various types of involvement, from informal parent–staff relationships to parent education and support programs, are discussed. Particular attention is placed on ways to strengthen the home–school mesosystem.

QUESTIONS FOR THOUGHT

1.   Using materials from Chapters 4, 5, and 6, list several ways that the father, siblings, and other family members can make a positive contribution during pregnancy, labor and delivery, and the early postpartal period.

2.   Consider the childbirth alternatives discussed in the chapter. Formulate and justify your own personal preferences.

3.   Discuss the relative contributions of family members, the peer group, television, and the schools to individual development from infancy through adolescence. Use examples from your own childhood.

4.   Parenthood is one of the most important roles we can assume in life. Often, however, individuals enter the role without the preparation necessary to meet its demands and responsibilities. What are the greatest challenges facing American parents? Discuss ways that childrearing practices and school curricula can be modified to help prepare children for later parenting roles. Suggest a number of different ways that both formal and informal support systems can provide promotive services to parents.

5.   What changes in parents' lives are presented by their child's passage from infancy to childhood and on to adolescence and young adulthood? How

must life-styles be altered to meet the changing needs of both the parents and the child?

6. Imagine that you have been asked to talk to a group of teachers, case-workers, or judges about helping families adapt to divorce. What recommendations will you make regarding child rearing by divorced parents and the maintenance of strong parent–child relationships?

7. This chapter mentions that although Americans celebrate Mother's Day and Father's Day, there is no official Children's Day. Japan, however, does have such a holiday. Consider the significance of a day set aside to observe the value of children.

8. How do current policies and practices about surrogate parenthood, adoption, and child custody illustrate how people weigh the role of biology in parenthood?

9. What factors would you weigh in making a recommendation in a child custody case?

10. How would you adapt Family Focus for a poverty community?

7

Cultural Diversity
and Identity Formation

James Garbarino and Kathleen Kostelny

In English my name means hope. In Spanish it means too many letters. It means sadness, it means waiting. It is like the number
nine. A muddy color. It is the Mexican records my father plays on Sunday morning
when he is shaving, songs like sobbing.

It was my great-grandmother's name and
now it is mine. . . . At school they say my
name funny as if the syllables were made
out of tin and hurt the roof of your mouth.
But in Spanish my name is made out of a
softer something like silver, not quite as
thick as sister's name Magdalena which is
uglier than mine. Magdalena who at least
can come home and become Nenny. But I
am always Esperanza.

I would like to baptize myself under a new
name, a name more like the real me, the one
nobody sees. Esperanza as Lisandra and
Maritzza or Zeze the X. Yes. Something like
Zeze the X will do.

"My Name" from *The House on Mango Street*

Who am I?

Identity is the answer to this question, a question that is one of the
fundamental issues in human experience. As Americans we are inclined to

179

answer this question as individuals. Our culture points us in the direction of individual identity—"I am John Smith." "I am Jane Doe." But there is more to identity than individuality. This chapter explores the role of ethnicity and race in the formation of identity. The United States is a diverse and multi-cultural society. Its political ethos is based upon plualism—the concept that diverse social groups can exist—and even compete—in arenas governed by mutual respect and tolerance.

The demographic changes occurring in the United States pose both new opportunities and risks for minority children and families. What is the experience of minority children and families in America? What role does ethnicity and race play in identity formation? How do minority children and families adapt to the dominant culture? How does the dominant culture adapt to them? Our goal is to know and understand the growing cultural diversity in our society, and by so doing enhance the development of children.

American society has experienced significant social, cultural, and demographic changes since the 1960s. Changes in the social and economic conditions have stimulated, and changes in immigration laws have permitted new waves of immigrants and refugees to the United States from Latin America, the Caribbean, Africa, and Asia. Minority groups now comprise 14% of adults and 20% of children under the age of 17 in the United States. It is estimated that by the year 2000, one-third of all school-age children will be minorities (U.S. Bureau of the Census, 1987). California is already called "The Third World State," and the three largest cities in the United States, New York, Los Angeles, and Chicago, have majorities of minorities. In many other areas Asians, Hispanics, and Africans are a significant local presence. In view of these changes, the majority Anglo-American group (Caucasians of Northern European descent) will become an even smaller presence in American society.

Minority Groups in the United States

Minority groups in the United States have historically suffered from multiple disadvantages, having unequal access to power, less opportunities in education, employment, and upward mobility, and insufficient access to health services. Furthermore, minorities are often stigmatized as possessing inferior characteristics, such as inferior intelligence, laziness, and dishonesty (Mindel & Habenstein, 1981). Such conditions produce alienation, social isolation, and stress for children and families, often resulting in psychological consequences (Garmezy & Rutter, 1983). Identity is one casualty of this process.

Indeed, identity is inextricably bound up in the essence of these issues. The labels we apply reflect complex political and cultural negotiations. "Negroes" became "Blacks," then "African-Americans" in popular
usage (with a variety of deliberately derogative terms surviving all the
changes made "official" by mainstream publications such as the *New
York Times*). Debate continues over the validity and ramifications of "Indians" vs. "Native Americans" and "Hispanics" vs. "Latin Americans."
In some areas "Anglos" includes all Caucasians of non-Spanish-speak-
ing background. In the United States, a person with any African ancestors is "Black", but in Brazil a person with any European ancestry is
"White." And what makes white people "White" anyway? Culture,
ethnicity, race, and identity are bound up in the full range of ecological
influences. Few issues are more difficult to make sense of *and* more
important.

Minorities living in the United States are composed of resident (indigenous) groups, refugees, and immigrants. The resident groups have
lived in the United States for an extended period of time (such as African-Americans who were imported as slaves, and Native Americans
who are indigenous). A second group of minorities are refugees (such as
Southeast Asians, and Central and South Americans) who have fled
their home country because of war, or political, religious, and racial
persecution. These refugees, in addition to learning a new language,
new culture, and a new set of behaviors, must also process their traumatic experiences of war, persecution, abandoning their country, and
the loss of family and friends. A third group of minorities are immigrants (such as Mexican-Americans and Puerto Ricans) who came vol-
untarily to the United States for better employment or educational opportunities, although conditions are often so bad in their homeland that
they might be termed economic refugees.

Demographic Characteristics

African-Americans, Hispanics, East and Southeast Asians, and American Indians represent the four largest minority groups with the longest
period of residence in the United States. African-Americans are the largest minority group in the United States, numbering 29.3 million (U.S.
Bureau of the Census, 1987). The median income for African-American
families in 1986 was $17,604 compared to $27,000 for white Americans.
African-Americans also have one of the highest levels of poverty. In
1984, 30.9% of African-Americans lived in poverty, compared to 9.1% of
the white population, and one in every two African-American children

was poor, compared to one in five for the nation (U.S. Bureau of the Census, 1986). The school dropout rates for African-Americans range from 40 to 60% in many urban areas (Reed, 1988).

Hispanics are the second largest minority group in the United States, numbering 16.9 million as of 1985 (U.S. Bureau of the Census, 1985). The largest Hispanic subgroup is formed by Mexican-Americans (11.8 million). In 1984 the median income for Mexican American families was $19,200. As of 1984, only 42% of Mexican Americans age 25 and older had completed high school compared to 74% of the total United States population (U.S. Bureau of the Census, 1985).

The second largest Hispanic subgroup are Puerto Ricans (2.6 million). Puerto Ricans have one of the highest poverty rates in the nation, with 42% of Puerto Rican families living below the poverty level in 1984, compared to 11.6% of the total population (U.S. Bureau of the Census, 1985). In 1984 the median family income was $12,371—the lowest of all Hispanic subgroups. Only 46% of Puerto Ricans age 25 and older had completed high school in 1985.

Asian-Americans represent the third largest minority group. Chinese-Americans constitute the largest Asian-American subgroup, numbering 812,000. Of these, 63% are foreign born (U.S. Bureau of the Census, 1983a). Although the median household income was $19,561 in 1980, 12% of all Chinese-American families had an income below $5,000 (U.S. Bureau of the Census, 1983a). As of 1980, 71.3% of those 25 years and older had completed high school.

There were 716,000 Japanese-Americans living in the United States in 1980. Of these, 72% were native born and 28% were foreign born (U.S. Bureau of the Census, 1983a). Japanese-American families have one of the lowest poverty rates in the United States, at 4.2%, and one of the highest median family incomes at $27,354 in 1980. Japanese-Americans have the highest rate of completion of high school of all minorities: 96% of Japanese-Americans aged 25–29 had completed high school, and 26% of those age 25 and over had at least 4 years of college. This is a better record than the majority white population.

In addition to the Asian groups of the Japanese and Chinese, over 800,000 refugees from Southeast Asia have come to the United States from 1975 to 1986, as a result of the Vietnam War and the fighting in Cambodia and Laos. It is estimated that children comprise 40–60% of these refugees (Lee, 1987). The median household income varied according to when families immigrated. In 1984, the median income was $16,377 for refugees who came in 1975, and $11,105 for refugees who came during the period 1976–1979 (U.S. Department of Health and Human Services, 1987).

Native Americans represent one of the most diverse minority groups in the United States, with 517 native entities and 200 tribal languages. The Native American population is estimated at between 1.5 and 1.8 million. The median family income is $13,678, compared to $29,152 for white families. School dropout rates are high, reaching 85% in urban areas and 50% in boarding and reservation schools.

Social Historical Context

Understanding the historical and social context of ethnicity and race is necessary for understanding the role they play in the formation of identity. Minority groups in the United States represent a range of customs, beliefs, acculturation experiences, linguistic diversity, and family structures. Moreover, each group has a unique history in this country.

For example, it is important to understand the special circumstances produced for the Japanese-American community by their internment during World War II. Families living along the West Coast were taken from their homes and forced to live in internment camps for up to 4 years, affecting more than 110,000 Japanese-Americans. While Japanese-Americans living in Hawaii were not interned (because of their local political power), some Japanese-Americans were nonetheless displaced and discriminated against for "security" reasons. The impact of this experience—where families had little time to prepare for the move—was enormous. This experience is chronicled well in a book by Houston (1973), called *Farewell to Manzanar* (an account of growing up in an internment camp). Because families had to live in communal barracks, a change in family structure and the disruption of traditional family roles occurred. Economic hardship and psychological problems also resulted from being expelled from their homes, incarcerated, and victimized (Mass, 1986).

The social–historical context of African-Americans has been marked by slavery, discrimination, and poverty. African-Americans were historically forced to maintain separate social institutions (such as churches, schools, and health services) that were generally inferior to the institutions of Anglo-Americans. Even though segregation has been declared illegal, many separate and unequal institutions still remain (Gibbs, 1989). In spite of programmatic efforts to rectify such inequalities in education, housing, and employment, many observers argue that such programs have helped only those African-Americans who were more advantaged to begin with. There remains a large, poor, disadvantaged African-American underclass (Wilson, 1987). This point was once made evident to a civil rights leader who had given a speech proclaiming the gains made by his organization to a group of poor people. One responded by saying, "See that store over there? Because of what you have done, I could take a dollar into that store and make a purchase. But I still don't have a dollar."

Native Americans have suffered immeasurably at the hands of the dominant culture. The reduction of the Native American population from 10 million to less than 2 million has been called "cultural genocide" by some (LaFromboise & Low, 1989). Native Americans have also endured being uprooted, relocated, and "socialized" by mainstream society in an effort to wipe out their tribal traditions and identity.

With regard to the social–historical context of Southeast Asian refugees, it is necessary to understand that different waves of refugees came from different socioeconomic groups and have had different experiences. For example, Southeast Asian refugees who did not leave Vietnam or Cambodia until after 1977 suffered loss of family members, forced internment in labor camps, and experiences with violence—events not experienced by refugees who left earlier (Sheehy, 1986). Additionally, these refugees were from rural backgrounds, having less education, fewer occupational skills, and little prior contact with Americans and their culture than the refugees who had come before.

These social facts—of demography, history, and economics—are not the whole story, of course. They provide the raw material for the more important developmental story of how ethnicity translates into personal identity, how the facts of group history influence personal history. To understand this important connection we must understand identity formation. To this we turn next.

Identity Formation

Part of the developmental process of becoming a competent person is forming an identity—of knowing who you are, and where you stand amidst the micro-, meso-, exo-, and macrosystems of life (Garbarino, 1985a,b). This identity formation is brought about when disparate aspects of the self are integrated by one's ego into a coherent and distinctive whole (Josselson, 1980). This process begins in infancy when the ego first experiences the self as unique and separate from "the other" (i.e., the mother in most cultures). By 2 years of age most children demonstrate that they have some form of self-awareness (e.g., if rouge is applied secretly to a child's forehead and he is placed before a mirror, he reaches up to touch his forehead in recognition that the child in the mirror is not someone else, but himself).

The identity process continues throughout childhood as childrearing patterns and family experiences play a significant role in the formation of identity. Children first see themselves within the context of their families, and thus through the eyes of parents and siblings. In this context, positive but traditionally authoritarian families tend to produce youth who have not explored identity options. Conflicted and nega-tivistic families tend to produce youth who do not have a strong identity. Positive, expressive, and flexible families tend to produce youth who successfully achieve identity (Marcia, 1980).

In addition to parents, a child's perceptions of what his teachers and other supportive people think of him influences identity. A study by Rosenberg and Simmons (1971) found that both African-American and white children who believed that significant others viewed them posi-tively also had a positive identity.

Children's Culture

In addition to childrearing styles, family experiences, and a child's support system, peers also play a significant role in identity formation. Children have a unique culture of their own that contributes to indi-vidual socialization and the development of identity (Price, 1991). Only recently has this "children's culture" been recognized by anthropo-logists, sociologists, and psychologists. Children's culture is "a stable set of activities or routines, artifacts, values, and concerns that children appropriate, produce, and share in interaction with peers" (Corsaro & Eder, 1990). Children's culture is characterized by a unique social struc-ture, idiosyncratic language, and often risque content.

For example, consider the "almost naughty" game of "Miss Susie," a rhyming and clapping game, played by young girls: "Miss Susie had a tugboat, the tugboat had a bell, Miss Susie went to heaven, the tugboat went to Hell-o operator, give me number 9. . . ." Girls from all parts of the United States have played this game for generations, learning this game from other young girls, demonstrating how timeless and wide-spread certain characteristics of children's culture are. An additional motive behind children's culture is the subversion of adult authority, as demonstrated in the use of "forbidden" words in "Miss Susie."

Another example of children's culture is illustrated in research con-ducted of boys' Little League. A study by Fine (1986) found that whereas the adult culture of Little League was aimed at having children learn competitive values, sportsmanlike behavior, and losing gracefully, the boys' culture had different goals. In their culture, the boys uttered derogatory racial comments and exhibited sexist behavior. Price has hypothesized that for most boys, these are transient characteristics of a children's culture that is rebelling against adult socialization while exploring their identity as it relates to differences in race and gender (Price, 1990).

Identity formation also reflects the different values for males and females in a culture. For example, in North American culture, girls' identity includes an emphasis on the interpersonal, communal characteristics, whereas for boys the emphasis is on individuation (Block, 1973).

Adolescence and Identity

In adolescence, identity formation assumes profound significance in social relations. Identity formation is one of the most important developmental tasks for adolescents, providing direction and meaning in their lives. Adolescence is the time to sharpen the boundaries between self and nonself, to become a distinct, autonomous individual. Such autonomy allows the youth to function as a separate person, to make decisions, to act without direct guidance, and to display a sense of self-determination. As adolescents develop a more stable sense of self, they can then sort through and synthesize childhood identifications and change physical, social, sexual, and emotional selves into one coherent identity (Garbarino, 1985a).

Influences on identity formation can come from individual characteristics (e.g., self-esteem, independence, anxiety), interpersonal factors (e.g., reactions of peers and family), and societal factors (e.g., cultural and ethnic influences on the goals, tone, and structure of day-to-day social experience). Additionally, identity formation depends on an individual's developmental history (having resolved earlier development conflicts) as well as the historical period he or she is in—both past and future are connected to the individual and society (Erikson, 1968).

Identity formation also involves an ongoing process of judgments and comparisons that requires the ability to observe oneself in relation to others (Erikson, 1968). The judgments individuals make about themselves are based on what they believe others think, as well as their own comparison of themselves with others. Identity includes mutuality between self and society—a public statement of the self to which the individual intends to be committed. This identity moves from the family to a more public presentation in society as youths display "this is who I am" to the others they interact with in their microsystems (Garbarino, 1985b).

Ethnicity

Identity formation is also influenced by the ethnic and racial groups with which one identifies, which groups are preferred, and what one's attitudes are toward one's own group and the majority group (Spencer & Markstrom-Adams, 1990). Being part of an ethnic group contributes to personal, social, and ethnic identity for its members—for better or for worse. It cannot be avoided—even if it is taken for granted, as it is so often for the dominant majority group in a society.

Ethnicity—belonging to a group that shares unique cultural and social traditions that continue across generations—is an important factor in shaping identity (McGoldrick, Pearce, & Giordano, 1982). Ethnicity is linked to the way an individual thinks, feels, and behaves because of membership in such a group. Race and ethnicity are not identical. For example, Hispanics have the common cultural heritage of Latin America and the common language of Spanish, but may be White, Black, Indian, or a mixture of the above. However, race and ethnicity can overlap, as in the case of African-Americans and Chinese-Americans.

Members of ethnic groups view their differences in language, customs, and beliefs as distinguishing them from others in important ways. Membership in an ethnic group gives the individual a cultural identity, a sense of belonging and continuity, and a belief and value system with established norms, values, and social behaviors (Gibbs & Huang, 1989; Spencer & Markstrom-Adams, 1990). Successful identity formation is achieved by exploring an ethnic identity, and then choosing to commit to it (Marcia, 1980). This is why group pride is crucial for individual positive identity. If you reject your group, you may come to hate yourself.

Ethnicity enables children to form a map of how they perceive themselves and their world, and bestows meaning on their experiences. Ethnicity influences such factors as a child's role in his or her family, how he or she is perceived at school, how he or she is treated by peers, and how he or she is accepted by the community. Ethnicity may also affect what language a child will learn first, what kind of family a child grows up in, the community he or she lives in, as well as which church or school he or she attends.

Ethnic and racial pride based on success within a subgroup has both costs and benefits for developing adolescents. A clear benefit is that cultural roles are more clearly defined by the subgroup and that they know what they must do during adolescence to become an adult. In their usually tightly knit neighborhoods where they live, there is also a sense of closeness and interdependence among neighbors. Thus, young people can gain support and learn strategies for approaching life, all of which make establishing a positive sense of self somewhat easier. There is a sense of rootedness and acceptance.

However, as Rosenberg (1965) writes, "there is no indication that the distribution of self-acceptance in a group is related to the social prestige of that group in American society." Thus, there may be a negative reality in the social environment beyond the neighborhood with which adolescents must eventually come to terms if they are to succeed in the larger society. The beliefs, values, morals, and behaviors that are learned in the neighborhood may not be ones that are accepted by society at large. This may compound the problem of developing mainstream social competence (Garbarino, 1985a).

Until recently in the United States, a typical view held by mainstream society was that black culture did not exist except as a deviation from "middle-class white culture" (Howard & Scott, 1980). Only relatively recently has black culture been accepted as valid in itself.

However, whereas Blacks were seen as being cultureless, Mexican-Americans were seen as having a damaging culture (Ramirez & Castaneda, 1974). The majority culture viewed Mexican culture as socializing individuals to be lazy, criminally prone, unreliable, intellectually inferior, and dishonest (Ramirez & Castaneda, 1974).

Under the best of circumstances, establishing one's identity is a difficult and complex process (Erikson, 1968). However, for ethnic and racial minority youth who differ in color, language, and physical characteristics from the dominant group in society, successful identity formation is an even more challenging task as it is jeopardized for them by prejudice and discrimination by individuals and institutions.

Minority youth must cope with the stresses that result from "being different," and that often means being perceived as inferior. Such stressful experiences often include verbal aggression and physical attack. For example, researchers have observed that in California where Asians are a significant force, racial tension is a regular aspect of school life for Asian children. In one study, all the children in the sample reported being punched, mimicked, harassed, or robbed by non-Asian students (*San Francisco Chronicle*, March 28, 1987). Often a minority youth's "normal" experience includes adapting coping strategies to deal with prejudice, discrimination, and stereotypes as a function of race or ethnicity.

Whereas positive ethnic identification can fulfill a sense of pride and belonging and contribute to psychological well being, negative identification can result in feelings of futility and powerlessness. When a child's ethnic identity is combined with belonging to a minority race, there often occur risks to the child's development. Certain ethnic groups in the United States—such as Italians, Lithuanians, or Irish—can maintain their cultural customs at home and in their ethnic institutions, but still be able to blend inconspicuously into such mainstream institutions as school and business. Minority groups of color are not able to achieve this anonymity: to a large degree you can be selectively Italian or Irish (and just plain "white" as needed) but this option is not open to people of color.

Because identity formation is influenced by an individual's communal culture, Erikson (1968) speculates that minority youth may develop a negative identity as a result of accepting the negative images given them by the dominant society as well as by their own group. Identity conflicts can occur when the dominant group is portrayed in a positive manner and the minority group in a negative one. For example, Mexican-American adolescents are presented with images of white middle-class Americans as successful and powerful, while Mexican-Americans are stereotyped as primitive and powerless. Accepting negative stereotypes can thus lead to a sense of futility and powerlessness (Mendelberg, 1986).

However, when stereotypes are *not* accepted, pride and self-esteem are evident. Research indicates that Blacks, Mexican-Americans, and Puerto Rican children and adolescents report equal, and sometimes higher, senses of identity and self-esteem than do nonminority children (Powell & Fuller, 1970). Powell and Fuller found higher self-concept scores for black students in all-black schools and integrated schools than for white students, a phenomenon attributed to the cohesiveness of the black community and as a defense against a hostile world (Powell, 1985).

Soares and Soares (1971) in their study of elementary and high school students found that minorities view themselves more positively and attribute more positive views of themselves to others (i.e., their classmates, teachers, and parents) than do nonminorities. Frazier and De Blassie (1982) found that given equal levels of academic ability, Mexican-Americans and non-Mexican-American adolescents do not report discrepant self-concepts in terms of either academic success or self-esteem. Furthermore, a study of ethnic identity among black and white eighth graders found that black students had more understanding of their own culture than did white students. They were also more aware of prejudice, and the researchers concluded that the process of coping with prejudice necessitated a better understanding of one's culture. Responding to challenge can be growth inducing.

One group of minority children who face unique problems in identity formation are biracial children. Because their parents do not share similar racial or cultural heritages, biracial children must integrate two different ethnic identities and two different cultural heritages. Clinicians working with biracial adolescents have reported that conflict over racial identity is the major issue that emerges during therapy. Biracial youth experience problems with family approval, community acceptance, and social isolation (Gay, 1987). These youth often may identify with one parent and reject the other as a "solution" to their problem. Integration of the racial backgrounds of both parents is necessary before successful identity formation can occur.

Ethnic Identity and Intergroup Conflict

Situations in which ethnic diversity are present pose a special challenge for students of human development. In such situations the partisans often have powerfully divergent views of social reality. In these discrepant world views differences are debated fiercely and often lead to conflict. Even humor is brought to bear to highlight group identity and reinforce negative stereotypes: most societies have a set of jokes that focus on the clumsy stupidity of one group, the greed of another, the sexual excesses of a third.

For example, in South Africa there is a Black world view and a White world view. In the Israeli Occupied Territories there is an Israeli world view and a Palestinian world view. In Northern Ireland there is a Catholic world view and a Protestant world view. Most conflicts between world views are not very engaging to most people: few Americans appreciate the passion in the contrast between Croatian and Serbian world views, for example. But almost any American who lives in a city with racial cleaveages can understand the intensity of conflicts between African-Americans and whites. Only when differences affect one's self and one's identity do strong passions become elicited.

According to Tajfel (1978), all societies engage in a process of social categorization. Social categorization simplifies life by reducing large and overwhelming amounts of social stimuli into smaller, and more manageable categories, minimizing differences within categories and exaggerating differences between categories. Thus, two people who belong to different ethnic or racial groups are perceived as more different from what they are in reality, whereas two people from the same ethnic or racial group are seen as more similar than they really are. Indeed, research data generally reveal that on most characteristics the differences within groups (in statistical terms, the "variance") are greater than the average difference between groups (in statistical terms the "mean").

Because people see themselves as belonging to some social categories but not to others, intergroup conflict can result. To hate or discriminate against individuals belonging to an ethnic or racial group, individuals must first perceive themselves as belonging to a group distinctly different from the group they hate or discriminate against (Tajfel, 1978).

In addition, intergroup conflict also results from the need for individuals to enhance their self-esteem by making sure that their social identity is viewed positively. This is accomplished by making comparisons between their own social group and other social groups and ensuring that through these comparisons their group achieves "social psychological distinctiveness" (Cairns, 1987). Thus, intergroup conflict is more likely to occur in societies where the "if you can't beat 'em join 'em" option is virtually nonexistent. When individuals are locked into membership of a group that plays a role in determining where they live, where they go to school, and who they marry, the only way for individuals to achieve a more positive social identity is for them to ensure that their social group gains an advantage over other social groups (Cairns, 1987).

Consideration of Cultural Characteristics

The cultural characteristics of minority groups will influence their experiences in the majority culture. Groups emigrating from societies with a traditional value orientation will have different experiences from groups emigrating from societies with a modern value orientation. In certain ethnic groups, the age and sex of the family member determine each person's role in the family; in other ethnic groups there is more equality in age and sex roles. In the former, obedience to parental authority, respect for elders, acceptance of male authority, loyalty to the extended family, and strong conformity to community norms and expectations can be observed, while the latter is characterized by greater egalitarianism in age and sex roles, greater emphasis on shared household responsibilities, individual decision making, flexibility in marital roles, and moderate conformity to community norms and expectations.

In Japanese culture, for example, politeness and good behavior are valued and encouraged over self-direction and independence (O'Reily, Tokuno, & Ebata, 1986). Furthermore, the values of group loyalty, nurturance, and dependence are as important as success and achievement. Parents and elders are held in high esteem, and the concept of repaying one's parents for their sacrifices, usually through social responsibility for their cultural group, is stressed (Slaughter-Defoe et al., 1990). These values, although different from American middle-class values, are none-theless compatible with them and viewed positively by the dominant culture (DeVos, 1973). Such shared and compatible cultural values have facilitated Japanese-American acculturation within mainstream America (Slaughter-Defoe et al., 1990).

However, when cultural values conflict, risk is possible. Teachers and observers of Southeast Asian immigrants have reported how cultural characteristics can conflict with traditional American educational ac-tivities. In their home culture the teacher is the "expert." Parents do not question the teacher, nor are they involved in school-related matters. Thus, parental participation in activities such as PTA is often in-comprehensible to them.

Another example of cultural difference is the concept of "saving face," a cultural characteristic highly valued in Asian culture. Saving face in-volves not only the individual, but a child's entire family as well as his dead ancestors. Thus, even a mild reprimand can be highly stressful for an Asian child, bringing shame on his entire family as well as past generations. Still another cultural characteristic that can cause misunder-standing is self-effacement. Positive reinforcement, if given in front of others, is embarrassing, as receiving notice for one's self publicly is undesirable (West, 1983). Furthermore, revealing personal circum-stances or problems to people outside of one's family is equally undesir-able, a factor that may inhibit children from communicating with teach-ers (West, 1983).

For Southeast Asian refugees, the extended family is crucial, even though many have often had to leave their extended family behind. Though not physically present, these family members are nonetheless psychologically present as refugees suffer from guilt, regret, and worry about their relatives remaining in the home country (Huang, 1989). The psychological reality of the absent "ancestors" may also serve as a powerful motivation to achieve (Garbarino, Kostelny, & Dubrow, 1991).

An area of conflict for Native Americans with the majority group involves their cultural traditions. Native American parents expect their children to participate in traditional ceremonies that often conflict with the Anglo-American school calendar. The Native American belief sys-tem also comes into conflict with the Anglo-American belief system. For example, the Hopi believe that repetitive "bad" behavior has a cumu-lative effect and will eventually lead to a change for the better, in opposi-tion to the dominant culture's belief.

Another conflict which can arise is due to differences in childrearing styles. For example, Native Americans emphasize the value of autono-my in their children, and children are expected to make their own deci-sions and be semi-independent from an early age. This difference from the majority Anglo group has been perceived as permissive and even negligent by social service agencies (Gray & Cosgrove, 1985).

African-American culture also comes into conflict with the dominant culture regarding childrearing styles. Strict sex-role distinctions are not stressed—girls are encouraged to be assertive and aggressive and boys are encouraged to be nurturing and to express emotion (Lewis, 1975). Anglo-American teachers have frequently considered such behavior inappropriate in their classrooms.

Research indicates that parents from different cultures respond differently to their children's temperament and activity levels (Thomas & Chess, 1977). These cultural differences can decrease or increase the risk of child maltreatment (Garbarino & Ebata, 1983). However, there are difficulties in identifying cultural and ethnic differences in child maltreatment because social class and cultural differences are often confounded; there are more minorities in the lower socioeconomic group. In a national incidence study it was found that ethnic differences in child maltreatment were small when groups were economically secure, but large when groups were living in poverty (Bergdorf, 1981). This is a general finding: the lower one goes on the social class ladder, the greater are the cultural effects on belief and behavior (Garbarino & Bronfenbrenner, 1976b).

The social support system of a culture (i.e., the degree to which childrearing is embedded in family and community networks) and the cultural values are also linked to the risk of child maltreatment. These values are the worth of children, beliefs about special categories of children (e.g., physically handicapped or illegitimate), and beliefs about age capabilities and developmental states (Korbin, 1981). It is the values, practices, and institutions for coping with economic stress that make up one of the most significant factors in ethnic and cultural differences in child maltreatment (Garbarino & Ebata, 1983).

Acculturation

A minority member's ability to function within the dominant culture's value system is acculturation. When acculturation is made possible by openness of the dominant culture and complementarity with minority culture, children tend to thrive—literally getting the best of both worlds. When the dominant and minority cultures are at odds, hostile, and competitive, the child's development may suffer.

For now, and unless there are major shifts in the macrosystem of America, ethnic and racial minorities in the United States must learn to function in two different cultures—their home culture and that of the larger Anglo-American culture. The ability of an individual to function both in the culture of origin and in the host culture has been referred to as bidirectional acculturation and bicultural socialization (Szapocznik & Kurtines, 1980). A study of Vietnamese, Chinese, and Cambodian children discovered that at home the children perceived themselves as more ethnic, whereas at school they saw themselves as more American. With their good friends, they considered themselves equally American and ethnic. These shifts in identification did not affect their self-esteem or sense of competence (Huang, 1989).

The ability to live successfully in two cultures simultaneously includes such factors as (1) the two cultures sharing norms, values, and beliefs; (2) having cultural translators, mediators, and models; (3) providing feedback by each culture about one's behavior; (4) similarities in both cultures in conceptual and problem-solving style; (5) having language facility in both cultures; and (6) similarity in physical appearance to mainstream culture (DeAnda, 1984). As we have seen, when the value systems of both cultures are similar, the child finds opportunities to grow and develop.

However, even when value systems are different, there is still opportunity for growth and development. In a study by Gutierrez and Sameroff (1990) comparing highly acculturated Mexican-American mothers, moderately acculturated Mexican-American mothers, and Anglo-American mothers, they found that mothers who were both highly acculturated *and* bicultural (vs. monocultural) were more able and inclined to interpret their child's development as a function of the interplay between constitution and environment over time ("perspectivisitic"). Furthermore, these mothers believed that different factors could produce the same developmental outcome.

In integrating two cultures, an individual must transcend rationalizations for behavior to appreciate that each culture has different forms of acceptable behavior. Such integrations require a perspectivism that appreciates the relativism of belief systems in each specific culture.

Impediments to Acculturation

Unsuccessful identity formation can be linked to failures in acculturation, including conflicting values between mainstream society and one's reference group. Risk occurs when children and youth are not able to blend the two cultures into a single identity. For example, observers have reported that many Native American youth go back and forth between their tribal identity and an Anglo identity without successfully merging the two.

An impediment to acculturation is the fear of rejection by the dominant society. For example, Vietnamese refugees may fear rejection by Anglo-Americans because of the negative association with the Vietnam War (Huang, 1989). Another obstacle to acculturation can come from unresolved anger. The Vietnamese may also harbor resentment for the American role in the Vietnam War that forced them to flee their country and leave their families behind. Such feelings may complicate formation of an identity and a positive self-concept.

In minority families, children and youth often experience conflict between the beliefs and values of the culture of their parents on the one hand, and those of their peers and school on the other. To be accepted in both cultures, the child must often perform a delicate balancing act. Frequently, stress and psychological problems result (Huang, 1989). These are manifest in behavior problems, school adjustment problems, delinquency, somatic symptoms, depression, and anxiety (Gibbs, 1989). A study by Nann (1982) found that adolescents suffered stress from the clash between their old and their new culture, appearing as self-depreciation and low self-worth.

Often an "acculturation gap" results when children adapt to their new environment faster than their parents (Huang, 1989). After migration, the first generation often experiences culture shock in their new society, and often reacts by trying to keep the family closer together by holding strongly to their original cultural values, beliefs, and language. Similarly, ethnic communities are recreated and preserved in their new environments.

Children and youth acculturate more rapidly than their parents, and often take on an active role in the process of adaptation, serving as negotiators and translators for their parents. Adolescents are more willing to explore the new roles and customs and adapt to new values and language (Inclan, 1985). As they reshape their values and self-concept, they also create differences in behavioral and cultural expectations.

Children often receive conflicting messages from their parents—they are expected to succeed in America, but not to become American. Although proud of their children's achievements, parents may find it difficult to accept the new values and behavior that go along with their children's acculturation and success. Or behavior that is considered typical for a child's age from an Anglo-American perspective can be viewed as deviant from the parents' perspective. Parents can interpret their children's acculturated lives as being less caring toward them and their values (Inclan, 1985).

A study by Ou and MacAdoo (1980) found that fifth- and sixth-grade

American born boys of Chinese immigrant parents who spoke Chinese at home had higher levels of anxiety than boys whose parents home language was English. Furthermore, boys whose parents had more positive attitudes toward Chinese culture had lower self-concepts than boys whose parents had less positive attitudes. The researchers concluded that speaking Chinese and adhering to Chinese values increased bicultural pressure on the children of immigrant parents. Is the maintenance of ethnic identity worth the cost? Each individual and group must decide.

Risk of Psychological Problems

Psychological problems are often linked to experiences in a new culture. Lin, Masuda, and Tazuma (1982) in a longitudinal study of 115 Vietnamese refugees found high rates of physical and psychological dysfunction during the first 2 years of resettlement. Loss and culture shock were the main factors these families experienced, resulting in depression and anxiety. However, even after the refugees had settled, their problems continued. Why?

Sluzki found that refugees suffered more psychological problems once they had found order in their lives and were in control of their day-to-day affairs. Studies of refugees found that immediately after migration, their energy focused on meeting basic survival needs. Once this was accomplished, however, emotional distress, depression, and anxiety often followed (Sluzki, 1979). Furthermore, Williams and Westermeyer (1983) found that when parents—especially single or widowed mothers—did not have a culturally similar and mutually supportive network, as in the case of refugee families living in rural areas and isolated from peers—conflict between parents and their children was severe.

Bloom (1975) noted that the psychiatric hospitalization rates for Spanish-surnamed individuals were significantly higher when they were a minority in an area than when they were a majority. In another study of Whites, Blacks, and Puerto Ricans, Rabkin (1979) found that for minority groups, the smaller their size in a community, the higher their rate of psychiatric hospitalization. These results may parallel the findings reported earlier about segregated schools: the need to find positive identity is primary.

Moritsugu and Sue (1983) suggest that because members of ethnic and racial minority groups encounter hostility, prejudice, and lack of effective support during crises, they may develop ineffective cognitive coping styles as a reaction to these experiences. With Southeast Asian refugees, it is necessary to understand the developmental, social, psychological, and moral consequences of war. Children whose only experience has been war may be fearful, suspicious, and anxious in their new culture, not believing that peace can be a lasting condition. Because of the extreme conditions in a "trauma culture," many refugees developed adaptive coping strategies in the situation of war and flight, such as mistrust and psychological numbness, which proved detrimental in their new culture. Previously unacceptable behaviors were assimilated into their self-concept, such as assuming the victim's role and easily surrendering to more dominant personalities (Huang, 1989).

"Unaccompanied minors"—children who migrated without their parents or other adult relatives—are at most risk (Huang, 1989). Having suffered the loss of both family and homeland, these children must at the same time adapt to a new culture without the help of a supportive family. As a result, they are often depressed, angry, or withdrawn. Frequently the youth's anger toward the biological parents for abandonment is displaced onto the foster parents. The Anglo-American concept of foster parenting by unrelated strangers has no counterpart in Asian culture, as this task is usually assumed by the extended family. Consequently, refugee youth may have difficulty comprehending this Western form of "family" and determining their role in this structure (Huang, 1989).

Conclusion

As the United States experiences new waves of immigrants and growing cultural diversity, mere "acceptance" is not enough. We must go beyond to embrace these differences and appreciate multiculturalism. Knowing what those differences are, and understanding them, will facilitate the development of all children and families. Each of us must address and answer the fundamental questions of identity: "Who am I?" Who are we?" Cultural diversity can enrich our answers to the identity questions. Ethnic differences are a fact of life in American society. If we resist, reject, and deny these differences we imperil the development of all children, both those in minorities as well as the development of the majority group.

RESEARCH CAPSULE

Brice-Heath, an anthropologist, used a cultural/ecological approach to conduct an ethnographic study of language socialization of black children in a school system that had recently undergone desegregation.

Both teachers and parents reported that verbal communication between children and teachers was poor. Whereas teachers reported that children did not answer their questions, parents reported that the teachers "asked dumb questions" and did not listen to children.

Brice-Heath found that members of the black community and the teachers in the classroom used questions differently. For teachers, the purpose of asking questions was to promote conversation and develop language skills. These questions were outside the children's experience or else were "obvious." Parents and other adults in the community, on the other hand, did not ask questions that they believed the children knew answers to. Instead, questions were asked to obtain new information from children, as a method of informing, or to accuse. All this provided a context for understanding how cultural/ecological differences shape how questions were used with children.

PRACTICE CAPSULE

Educators in American schools have traditionally sought to assimilate immigrant and refugee children into mainstream culture. Beginning in the 1980s, however, many educators began taking steps to raise the public awareness of the importance of a multicultural curriculum as ethnic groups such as Asians, African-Americans, and Hispanics become more prominent.

Educators began broadening school curriculums to reflect the growing diversity of America's population, recognizing that America is composed of a variety of groups and draws on many diverse heritages and cultures. While assimilating groups to their new country, educators are taking steps to preserve minority children's ethnic culture.

In some predominantly African-American schools, the curriculum uses African elements in music, art, history, and social studies. In a Chicago public school serving a nearby housing project, each year a group of students is taken on a study trip to Africa in order to give African-American children an awareness of their cultural heritage.

In elementary schools where there are majorities of minorities, traditional Anglo readers have been replaced with books with stories from Laos, Guatemala, and Zimbabwe. By incorporating and adding to the traditional curriculum, educators are seeking to enrich and strengthen, creating situations where minority students can learn and gain self-respect.

FOR FURTHER READING

Gibbs, J. and Huang, L. *Children of Color: Psychological Interventions with Minority Youth.* San Francisco: Jossey-Bass, 1989.

This book provides a framework for assessing and treating the psychological and behavioral problems of minority youth. The authors present intervention strategies that are sensitive to the cultural and linguistic differences of minority groups in the United States. Additionally, the various ways children and adolescents cope with macrosystem issues such as discrimination and poverty are illustrated in rich case material.

Peshkin, A. *The Color of Stranger, the Color of Friends: The Play of Ethnicity in School and Community.* Chicago: The University of Chicago Press, 1991.
This book, written by an anthropologist, is a study of a multiethnic high school in California. The author participated in the life of the community and its high school, observing the behavior of students, families, and neighbors. In this school, students "mingled" with others of different ethnicities and races, and formed a united group against people from outside communities who were prejudiced against their predominantly working-class and nonwhite community. As a result, this school achieved integration at a level of social interaction and friendship rare in other multiethnic communities.

QUESTIONS FOR THOUGHT

1. Some observers argue that the positive side of group identity is outweighed by the negative side (chauvinism, discrimination against "the other" etc.) and cite as examples Serbs vs. Croats in Yugoslavia, Catholics vs. Protestants in Northern Ireland and African Americans vs. Anglo-Americans in the U.S. How do you deal with this?

2. How is the process of identity development understood in terms of Piaget's concepts of "assimilation" and "accomodation?" How is it a matter of what in this book we have called the child's emerging "social maps?"

3. If you were devising a program to strengthen identity formation among minority youth what activities and techniques would you employ?

4. Some observers argue for the need to encourage identity as a "citizen of the world." Is this psychologically realistic? For children? For adolescents?

5. Consider times and places when you have felt most strongly your identity in ethnic, racial, or national terms. What do these situations have in common?

6. Urie Bronfenbrenner reports that his ability to analyze American society arises in part from his experience growing up as a child living in two worlds—the world outside his home and the world inside his family. Such a person is a "Zwischen mench" (a "between person"). Why should this assist in social analysis? Do you have any experience with this phenomenon?

8

The Territory of Childhood

James Garbarino, Nancy L. Galambos, Margaret C. Plantz,
and Kathleen Kostelny

> In building a neighbourhood that meets hu-
> man needs, we start with the needs of in-
> fants. These give us the groundwork on
> which we can build for contact with other
> human beings, with the physical environ-
> ment, with the living world, and with the
> experiences through which the individual's
> full humanity can be realized. For every
> culture, the criteria must be modified. We
> cannot set our sights too low, but we can aim
> at any height, for we have as yet scarcely
> begun to explore human potentialities. How
> these are developed will depend on the
> learning experiences we can provide for chil-
> dren through the human habitat in which
> they live.
>
> Margaret Mead, "Neighbourhoods and
> Human Needs"

We have moved from an introduction to the ecology of human development through the examination of issues that bear directly on the parent–
child relationship and the family as a whole. Throughout history, human
beings have collected together and shared their energies to survive. Families have fought their environment, shaped it, and loved it. It is to the
geographic side of the environmental context of families that we now turn.
We begin with an exploration of the modern community, and will examine
the neighborhood as a major influence in the lives of families. Our ecologi-

cal perspective leads us to look at the various settings in which families grow and develop. We then focus on various social problems as expressions of the physical and social environment. Our goal is to gain a better understanding of the dynamics relating families and their contexts, an understanding that will lead to implications for improving the welfare of families.

A Child's Turf

The territory of childhood—the neighborhood and community— plays an important role in molding the child's experiences and in determining how well the child adapts to many individuals and situations. The child's first turf is the neighborhood. It is the child's to explore, become a part of, and use. The neighborhood in which a child lives is an early and major arena for exploration and social interaction, and serves as a setting for the physical and emotional development of the child. It plays an important part in determining with whom a child will come in contact and how safe the child will be in those contacts. At first the child's turf hardly extends beyond the front door, but it expands gradually as the child roams farther from home. Later, in adolescence, it may range over the entire community, particularly if the child has access to mass transit or an automobile. But the characteristics of that larger community territory and the decisions of the community power structure significantly affect the resources and experiences available to the child of any age.

The territory of childhood also influences adults, particularly as they function in their roles as parents. Neighborhood safety, recreational facilities, health and social services, schools, economic conditions, and opportunities to develop supportive relationships are all factors that affect the lives of families. In a reciprocal manner, the community responds to—and is shaped by—the needs and demands of individuals and families within it. Their choices about staying or moving, participating or not participating, and seeking change or accepting existing conditions affect many aspects of the community as it is and can become.

In this chapter we explore the geography of family life and child development, beginning with the community as the joint expression of the social and physical environment. Of particular interest to us is the nature of social support for families. As noted in Chapter 3, social support systems are networks of individuals that nurture and care for people and serve as resources in times of physical and emotional need. We consider both formal support systems (organizations structured for the purpose of giving care, such as social service agencies, child care centers, and community mental health centers), and informal support systems (nonprofessional care giving, such as neighbors, family, and friends). As we shall see, communities differ in the amount of formal and informal social support that they provide, thereby affecting the extent to which families can rely on others for help.

The Community and Human Ecology

The term "community" has taken on a fuzzy warm glow in loose public and professional usage, as in the amorphous way people use "sense of community" to convey a feeling of fellowship. The term does have a core meaning for many students of human development, however. Although one can speak of a community that is not linked to a geographical setting, such as "the academic community" (Toennies, 1957), our concern with families directs our attention to territory-based "place" communities (Anderson & Carter, 1978).

Hillery's (1955) classic distillation of the common elements of community endures: "Community consists of persons in social interaction within a geographic area and having one or more additional common ties" (p. 111). R. Warren (1973) characterized a community as a collection of social systems that performs the "locality-relevant functions" of social control, social participation, socialization, mutual support, and economic production, distribution, and consumption. A community, thus, has both social and economic components. The characteristics of a specific community arise in part through its own history and geography, in part through decisions of the local power structure and community residents, and in part through trends and influences that originate outside the community.

We know that community differences exist in many important ways relevant to families. In a segregated city such as Chicago, an individual has only a 1 in 25 chance of encountering a person of a different race within his or her "home" neighborhood. Is this a community effect or simply a coincidence? Whose interests are served?

The characteristics of a community, in turn, exert powerful influences on the quality of life for the families that live within it. These influences are of many types, and our ecological perspective reminds us to consider both direct and indirect effects at all levels of a family's environment. This perspective directs our attention to how the community affects the internal dynamics of family microsystems. For example, it leads us to be concerned with how disruptions of the community's primary economy (e.g., the closing of major industrial plants) affect rates of domestic violence (cf. Steinberg, Catalano, & Dooley, 1981; Straus, Gelles, & Steinmetz, 1980). It reminds us, too, to consider the impact of communities on microsystems such as schools and neighborhoods. Furthermore, an ecological perspective leads us to explore ways in which the community affects relationships *between* families and other contexts. These intersystem relationships—mesosystems—play an important part in defining the day-to-day lives of families, as in the way school and home relate in the education of children. An ecological approach also causes us to inquire about the way families are treated by the institutions of the community, a matter of exosystems. Are local employers sympathetic to the needs of children as regular customers? Does local government seek to serve family interests in zoning and tax decisions (Garbarino & Plantz, 1980)? In addition, we can also view the community as an important force in carrying out the ideologies and beliefs of the larger macrosystem. For example, tacit societal acceptance of domestic violence filters down through communities to families. If a community ethic against violence existed, abuse in families would probably decrease (Garbarino, 1977a). All of these issues deepen our appreciation of the ways in which various characteristics of the community affect the lives of its members.

Community-Level Effects on Children and Families

One of the issues facing researchers interested in community effects on families is the issue of just what *is* a "community" effect. Many studies simply aggregate or group together the data on individuals in the community and call that aggregate a "community effect." However, if we know that inadequate income is associated with child maltreatment at an individual level, then calling the relationship between average income in a community and overall community rate of child maltreatment a "community effect" is using the term in its simplest sense. We can observe a more theoretically interesting and significant community effect in situations in which community factors override individual characteristics in producing an effect on families. Although there are many community effects of this type, we are particularly interested in four: the economy of the community; its character as an urban, suburban, or rural setting; the social density of the family's environment; and the stability of that environment.

Community Economy

Economic factors play a central role in shaping the day-to-day life of families. Although the overall economy of the nation influences every community in the United States, there are wide variations *among* communities in the composition and vitality of their primary economies. As one of our colleagues (Rockwell, 1978) is fond of reminding us, "No one lives in America. People live in Boise, in Newark, in Chadron, in Atlanta, in Los Angeles or in Waco." Although this somewhat overstates the point, it is basically correct. The effects of the national economy are certainly mediated by community differences. Local economic systems vary depending on the jobs, goods, and services provided by businesses and industries in that community. The substantial intercommunity variation in unemployment rates indicates the magnitude of economic differences in communities. For example, in 1991, the unemployment rates among counties in New York State varied from a high of 12.5% to a low of 5.0%.

The 1980 census revealed community effects in population change between 1970 and 1980. For example, Florida experienced a 40% increase in population, whereas Rhode Island's population actually declined. Although most communities within these states show trends that match overall state data, some communities show reversals (U.S. Bureau of the Census, 1981). In Florida, for example, some cities grew less than 10% in population (e.g., Jacksonville's 7.3%) whereas others grew more than 50% (e.g., Coral Gables' extraordinary 90+%). The shifts in political power that follow these economic and demographic changes have important effects on families. In 1981, the President's Commission for a National Agenda for the Eighties tacitly recognized this "community effect" when it urged the federal government to cease its efforts to maintain artificially the primary economies of "Snow Belt" cities of the Northeast and Midwest and instead to facilitate the natural expansion of the "Sun Belt" cities in the Southeast, Southwest, and West. Such a policy is derived from the premise that the population and vitality of a community depend on the nature of its primary economy, and federal efforts to override this dynamic are ineffective at best.

Shifts in the work force are an important community-level economic event with family-level effects. For example, Elder (1974) reported that severe income loss during the Great Depression of the 1930s was partly a community-level effect, independent of the characteristics of individual workers. That is, a downturn in a community's primary economy produced unemployment randomly or nearly so among workers in the community, as opposed to being systematically based on worker performance. Thus a clerk in Ithaca, New York (which was shielded from unemployment as the home of a large university) had a much better chance of holding onto his job than a clerk in Detroit (where heavy industry was hit hard). Some communities, and thus some occupations and individual workers, were spared. In other efforts to identify community characteristics that affect families regardless of their individual attributes, Steinberg et al. (1981) demonstrated a negative relationship between the number of jobs in a community and its rate of child maltreatment. A community's primary economy determines its vulnerabilities to hard times.

Community-level effects also could be demonstrated by findings that the relationship between income and child maltreatment is different for different communities, or that the degree of economic homogeneity versus heterogeneity affects the rate of maltreatment uniformly among communities. Unfortunately, there is little research that addresses this sort of community effect. Much community research has methodological limitations such that one mistakenly infers individual-level effects from aggregate data analysis. However, where the units of analysis are relatively small (e.g., census tracts) and the effects large, we can draw some conclusions about what individuals are doing, based on what the community is doing (Bogue & Bogue, 1976).

Urban, Suburban, and Rural Settings

The economy of a community clearly is an important determinant of the quality of life for its families. Another major community-level effect derives from a community's status as an urban, suburban, or rural setting. The traditional urban–rural dichotomy for classifying communities became increasingly obsolete in the period following World War II (VanEs & Brown, 1974; Photiadis, 1970). The rise of the "automotive society" gave birth to new residential forms that have altered the foundations of both urban and rural life. The automobile and the cheap-energy economy it represented made possible new and attractive suburban, rural, and urban patterns that by their very existence undermined the older forms (cf. Kowinski, 1980; Wynne, 1977). With the new mobility, members of families have become increasingly separated from each other, an occurrence that has probably increased their need for community- and neighborhood-based support systems at a time when many of these systems are declining (Bronfenbrenner, 1975).

The automotive era appears to have had its clearest and most profound effects on the evolving patterns of suburban life. Wynne (1977) distinguished between "old" and "new" suburbs, concepts that seem to apply most readily to older cities, particularly in the Northeast and Midwest. "Old" suburbs were formerly small towns on the periphery of a city, having railroad stations as focal points. "New" suburbs are bedroom communities without a primary economy of their own that depend on automobile-based commuting for economic activity. In 1956 about 80% of America's suburbs were of the old type, whereas the figure for 1980 was about 45% (Wynne, 1977). By 1990, for which data are not available directly, we expect that figure was higher still. Wynne speculated that new suburbs may be less supportive of families because they overemphasize peer group relations, and because they lack sufficient formal and informal activities (e.g., Chamber of Commerce, service clubs) to offer children a socially rich and varied existence. Thus, they place greater demands on parents to act as socializing agents.

The 1990s have seen crystallization of two additional trends: cross-suburban commuting and "reverse" commuting. The former refers to the large and growing number of people who drive to jobs in other suburbs (rather than in the city). The latter refers to people who live in the city and drive out to the suburbs to work. Neither really contributes to community "completeness."

The automotive era's main effects on cities have been movement of the population away from the core of old cities to new cities and suburbs, and increased noise and accident hazards (Michelson & Roberts, 1979). Both of these may have adverse effects on young children (Aiello, 1985). Furthermore, erosion of the urban tax base and increasing concentration of high-risk populations have jeopardized schools, governments, businesses, and neighborhoods—the essential infrastructure of community (Jacobs, 1961). The effect of this sort of breakdown on families is of undetermined magnitude, although we presume that its direction is negative. We assume that these problems affect some families more than others and are of greatest concern for families with young children otherwise at social risk. Of course, increased mobility has allowed many families to leave socially stressed environments and move to areas that are more conducive to a healthy family life. They may, for example, leave poor urban areas and relocate to small communities or suburbs with better schools for their children, leaving those with the least resources to fend for themselves in the center city areas. This has been a big problem for African-American neighborhoods, where middle-class families (who used to be confined to ghettos because of racial segregation *and* who used to exert a stabilizing influence on neighborhood life) have left behind an increasingly marginal low-income population (Wilson, 1987).

Although industrialization has led to a shift in families from rural areas to suburban and urban environments, some regions of the United States can still be considered "rural America." Southern Appalachia, for example, has maintained a relatively isolated and semiautonomous existence. However, values from the larger society have infiltrated the traditional social system, thereby creating changes in the social equilibrium (Photiadis 1970). The desire for economic achievement that produced migration to cities has increased stress on the family and has increased the need for reorganization of the social system. Schwarzweller (1970) emphasized that the family has withstood the social change. In support of this view, Heller and Quesada (1977) found that families in the rural southeastern United States are characterized by strong ties and close geographic location to members of the extended family, little support for geographic mobility, and more participation in kinship rather than in community activities. Rural society in the western United States, on the other hand, is composed of strong nuclear families, dependence on the community for activities and support, and more geographic mobility. Heller and Quesada (1977) concluded that the two distinct forms of rural families evolved as a result of different ecological conditions. That is, greater numbers of kin in eastern settlements and fewer numbers in the west because of their recent migration.

Social Density

One of the most intriguing community effects seems to be on the "social density" of the family environment (Garbarino, 1985). By social density we mean the degree to which an environment contains a diversity of roles for children to learn from and for parents to draw upon. The density of roles—that is, their relative homogeneity versus heterogeneity in the setting—is an important issue. It goes beyond racial, ethnic, and religious issues. A heterogeneous setting is one in which multiple roles exist; in a homogeneous setting few roles predominate. In this and many other respects, we believe that homogeneity tends to be simply reassuring but developmentally stultifying, while pluralism is challenging but invigorating (Garbarino & Bronfenbrenner, 1976).

Multigeneration households or neighborhoods offer greater social density than those in which children encounter only one generation of adults. Microsystems can capitalize on the fact that members play multiple roles (e.g., homemaker, provider, and organization officer). The presence in a child's environment of adults who fill several roles contributes to the social richness of the child's experiences.

The spectrum of roles in the immediate social environment of the child contributes to development. Most students of human development seem to agree that children do best when they are set within a community environment that offers stable opportunities to observe and practice basic human roles (Aldrich, 1979). A dense setting with respect to roles may be developmentally enhancing, as when the neighborhood contains shopkeepers, retired persons, and a variety of kinship and friendship relations. As we shall see, the fragments of data available to us suggest that it is typically small towns or coherent neighborhoods nested within communities that are the best vehicles for providing these experiences. Aldrich (1979) speculated that "a complete community of around 5,000 people allows a child to get a rather good idea of what community relations are all about" (p. 87). A coherent neighborhood can meet these criteria—and offer the cultural riches of the city.

A socially dense environment also may provide social resources that parents can draw upon. One necessary resource is the availability of adults who are "free from drain." Adults who are "free from drain" are those whose energies are not totally consumed by day-to-day responsibilities, and who, therefore, can devote time and energy to serving in the informal helping networks that support neighborhood life and families in need (Collins & Pancoast, 1976; Gottlieb, 1980; Pancoast, 1980; Tietjen, 1980). Thus, the social density of the community has an effect on the amount of support that families receive.

Investigators have reported that children in a small town have more knowledge of people and roles than do urban children living in an area without a well-developed neighborhood, while those in a well-functioning urban neighborhood stand somewhere between the town and city in this respect (Gump & Adelberg, 1978). The term used by the ecological psychologists working in Kansas in the 1950s for situations with many people in relation to the number of settings is overmanned, and undermanned referred to the opposite situation. We updated their language, and would say that the small town tends to be "underpeopled" in that it has a low ratio of people to roles needing to be filled. As a community, it has the full range of community activities to maintain and, thus, is very "dense" or heterogeneous with respect to roles and mesosystems. The less well-developed urban neighborhood is not a complete community; it must rely on the larger city for many functions, including the provision of jobs. We speculate that because adults are drawn away from such a neighborhood, children see less of life's basic social functions in it. It is less socially dense. As a neighborhood it tends to be "overpeopled" in the sense that there is little to do and many people to do it. Thus, kids are unneeded.

The well-developed urban neighborhood, although not a complete community, may approximate the small town in its social density. There are neighborhood activities beyond residing. The socially undeveloped urban neighborhood may have so little going on that it impoverishes the social experience and knowledge of its children. Even further, what *is* going on may not enrich their lives.

Environmental Stability

Just as the community context of the family's immediate setting is important in determining the richness of the child's and parent's social experience, so is the stability of that setting and context. We know from informal observation that neighborhoods are hard to transplant because relocation disrupts the "natural" social systems of the area (Jacobs, 1961). These informal networks are important community characteristics that can compensate for, and override the effects of, individual situations.

Decisions of the community power structure often affect the vitality of these personal support systems. When natural disaster strikes a community (e.g., a flood or tornado), the biggest problem is how to recreate not the physical, but the *social* landscape (Nuttal, 1980; cf. Erikson, 1976). When the "disaster" results from social policy, such as industrial, highway, or dam development that requires relocating residents, we face the same issues. Rebuilding social networks often is more difficult than physical reconstruction. Warren (1968), for instance, reported that when a small town was relocated because of a dam project, only one quarter of the town's accustomed settings for social interaction survived the move. In 1981, the case of Hamtramck, a Polish-settled neighborhood in Detroit, received national attention as the municipal administration exercised eminent domain to tear down the 1500 private homes, schools, businesses, and churches in the neighborhood and sell the land to the General Motors Corporation to build a massive industrial plant. Whatever its economically salubrious effects on the rest of the community, the decision meant social annihilation for the neighborhood, relocation of 3400 people (one-half of whom were elderly), and confrontations between neighborhood members and the corporation (Kelly, 1981). Its longer term effects on families are as yet undetermined.

Community effects resulting from a lack of stability can also occur in less drastic situations. The closing of schools, decisions to bus children to different neighborhoods, and shutdown of businesses and industries can affect the social interactions within and among individuals in the community. As Devereux (1977) demonstrated in his critique of ecological psychology, community changes are probably the principal forces affecting the quantity and quality of settings in which social behavior occurs. While we have some research documenting such community changes, we have virtually no documentation of how they affect families.

Family–Community Interface

There are several aspects of the family–community relationship that affect children and parents in the community. Local government practices, the parent's place of work, the relationship between home and school, and community response to the need for child care services determine the nature of the environment's support for families. Although it is the combined interactions within and among these systems that comprise the family–community interface, we will present each aspect separately in order to examine some important issues.

Family–Local Government

Local government exerts an important influence on families. Through their zoning and planning agencies, local governments do much to shape the community contexts of families. They are involved, for instance, in balancing the desire of children for open spaces to use as playlots vs. the desire of adults to fill in the holes in the neighborhood or in the desires and needs of adult-only and adult-plus-children households. Local government policies may permit or even encourage landlords to exclude children from rental housing. There are areas in the United States where adults may reside only if they have no children at home. By limiting their options, this discrimination puts psychological, and perhaps even financial, stress on some families. It also increases age segregation and reduces the adult-to-child ratio in residential areas. Of course, some older adults desire age-based residential segregation. They seek to avoid the stress of sharing their neighborhood with children. Some would argue that this is their right.

Local governments also play central roles in decisions that disrupt existing neighborhoods. A neighborhood is vulnerable to external assault in a variety of ways. Urban renewal and highway projects, like natural disasters, can seriously disrupt the ability of a community's neighborhoods to serve as family support systems. One of the important aspects of the government–family interface is the extent to which local governments are protective and restorative in their efforts to control the residential environments of families (Michelson & Roberts, 1979). The protective function of a local government was exemplified by the successful fight against developers who wished to build a large jetport in a small community in western New York. Citizens in the community were concerned that the noise and pollution would disrupt their lives. The battle between local citizens and outside officials continued for a few years until the local government, aided by community support, succeeded in preventing construction of the jetport. If the local government had placed a higher priority on the financial reasons for supporting the jetport than on the comfort of local families, the result might have been much different.

We see that the restorative function of local government varies in policies that promote renovating or restoring old buildings, homes, or areas. The government that razes impossibly deteriorated buildings, constructs new housing, and restores run-down homes is improving the quality of the community. Some communities are attempting to improve residential life through a policy that allows families to rent or purchase, at very low prices, old homes that need renovation. Families move into these homes with an agreement that their responsibility is to restore the homes. Through such policies, government and families work cooperatively to enhance neighborhoods. On the other hand, a government that allows the continual decay of buildings within a community is potentially harming the community. Children may be injured by playing in dangerous areas, businesses may not be attracted to the area, and the community may become a breeding ground for crime. These effects will diminish the financial and aesthetic value of the community. Clearly, the local government has a large effect on families in a variety of ways.

A government that allows functioning residential areas to be weakened or even eliminated in the service of commercial or industrial development often unwittingly (or even wittingly) effectively eliminates low cost housing. This action displaces the families with the least means to relocate to other—usually more expensive—housing. This dynamic plays a major role in creating the problem of *family* homelessness (as opposed to the problem of homelessness as it affects single adults, whose lives may be responding to other forces, such as alcoholism and serious mental health problems (cf. Bassuk & Rosenberg, 1988).

Family–Work

The family–work interface is a critical feature in any review of family life and its effects on child development (Bronfenbrenner & Crouter, 1982). Here, as elsewhere, community factors mediate the relationship. Because work and work-related factors are near or at the top of the list of day-to-day stresses for parents, anything a community does to provide work-related support and reduce work-related stress is important. House (1981) emphasized the need to build work-related supports into organizations and made several recommendations, such as sensitizing supervisors to employee problems. As we noted at the outset of our discussion, community differences in primary economy account for significant variations in unemployment—in many ways the ultimate work-related stress. Naturally, the nature of the community's primary economy also affects the types of available jobs—blue versus white versus pink collar (i.e., jobs such as waitressing that are traditionally taken by women). The wage levels associated with these variations produce different socioeconomic mixes. The impact of this variation on families is undetermined, but we can assume that the child exposed to very homogeneous populations of working individuals will have different experiences from the child whose parents have contact with a number of people from different backgrounds.

The very centrality of the work–family relationship means that many community policies and decisions relevant to working conditions, such as those affecting mass transit and zoning, have direct effects on the family. We mentioned previously the effects of opening or closing industries and businesses. In communities that already have mass transportation systems, the effects of strikes by transit workers are great on both the community and individuals within the community.

Home–School

The home–school interface is perhaps the most widely recognized aspect of the family–community relationship. However, for all the professional, political, and public attention it receives, it is not adequately understood. We know that the congruence between home and school can have a large and significant effect upon child development—particularly upon academic success. Where this mesosystem is strong, the child benefits. A strong home–school mesosystem is a set of multiple and mutually respectful relationships between families and school officials. Naturally, the nature and strength of the home–school relationship are variable from community to community.

Community factors impinge upon the home–school mesosystem in several ways. First, the community partially defines the degree to which schools are neighborhood based. Many studies document the importance of a school's catchment area (i.e., the area served by a school) in shaping its success as an academic socializer (Jencks, 1972). However, the strength of this relationship appears to be greater in some settings than in others (Coleman, 1966): the more socioeconomically deprived the community, the greater the difference that the school's efforts produce (Garbarino, 1981b). The size of the community's schools can also have important effects on families. As a result of pressure to stay in school, urban and suburban concentrations of students, and academic and economic policies that favor consolidation of smaller schools into larger ones, the *average* American high school has 1500 students, and most secondary schools (grades 9–12) have more than 750 students. This imposes psychological and social costs on the community and its young people. According to research (Barker & Grump, 1964) a high school with more than 500 students is large, and large schools breed impersonal and elitist relationships and discourage participation. Large schools have their worst and strongest effects on academically and socially marginal students. These youth tend to become alienated, unappreciated, and unsuccessful (Garbarino, 1980d).

Community factors can also affect the congruence of school and home. Policies concerning bilingual education, for example, may affect the degree of respect for the home's culture, a factor more relevant in the many communities such as Miami or Los Angeles that have large concentrations of non-English-speaking families. The federal government's 1981 decision to discontinue national efforts to promote bilingualism and leave the matter to local discretion increased the differences among communities in this and other cultural matters, such as the use of physical force as punishment and the provision of sex education in schools.

The community affects the home–school relationship by encouraging or discouraging academic success in children of low-income families. The Children's Defense Fund (1974) reported that most of the school-age children out of school on a regular basis were in effect excluded from school—often because of economically related requirements such as paying for books or transportation. They reported substantial variation among communities on this score. On the other hand, community efforts to promote school success (e.g., by special enrichment programs) for low-income children can significantly modify the mesosystem mismatch that often occurs between low-income families and middle-class oriented schools (Committee for Economic Development, 1987; Garbarino, 1981b). Head Start, a national program for young children of low-income families, was designed to overcome the academic impoverishment that these children experienced. The object was to give them the skills and experiences they needed to succeed in America's schools, or in other words, to improve the school–home mesosystem.

The issue of desegregation also shows how families affect and are affected by the school, community, and local government. The decision about whether to bus students to schools that are outside of their neighborhood is often made after considerable debate. Many residents do not want their children bused, while community leaders often desire integration of racial groups. It is obvious that community decisions affect interactions within the home–school mesosystem that, in turn, have direct effects upon children and their parents.

Child Care

One indicator of the quality and quantity of community support for families is the provision of child care. Indeed, international studies of community development often use provision of child care as a social indicator. We know that there is a substantial need for child care, given the dramatic increase in the number of mothers working outside the home who have young children. We also know a substantial proportion of child care providers are part of the informal (friends, relatives, and neighbors) rather than the formal (licensed child care and family day care programs) support systems of the community. In the early 1970s, the National Childcare Consumer Study (Unco, 1975) found that for children under 6, in-home babysitter care was most common (26%), followed by care in someone else's home (16%) and nursery school (8%), with care in child care centers trailing far behind (3%).

In the fall of 1987, informal support systems continued to provide much preschool child care. Of children under age 5 with employed mothers, 45% received care in their home or care by a relative in another home (U.S. Bureau of the Census, 1990). The importance of formal child care arrangements had grown substantially, however. More than one-fifth of the preschoolers (22%) were cared for in another home by a nonrelative, some in essentially a babysitting arrangement in the sitter's home, but many in formally licensed or regulated family day care. Organized child care facilities, including group care programs, nursery schools, and preschools, cared for 24% of preschoolers with employed mothers (U.S. Bureau of the Census, 1990).

Community characteristics are relevant to both the informal and the formal systems assisting families in meeting their child care needs. The richness of the informal support systems surrounding home-based child care is one of the most important dimensions of the community–family interface (Collins & Watson, 1976; Unger & Powell, 1980). Social networks and neighborhood interaction serve a vital function in making this link work well.

Formal community support systems also are essential to ensuring the availability of quality child care. Informal child care supports for children of employed parents have shrunk as families have continued to move away from longstanding social networks and relatives and neighbors have themselves entered the labor force. Concerns about the care given in informal home-based day care arrangements have increased the demand for background checks, training, monitoring, and other forms of quality assurance. Interest in center-based programs, which generally offer more resources and activities—such as toys, books, and field trips—than does home-based care, also has risen. As the data cited above indicate, the role these formal child care arrangements play has increased markedly since the mid-1970s.

Communities greatly influence the quality and responsiveness of formal child care support systems for families. Financial support for child care is only one factor. Local ordinances and regulations expand or constrict the diversity of child care settings and arrangements that the community supports and monitors. Zoning regulations can affect the availability of family day care in certain neighborhoods. Communities have some discretion in how State and Federal child care funds are used locally. They also can encourage local coalitions or partnerships among public, private, and voluntary interests to address child care issues.

Another difference among communities with respect to support for child care is the existence of services that help families address child care questions and needs. Resource and referral agencies, family services programs, employer-sponsored family support programs, and other services exist in many communities to help parents evaluate various child care options, locate certified or licensed providers, assess providers' fit with their own needs, explore the availability of subsidies, resolve problems that may arise with the chosen provider, and deal with other problems related to parents' child care responsibilities.

One of the newest aspects of the community–family interface is the provision of before- and after-school care for children in the 6- to 13-year-old age range (Levine, 1976). A report by the U.S. Bureau of the Census (1976) indicated that in 1974 roughly 13% of the children aged 7 to 13 whose mothers were employed cared for themselves after school. Thirteen years later, of children aged 5 to 14 with employed mothers, 22% who were in school most of the time their mothers were at work were in self-care before or after school. Another 4% were at home alone most of the time their mothers were at work because their mothers were not employed during the school hours (U.S. Bureau of the Census, 1990). Thus, over two million school-age children are possible candidates for supervised care. Unsupervised children are about twice as likely to come from single- rather than two-parent families (U.S. Bureau of the Census, 1976, 1980). If a community has many single parents, there will be an especially pressing need for informal and formal child-care systems for school-aged children that are affordable and easily accessible. The same trends that have eroded the informal systems of care for preschool chil-

dren have made consistent informal care for school-aged children difficult to arrange. Formal support systems for school-aged child care have
lagged behind those for younger children in most communities. Some
communities are taking innovative steps, however (e.g., Gannett, 1989),
to address this important need for families and children (Seligson &
Fink, 1989).

The Neighborhood and Support Systems

To examine the relationship between social support systems and families, it is helpful to focus on the neighborhood. As we said in Chapters 2
and 3, the neighborhood is the place in which parents interact with their
children and also interact with others, independently of the children.
The children are participants in the neighborhood, too, and are often
given the freedom to socialize without the presence of the parents. The
quality of the support, encouragement, and feedback given by the
neighborhood to the family has an effect on the child's development.
What are neighborhood characteristics that influence families?

Keller (1968) identified functions of a neighborhood as those fulfilled
by members within it. A neighbor is characterized as "the helper in
times of need, who is expected to step in when other resources fail"
(p. 29). The occasions of sickness, death, and emergencies, as well as
weddings and other festivities, call neighbors together. Therefore,
neighboring is a socially defined relationship that involves the duties of
exchanging resources, information, and help. Neighbors form an informal support system that a family can look to in times of need. Another
function of the neighborhood is to maintain social control and standards. Neighbors provide feedback to one another about moral conduct,
the appearance of the home, and child care.

A good neighborhood in Kromkowski's (1976) terms enhances development by providing the kind of multiple connections and multiple
situations that permit children to make the best use of their intellectual
and social equipment. It also gives them a sense of familiarity and belonging, a territorial base. What Bronfenbrenner calls "cross-contextual
dyads" (relationships that exist in more than one situation) flourish in a
healthy, well-developed neighborhood. Likewise, a strong neighborhood offers a sense of security and peace of mind for the parent, feelings
that translate into a more relaxed and positive stance toward the task of
child rearing and toward the child in particular.

Neighborhoods differ in how strong and healthy they are. We can
attribute these variations in part to conventional economic influences.

Across different economic levels, we find strong and weak neighbor-hoods—they exist among both the rich and the poor (Warren & Warren, 1977). However, the importance of the neighborhood as a factor in family life and in child development is probably greater among the poor (Smith, 1976). While the rich have a wider community to draw on and can use their material resources to purchase other avenues of support, encouragement, and guidance, the less affluent are more likely to depend on whatever informal support systems are available to them in the neighborhood. A high-risk neighborhood is one that weakens rather than strengthens families by virtue of the character of the neighborhood. This leads us to consider community ecology and family social pathology.

Community Ecology and Family Social Pathology

Families are subject to a variety of social pathologies. Social pathologies are problems or dysfunctions that are related to the quality of the social environment. Research has shown that there is a relationship between social pathology, stress, and support (Cooper & Gath, 1977). "Where the environment is supportive, creative adaptation and growth occur. Where the environment is nonprotective or depriving, stress is created, and adaptive functioning may be impeded" (Germain, 1978, p. 522).

Both the availability of effective supports for families and the level of environmental stress they face derive in part from community factors—characteristics of the community as well as decisions made within it. Individual neighborhoods add their own mix of pressures and protection. We should expect, then, that the qualities of a family's neighborhood and community, its community ecology, are important forces in the patterns of family social pathologies. We should expect that areas with high concentrations of pathology will be areas where the balance of environmental stresses and supports tips against families. Conversely, if we can identify communities and neighborhoods with characteristics that make them high-risk places for families, then we can predict that rates of social pathology among their families will be high.

A geographic approach to family social pathology is new ground for many, if not most, students of child development. The value of mapping the incidence and distribution of disease—following epidemiological methods—is revealed in this instance of medical sleuthing. During the 1960s, a high proportion of cases of cleft palate in various counties in upstate New York came to the attention of the U.S. Public Health Service. As was the accustomed procedure of public health physicians, the local director of the Public Health Service placed a pin for each case of cleft palate and all other congenital malformations on a map of New York, denoting the location of each case. The resulting pattern corresponded to the pattern of igneous rock formations in New York, revealing the probable source of the health problems. Igneous rock emits natural radiation and had been associated with deformities present at birth, such as cleft palate (Bronfenbrenner & Mahoney, 1975). The mapping technique, in this case, led to the root of the physical problems. The usefulness of a geographic orientation goes beyond physical disability and illness, however. It extends to psychological and social dysfunction as well, to mapping *social* radiation.

Some of the impediments to the general use of a community approach to family social pathology are technical and others are conceptual. The technical problems include the fact that data are often difficult to obtain in a form that permits efficient geographic mapping. It seems that our individualistic conception of pathology and the necessity of protecting confidentiality lead to data that are detached from their geographic location. One technological innovation has been the development of computer programs to perform "geocoding" of family data by translating addresses into mapped data points. The investigator, thus, can plot data to correspond with other data sets that describe census-tract or neighborhood-level indices of economic or demographic stress and support. The investigator can then determine the relationship between these data sets. Geocoding can become a vital resource for social workers, health planners, students, and others seeking to obtain more knowledge of communities (Kromkowski, 1976).

A second technical innovation that can aid in analyzing community effects is "social area analysis." Pioneered by Shevky and Bell (1955), and refined and expanded in the past 20 years by many researchers (Janson, 1980), social area analysis promises a systematic way of classifying and categorizing the sources of socioeconomic and demographic stress and support. The technique gives specific criteria for judging when a particular pattern of data is abnormal or deviant. It relies on routinely available data and does not require the special surveys and field study demanded by other approaches to neighborhood analysis (e.g., Warren & Warren, 1977). The major limitation is the quality and quantity of the data base. The approach depends on contemporary accuracy of data that often must come from census reports. These data rapidly become outdated for unstable communities and changing neighborhoods—precisely those areas that are often of greatest interest and concern in matters of family social pathology.

There have been other efforts to relate community factors to family social pathology using existing data and techniques. These efforts view the extent of various family social pathologies as indicators of the social habitability or quality of life in communities (Brim, 1975; Garbarino, 1991).

Kogan, Smith, and Jenkins (1977), for example, created a multivariable index of stress indicators. Its acronym is DIPOV, and it includes a mix of measures that tap health and socioeconomic deprivation: Dependency (proportion of children under 18 in families receiving AFDC—Aid to Families with Dependent Children); Incomplete Families (proportion of children under 18 not living with both parents); Premature Births (rate of infants with birth weight under 2501 grams per 1000 live births); Out-of-Wedlock births (as a proportion of all live births); and Venereal Disease, Juvenile (rate of reported cases of primary or secondary syphilis or gonorrhea among persons under age 20 per 100,000 population under age 20). The investigators calculated DIPOV indices at county, census-unit, and neighborhood levels.

The researchers then sought to verify DIPOV by conducting an interview survey of families in areas with different scores on the index. Their analyses showed that the DIPOV Index performed progressively better as a predictor of difficulties of children (e.g., antisocial behavior) and parents (e.g., punitiveness) as the level of analysis moved from the larger (county) to the smaller (neighborhood) unit. Thus, preliminary use of DIPOV suggests it does have some validity as a correlate of family social pathology.

Four of the more significant social pathologies involving families are obstetric and pediatric illness, child maltreatment and domestic violence, juvenile delinquency, and teenage pregnancy. Each reflects the nature of transactions between the family and the social environment and demonstrates the nature of social stress and support in that environment. It is likely that community factors affect the prevalence of these pathologies. However, few community studies of these or other family social pathologies employ the DIPOV index, social area analysis, or any alternative social indicator approach. Greater use of such approaches is part of a more general need for empirical studies exploring the nature and power of relationships between communities and families. This need is reflected in, and supported by, the following brief review of these four types of family social pathology.

Infant Mortality and Morbidity

Infant mortality (death in the first year of life) and morbidity (illness) are two of the traditional indices of social pathology (Kessner et al.,

1973). Differences among countries are often large and community effects are common. We can begin with the "natural" variation evidenced in standard descriptive statistics. Among nations, the differences are associated with two major factors: level of economic development and public commitment to support mothers and infants, prenatally and in the first year of life. Thus, for example, most poor nations have very high rates—about 100 per 1000 births—and most rich nations have low rates—less than 10 per 1000 births. But some poor countries have lower rates than others (e.g., 30 per 1000 vs. 150 per 1000), and some rich countries have higher rates than others (e.g., the rate in the United States in the 1980s was 12 per 1000 vs. the Netherlands 8 per 1000). Among communities we see these same two sources of variation—i.e., resources and policy.

Among communities in the Chicago metropolitan area, for example, we see variation from 4 per 1000 on the low end to 34 per 1000 on the high end (a figure that is actually higher than some Third World countries!). Research indicates that these differences correlate mainly with the degree of poverty in these communities and the degree to which resources are programmed to reach mothers—particularly high-risk mothers (Garbarino & Kostelny, 1992b).

These gross differences are difficult to interpret and evaluate. They certainly reflect, at least in part, ecological correlations between low income and infant mortality and morbidity (Keniston, 1977; National Academy of Sciences, 1976). We have reason to believe that they indicate more than these aggregate community effects, however. The demonstrated effects of prenatal health care, coupled with community-level variation in provision of such care, testify to a genuine community effect (Kessner et al., 1973). In 14 communities where maternal- and infant-care projects were sponsored by the Department of Health, Education, and Welfare for low income neighborhoods in the mid-1960s, significant decreases in infant mortality were observed: from 34.2 deaths per 1000 live births in 1964 to 21.5 in 1969 in Denver, from 33.4 to 13.4 in Omaha, and from 25.4 to 14.3 in Birmingham. More recently, efforts to enhance the supportiveness of the prenatal and perinatal experience of young, high-risk mothers have resulted in decreased infant morbidity (O'Connor et al., 1977; Olds, 1980). Such results are appropriately considered community effects because the changes in policies, practices, and priorities they represent result from shifts in the direction of institutions, such as hospitals, that reflect community power structures and values. The whole movement toward family-centered childbirth has advanced community by community across the country (Garbarino, 1980a). These effects are equally apparent for teenage pregnancy.

Teenage Pregnancy

As a form of family social pathology, teenage pregnancy has received significant public and professional attention, but little systematic, quantitative analysis has addressed it as a community problem. We know that socioeconomic and ethnic factors seem to influence the rates of teenage pregnancy: low-income blacks have the highest rates (Baldwin, 1976; Bolton, 1980). One source of apparent community effects is the level and quality of support and guidance given to the teenager involved in a first pregnancy (Shelton & Gladstone, 1979). The response of schools, operating under community mandate, can influence the subsequent educational, occupational, and thus, of course, family prospects of the adolescent parent (Furstenberg, 1976). Community support for an active family-planning effort can prevent or delay second pregnancies among teenagers (Bolton, 1980; Furstenberg, 1976).

The principal community effect in this aspect of family social pathology is, thus, to moderate the effects of teenage pregnancies—on children, on parents, indeed on the very creation and maintenance of parent–child relationships. Historical trends in the United States suggest that another community effect on teenage parenthood is to influence the likelihood of teenage *marriage* as a consequence of teenage pregnancy.

Some observers (Shelton & Gladstone, 1979) note that much of the medical and social pathology associated with teenage pregnancy derives from the community's response. As evidence, they cite both a decrease in adverse consequences—as society has become more supportive and less punitive with respect to teenage pregnancy—and the fact that among well-supported groups, the level of medical pathology and social disadvantage is minimal. Community effects are observable in the availability of sex education, contraception, and abortion to teenagers. Of course, measures of maternal and child health at birth do not address consequences to the child of growing up in a teenage-parented, often, single-parented household, so we should not overgeneralize the significance of these findings.

Juvenile Delinquency

Juvenile delinquency was one of the earliest interests of human ecologists working at the University of Chicago in the 1920s and 1930s (Hawley, 1950; Lander, 1954; Shaw and McKay, 1942; Shaw et al., 1929). Extensive data exist documenting community differences in the reported incidence of juvenile delinquency and crime generally.

Studies such as the Nebraska Social Indicators Study report a correlation between community size and "fear of walking alone at night near one's home" (a good measure of social climate). Using these data, Eells (1981) reported that as community size increases, so does the percentage of residents expressing this fear: rural, 9%; towns under 2500 population, 16%; small cities, 24%; cities 10,000–50,000, 32%; city of 100,000, 41%; city of 300,000, 49%. This phenomenon reaches its maximum point in inner city "war zones" where violent juvenile crime in the form of gangs literally places families under a kind of "house arrest" (Garbarino et al., 1991).

The rich community case study literature (e.g., McKay, cited by Short, 1966) suggests that local decisions regarding zoning, law enforcement strategies, schooling, youth employment, curfews, recreation, and the like all can have the effect of mediating the family dynamics, peer relationships, personality shifts, and behavioral contingencies that generate or suppress juvenile delinquency. Neighborhood-oriented research of this sort reports that stability is associated with lower delinquency, while disruption is associated with increased delinquency (McKay, cited by Short, 1966). Social cohesion appears to be a precondition for social control, but it is the effective power of prosocial forces within the neighborhood or community that tells the story (Short, 1966). More specifically, investigators have found that juvenile delinquency rates differ between neighborhoods that are socioeconomically and demographically comparable if the neighborhoods differ in how capable they are of exerting social control, with the critical dimension being degree of social cohesion on behalf of prosocial goals among residents (Maccoby, Johnson, & Church, 1958). Research on child maltreatment has taken this finding and moved toward a more comprehensive conception of how community and neighborhood influence family social pathology.

Child Maltreatment

Following earlier neighborhood-oriented work (Sattin & Miller, 1971), Garbarino and his colleagues (Garbarino, 19976; Garbarino & Crouter, 1978; Garbarino & Kostelny, 1992a; Garbarino & Sherman, 1980) undertook research designed to illustrate the use of child maltreatment report data as a social indicator of the quality of life for families. This research addressed the feedback function of family support systems, and linked maltreatment to the overall balance of stresses and supports in the neighborhood context of families. The first study provided county-level correlations relating socioeconomic and demographic stress on mothers to rates of child maltreatment (Garbarino, 1976).

Further study focused on the reported incidence of child abuse and neglect in 93 neighborhood areas in a single metropolitan county. The statistical technique of multiple regression analysis was used to develop equations to predict abuse and neglect rates from socioeconomic, demographic, and attitudinal data (Garbarino & Crouter, 1978). For the 93 neighborhoods, 52% of the difference in reported rates was accounted for by five variables—two measuring family income, one assessing the presence of single parent households, one indexing transience, and one indicating the presence of mothers working outside the house who have young children. This study extended and validated the earlier research reporting similar results using counties as the units of analysis (Garbarino, 1976) and formed the basis for more in-depth neighborhood-focused studies (Garbarino & Kostelny, 1992b; Garbarino & Sherman, 1980).

The multiple regression analyses identified low-income neighborhoods that, although matched in socioeconomic level and demographic character, differ significantly in the rates of child maltreatment. Neighborhoods with a child maltreatment rate greatly exceeding what would be predicted by their socioeconomic and demographic profile are termed high risk, whereas other neighborhoods in which the actual rate was much less than the predicted rate are termed low risk. For example, one pair of such neighborhoods had 72% of their families in the low-income category, but the first had a rate of child maltreatment eight times that of the second: 130 per 1000 versus 16 per 1000 families (Garbarino & Sherman, 1980). Interviews with expert informants, ranging from elementary school principals to mail carriers, were used to develop profiles of the two neighborhoods. Samples of families were drawn from each neighborhood and interviews were conducted to identify stresses and supports, with special emphasis on sources of help, social networks, evaluation of the neighborhood, and use of formal family support systems. Table 8.1 presents some of the results.

As shown in Table 8.1, families in the high-risk neighborhood, though socioeconomically similar to families in the low-risk neighborhood, reported less positive evaluations of the neighborhood as a context for child and family development. Furthermore, they revealed a general pattern of "social impoverishment" in comparison with families in the low-risk neighborhood. These findings lend support to the assertion that there are neighborhood effects related to child maltreatment, and studies exploring this pattern further (Garbarino & Kostelny, 1991a,b) extend these findings (e.g., to show the effects of local politicians, hospital closings, and effective family support programs).

The approach used in these neighborhood studies represents, along with geocoding, social area analysis, and the DIPOV Index, an addi-

Table 8.1. Illustrative Data Comparing Families in Two Neighborhoods

	Low-Risk Neighborhood (21 families)	High-Risk Neighborhood (20 families)
1. Percent of school-age children cared for by parents in after-school hours	86%	25%
2. Percent of those interviewed who never engage in neighborhood exchanges	8%	32%
3. Percent of children for whom neighborhood children regularly serve as playmates	86%	40%
4. Average number of people mothers name as taking an interest in their child's welfare	5.3	4.1
5. Mean score on Holmes–Rahe Social Readjustment Scale (200+ indicates moderate or major crisis)	166	258
6. Average rating by mothers of neighborhood as a place to raise children (−4 to +4).	1.66	.09

Note: All differences are significant at *p* less than .05. After Garbarino and Sherman (1980).

tional method of analyzing community effects on families and children. These and other ecologically oriented research techniques enable us to document in greater detail the relationships between various community characteristics and the well-being of residents. With enhanced understanding of these connections, we can identify community attributes that are most closely related to the quality of life for families and spot areas that may be high-risk places for children. This will enable us to act more effectively in minimizing the risks and maximizing the opportunities presented to the developing child by the territory of childhood. This leads us to consider the nature and structure of human services, and that is the topic of our next chapter.

RESEARCH CAPSULE

The importance of the environmental context and its effects on family functioning have been explored in this book. One of the aspects of the environment that deserves mention is density. Density usually refers to the number of individuals per unit of space. However, various indices of density also include the number of rooms per house, the number of houses per acre, and so on. Galle, Gove, and McPherson (1972) found that of the above indices, the number of persons per room best predicted rates of social pathology. As the number of persons increased, so did mortality, juvenile delinquency, and public assistance rates. Lower cognitive development is also associated with a large number of persons per room (Wachs, Uzgiris, & Hunt, 1971). In a review of residential density and child development, van Vliet (1985) concluded that there appears to be a relationship between crowded households, on the one hand, and behavior problems and maladjustment in children, on the other. The environmental impact of density on the child seems to be such that too much social stimulation may be harmful to adequate development.

Wohlwill (1983) noted that the existing research on density points to a greater effect of density on children than adults. He hypothesized that adults have learned to adapt to adverse living conditions, but children have not had the experience or opportunity to know how best to fit in with their surroundings. One of the variables that may affect the family's adjustment to dense households is housing preference (Booth, 1983). For those families who prefer to live in close quarters, there may not be any stress associated with that situation. This suggests there is a strong cultural component to the "developmental psychology" of density.

In those cases where families would prefer to live in a less crowded household but have little choice in the matter, stress in the family and in the parent–child relationship may be experienced. Poor families may be most at risk, as they do not have the economic resources to be able to make a choice in housing. Research on density needs to examine more fully the relationship between poverty, density, and adjustment to density levels.

Density is clearly an important issue that needs further research. It has implications for policies concerning housing, land use, and population distribution (Booth, 1983). Planners can use information on density to guide their decisions in ways that improve the social environment of children through their physical environment. Social welfare agencies, schools, and other human services can also benefit from research on density, as all are involved in serving the needs of families.

PRACTICE CAPSULE

Pancoast (1980) and Collins (1980) have developed a community-based preventive program aimed at strengthening support systems in neighborhoods to reduce the risk of child maltreatment. They call their approach "the neighborhood consulting model," so termed because of the importance of consultation to central figures or adults who are "free from drain" in the natural helping network of a community. Generally, a community agency supports a consultant whose role it is to become knowledgeable about the supportive networks within a given community, gather information about the central figures in the network (those members of the neighborhood who serve as informal helpers through their frequent contact with families, e.g., school personnel, merchants, or the local busybody), establish rapport with the central figures, and serve as a consultant to the central figures through listening, empathizing, and giving support, information, and advice.

From the initial attempt to identify a neighborhood that has a high risk of child maltreatment to identifying those people who are central figures and to finally establishing trusting relationships with central figures, the process takes many months. After achieving these goals, the consultant regularly meets with each central figure and listens to his or her concerns about families in the neighborhood. The consultant, through contact with the central figure, is able to influence families at risk. Reporting neglect and abuse cases can be encouraged, particularly when children are in dangerous situations. Information about healthy childrearing attitudes and practices can filter down to the parents, suggestions for referrals to local human service agencies can occur, and strategies for involving isolated families in a social network can emerge. The consultant's precise goals will vary from neighborhood to neighborhood, across different informal helping networks and involved families.

The strengths of this consultation model are that it takes advantage of the support systems that already do exist, it minimizes professional interference into family lives, and reaches families in a cost-efficient manner. This model has exciting possibilities as an approach for dealing with child maltreatment (Garbarino & Kostelny, 1991a). The U.S. Advisory Committee on Child Abuse and Neglect has gone on record supporting it as a strategy.

FOR FURTHER READING

Fandetti, D. V. (1978). Ethnicity and neighborhood services. In D. Thursz & J. L. Vigilante. *Reaching people: The structure of neighborhood services.* Beverly Hills: Sage, 15 pp.

Stressing the pluralism of our communities, Fandetti explores the relationships between ethnicity, social class, and the emotional significance ascribed to one's neighborhood. Discussing implications for service delivery strategies, he suggests that programs can build on neighborhood attachment by affiliating with local places and institutions and by strengthening traditional mechanisms of assistance, such as families and churches.

Garbarino, J., Dubrow, N., Kostelny, K., & Pardo, C. (1992). *Children in danger: Coping with the consequences of community violence.* San Francisco: Jossey-Bass.

This book deals with the problems faced by children in high-crime, inner city neighborhoods plagued by chronic community violence. It focuses on the crucial role of adults in buffering the stress and in interpreting the experience of young children who encounter urban violence on the streets as well as in their homes.

Jacobs, J. (1961). *The death and life of great American cities.* New York: Vintage, 458 pp.

Jacobs presents a lively analysis of the workings of city neighborhoods from the perspective of their residents, including their youngest residents, the children. She disputes much "common wisdom" about what makes successful neighborhoods. The importance of an active sidewalk life is a recurring theme. Implications for city planning are presented.

Keller, S. (1968). *The urban neighborhood: A sociological perspective.* New York: Random House, 201 pp.

Neighborhoods, neighbors, and neighboring in the urban setting are addressed as distinct, but related, phenomena in this readable classic. Keller charts many of the changes occurring in these phenomena as cities, families, and the general social order change over time. She finds that increased heterogeneity in urban neighborhoods, less dependence of families on their environments, and more impersonal forms of social control lessen the traditional importance of neighborhoods.

Michelson, W., Levine, S. V., & Michelson, E. (Eds.) (1979). *The child in the city: Today and Tomorrow.* Toronto: University of Toronto Press, 272 pp.

The situation of the child in the metropolis is discussed in chapters by scholars representing history, law, social welfare, medicine, developmental psychology, and sociology. The companion volume by W. Michelson, S. V. Levine, and A. R. Spina, (1979) *The child in the city: Changes and challenges* (520 pages), contains discussions of specific urban-child issues such as community services, the adolescent in the city, and ethnic diversity and children.

Stack, C. (1974). *All our kin: Strategies for survival in a black community.* New York: Harper & Row, 175 pp.

This is a white participant-observer's vivid account of the resilient support networks operating in a poverty-stricken black neighborhood and the elaborate rules and protocols governing network functioning. She shows how the effects of severe economic impoverishment are mitigated by active social networks that provide some reasonable assurance of survival.

Warren, R. L. (1973). The community's vertical pattern: Ties to the larger society and culture (and) The community's horizontal pattern: The relation of local units to each other. In R. L. Warren, *The community in America* (2nd ed.). Chicago: Rand McNally, 65 pp.

In these two chapters, Warren presents the concepts of the vertical and horizontal ties of a community and discusses different types of ties and their influences on communities. A useful perspective on closed versus open communities and local versus extra-local demands and standards that can help to explain how and why some communities are more responsive to their residents' needs than others.

Wynne, E. (1977). *Growing up suburban.* Austin: University of Texas Press, 236 pp.

Wynne clearly and concisely addresses issues associated with suburban children and parents, and focuses on the school and community as settings that can facilitate the child's development. The fundamental assumption is that life in suburbia may not be ideal for the development of the child. Suggestions for improvement include fostering better community–school relations, selecting teachers with affective skills, and increasing the diversity and residential stability of the community.

QUESTIONS FOR THOUGHT

1.   We have presented evidence that communities differ in their effects on families. Unemployment rates, local economy, and social density are but a few of the factors that affect family functioning. What other factors can you think of that could have effects on families as a result of different communities?

2.   The chapter suggested that social density (the variety and number of roles in a community) affects the development and experiences of children. Are children better off in a large city with people of all ages, professions, and nationalities or in a small town where there are a limited number of roles to be observed? Be sure to take into account other aspects of a community that affect

child development (e.g., number of people, amount of social contact). What are the tradeoffs?

3. Imagine yourself as a member of a local government that is receiving pressure from the state to allow a major highway to be built through a section of town. The highway, if approved, will disrupt a close-knit neighborhood consisting of many families with small children. If you vote for the highway, what policy would you adopt toward relocation of those families? If you vote against it, explain the reasons for your choice.

4. The lack of availability of day care for children while parents are working presents difficulties to parents. Suppose that you are the president of a large factory and have the power to make decisions regarding the implementation of on-site day-care facilities and/or support for parents who wish to use community day-care facilities. Draw up reasonable plans of action that would allow parents the comfort of working without having to worry about the safety and care of their children.

5. In examining the influence of informal support systems on the welfare of families, we have found that neighbors serve several important functions. Describe five stressful situations that families might encounter and give examples of ways in which neighbors could help.

6. We have looked at infant mortality, juvenile delinquency, teenage pregnancy, and child maltreatment as indices of social pathology in a community. What other indices can you think of that might be useful in pointing out community variation in social pathology? After you have identified other indices, describe what you could do to improve situations in a community that does indicate high levels of such social pathology.

7. The importance of the home–school relationship cannot be overemphasized. Think about ways in which parents could be convinced to become more a part of the school and community. Describe the effects that such involvement might have on parents and their children.

9

Developmental Issues
in the Human Services

James Garbarino and Florence N. Long

Margaret W. is a divorced parent with 3 children, ages 10, 5, and 2. The 5-year-old was born prematurely and has speech and hearing defects. His kindergarten teacher told Margaret that he is a slow learner; speech therapy and a hearing aid would help him. Margaret's ex-husband's alimony payments are often late, if they arrive at all.

Margaret works from 10:00 A.M. to 4:00 P.M. in a school cafeteria, where she earns the minimum wage. She leaves the 2-year-old and the kindergartner with a neighbor who goes to work at 2:30. By then, the 10-year-old is home to care for the younger children. Susan complains that it's not fair that she has to stay home with her brothers while her friends can play after school.

Margaret's father had a mild stroke several weeks ago. She would like him to live with her so he could watch after the kids. But she doesn't have room in her apartment; Medicaid would pay for him to go into a nursing home, but it won't pay the rent for a larger apartment.

Margaret W. represents a common situation in the United States today—families who are scraping by on their own in less than optimal
conditions. Her family could benefit from many social services: day care,
therapeutic services for the 5-year-old, housing assistance, legal assistance
to secure alimony. Perhaps Margaret W. lives in a community where these
services are available, but she is not aware of them or not eligible because
her marginal income disqualifies her.

In this chapter, we examine dimensions of the human ecology that
influence how human services are delivered. We will explore the historical
roots of social services in the United States and consider the ideological
bases for these services. We will discuss some of the issues involved in
delivering services that meet the developmental needs of children and
families. Finally, we will present examples of human services that we feel
are meeting these needs.

Concepts of Helping

The term "human services" encompasses a broad range of activities,
programs, and agencies designed to meet the physical, intellectual, and
social–emotional needs of individuals and families. These services are
encountered primarily in microsystems (e.g., dyadic counseling) or
mesosystems (e.g., referral or liaison between agencies). Community
services, on the other hand, are those that directly address larger social
forces—for example, controlling crime or building sanitation facilities.
They are thus mainly found in exosystems (with respect to children).
Many services fall somewhere between the extremes of direct service to
individuals and indirect service through management of the physical
and social environment. Both human and community services can deal
with a wide range of life domains: education, mental and physical
health, safety and sanitation, religion, transportation, housing, employment, legal services, and recreation (Urban & Vondracek, 1977). Not
all of us do, or will ever, require some of these services: mental health
services, unemployment benefits, or the medical care of a coronary re-
suscitation unit. But all of us use some of them, at one time or another.
And one measure of the quality of our community is whether it comes
fully equipped with human services.

We can classify human services on the following dimensions:

1. *Timing:* Do they aim to prevent a problem from occurring or to
   repair it after it occurs? Do they address families before risk factors
   are present or only after they are evident?
2. *Goals:* Do they seek to minimize negative factors or to optimize

positive factors; are they oriented to reducing risks or increasing opportunities?

3. *Scope:* Are they single purpose or comprehensive?

Beyond these three dimensions, there are others. Human services can be offered directly (e.g., education) or indirectly (e.g., guarantees for banks to offer mortgages for restoring dilapidated homes). They are public (e.g., Aid to Families with Dependent Children), private non-profit (e.g., the March of Dimes), or private for-profit (e.g., a child care center run as a profit-making business). Human services can also be formal and bureaucratically created or informal and spontaneously occurring. The formal services include all those offered by federal, state, and local government agencies as well as programs, voluntary organizations, and private groups and institutions officially recognized as providers of support to children and families. By "informal" we mean the activities of those systems that we discussed in Chapters 2, 4, and 8—families, friends, neighborhoods, and other social connections (cf. Whittaker, Garbarino, & Associates, 1984).

These informal connections or support systems provide both tangible and intangible services: child care exchanges between neighbors (Unger & Powell, 1980), for instance, or emotional support after the loss of a family member (Caine, 1974). Most of us turn for help to our informal support systems far more quickly and more frequently than we look to the formal helping services (Gottlieb, 1980). For many of us, the informal support systems are a natural part of our daily lives, and, therefore, we do not often recognize their role as "human services." We take them for granted, whether we give or receive them. But for others, these supports are lacking. The lives of these individuals may be less successful and satisfying because of the absence of support. What is more, this lack may be related to the "distancing" interpersonal style of the parents as much as it is to the quality of the informal support systems (Gaudin & Polansky, 1985).

Our lives would be significantly less satisfying without the feedback, nurturance, and guidance we receive from our support systems. Earlier chapters suggested some ways to meet this need. Later in this chapter, we will develop further the notion of informal support systems as helping services.

Social services can be described on several dimensions that relate to the goals of intervention. In this discussion, we describe the end points of these dimensions, recognizing that actual service delivery often falls between the extremes. The first dimension concerns whether one seeks to *minimize* negative outcomes or *optimize* positive ones. Minimizing interventions start with an individual or family who is perceived as malfunctioning or functioning inadequately. Thus, the client must step over an invisible line of failure or inadequacy before service begins. Even then, the intervention offers only those services necessary to bring the individual or family back across the threshold to an acceptable level of functioning. For instance, families receive financial support from most public assistance programs when their incomes fall below a prespecified criterion set at the lower end of the continuum of economic adequacy. Once they reach the defined level of adequacy, the program disengages from them.

We find a particularly graphic example of this in the Special Supplemental Food Program for Women, Infants and Children (WIC), which offers food supplements for pregnant women and children up to 5 years of age. Need is determined jointly by income and by the child's nutritional status and placement outside an acceptable range on a growth curve (measuring height and weight by age). When children enter the acceptable growth range, they are dropped from the program. The subsequent loss of food supplements may mean that the family will have difficulty continuing to provide fully nutritious meals to the child. Thus, a minimal approach to the delivery of social services may leave many families functioning marginally, just over the threshold of need, or may result in families bouncing in and out of the eligible range, over and over again.

Those who advocate the minimizing approach make several assumptions (Berger & Neuhaus, 1977; Kadushin, 1978). First, they see individual or family functioning as being on a continuum, and assume that we can determine a critical point beyond which conditions are inadequate or maladaptive. Second, advocates of minimal intervention usually argue that we have limited resources for intervention but many people in need of services. Therefore, we can guarantee minimum services only to those beyond the critical point, for whom intervention is clearly needed. Finally, they argue that although we do not know how to optimize development, we do know how to remedy dysfunction. When these four points are put together, they justify a human services safety net to catch individuals who fall out of acceptable social and economic patterns, a net that releases them once they bounce back into the normal range.

In contrast to this, the optimization position advocates efforts to maximize an individual's or a family's potential to achieve the best possible outcome—for that individual or family. Although advocates of optimization agree that resources are limited, they argue that these resources are well spent in pursuing optimal functioning for all families rather than targeting specific problems when they occur. (This implies a prevention approach that we will discuss later in more detail.) Those who favor an optimizing approach believe that we *do* know enough to intervene to facilitate development in some ways, and that a positive approach will have greater long-term payoffs than a minimizing approach. Thus, for example, they may argue for expanding protective services to ever wider domains of family relations rather than limiting coverage to the families exhibiting life-threatening abuse.

The philosophy of optimization motivated enactment of Public Law 94-192, the Education for All Handicapped Children Act of 1975. This federal law called for integrating handicapped children into settings as nearly like those of nonhandicapped children as possible. Thus, for instance, it provided that handicapped children be allowed to live in homes or homelike environments instead of institutions, attend regular school classrooms for as many activities as possible, have access to public transportation and buildings, and have the recreational experiences that other children have, such as field trips and sports. In the years since its enactment, this law has been expanded and refined in many ways. It has come to serve as an important foundation for improving human services for a broad range of children at risk. This is an example of optimizing the at-risk child's experience to produce the best possible quality of life and the best possible developmental outcome for the child.

This minimization–optimization distinction is insufficient by itself. We also need to consider whether services address the whole child or whole family rather than just one narrow aspect or problem. Services that deal with only one aspect of the client's life are called categorical. For instance, an agency that arranges foster placements for abused children takes a categorical approach to child abuse. Another agency may provide emergency child care, accompanied by counseling to the abusing parent and abused child, and social services required to reduce the family stresses that may have contributed to the abuse. A preschool intervention program may seek only to optimize cognitive development, or it may seek to increase general social and intellectual competence of children while also addressing nutritional and financial issues.

The latter agency in each example is taking a more comprehensive or generic view of the client's situation. In other words, a comprehensive service approach takes into account several influential systems in the client's life. The intervention may focus on multiple aspects of the individual, as in a comprehensive health program that considers both mental and physical well-being. We can also consider systems on several

ecological levels, as in a child abuse prevention program that incorporates individual counseling, family social services, and a community
awareness campaign.

Although some (e.g., Kadushin, 1978) argue that comprehensive approaches are too costly to be feasible, others believe that categorical
problem-oriented service delivery tends to fragment people's lives, and
ultimately to dilute overall effectiveness. Think of the family that must
go to one office for food stamps, another office for infant food supplements, and yet another office to arrange for meals on wheels. The categorical approach can also lead to inefficient duplication of services and
removing people from service rosters if they no longer meet the categorical requirements, but are still in need. The sum of the family's problems may put them in real need while no single problem does. A categorical approach also leads to focusing on problems outside the context
of total family functioning. Comprehensive approaches to services are
often termed unrealistic because of fiscal restraints, and most social
service agencies make efforts to refer their clients to all necessary services. However, having an understanding of how mesosystems affect
individual development may help us avoid fragmentation of clients'
needs.

Another dimension of service delivery to consider is *when* services will
be delivered: that is, whether they prevent or remediate problems. The
goal of preventive programs is to reduce the incidence of a problem (the
number of new occurrences) or even to promote positive outcomes.
Remediation, on the other hand, seeks to fix problem behavior or characteristics. Prevention can aim at reducing negative events or facilitating
desirable ones. The preventive–remediation dimension of service delivery can be distinguished from the optimizing–minimizing dimension on
the basis that the first has to do with the *timing* of intervention, whereas
the latter is related to the *goals* of intervention. Using another example,
one of the debates in the study of child abuse is whether to prevent
abuse by attacking the known risk factors (a preventive and minimizing
approach) or by building up the positive styles of family life thought to
be incompatible with maltreatment (a preventive and optimizing approach).

Many examples of prevention come from the field of public health:
innoculation against disease, introducing fluoride in drinking water,
sanitary control of water and food, educational campaigns to encourage
physical fitness or discourage smoking. In the area of social services, it is
more difficult to specify what is necessary to prevent negative outcomes.
Causes of physical illness are often easier to define and eliminate than
causes of poverty, instability, or family disruption. This is one reason
why many people opt for remedial approaches to social services.

Staulcup (1980) has described two models of preventive intervention. The first involves external control of individual behavior. For instance, laws are passed to prevent speeding on the highway or smoking in public places. These are measures taken in the name of public welfare and enforced through the state's police power and citizen initiative. Internal control models, on the other hand, provide individuals with information to guide their decisions and to encourage them to act in a manner that will have positive outcomes. For instance, parent-education courses teach parents how to establish positive relationships with their children and public-education campaigns educate adolescents about the dangers of drug use. But the responsibility to implement the knowledge, in each case, rests on the individual.

A related distinction comes from efforts to prevent childhood injuries. A passive control is one in which the individual need do only one thing, once, to achieve protection—such as install air bags in a car that work automatically. An active control requires constant behavior—such as fastening seat belts each time one drives the car.

Because of the difficulties involved in specifying desirable outcomes in social welfare, American ideology about independence and private responsibility, and the problems in defining the methods for achieving these outcomes, most service delivery relies on a remedial model. Where prevention is the goal, it is most often what Caplan and others call secondary prevention. Secondary prevention occurs when one has identified a group of high-risk people and seeks to prevent that high-risk status from being translated into occurrence of the problem itself. This is distinguished from primary prevention (preventing the problem by preventing the conditions that produce risk) and tertiary prevention (preventing the problem from recurring). Thus, delivering treatment to a parent who has abused a child is remedial, or tertiary prevention. Identifying families at risk for abuse and offering them services to reduce this risk is secondary prevention. Promoting nonviolent and emotionally supportive childrearing is considered primary prevention for child abuse.

The remedial and preventive approaches have very different implications for how, when, and to whom we deliver services. The remedial approach is typically applied on a case-by-case basis. Intervention occurs when a problem arises. Often this leads us to cure symptoms rather than causes. For instance, we treat poverty-stricken individuals by offering individual solutions (welfare) rather than seeking societal changes that will eliminate poverty (Ryan, 1976). This remedial perspective views the client as incapable of solving his or her own problems. Thus, the state is justified in assuming the role of surrogate caregiver because the family cannot adequately care for itself. This view sees social problems as the result of individual failures, rather than social misdirection. As we will see in the historical development of the human services, these orientations have their basis in the sociopolitical climate of our society.

Preventive models can also offer solutions based on attempts to change individuals. This is especially true when problems in development can be prevented by educating the public or providing adaptive behavioral skills. By taking the preventive focus over a remedial approach, however, we are more likely to seek the responsibility for family disruption in larger social forces over which individuals have little control. These forces affect everyone, not just the relatively few who fall victim to them. Promoting individual welfare becomes a legitimate concern of the state to help individuals gather resources that may otherwise be unequally distributed (Moroney, 1980). Because a strategy of optimizing outcomes also requires looking into the future, preventive approaches and optimizing approaches often, but not always, join hands in intervention. One example of this is found in innoculation programs for childhood disease. Innoculations prevent illness and promote good health.

The debate over where we put our money is crucial to the debate between advocates of remedial and preventive intervention. Proponents of remedial approaches argue that because we have limited funds we must treat the most serious cases first (and the advocates of minimal intervention would add "only"). Some would go even further, to argue that some cases are so dysfunctional as to be hopeless. Any investment in these cases is wasted, they argue. Thus, they believe we must undertake a process of "triage" to identify those in greatest need who are not beyond help. This does not leave any room for prevention. Besides, they argue, why spend money on unproven preventive strategies when we know what works in crises?

Those who argue for prevention counter with the proposition that funds invested in prevention will reduce or eliminate the vast expenditures incurred in intervening after the fact and are thus more cost effective. If we strengthen teeth—or families—now, we will not have to clean up dental—or social—decay later. A related point of view argues that if we remove obstacles to effective and powerful family functioning, families will provide services that otherwise the state would have to provide. It is more costly for the state to provide these services than for the family to do so.

In 1988, Lisbeth Shorr published a book entitled *Within Our Reach.* In it she marshalled an impressive array of evidence in support of the proposition that we as a professional community know what works to prevent problems of family functioning and child development. She cited numerous examples of successful programs that are cost effective. Her book became required reading for students of human services. However, even friendly critics have acknowledged that these programmatic efforts do not really address the structural inequalities and other macrosystem problems that generate such large numbers of high-risk children and families (Halpern, 1991).

Unfortunately, limited financial and staff resources mean that we cannot always provide a service to all. In the event of limited resources, we must take two steps: (1) define the population most likely to suffer from the problem and (2) evaluate the net gain to be achieved from the intervention. We can approach this second task in two ways. The first is cost–benefit analysis: measuring the estimated benefits of the intervention in comparison to its costs. For instance, suppose the cost of arresting, trying, providing child welfare services (e.g., foster care), and incarcerating drug-abusing mothers for future offenses, if they are not rehabilitated, is estimated at $2,000,000, and a program to rehabilitate these mothers costs $1,000,000. Thus, the rehabilitation program has a cost–benefit ratio of 2:1—it would cost half as much in the long run to intervene than not to rehabilitate drug-abusing mothers.

The second way to assess the economic feasibility of intervention is to look at its *cost effectiveness* in comparison to other means of achieving the same end. For instance, suppose we want to reduce the rate of juvenile delinquency in our community. Three approaches have been proposed, all with equal likelihood for success; that is, each will reduce juvenile delinquency among the youth who participate in it by the same amount.

	Approach	*Cost*
1.	A community center for all young people, with meeting rooms and recreational equipment.	$500,000
2.	A psychiatric therapy program unit serving 20 troubled youth.	$200,000
3.	A program coordinated between schools and churches to provide after-school athletics and community service employment.	$100,000

If cost effectiveness is the basis for decision making, the last option would be most likely to be chosen since it is the least costly as well as the one that would reach a large number of adolescents. It has the additional advantage of working from agencies and resources that are already available. Of course, if other considerations rule (such as the interests of investors in psychiatric services) the second option might win out.

In choosing between preventive and remedial approaches, the economic feasibility of a program must be considered along with its short- and long-term consequences. We must also consider who will be most likely to benefit from the intervention. Our inability to predict who will develop a particular problem often limits the usefulness of prevention. Although we would often prefer to advocate the preventive approach, the optimal means of husbanding our resources to meet the most pressing needs of the target population may require a remedial approach. This is especially true when successful treatment methods have been developed, but the effectiveness of preventive approaches is not yet clear, as would be the case in our example if the success of each program is undemonstrated.

Another dimension of service delivery relates to one's view of the roles of client and provider. The medical or corrective model views the client as having something wrong that a professional intervener can fix with his or her skills. This model has also been labeled an "illness" or "pathology" model since the client needs an expert "cure." For instance, an individual seeking psychotherapy because of a personal problem is "cured" by the psychiatrist, social worker, or psychologist who helps the person overcome the problem. This approach empowers the helper and casts the client as being incapable of solving her or his own problem. This model can also be applied to families. Some professionals view families as causes of their client's problems or as impediments to the delivery of services. An example of this is found in theories attributing schizophrenia to unhealthy family dynamics. And sometimes such a model is an accurate portrayal of reality. But it is rarely complete.

In the collaborative model, on the other hand, the client and professional share resources and competence (Moroney, 1980). The helper may have some skills that the client lacks in defining problems, resolving conflicts, or locating services, but there is no assumption that the client is helpless. The helper assists in defining the client's needs and assists the client in identifying and locating the resources or support systems that can fill those needs. The distinction between counseling (clients) and therapy (patients) reflects the important distinction between a situation where two parties have nearly equal status and share resources (counselling) versus a situation where a competent resource-rich party helps an incompetent, resource-impoverished party (therapy). Self-help groups such as Parents Anonymous, contrast with psychotherapy on this dimension.

There are situations where each model (the corrective or the collaborative) is appropriate. In certain families, where a coercive style of family interaction has developed, the most fruitful solution may be to teach the parents and children to interact with each other in a positive manner. In other words, the corrective model would replace inappropriate behaviors with acceptable ones. In a single-parent family, where the parent feels isolated and unable to cope with childrearing difficulties, bringing the parent together with a support group of other single parents and providing relief from child-care responsibilities may solve the problem. In some families, both corrective and collaborative approaches may be necessary to reduce the family's stress. For instance, a physical therapist can work with a handicapped child and train the parent to take over the treatment. These viewpoints have a major influence on how the professional interacts with clients.

One final concept relevant to human-service delivery that we will consider here is enhancement. Enhancing interventions aim to increase competence in dealing with future life events by using knowledge and skills to solve problems. During a major personal event such as acquiring a new job, for instance, an enhancing intervention would help the individual to marshal resources and skills developed from previous transitional experiences. Enhancing interventions pinpoint skills needed to pass critical life events adaptively and ensure that the individual learns these skills so that they will be available in similar future situations (Danish, Smyer, & Nowak, 1980). For example, one might teach teenagers techniques for nonviolent conflict resolution as the basis for improving future conjugal and parent–child relationships (Garbarino & Jacobson, 1978; Garbarino, Schellenbach, Sebes, & Associates, 1986).

Any human-service program must consider several issues. First, we need to define the desired outcomes. Second, we need to define the steps to achieve these outcomes. This may involve changing individual characteristics or interpersonal behavior (microsystem), providing resources or creating support systems (meso- and exosystem), or even advocating social change (exo- and macrosystem). Third, we have to decide at which of these levels we can intervene most effectively. The history of human services reveals these issues in action, and shows how the United States has emphasized categorical and remedial approaches at the individual or microsystem levels.

The History of the Human Services

Several philosophical and political trends have contributed to the development of helping services in the United States. As we shall see,

economic concerns have motivated our desire to help as frequently as
has humanitarian inspiration. In the long run, the former may be more
persuasive than the latter. Our hope, of course, is that these two interests will be congruent rather than discrepant.

Historically, families have provided many of the resources we now
consider the domain of social services. A rural subsistence economy
provided the means for most families to provide for themselves. When a
family could not support itself, relatives usually helped out. Orphans
and the elderly were absorbed into the extended family and community.
When an extended family network was not available, neighbors, church
congregations, or charitable groups stepped in. In other words, "social
services" were provided by the family's informal support systems. This
"system" was based on low expectations for personal growth and development, but did function to meet those low expectations.

During the early 1800s both government and voluntary agencies
began providing services to children and families. Two major social
changes provided impetus to this rise of *formal* services. The growth of
the cities, as a consequence of industrialization, created larger numbers
of families who suffered from poverty and disruption of their life-styles.
Cut off from many traditional sources of social support, and the subsistence agrarian economy, they faced the multiple pressures of urban life,
factory work, and adaptation to a new culture. All three contributed to
family disorganization. Informal helping networks were disrupted by
increased geographic mobility of families, leaving many children and
adults isolated without traditional sources of assistance. Loss of cohesive primary groups also weakened previously powerful mechanisms
of informal social control. Formal social services were devised and supported to counteract these effects.

Charitable care for families stemmed from a humanitarian desire to
care for the unfortunate, and from a political concern for antisocial behavior. Social agencies intervened in an effort to reduce the likelihood
that indigent children would become delinquent or a permanent social
burden. Two types of services developed from this goal. Institutional
care for children developed out of the philosophy that the community
has the right and an obligation to intervene when the family does not or
cannot properly support children or monitor their behavior. In addition,
as industries sought to expand their work forces they drew greater numbers of women to work outside the home. In service to this, day-care
nurseries were established to meet the child-care needs of working
mothers. Thus, nurturance and control—often in service to economic
goals—were themes that arose early in the history of human services
and remain issues to this day, particularly in the United States.

The second major impetus for child and family services derived from the goal of universal education. Once again, economic forces underlay social reform. Education became widespread in an effort to prepare people for productive roles in industry and to integrate immigrant populations (Greer, 1972). Public education also removed children from the labor market and provided daytime supervision for them. Both of these activities improved employment opportunities for parents, especially mothers. Compulsory education also had a socializing effect on immigrant children, teaching them how to be "good Americans." Social reformers saw the schools as a means for providing the literate public required to run a democratic country. Today, some see this as a humanitarian enterprise. Others see it as a kind of conspiracy to downplay ethnic diversity and control deviants through a process of homogenization.

The social philosophy of the 1800s and the early 1900s contained two opposing trends that help illuminate the control-nurturance issue. The first is represented by the doctrine of Social Darwinism: social philosophers broadened concepts of biological evolution to justify a view of society being ruled by the principle of "survival of the fittest." That is, those who are not able to fend for themselves will drop out, and those who are more skilled, competent, and fit will succeed in providing for their own needs. This philosophy supported an attitude of "hands off" or *laissez-faire* toward social problems. It also fit well with the American tradition of individualism and pulling oneself up "by the bootstraps."

On the other hand, American ideals include an emphasis on equality and fairness that extends to economic as well as political rights. The struggle to implement this value tells much of the American story. Despite the rhetoric and the real progress our society has made toward offering equal opportunity, major inequalities remain. Equality is supposed to go hand in hand with opportunity, although differences in outcome are a natural consequence of differences in individual capacity to capitalize on opportunity. Social reformers have sought ways to provide materials and skills that will equalize the opportunities of the less fortunate. These efforts have met with only limited success. The struggle to determine who will control the content and direction of the American macrosystem continues.

In their provocative history of the helping services, Levine and Levine (1970) showed that the orientation of the helping services fluctuates with the political mood of society. Thus, when the climate is conservative, the majority emphasize social order. Social problems are treated as failures of the individual rather than as qualities of society. When society enters a reformist period, people are more likely to seek solutions to social problems by changing social structures and institutions. During the late 1800s, the Depression years (1930s), and the Decade of the Great Society (1960s), concerned groups attempted to institute progressive social change. During the intervening periods, the climate was more conservative, and a focus on changing individuals predominated. The 1980s—the "Reagan Years"—was such a period.

Charity

Social services had their beginnings in the voluntary, charitable organizations that began to flourish in the late nineteenth century. These charities typically had a neighborhood base and emphasized meeting the survival needs of families through employment rather than alms (Kahn, 1976). Levine and Levine (1970) provided examples of settlement-house workers who lived in poor neighborhoods and got to know the problems of the families surrounding them. They would visit and care for the elderly and ill, give their sewing or laundry to a widow who had no means of support, or facilitate support arrangements between families. Church charities operated in a similar manner—identifying the needs of the local congregation.

Originally, social services were delivered to remediate problems or correct deficiencies. One problem that was addressed within this framework was the problem of child maltreatment. In the late nineteenth century private agencies arose to rescue children exposed to severe abuse and neglect—much as other "humane societies" had arisen to protect mistreated animals. The case of Mary Ellen—a little girl in New York City—served as an impetus for this movement. Intervention to save her from the severe mistreatment inflicted on her led to a national outcry and a corresponding philanthropic response. Mary Ellen became a symbol for child protective services, and still serves that function a century later. At the turn of the century, social workers began to recognize the value of preventive intervention (Ford, 1974). The first White House Conference on Children was a meeting of social workers concerned with the care of dependent children (Proceedings of the Conference on the Care of Dependent Children, 1909). They asserted that the public should take responsibility not only for children who were potentially delinquent, but also for children who were simply unfortunate—the worthy poor. The conference participants concluded that a solid home life was the basis for good character development. They recommended that income supports be given to parents

> of worthy character, suffering from temporary misfortune, and children of reasonably efficient and deserving mothers who are without the support of the normal breadwinner . . . such aid being given as may be necessary to maintain suitable homes. (p. 17)

Their recommendations set the precedent for the later Aid to Dependent Children programs. By 1935 Title V of the Social Security Act created Child Welfare Services and Aid to Dependent Children programs (now Aid to Families with Dependent Children) in every state.

In the 1930s and 1940s, as social service became a "profession," service agents moved out of the neighborhoods into centrally located bureaucracies. These agencies continued to deal with the same sorts of problems: meeting the needs of dependent children and adults, employment referrals, adjustment of probationers and parolees, placing the mentally disabled. With the rise in popularity of psychotherapy, professional expertise became valued; expert diagnosis and treatment of problems were demanded.

After World War II, delinquency became a major concern of social service professionals. Delinquency was linked to "multiproblem families," a small number (6–8%) of families who consumed over half the social services provided in urban areas. These problems brought case workers back to the neighborhood in intensive efforts to gain insight into delinquency and other social problems of the slum. The street worker of the 1950s developed into the "grass roots" organizer of the 1960s. Thus, the delivery of social services had two emphases: a vast bureaucracy of impersonal services whose delivery depended on needs determined by experts, and local outreach movements that emphasized community representation, control, and action. (For a more detailed presentation of this development, see Kahn, 1976.) These themes continue in contemporary human services.

The Safety Net

The notion that we have a social responsibility to meet the needs of the underprivileged has traditionally been paired with the idea that we can step in when we believe that a child is being improperly cared for. The traditional model of service delivery has been remedial, minimal, and corrective. As a last resort, if a family needs help to meet its physical needs, service agents may define the parent as inadequate to guide or socialize children. The state's responsibility to guard the welfare of children implies a right to judge parents' skills.

In the United States, most programs are built on the belief that autonomy and independence are signs of maturity and mental health, but that dependency is a sign of failure and illness in the individual. These standards are projected to the family as well. Thus, much of our service system seems based on the premise that parents are solely responsible for raising their children, and any problems that might develop result from insufficient parental guidance and caring.

This view postulates the healthy, mature family, like the mature individual, as a self-sufficient, autonomous entity. It sees any manifestation of dependency, such as the use of problem-oriented human services, as an admission of failure or at least a sign of illness. This is especially true for the poor. Low-income families are still stigmatized by the antiquated philosophy of Social Darwinism; we are quick to label these parents as inadequate because of their economic defeats. However, current thinking about service delivery is shifting to focus on supporting family functions rather than correcting parental failure. One of the results of the "grass roots" efforts of the 1960s was the increasing emphasis on a supportive or collaborative role for professionals in working with families. This means taking a developmental perspective, identifying what families need in order to function successfully (Ford, 1974).

Kahn (1976) and Kamerman and Kahn (1976) have described a system of "personal social services" that has grown up beside the traditional case-work services for the needy. The personal social services include those supports all of us may need, regardless of income: support in socialization and development of children and adults through such programs as child care or family planning; counseling and guidance (including family problems, substance abuse, and other crises); community mental health programs such as self-help and support groups; programs guaranteeing basic life support to allow handicapped, elderly, or other incapacitated individuals to continue living in the community; and information, referral, and integration services. These services have blossomed in the past two or three decades, but they have not been well integrated with the large social-service system that focuses on case services for the needy. There is no doubt that these services are sought across the community, not only by those below a particular income level. Their expansion demonstrates that many people need and use the personal social services. However, there is much debate over whether the personal social services should be viewed as "public social utilities" to be provided to all citizens. The cost of doing so would be tremendous. Although some argue that families above a minimal income level should be able to purchase these services from the private sector, the uneven quality and availability of private services may make this unrealistic (Keniston, 1977). Kamerman and Kahn (1976) propose that we offer the personal social services to all, with clients' fees assessed on a sliding scale according to their ability to pay. Others, as we will see later in this chapter, are attempting to foster these services informally by promoting the informal helping networks that exist within communities.

We have discussed the historical development of the helping services as a result of political and philosophical influences. Contemporary human services find their focus in terms of five principles for promoting and maintaining the well-being of children and the integrity of families: (1) public education is a right of all citizens; (2) health care and sanitation are essential preventive interventions; (3) housing is a basic right; (4) full employment is a primary social and economic goal; and (5) financial and resource support should be provided to those who are deprived through misfortune. When coupled with formal and informal social supports (i.e., psychologically supportive and enhancing personal networks of friends, neighbors, relatives, and professionals), these principles make up a comprehensive range of human services, and they outline the ideological and resource allocation agenda for the coming years in American public life. The National Commission on Children set out this agenda in its 1991 report. And the political debate of that report illustrated the tough road ahead in realizing national policy and programming needed to implement it.

Issues in Human Service Delivery

We believe that optimizing the development of children and families is a valid goal of the human services. But what do we mean by "optimizing development," and how do we go about it? To answer this question, we must build on the concepts of development, opportunity, and risk presented in earlier chapters.

We believe society can sponsor intervention to improve the lives of children because we believe that we have some ideas about how children grow and that we can specify some preferred outcomes for children. We believe that the joint concepts of risk and opportunity help us specify what children need and what they cannot tolerate. And we believe that children have a basic relationship with the community (as citizens) that provides a foundation for prevention and intervention.

Developmental Influences

The human services have traditionally focused on negative influences. However, if we want to optimize development, we cannot ignore the events that present important enhancing experiences to children as they grow. We need to increase, if not ensure, the likelihood of experiencing these events. Optimization requires specification of our developmental goals for children. What are some of these goals?

1. That they develop a positive and accurate self-concept.
2. That they become socially and intellectually competent, and that they enjoy life.

3. That they grow into adults capable of providing for their own material needs and motivated to contribute to their community.
4. That they provide emotional support to others and receive it in return and that they can sustain intimate relationships.
5. That they learn the skills necessary to meet the needs of *their* children and families.

Together, these goals provide a capsule description of healthy socialization to adulthood (Garbarino & Gilliam, 1980). In Chapter 3, we discussed some of the factors that can promote these outcomes. We also pointed out some characteristics of the child's ecology that detract from her or his ability to grow and thrive. We know a great deal about what is *bad* for children. Our knowledge of what specifically is *good* for children is more limited. This lack of knowledge may exist precisely because children are flexible and adaptable and can thrive in diverse settings. In all this, we must remember, however, that children also need challenges to grow and develop well. In our search for ways to protect children from harm, we must be sure we do not deprive them of the challenges that induce growth. As always, and in nearly all things, moderation is the key. The risk of negative outcomes for children in difficult situations is reduced if they have adequate social and personal resources (Rutter, 1979). It is the accumulation of risk factors in the absence of compensatory opportunities that undermines development.

In planning, delivering, and evaluating the effects of human services, we can consider three influences on human development (Baltes & Danish, 1979). One set of influences comes from the typical, age-related experiences of most children. For example, the quality and consistency of parental care during infancy have important effects on children. Entering school has a major impact on most 5 or 6 year olds. All children need acceptance.

A second set of influences may only affect children of a particular historical period. As we saw in Chapter 3, the Depression of the 1930s had great impact on children growing up during those years through its dramatic impact on family resources and stresses (Elder, 1974). World War II did also in terms of the father absence it produced (Elder, 1980). The more subtle effects of postwar affluence and suburbanization on the socialization of youth are another example (Wynne, 1977). These events affect large groups of individuals in similar ways. And, they may affect children of different ages in different ways.

A third category of developmental influence contains those events that are more individual and unusual; that is, they are not the common experiences of most children. These events, like historical influences, can be positive or negative. Some examples of negative events that have an impact on the child's development include accident or illness and loss or incapacity of a parent. Positive events include improvement in previously unhealthy circumstances and resolution of a family conflict. As we shall see shortly, both positive and negative events can present developmentally enhancing challenges if they occur in a supportive context.

We know that a buildup of stress factors in a child's life generally bodes ill for the child's development (Rutter, 1979). The risk to the child and to the parents is greater when illness, unemployment, separation, and conflict come together. Of course some families and individuals cope better than others. Indeed, skills for handling or coping with events are a primary resource in dealing with stress affecting family members (Burgess, Garbarino, & Gilstrap, 1983). Overall, however, families and individuals can grow from dealing with stress if they experience it as a challenge. Although the details of this idea are not worked out well in existing research, it seems that children and parents will experience stress as a challenge if their primary social and psychological resources are strong. Thus, as we saw in Chapter 3, couples with strong marriages pulled together and produced stronger families when hit with the income loss produced by the Depression. Weak marriages were associated with nonproductive psychological crises for family members. Likewise, hospitalized children need not suffer serious psychological disturbances if parents remain with them, even if more than one hospitalization is required (Rutter, 1979). In our efforts to protect and enhance development, we should be careful to concentrate on maintaining basic social and psychological resources and not inappropriately seek to insulate the child from growth-inducing challenges. Human services should seek to be enabling: they should support children in meeting challenges.

This message finds expression in the following words found taped to a wall at a summer camp some years ago:

> Have you only learned lessons from those who admired you and were tender with you and stood aside for you?
> Have you not learned great lessons from those who reject you and brace themselves against you or who treat you with contempt or dispute the passage with you?

Challenge within a larger context of support is a positive influence, particularly if we take a life-course perspective. Jones (1965) and others have reported, for example, that youths who experience the stress of being either an early maturing female or a late maturing male in adolescence show signs of disruption during adolescence but in adulthood demonstrate signs of greater sensitivity, insight, flexibility, and humor.

Characteristics of the child contribute to his or her development. A positive, happy, responsive temperament may encourage significant others (parents, siblings, teachers) in a child's life to be supportive. A negativisitic, irritable, or apathetic temperament may alienate these same significant others. The child may be more or less adept at coping with disadvantages, more or less vulnerable to stress. These characteristics of the child are not always malleable. Our growing understanding of the role of the abused child in eliciting his or her own abuse demonstrates this (Kadushin & Martin, 1981). Besides abused children, some premature infants and handicapped children also appear to have characteristics that make them more difficult to care for. These characteristics can serve as cues for identifying caregivers who may need greater than average support to care for their child.

Family Effectiveness

Family and outside factors that influence the child's development have figured prominently in this book. Where one system is weak, others may meet the needs of a child for emotional support or for feelings of self-esteem. For instance, a child whose family microsystem is not emotionally supportive may receive positive feedback from teachers to compensate for what is not happening with parents. This process of systems compensating for one another is vital. However, in some instances, the family or individual is not lacking resources but instead has inappropriate means of coping or adapting. Consider the support system of a street corner gang that rewards members for vandalism, the teaching of a boy who guides his younger brother in the arts of shoplifting, or the coercive interactions of the families of aggressive boys (Patterson, 1979). Research with coercive families has shown that it is possible to replace coercive interactions with positive ones through programs of modeling and feedback (Burgess et al., 1980; Patterson, 1979). The Homebuilders program, described later in this chapter, provides another example of skill training (either to build skills that are lacking or replace inappropriate interactive styles) as a form of intervention in situations of family crisis.

Even in the most negative circumstances, we can find ways to strengthen the supports that guide the child's development by meeting basic needs. Meeting these needs sometimes requires direct intervention to supply the family with resources. In the most unfortunate situations, it requires placing the child away from the family in an alternative environment, with the hope that services may pave the way for successfully reuniting the family at an early, opportune moment. This is a drastic step, however, with many risks inherent in the separation. In most circumstances, our role should be indirect. After all, the family, not the social service system, provides the primary context for human development. The overwhelming majority of children grow up within the confines of a family (Bane, 1976). A healthy family meets its basic responsibility to bear and rear prosocial children successfully.

What are some of the ways in which families fulfill their obligations to society? In brief, an effective family is one that provides

1. A stable setting for childbearing.
2. A stable setting for childrearing.
3. A setting that reinforces prosocial behavior and the development of competence and positive self-regard.
4. A setting that provides intimacy and sexual satisfaction.
5. A setting that serves as an economic unit—for consumption and income transfers (and for production to some extent).

These functions are rooted in the evolutionary history and contemporary purposes of families (Garbarino, 1981a). Three of these obligations focus directly on the child's development; the others have indirect influence. We give the family primary responsibility for fostering the development of children. Yet the family's ability to do so depends in part on the social environment we create or tolerate around the family, in part through human services.

We believe that the notion that each family functions as a totally independent unit is in error. This notion exacts serious human costs, and we should reassess it. Specifically, the social isolation fostered within a privacy-seeking ideology can constrict the necessary functioning of kinship, neighborhood, and institutional feedback loops, rendering them inoperative (cf. Bronfenbrenner, 1975). Support systems function on the premise of exchange between members of both tangible (e.g., child care) and intangible (emotional support in a crisis) items. When individuals are hesitant to offer support, they are less likely to receive it (Unger & Powell, 1980). We are presently faced with the task of reducing the negative aspects of family privacy without incurring unacceptable costs to freedom and individuality. We are trying to have our cake and eat it too, some would say. One way to discover some strategies for accomplishing this difficult balancing act is to look at how other cultures have dealt with the problem.

Efforts to look at human services for families cross-culturally demonstrate the merit of an "activist" stance. Such an activist approach results in lower infant mortality for example. More broadly, an activist approach to human services in other countries produces a reduction in the number of multiproblem families who need specialized rehabilitative and therapeutic services. Broadly based human services that are activist in their approach can prevent risk from accumulating and thus reduce the demand for intensive and costly treatment (tertiary prevention).

Korbin (1977) reviewed cross-cultural studies of family life. She pinpointed several factors that enhance the abilities of parents to provide a supportive emotional environment for their children. The availability of multiple caregivers relieves stress on the primary caregiver and provides multiple role models for the child. Multiple caregivers serve as sources for additional positive relationships in case the parents cannot adequately meet the child's emotional needs. The primary caregiver needs not only occasional relief from caretaking responsibilities ("babysitting"), but access as well to career opportunities and support systems outside the home. Furthermore, caregivers need information about child development and behavior that can be obtained through contact with others who have reared children. Thus, both child and parent can profit from having other adults intimately involved in childrearing. In our society, where families have become isolated from traditional primary groups, we need to promote new social networks that will provide childrearing relief and support. Studies of high- and low-risk neighborhoods (see Chapter 8) may offer clues to the key factors we need to emphasize in building these networks.

This discussion may appear to have taken us far afield from the subject of the human services. But the first "service" we can provide to families is to recognize the need to go beyond remedial intervention to embrace optimizing the child's development. This does not mean that families have to do this alone. Supporting parental competence should be a major function of informal and formal support systems. This was and still is the motivation and rationale for Head Start and related programs of the Great Society era.

The Family as a Social Service

Moroney (1980) argues that the family is a social service. Taking this unorthodox view can shed some light on the proper relation of informal and formal helping. Families meet some of the basic needs of individuals and, thus, promote their well-being. Families also care for the majority of the dependent members of our society (children, the elderly, the handicapped). In the first part of this chapter, we described several dimensions of service delivery. Moroney has applied these dimensions to professionals' views of families. In some cases, the family is considered part of the client's problem. This is very common with the mentally ill. Families are perceived as obstructing the professional's ability to treat the patient and may even be accused of contributing to the cause of pathology. From another point of view, family members are considered as a resource only to the client. No thought is given to the needs of other family members. A third perspective casts the family as extenders of professionals. They carry out professionally supervised treatments. The final perspective characterizes the family as the primary care giver. Professionals exist to provide the services families need to carry out this role. From this perspective, families may need resources that professionals have, either to provide care to a member with special needs or to relieve stresses associated with the demands this care places on them.

If we view families as both responsible for rearing children and as *capable* of doing so when they have access to appropriate community supports (even as we acknowledge they are sometimes problematic), then the last perspective on service delivery is the one we must adopt. This means that our role as professionals is not primarily one of treating pathology but rather that of supporting, creating, relieving, or assisting families in their efforts to cope. These are not simply semantic differences; they reflect a basically different approach. They require that we redefine our professional roles away from a stance as "experts" toward one as "facilitators and intermediaries" (Moroney, 1980, p. 155). These differences have very real implications for where, when, and how we choose to intervene.

Redefining our professional roles as supporters of families means that we have to reconsider not only what constitutes services to families but also the most appropriate targets of intervention. Recognizing the family's role as the principal nurturer of children means that we take the focus off children and put the spotlight on *families*. Rather than focusing on developing institutions for housing handicapped children, for example, we should develop supports such as respite care, visiting homemakers, and parent-support groups for families with handicapped children. Many of these same services would reduce the necessity to remove most abused children completely from their homes. These services relieve some of the strains of constantly caring for a special child, and they allow the family to continue functioning as the child's primary caregiver.

Most families do not encounter problems as severe as having a handicapped child. But most families can benefit from supportive interaction with other individuals and groups who offer support in times of crisis, when they need information or need simply to overcome everyday problems in living. Although the network of personal social services described previously is one way of filling this need, fostering informal support systems is equally important.

There are other important targets of intervention beyond the family, however. Each of us is influenced by multiple levels of systems interact-

ing with each other. Recognizing this ecological perspective is fundamental. Because of these interactions, an intervention on one level can
have an impact on other ecological levels. In addition, how we choose to
intervene reflects where we think the problem lies and what our goals
and values are. We have stressed family-centered interventions because
the family provides the primary context for the development of young
children, but one can intervene on the exo- and macrosystem levels as
well.

Intervention in the exosystem means structuring community organizations to meet families' needs for support. It can mean making the
world of work more consonant with the needs of parents. It can also
mean enhancing the stability and cohesiveness of neighborhoods. It
means creating a pro-family consciousness in local government. These
changes require structuring our social values and policies to reflect the
value of children.

Supporting families in meeting the developmental needs of children is
not something that can be done by entering the picture only when a
problem arises. If our goal is to facilitate the best possible outcome for
children, we have to lay the groundwork beginning before the child is
born by making available to families the skills and resources they will
require. A preventive approach is indispensable to optimizing child development. A full range of formal and informal support services is necessary to minimize the negative effects of family disruption.

When you put it all together, you begin to see a picture of what the
complete community looks like with respect to human services. It is
worth our time to briefly outline such a community. It has a sustainable
economic base. Its primary economy is stable and sound, not subject to
wild fluctuations that disrupt families. It has a system of comprehensive
maternal and child health care. It has a strong system for providing
substitute and alternative child care for families who need it—including
infant day care and after-school care for children of elementary school
age. It has a strong network of home-based services to support families
in crisis and prevent placement of children in foster care. It provides for
all families an active health-visitor program that is available when children of working parents are home sick from school. It has employer
policies that facilitate flextime and part-time work arrangements. It has
generic social service providers assigned on a permanent basis to specific neighborhoods, who are charged with working as consultants to social networks and natural helpers. It has a school system that emphasizes basic skills and social competence, and serves as a family–
neighborhood center. It has a network of individuals within agencies
willing and able to work with families having trouble with their offspring's adolescence. A secure and family-oriented runaway shelter system is also part of such a network.

Is this an unrealistic utopian dream? Or, is it a realistic conception of our goals in this world? We think it can be achieved if we incorporate some basic principles about the relationship between the formal and informal human services. The keys are integration and appropriate scale, fitting professional and lay helpers together in manageable tasks and organizations. Can we do it? Abe Kaplan is said to have remarked: "An optimist believes this is the best of all possible worlds. . . . A pessimist is afraid he's right." We need to make a better world and, thus, disprove both the optimist and the pessimist.

Programs that Support Children: Case Studies

In this section, we return to elaborate on the concepts presented in the first part of the chapter by describing several human-service programs. We begin with an example of how services should *not* be delivered. We begin with foster care. The foster child care system has been lambasted frequently; unfortunately it appears that most of the criticism is deserved. The goals of foster care and protective child services are often in direct conflict with the outcomes they achieve.

Hundreds of thousands of children are placed in foster care—many for years. In 1991, 407,000 children were in out-of-home placement (American Public Welfare Association). Most are placed because of abuse or neglect at home—including incapacity due to drug abuse. The number of children in foster care has grown since the 1970s as protective service interventions have increased as a result of greater public awareness and deteriorating conditions for families.

Foster care provides *temporary* care when the child cannot be cared for in his or her own home, even with supplementary or supportive services (Kadushin, 1980). This happens most often in cases of illness of the primary caregiver, death of a parent, divorce or desertion, inadequate financial support, abuse or neglect, or child behavior problems or handicaps with which the parent cannot deal.

The goals of foster care have been delineated by the Child Welfare League of America in their *Standards for Foster Family Services* (Wiltse, 1978). These goals include the following:

1. To maintain and enhance parental functioning to the fullest extent.
2. To provide the type of care and services best suited to each child's needs and development.
3. To minimize and counteract hazards to the child's emotional health inherent in separation from his or her own family and the conditions leading to it.

4. To facilitate the child's becoming part of the foster family.
5. To make possible continuity of relationship by preventing unnecessary changes.
6. To protect the child from harmful experiences.
7. To bring about the child's ultimate return to his natural family . . . or . . . develop an alternative plan that provides a child with continuity of care (Wiltse, 1978, pp. 63–64).

Unfortunately, for many foster children—perhaps for most—these goals are often not met. Goal No. 1 intends to prevent placement of the child in foster care, to begin with, yet once social service agencies intervene in family problems, separation of the child is often the only recourse from the agency's point of view. The serious multiple problems of families and the inadequate resources of agency personnel to cope with these problems make unlikely such creative options as respite care, homemaker service, counseling, and environmental supports. This same lack of alternative solutions reduces the probability that children will return to their homes. The Children's Defense Fund survey (1978) found that 51% of foster children had been out of their homes for more than 2 years, and this exceeds the common sense meaning of "temporary."

On the other hand, there is little attempt to provide permanent placement for the child outside of his biological family, thereby violating Goals Nos. 2, 3, 4, 5, *and* 7. There is no reasonable vehicle for terminating parental custody, making permanent adoption impossible. The macrosystem of "biological parenthood" rights ensures this. Foster parents are admonished not to form attachments to their wards since the arrangement is temporary; in some places, policy demands that children be moved periodically so that these attachments do not form. The lack of continuity for children in foster care has led some (e.g., Goldstein, Freud, & Solnit, 1979; Wald, 1980) to advocate swift and permanent termination of legal custody of the biological parent as soon as the child is placed outside the home.

These problems came to light in the 1970s and the 1980s, which saw the testing of a variety of reform measures. Foster care is one social service area in which prevention can have a high benefit-to-cost ratio (because foster care is so costly). However, the legal issues and personal tragedies involved in foster care create many controversies that are not easily resolved. Protective service workers particularly feel they are caught in a dilemma that sometimes becomes a double bind in which every decision has the potential for backfiring and opening them for criticism—if not legal action. They are told to preserve families *and* rescue children. A cartoon that struck a responsive chord with protective service workers contained two pictures. In the first is someone being hanged. The caption reads: "Social worker who didn't remove child from abusive family." The second picture shows the same hanging. The caption reads: "Social worker who did remove child from abusive family."

In spite of the bleak national picture for foster care, there are some agencies that are striving to reduce the problems of extended placement and family dissolution. An excellent example is the Lower East Side Family Union (LESFU) in New York City. LESFU serves a mixed ethnic community, one of the poorest in the city. When LESFU was begun with a grant from a private foundation, area residents were characterized by a history of family disruption over generations. Social services were fragmented, with numerous agencies often offering duplicate services to families. Of particular concern to social welfare agencies was the very high rate of foster placement in the city with tremendous costs to the public ($280 million in 1977). The goals of LESFU are to support and strengthen families threatened with disruption and to avoid the intervention of the juvenile justice and child welfare systems, since contact with these agencies often leads to placement of children outside the home. The project seeks to place children within the community when placement is necessary.

LESFU acts as a coordinator of services by connecting clients with the agencies who will best meet their needs. After several meetings with family members, the Family Union workers draw up contracts stating the family's, agencies', and LESFU's responsibilities in meeting the family's goals. An example of this is provided by Dunu (1979). The case involved an alcoholic mother who had been illegally excluded from welfare. She was without housing for herself and her youngest child. Five other children were in foster care, and the youngest son needed regular medical care for sickle cell anemia. The agreements made involved the following:

1. She was to enroll in a treatment program for alcoholism.
2. She had to make permanent plans for her children in foster care.
3. She had to keep all appointments and cooperate with agencies.
4. The hospital agreed to schedule all appointments conveniently.
5. The foster care agency agreed to accept a temporary placement for the youngest child contingent on the mother's finding housing.
6. LESFU agreed to oversee and coordinate the efforts of all agencies involved in providing housing, health care, and welfare payments.

In addition to social workers, LESFU also employs a cadre of homemakers who teach home management, child care, and parenting skills.

They can fill in during an emergency and may prevent the break up of a family. LESFU also has a community development team that deals with broader issues of housing, employment, and so on.

LESFU appears to be an effective, preventive program reducing family disruption. In 1977 it served 420 families, 193 of whom were at risk of family breakdowns. During that year only 11 of these families required foster placement. While the duration of foster placement in New York City averages 6 years, no LESFU child has been placed for more than 18 months. The economic savings are tremendous—the per-family cost of $1500 a year is much less than it would cost to put the 1000 or so children of these families in foster care. Foster care for the same children would have cost $5000 to $30,000 per child per year in 1977 dollars (Dunu, 1979; "New York City Agency Keeps Families Together," 1980).

Homebuilders (Haapala & Kinney, 1979; Kinney, Haapala, & Booth, 1991) is another program that deals with families in crisis, and has 24 hour a day intake. Clients are seen in their homes within 24 hours. The program is based on two assumptions: first, that no family is "hopeless," and second, that "families are trying, in their own homespun, beautiful, error-filled ways, to make things work" (Haapala & Kinney, 1979, p. 254). Homebuilders is a family preservation program.

Staff are trained in communication skills and behavior change techniques as well as therapeutic skills. They enter the home of a family in a time of crisis—when regular agencies have given up. Each team member represents the position of one family member in negotiations designed to air grievances and reach agreements over steps to a solution.

The families that Homebuilders typically serve are threatened with family disruption because of foster placement of the children or psychiatric placement of an adult. In the first 3 years of the program, 86% of the families served were still intact 1 year after intake.

The main purpose of Homebuilders is to enable family members to work together to solve problems. They accomplish this by serving as a "negotiating" team and by teaching family members skills that will enable them to resolve interpersonal conflicts peacefully. However, Homebuilders staff members also help to contact and coordinate the social services the family needs.

Although both Homebuilders and LESFU aim to keep families together, they represent opposite poles on several of the dimensions of service delivery discussed earlier in the chapter. Homebuilders is a remedial program. In fact, Haapala and Kinney (1979) state that Homebuilders prefers to serve a family in crisis, since this family will be more receptive to new ideas and behaviors. Although LESFU certainly encounters many families in crisis, its intent is to avoid this situation by coordinating the delivery of services before the family enters a crisis stage. LESFU tends to be more comprehensive in service orientation. Homebuilders, while coordinating all necessary services, focuses on interpersonal conflict resolution as a first step to dealing with more global family problems. Both programs adopt the collaborative or supportive model of professional service. Homebuilders is especially strong in this regard, stating that every family has the capacity to resolve its problems, if it has the required skills and resources. Since its inception in 1974, Homebuilders has grown. By 1990, there were Homebuilders programs in 30 states and several foreign countries (Kinney, Haapala, & Booth, 1991). Small caseloads, highly skilled staff, a strong community focus, and a commitment to family preservation characterize the program.

The next program we will describe blends formal and informal support systems in an attempt to strengthen an already existing system of child-care support (in Portland, Oregon). The family child-care network described by Collins and her colleagues (Collins, 1979; Collins & Pancoast, 1976; Collins & Watson, 1976; Pancoast, 1980) has become a model for supporting networks of "natural helpers" in the community. A natural helper is someone who has many connections to others in the community. Many turn to her for advice because she is well informed and knows who can do what and how to get it. They are often individuals who have the energy, time, or special interpersonal skills needed to help or to bring people together.

The program developed by Collins and her colleagues places the professional in a consulting and supporting role with the natural helper. In some cases, information provided by the natural helper can identify families in need of formal intervention. However, the emphasis is on giving the natural helper support in acting on her or his instincts to help. The process of locating and assisting natural helpers was described in the practice capsule in Chapter 8.

The network consultation model is the ultimate in the collaborative role for the professional. The target of the intervention is not a particular family, but a neighborhood or social network. By locating the strong links in the network—the natural helpers—and by strengthening their role, the network is strengthened. Collins and her colleagues have applied this model to several problems (e.g., discharged mental patients, child abuse). In the case of family day care, the goal was to develop a network of neighbors and friends who could provide informal child care along the lines of an extended family (Collins, 1979). Natural helpers were identified by inquiring around the community about who offered child care. People who had contact with children and with a wide range of community members (the school secretary, public health nurse, church staff) were asked, as well as working mothers (waitresses, grocery clerks). Once a list of several names was established, day-care neighbors (natural helpers with special knowledge of child-care resources) were contacted and recruited. The relationship between day-care neighbor and professional consultant was formed with the goal of ensuring the best possible care for children. The consultant and natural helper worked together to match families in need of child care with day-care providers who best served their needs. As the consultant-helper relationships became firmly established, other agencies and individuals turned to the day-care team for referrals and suggestions on successful delivery techniques.

Integrating Formal and Informal Supports

To support and protect families and professionals, we must lose ourselves in the social landscape, blend in with the human terrain, and become part of the natural social systems of families and communities. At present, far too much of what we call the human-service system sticks out above the natural social horizon or is out of harmony with the social scene it seeks to aid. What can we do to blend into the social landscape and, in so doing, find the power to do the good that we seek? We have a series of suggestions, all of which are deceptively simple. We say deceptively simple, because each requires diligent, intelligent, sensitive, and loving action by each of us who is committed to improving the quality of life for children. With this in mind, here are our thoughts on what we need to do.

Recognizing the Limits of Professionalism

Recognize the limits of professional intervention. Just as our economy depends on private initiative and hard work to keep it going, the bulk of human services are delivered to families by the "free enterprise system of helping"—by friends, neighbors, and relatives. We forget this at our peril. At best, we will overlook a great potential resource. At worst, we will disrupt the bread-and-butter services to children that these informal support systems and natural helping networks provide. What does this imply for our behavior? Two things are paramount: consultation and advocacy (Whittaker, Garbarino, & Associates, 1984).

Consultation

Become consultants to informal family-support systems and natural-helping networks (Collins & Pancoast, 1976). One of the greatest obstacles is the idea that *"we"* need to help *"them."* We recall a conversation with a woman from Western Europe who had been through a program that combined nursing with social-work training. She now served families in a well-defined area of a city. We wondered if her clients thought of her as a social worker or as a nurse and so asked her, "When you are visiting a family, how do they refer to you?" (thinking this would reveal how the clients perceived her professional role). She looked a bit surprised and responded, "Why, they call me Elizabeth!" By becoming an accepted part of the social environment, she had become a powerful consultant to the informal family support systems and natural helping networks. We believe the most pressing task we face is to strive for this kind of relationship.

Advocacy

Become advocates of the parent–child relationship in the community power structure. This means seeking funds for formal services, of course, but it means much more. It means getting hospitals to adopt "family-centered" childbirth as the norm. It means making sure that the needs of children for safe, convenient places to play have a high priority with zoning boards and other government agencies. It means ensuring that residential development fosters and maintains the integrity of neighborhoods rather than destroying it. It means getting public officials to become models of how to serve the interests of children. All these things help provide a climate where caring for families is a "natural" phenomenon. We use the term "child centered" to mean a community where the obstacles to being an effective family are removed and are replaced by a web of forces encouraging parents and children to become effective families. Such a community is the necessary foundation for specific efforts to help individual children and parents become better family members.

Using Existing Social Resources

To help children and parents become better families we need intervention programs that *use the target's own strength to make things happen*. To do this we must avoid grand schemes, elaborate projects, expensive technology, and artificial programs, in favor of "appropriate social technology" (Rogers & Shoemaker, 1971). We need to develop and advance efforts that are *effective* (much of what we do is not of proven effectiveness), *inexpensive* (the high-cost demonstration program provides useful information, but we also need programs that can be done on a shoestring budget, i.e., in the *real* world), *locally relevant* (local responsibility is an essential complement to natural leadership, for we are a nation of thousands of communities when it comes to children and families), *flexi-*

ble (we need models that can be readily adapted to local conditions—be they Indian reservations or immigrant ghettos), *sustainable* (programs should not require or consume scarce resources, such as expert professional time or special funding), *simple* (they must be described in sufficient detail to be replicated by an "ordinary" user—you cannot empower people to help themselves if they cannot understand the directions on the label), and *compatible* (whatever we propose must build on—even if *away* from—existing values, past experiences, and presently perceived needs). All this is a tall order, but it is the only order that will do the job. It does require a social policy climate that supports and encourages families, however. We deal with the nature and character of such a climate in our next chapter.

RESEARCH CAPSULE

The Children's Defense Fund (CDF) is a national advocacy organization seeking to develop policies and practices that are beneficial to children. One arm of the organization conducts research on practices and programs that potentially cause mistreatment of children. One such study was conducted in 1975, when CDF looked at the status of foster care in this country. They considered

1. Public and family responsibility for children.
2. How the child's need for a family is supported or ignored.
3. What practices and policies may be harmful to children.
4. How to define governmental responsibility to children in foster care.
5. What can be done to improve the situation of children in foster care, including information, programs, legislation, and advocacy.

(Researchers conduct surveys to discover the current incidence or distribution of a variable. Surveys can also assess the relationships between variables, as in surveys to measure party affiliation and voting patterns. The survey conducted by CDF is of the first type.)

To collect this data, CDF surveyed the status of children in foster care in 140 counties throughout the country. They studied seven representative states in depth. Finally, they surveyed all 50 states to learn about placement of children in institutions outside their home states.

Large-scale surveys, such as those done at the national level, cannot reach all members of a population because of the costs involved. Instead, sophisticated techniques for selecting representative samples from the population of interest have been developed. For instance, in the CDF study, since it was not possible to survey all counties and states in the United States, the sample selected represented a range in population, geographic location, and urban/rural balance. Such samples, if chosen correctly (by using the appropriate criteria for selection) can provide very accurate information that can be generalized to the entire population.

Here are some of CDF's findings:

1. Placement of children outside the home usually occurs without consideration of less drastic alternatives such as day-care or homemaker services. These alternative supports do not exist in most communities.

2. Placement with a relative is rarely considered, and many states do not pay for foster care with a relative.
3. Only one-half of the counties surveyed specifically encouraged visitation by parents. CDF estimated that 10,000 children are placed out of their own states, making regular contact with their families virtually impossible.
4. Of children in foster care 52% had been out of their homes for 2 years or more; 18 percent had changed placements more than three times.
5. Monitoring of children in out-of-home placements is very poor. In the counties surveyed, welfare officials could not give information for one-half of the children on their ages or how long they had been in foster care.
6. Legal statues are poorly defined; none of the seven states required re-unification efforts. Only South Carolina included efforts to ensure permanent placement for a child, and no state gave priority to relatives or foster parents as potential adoptive parents.

In analyzing the results of the study, we have to keep in mind that CDF is an advocacy organization with a particular point of view to put forward. Still, this study is significant because of its interstate comparisons. Other attempts to make comparisons using the data collected by each state have been difficult to interpret because each state uses different data-collection techniques. Because record keeping in many states has been poor, the CDF study is one of the first to provide documentation for the criticisms of foster care in the United States. Of course, the quality of the foster-care system varies from place to place, but CDF's findings paint a grim overall picture.

CDF advocates the development of alternative services to avoid placement of children outside their families. However, there has been very little research conducted on the effectiveness of these programs. Programs such as LESFU and Homebuilders (see text) are a step in this direction. LESFU especially seems to provide a model for effective services that can avoid family disruption.

PRACTICE CAPSULE

One of the important human service agendas that has emerged in recent decades is childhood injury control and prevention. Injuries have displaced disease as the leading cause of child death and disability (due to the success of public health efforts). An extended look at how this issue is conceptualized as a human service program provides some useful models for other applications (Garbarino, 1988).

Childhood injuries may be classified in four broad categories of harm along a continuum reflecting the degree to which they are random vs inflicted: random accidents, preventable accidents, negligence, and assault. Such a classification helps sharpen the issues for prevention programs and policies.

Random accidents. In random accidents, children are injured by accidental trauma. Of course, the term "accident" is a social label, reflecting a community-based judgment that such harm is not someone's fault. Because it is a social label, the definition of what is or is not an accident is subject to historical change and contemporary variation across geographic, social class, ethnic, and demographic lines. For example, most automobile-related injuries to young children were once defined as random accidents but are now understood to be preventable. More than 90% of fatalities and 66% of disabilities are avoided through the use of child safety restraints (Margolis & Runyan, 1983). Thus, an event can be redefined as community understanding changes, or can be defined differently from community to community and from culture to culture. Random accidents carry with them a spirit of unmitigated sympathy in the community's response to the adults responsible for the injured children. At this end of the continuum there is no question of infliction of the injuries.

Preventable accidents. When a knowledge base develops to demonstrate that informed caregiver and community action can significantly reduce the likelihood of specific accidental injuries to children, those events become redefined as preventable accidents. This redefinition is a social process reflecting the interaction of community concepts and scientific expertise about what is and what is not socially and technically feasible. For example, many ingestions of dangerous fluids by toddlers are understood to be preventable through the use of "child-proof" caps on bottles. Preventable accidents elicit a spirit of regret but not official approbation in dealing with the adults responsible for the injured children.

Negligence. When children are injured because an adult has failed to meet the community's minimal standards for care and protection, we enter the realm of negligence. Consider the case of an injury to a young child sitting on the lap of a parent in the front seat of a car involved in a crash. After having been defined as a random accident 30 years ago, and a preventable accident 15 years ago, such an injury is now defined as negligence in many communities. Negligence-related injuries may invoke a spirit of anger or indignation, and often legal retribution for the adults deemed responsible.

Assaults. Assaults are intentional injuries inflicted on children. They stand at the opposite end of the continuum from random accidents. Physical abuse of children falls into this category. The community's response to assault-related injuries is often rage and vengeance directed at those responsible.

All of this may seem simple enough on the surface. But these four categories can mask difficult issues of science, ethics, and policy:

1.   Some intentional injuries are not socially defined as assaults. For example, many Americans favor the use of corporal punishment for children. Such discipline is often exempted from the category of assault, even when it produces specific injuries (which may be treated as accidental or as incidental to discipline). A Louis Harris poll found that only about 41% of adults believe physical punishment "often" or "very often" leads to injury to a child. On the other hand, 73% indicated that "repeated yelling at and cursing a child" "often" or "very often" produce emotional harm.

2.   Injuries may be classified as random accidents because lack of evidence precludes assigning blame. Recent research on Sudden Infant Death Syndrome (SIDS), for example, suggests that, at least among families living in poverty, many such diagnoses may be better classified as preventable accidents, negligence, or even assault (Bass, Kravath, & Glass, 1986).

3.   Some intentions may be unconscious and thus not directly accessible for review by caregivers. An unacknowledged desire to harm a child may be expressed not through assault, but by creating and fostering situations in which the child is exposed to elevated risk of accidental injury. Also, a child may seek out injury (e.g., poisoning) as a method for gaining attention, expressing anger, or demonstrating self-destructive intent.

4.   Any focus on intentionality with respect to individual caregivers should not deflect attention from the intrinsically social dimensions of childhood injury and prevention. Community-level actions can serve to increase or decrease the magnitude of individual responsibility for injury prevention, as well as the level

of risk experienced. For example, if a community permits controllable toxins (e.g., lead-based paint) in children's environments or if the community fails to control known child abusers (e.g., previously diagnosed pedophiles), then the protective task facing caregivers increases in difficulty and magnitude. If, on the other hand, the community seeks to defuse risk by assuming responsibility for providing safe environments (e.g., by building pedestrian overpasses connecting playgrounds and residential areas) it decreases the burden on caregivers (Aldrich, 1979). The same is true for spontaneous child behavior that produces the potential for injury in specific environmental contexts. For example, spontaneous random mouthing of objects becomes dangerous as adult supervision decreases or the presence of ingestible toys increases. This is evident in the dramatic decline in child deaths due to poisoning after the introduction of safety caps on bottles—an 80% decline among 1- to 4-year-old children between 1968 and 1979 (Baker, O'Neill, & Karpf, 1984).

This brief introduction establishes the origins of childhood injury in the social context provided for the child by community and caregivers.

Classifying and Evaluating Child Safety Programs

Knowing that the origins of childhood injury are multiple and diverse, that efforts to prevent childhood injuries are similarly numerous and different in orientation, and that multiple and often unforeseen consequences are likely, how do we proceed? One useful next step is to develop a scheme for classifying child safety programs on the basis of three factors: the type of risk to the child they address, the target for preventive intervention, and the method for delivering the intervention. Table 9.1 outlines the elements of this framework as a 5 (Dimension 1) × 3 (Dimension 2) × 5 (Dimension 3) matrix.

Table 9.1. A Framework for Classifying Child Safety Programs

DIMENSIONS
1. Source of Risk to the Child
   A. Environmental hazard
   B. Dangerous child behavior
   C. Inappropriate parenting
   D. Assaults by familiar persons
   E. Attacks by strangers
2. Target for Preventive Intervention
   1. Community
   2. Caregiver
   3. Child
3. Method for Delivering Preventive Intervention
   I. Legislation/regulation
   II. Mass media campaigns
   III. Programmed materials
   IV. Group instruction
   V. Individualized training

Sources of Risk to the Child

Environmental hazards. Children are at risk for injury from a wide range of environmental hazards, from automobile accidents to electrical outlets. The degree of risk varies with the child's age and level of competence, but the "cause" of the harm is always the child's encounter with a dangerous feature of everyday life. Some hazards exist equally for all children (e.g., air-borne radiation); others differ with social class, geography, or demography. This has implications for the timing of preventive efforts. Some efforts are best tied to a child's developmental milestones (e.g., messages about the risks of ingestion automatically sent to parents on the child's first birthday). Others are best tied to groups defined epidemiologically as being at risk because of a prior child injury (e.g., intensive efforts aimed at parents and children after an initial emergency room visit for an injury resulting from special circumstances, such as operation of an all-terrain vehicle).

Dangerous child behavior. Children are at risk for harm because of their own dangerous behavior. This ranges from the mouthing of objects by infants to substance abuse and reckless driving by adolescents, to even more self-destructive behavior arising from emotional deprivation or psychopathology. Most immediate causes of injury (e.g., high-energy impact, water, heat, and toxic substances) are through motor vehicle crashes, falls, drowning, burns, and poisonings. The issue here is the role of the child's own actions in creating or precipitating these injury-producing events. At the extremes these links are clear, e.g., in obviously self-inflicted injuries. In the middle ranges, the links become difficult to recognize and establish, and may only be evident after fine-grained epidemiological or in-depth psychological analysis, e.g., in the "carelessness" of a depressed child.

Inappropriate parenting. Children are at risk for injury because of inappropriate parenting. Parental negligence (e.g., lack of supervision for young children), assault, and exploitation (e.g., severe physical punishment or sexual molestation) are among the possibilities. The special role of parents in the lives of children warrants a special category for them in assessing adults as sources of risk (and prevention).

Assaults by familiar persons. Children are at risk from assaults by familiar persons, including adults acting *in loco parentis* (e.g., babysitters and teachers), as well as neighbors and acquaintances. The range of assaults runs the gamut from sexual exploitation (e.g., by pedophiles) to physical assault (e.g., by gang members).

Attacks by strangers. Children are at risk from attacks by strangers. These can include kidnapping (most often for purposes of sexual assault) as well as physical attacks.

Target for Preventive Intervention

Community. Child safety programs may be targeted at the community. Interventions can be legal (e.g., directing manufacturers on product safety, builders on construction codes, and professionals on improved monitoring of children's lives) or educational (e.g., informing citizens of such personal safety techniques as responses to a child who is choking, and institution of methods of assault prevention). Many of these efforts seek to implement passive preventive measures—i.e., automatic protection requiring no initiative by the ultimate beneficiary, in contrast to active measures that require the child to do something to avoid injury.

Caregiver. Child safety programs can be directed at caregivers. They may seek to reduce household hazards, to provide approved car seats for infants, to raise the minimum age and standards of supervision for babysitters, to recognize indicators of sexual assault, and to modify high-risk disciplinary practices (e.g., hitting a child on the head with objects).

Child. Safety programs may target children directly, addressing a wide range of topics such as ingesting unknown liquids, crossing streets, avoiding strangers, driving responsibly, or any other form of risk to which the child may be exposed.

Methods for Delivering Preventive Intervention

Legislation/regulation. Child safety programs may involve legislation or regulation aimed at controlling or preventing sources of risk to children. Such efforts can include laws governing product safety (and thus aimed at the community), laws aimed at caregivers (e.g., banning corporal punishment or sexual exploitation), and efforts to prevent children from danger by directly prohibiting risky child behavior (e.g., laws that establish age minimums for driving or being at home without adult supervision).

Mass media. Child safety programs may be delivered via local and national television and radio programs, as well as public service advertising.

Programmed materials. Child safety programs may utilize programmed materials such as workbooks, videocassettes for home viewing, comic books, and coloring books, all materials that can be used as free-standing activities.

Group instruction. Child safety programs may involve group instruction. Workshops, seminars, classes, theater and discussion groups, and community forums are examples.

Individualized training. Child safety programs can be presented through individualized training. Such efforts involve face-to-face training in concrete skills such as CPR training, defensive driving, stranger avoidance, telephone answering, response to fire emergencies, assertiveness in response to sexual advances, and self-defense techniques when assaulted. They also include one-to-one guidance given to parents by pediatricians and by child care providers to parents of children in their care. All share the common elements of tutorial experiences, usually with behavioral rehearsal.

The 75 possible combinations of these factors describe particular interactions of risk, target, and method. For example, some child safety programs seek to prevent assault at the hand of strangers (9.1) by teaching children to protect themselves against seduction through classroom workshops. Other programs address the same goal with children but seek to do so through televised public service announcements. Others address caregivers through legislation that establishes minimum ages for leaving children unattended.

In principle, all 75 combinations of risk, target, and method represent program options. However, in practice, some combinations may seem more promising than others. Indeed the whole task of evaluating child safety programs depends on an analysis of the potential impact of each approach as defined by a particular intersection of risk, target, and method. Conventional cost effectiveness analysis seeks to establish the dollar cost per injury prevented or per risk factor eliminated. For example, one analysis of safety seats for young children concluded that the cost would be $16,190 (at 1978 value) per fatal or disabling injury prevented, $614,400,000 being the total cost for equipping all child-occupied vehicles (Margolis & Runyan, 1983). What would be the dollar savings? Direct costs of care for one seriously injured child can run into the hundreds of thousands of dollars (not counting eventual loss in earnings). Similarly, a home health visitor program aimed at 50 high-risk families (Gray et al., 1977) was estimated to cost about $2,000 per family (thus $100,000 overall) and to have prevented injuries that over a lifetime would have cost many times that amount. Of course, such cost effectiveness analysis may be challenged for daring to use a financial measure in matters that bear on the quality and quantity of human life, particularly the life of a child. Such analyses are also unlikely to motivate changes in policy or practice so long as costs of injuries can, at least theoretically, be allocated elsewhere. Conventional economics speaks of "externalized costs," those that are not borne by the economic entity under discussion (e.g., when a manufacturer can dump waste untreated into a river and let someone else pay for processing it). Therefore, an ecologically valid cost effectiveness analysis must take into account efforts through the legislative and legal system to force the "internalization" of injury costs by every person and institution that plays a role in causing them or could play a role in their prevention.

FOR FURTHER READING

Caplan, G., & Killilea, M. (Eds.) (1976). *Support systems and mutual help.* New York: Grune & Stratton, 325 pp.
   This volume provides a number of examples of the development of informal mutual-help groups as well as presentations of the theoretical concepts behind this form of intervention. Going beyond social work, the contributors to the book represent fields as diverse as literature, administration, and religion.

Garbarino, J., Stocking, S. H., & Associates. (1980). *Protecting children from abuse and neglect.* San Francisco: Jossey-Bass, 222 pp.
   This book, oriented to practitioners and policymakers, discusses ways in which family support systems can be strengthened in order to prevent child abuse and neglect. It extends the mutual-help framework offered by Caplan and his colleagues by incorporating the ecological systems perspective. Contributions include discussions of the neighborhood, preventive services, and integration of formal and informal supports.

Goldstein, J., Freud, A., & Solnit, A. (1973). *Beyond the best interests of the child.* New York: The Free Press, 203 pp. Goldstein, J., Freud, A., & Solnit, A. (1979). *Before the best interests of the child.* New York: The Free Press, 288 pp.
   These two volumes represent a proposal by a lawyer and two psychoanalysts for the modification of our current child-custody system to support the needs of children. They apply psychoanalytic theory to child-custody decisions and advocate making permanent placement for children as soon as possible. Their view of the state's active role in decision making contrasts with Moroney's and has been heavily debated. The first volume lays out general principles; the second develops their implications for such situations as divorce, neglect, and foster care.

Kamerman, S., & Kahn, A. (1976). *Social services in the United States: Policies and programs.* Philadelphia: Temple University Press, 561 pp.
   This is one of the most complete resources available on social services in the United States. It reviews the "state of the art" of several different services and pinpoints problems of service delivery. Chapters on child care, children's institu-

tions, services for the aged, and family planning include discussions of the legislative framework for service provision, program descriptions, and research and evaluation. The final chapter develops the concept of the "personal social services."

Levine, M., & Levine, A. (1970). *A social history of the helping services.* New York: Appleton-Century-Crofts, 315 pp.

Levine and Levine review the development of community social services with special attention to the political and ideological influences that have led to reform. In chapters discussing the settlement-house movement and the development of the juvenile judicial system, among other topics, they portray the individuals involved in the development of services as well as the political and social events that influenced these developments. A very stimulating and thought-provoking book.

Moroney, R. M. (1976). *The family and the state: Considerations for social policy.* New York: Longman, and Moroney, R. M. (1980). *Families, social services, and social policy: The issue of shared responsibility.* U.S. Department of Health and Human Services, DHHS Publ. No. (ADM) 80-846, (monograph), 214 pp.

Pointing out that social programs often act to supplant rather than support the family as primary caregiver for its dependent members, Moroney offers a model of shared responsibility to guide family–state relationships in this area. He examines many of our cultural assumptions regarding the responsibilities families fulfill for the state and, based on a study in Britain, also examines whether social policies support family's functions or supplant them with formal social services. The monograph is based on the book and focuses specifically on these policies as they apply to handicapped children and the elderly.

Whittaker, J., Kinney, J., Tracy, E., & Booth, C. (Eds.) (1990). *Reaching high-risk families: Intensive family preservation in human services.* New York: Aldine, 206 pp.

This edited volume focuses on the Homebuilders model of family preservation. It does so in the context of reviewing more general conceptual and service delivery issues.

Whittaker, J., Garbarino, J., & Associates. (1983). *Social support networks: Informal helping in the human services.* New York: Aldine, 479 pp.

This book outlines what a social support approach means and traces its origins in social work and mental health research and programming. It then applies this approach to a wide range of human service delivery contexts—child welfare, delinquency, drug abuse, child protection, schools, etc.

QUESTIONS FOR THOUGHT

1.   Outline an ideal program for one of the following problems:

   * child abuse
   * juvenile delinquency
   * fetal alcohol syndrome (see Chapter 5)

Include the goals of the program, who the target population would be, and types of services provided. What might be some of the problems you would encounter in implementing your program?

2.   In the program you designed for question No. 1, did you incorporate

informal support systems? Why or why not? If you did not do so previously, redesign the program to incorporate informal support systems.

3.   The ecological approach to human development suggests that prevention cannot be achieved only at the individual level. Describe a program designed to reduce stress in single parent families that takes into account the ecology of the family. How would you need to intervene on each ecosystem level?

4.   One dimension of service delivery described in this chapter reflected the role of the professional. At one extreme, we find the corrective approach in which the professional is an expert who "fixes" the problem. At the other extreme is the collaborator who supports the client by providing the skills or information necessary for the client to solve the problem. Contrast these two approaches, applying them to the problem of unmanageable child behavior. What might be the parent's role in each approach?

5.   Moroney called the family a "social service." What did he mean by this? Give an example of a service provided by an agency that could be provided by a family with appropriate supports. Examine the program you designed in questions Nos. 1 and 2. Are there services offered by agencies in your program that the family could assume? Revise your program to incorporate these changes.

6.   The program examples offered in this chapter illustrated ways in which formal and informal support systems can work together. Give two advantages of developing informal social support networks as opposed to formal services as an approach to intervention. Identify two instances in which formal services would be more appropriate than informal services.

10

Social Policy, Children, and Their Families

James Garbarino, Mario T. Gaboury,
and Margaret C. Plantz

All systems of society must operate effectively together to make it possible for children to develop
adequately. . . . All systems of society must operate
together effectively if families are to establish and
maintain a climate that supports the continuing
growth and development of both children and adults.
. . . What is needed is better policy-making that includes awareness of the needs of families as dynamic
interaction units linked to all the social systems.
These more powerful systems need to protect and
support the family as a complex unit rather than de-
manding that families be strained and fragmented in
an attempt to cope with an inadequately organized
and only partially adequate society. These systems,
moreover, . . . need to be updated, modified, and co-
ordinated through enlightened public policies, planning, and programs if society and its families are to
weather the stresses of the years ahead . . . And persons concerned about the well-being of society and its
families need to add to their skills some knowledge of
the public social policy processes so that they can
affect the political and other governmental processes
that both create public policy and put it into operation.

(Chilman, 1973, p. 578)

271

In Chapter 10, we explore many "systems of society" that influence the well-being of children and their families and some of the diverse factors that direct policy decision making and program implementation. We will explore factors to consider in determining policy successes as well as policy failures. As enlightened policy practitioners, we need to know about cultural values, political realities, and economics. We need a feel for school systems and service agencies, as well as student and client characteristics. We need to know about grass roots, neighborhood organizations, and charitable, religious, and civic groups, as well as government entities. It is most important to realize that "policy" is not some amorphous entity engineered by unknowns in distant places. Policy is everybody's business, and everyone has an impact by way of his or her everyday actions. Certainly we all feel the effects of policies, whether we are conscious of them or not. We will supply a conceptual primer and some practical tools for participating more actively in the policy arena.

We consider ourselves a nation that cares about children and their families. Yet, this notion is something of a romantic or self-serving idealization: policies and practices at every level in our society reveal subtle biases against children and their families. At the federal level, for example, we find a "marriage tax" that makes it more costly for people to live as married couples than to cohabit out of wedlock and a welfare system that contributes to family dissolution (Bahr, 1979). Is our government antifamily? Is it antichild? With the federal government playing such a large role in shaping the social environment for children and families, we need to know.

Practices that undermine our country's families and children are not restricted to the federal government, of course. For instance, the adversarial nature of our courts and legal system in divorce proceedings maximizes the family-disrupting issues at hand, rather than negotiating ways to protect the family's integrity (Spanier & Anderson, 1979). Custody suits are well known for pitting parent against parent and "her" family against "his" family, with the fate of the child decided by outsiders. Is American family law antifamily and antichild?

What about agencies of local government? In some cases, zoning ordinances (abusive "spot zoning" creating "child-free" zones, and restrictions on the number of nonfamilial household residents) have caused tight-knit neighborhoods to decline by disrupting the traditional patterns of residential and commercial balance that provided stability. Neighborhood redevelopment programs have left people strangers on their own blocks. School boards have decided to close down smaller, more personalized neighborhood schools in favor of larger schools that seem more cost efficient. Can it be that the boards and commissions of our local governments are antifamily and antichild?

What about the private sector? Corporate policies that require executives and middle managers to relocate in order to advance into desired positions are disruptive of all-important family support networks. Furthermore, these new positions often increase already long working hours, shorten weekends and vacations, and make travel more frequent for persons already too often away from their families. Blue-collar workers face their own set of dilemmas. Mandatory overtime, swing-shift and split-shift hours, and a clock-in/clock-out (hourly as opposed to salaried) pay standard limit this group's time with spouses and children. These practices are doubly stressful for single parents who must choose between income and doctor's appointments, school conferences, and little league games. Plant closings often involving the export of jobs to other regions or countries put families on the unemployment lines. Are business and industry also participating in a nationwide effort to disrupt the lives of children and their families?

Consider the policies and practices of our human service agencies. Rather than working to restore children to their families, foster-care agencies often act to prevent their reunion (Children's Defense Fund, 1978). However, children may be taken from stable surrogate arrangements and returned to abusive families when a healthy balance is not struck between child and family interests. Child protective services may interfere in parent–child relations in an arbitrary manner because they do not understand or accept ethnic and cultural traditions that differ from their own or because of social class bias (Katz, 1971). Some local agencies administering the Aid to Families with Dependent Children program use criteria in making decisions about food, clothing, and housing that disrupt the informal social networks that are so vital to the poor (deLone, 1979). Could our human service agencies be antifamily, too?

Any treatment of social policy would be lacking without some mention of the powerful effects of mass media. During a normal childhood our young people are exposed to tremendous levels of violence and other social deviance. Despite the best efforts of child advocates to address issues ranging from guns and drugs in movies to nutritional messages conveyed in Saturday morning cartoon commercials, the media appear intransigent. The effects of this are clearly not positive. Are the mass media antichild and antifamily?

Is Our Society Antifamily?

Is ours a culture and a nation that is at its roots antifamily and antichild? Our answer is NO; it is not. Survey data make it clear that *as individuals*, Americans value their families and their children more than they do anything else. But the policies and practices cited above, and many others besides, make it more difficult for families to stay together, to take care of their members, and to build satisfying lives that contribute to a satisfying society. These policies limit access to economic resources and social supports. They reduce the range of choices available to family members, and limit their freedom to control their own lives and the development of their children. They displace the family as the unit with primary responsibility for the destiny of children and their parents. These policies and practices take their toll on our families and our children.

We do not believe that our country, governments, courts, businesses, industries, and human service agencies have instituted policies deliberately to undermine family unity and effectiveness. The policies and practices of these institutions certainly were not *intended* to have family-threatening effects. Their purpose was to address specific problems (sometimes problems that seem to be quite unrelated to families) with effective and cost-efficient solutions. In most cases, in fact, the potential family impact was not even considered when the policy decisions were enacted. And therein lies the problem. *In most instances, the potential impact of proposed actions or policies on families was not even considered* (Johnson, 1978).

But there is more to it than this. The American macrosystem reflects a very strong commitment to individualism. One way in which this translates into policy is a belief that some people deserve community support and assistance more than others, and a suspicion that "they" are not as trustworthy as "us." Indeed, one key to understanding the antifamily themes in American policymaking is to recognize that although we do not deliberately undermine "us," we sometimes do seek to punish or protect ourselves from "them."

Thus, one of the big underlying issues in American policymaking is a determination of who qualifies as "us" and who is relegated to "them." "They" must be controlled, guarded against, discouraged, and cannot be trusted. "We" need support, encouragement, nurturance, and aid. This all fits into our moral framework (e.g., of the "deserving" and the "undeserving" poor, or of "good immigrants" vs. "illegal aliens").

It should come as no surprise that racism and other forms of bias have a great deal to do with who qualifies as "us" vs. "them" in halls of government, in corporate boardrooms, and even in philanthropy, where white men continue to predominate.

So, in addition to some general problems of inadvertent or unintended antifamily and antichild policymaking, we must consider the consequences of racism, sexism, and classism on the way decisions are made about families and children. In these cases, the negative consequences for "them" may be interpreted publicly as either appropriate punishment or as necessary "costs" to sustain the values or interests of "us."

All this is particularly true in times of war. In the wake of the 1991 Gulf War, Kurds were "us" (and thus deserving of aid and protection). Iraqis were "them" (and thus on their own, their suffering "their own fault"). There are domestic parallels to this model (e.g., mothers on drugs are "them" whereas their bodies are still "us" for a few months).

We think that the impact of social policies and practices on all families should always be a primary consideration for this nation's institutions and decision makers. Creating and maintaining a sociocultural climate that actively supports all children and their families require purposeful, informed, and persistent efforts by many people at all levels of decision making in our society, people who are willing to uncover and confront their biases. We all can be part of that process, each in our own way.

Our purpose in this chapter is not to create social policy or political action experts. Rather, our intention here is to increase appreciation for the policy arena, increase consciousness about the effect of policies on both personal life and professional endeavors, expose and confront biases that define "us" and "them," and enhance the savvy necessary for making a positive impact on the social environment of children and families by affecting social policies. We intend to do this by

1. Demonstrating how powerful policy can be in shaping the day-to-day lives of both professionals and family members.
2. Heightening sensitivity to implicit values and assumptions about families and children that are reflected in policy decisions.
3. Increasing awareness of the diversity of social policies that affect families.
4. Identifying and expanding on the policy implications of some child-centered practices discussed in earlier chapters.
5. Increasing awareness of how much, and in how many ways, individuals who make a personal commitment to the well-being of children and their families can affect family-related social policies.

Our ecological perspective will help us describe both the multiple sources of child- and family-related policies and the multiple points of impact that are of concern to children and families. First, however, we need to clarify what we mean by "policy" and to present the ideas and concepts that figure prominently in the discussion that follows.

What is Policy?

For our purposes, a policy is a statement or a set of statements intended to guide decisions, activities, or efforts that generally describe either desired (or undesired) outcomes and/or desired (or undesired) methods of achieving them. We should point out some implications of this definition. Policies can address either the ends of an endeavor ("It is our policy to see that every child gets an adequate education") or the means that are used ("Parents will be fully involved in the development of educational plans for their children with learning disabilities"). In describing ends, policies can be either positive ("95% of all children will be immunized") or negative, expressing something bad to be avoided ("Vandalism in the neighborhood will not be allowed to rise above 1990 levels"). In discussing means, policies can either *pre*scribe what must be done ("Expectant couples must be told of their option for a family-centered birth experience") or *pro*scribe what must not be done ("Case-workers may not ask personal questions that do not pertain directly to the welfare of the child"). Finally, policies—as we are referring to them—are explicit and deliberately chosen and bear some relation to institutional power and authority.

Policies, then, are principles that guide actions. They are supposed to be more than personal opinion, although they may flow from the personal opinions of decision makers. They operate in every realm of society and vary widely in their specificity, from agreements on higher-order values ("We affirm a national policy of doing good for children") to specific policies that govern administrative practices ("It is our policy not to allow children under 12 years of age beyond the front desk"), internal family policies ("No one eats until Mom is served"), personal policies adopted in everyday life ("I make it a policy to offer my professional services at no charge to those who cannot afford to pay for them"), and to every point in between. Policies come in many forms and under many labels, including cultural norms, laws, regulations, judicial decisions, executive orders, administrative practices, and tradition ("We've always done it this way"). Policies also affect every level of society and every system in the social ecology of the child.

We find policies important to children and their families in the private sector (including for-profit—business and industry, as well as non-profit—civic, charitable, and religious entities) as well as in the public sector (government) and at the neighborhood and community levels as well as at the state and national levels. These include economic, health, employment, housing, banking, transportation, consumer protection, environmental regulation, criminal justice, recreation, and military policies, to name but a few (National Academy of Sciences, 1976). Other policy issues in the forefront in the 1990s include drug control and prevention, child care, homelessness and hunger, HIV/AIDS, and community violence.

"Social policy" is a broader term encompassing everything from a cultural consensus to a particular business policy. "Public policy," on the other hand, typically refers to social policies that are enacted by government agencies. Public policies are enforceable by the police and judicial powers of the state.

Having exposed the pervasiveness and many guises of policy, we now move on to a systematic discussion of social policies affecting children and their families. From our perspective, social policies are part of the ecology of child development. They arise from—and are shaped by—systems at each level of the family's social ecology, and they exert influence on the multiple systems that surround the developing child. In the next section of this chapter, we outline the role of ideological, cultural, and institutional macrosystems in providing the values and norms that shape policy. Following that, we discuss children and their microsystems and mesosystems as intended targets of some social policies and as unintended targets of many others. In the final section of this ecological view of child- and family-related social policies, we consider the broad spectrum of exosystems where cultural values translate into social policies and then are implemented, ultimately to affect the micro- and mesosystems of children.

Ideological, Cultural, and Institutional Roots of Policy: The Macrosystem

Policy finds its roots in the macrosystem (even as self and group interest may hitch a ride with these basic values). Notions of desired and undesired ends, of acceptable and unacceptable means, and of who has responsibility and priority flow from the shared belief systems of a society. Of course, as we said earlier, the degree to which these belief systems are *shared* is not the only issue. Power and resources are not shared equally in our society (nor in most others). Thus, some individuals and groups can shape policy more than others. Nonetheless, the democratic nature of our society means that these more powerful groups must at least give lip service to the common belief systems. They must couch their initiatives in the language of these values. At the very least, then, the shared belief system of the macrosystem exerts a moderating influence in a democratic society such as ours. Individuals and groups pursuing their own agenda must square that agenda with key concepts embedded in the macrosystem—"justice for all," "all people created equal," "due process," etc.

These belief systems are the blueprints of a society—its rules and general game plan—both a source and a reflection of its cultural consen-

sus on "the way things should be." From these systems arise the policies
and other mechanisms by which a culture enforces and reinforces its
fundamental ideology. It is these shared beliefs and assumptions and
the mechanisms enforcing them that give consistency to the aims and
actions of the many systems within a culture and distinguish cultures
with differing ideological roots. That these beliefs and assumptions
often are implicit rather than explicit does not make them any less influential. In fact, implicit, or unstated assumptions, may be some of the
most influential. Child development specialist Laura Dittmann said it
well:

> Although these cultural assumptions are used as guiding principles be-
> cause they have always been a part of our daily lives, we may not recog-
> nize our belief in them because they may not have been put into words.
> One such assumption is that hard work produces success. Another is that
> successful people are good people (and, by implication, that those who fail
> are weak or of doubtful moral fiber). Probably most of us believe that the
> rights of the individual supersede those of the state, except in times of
> war. Many other unspoken beliefs of this nature not only determine what
> we can accept or endorse on each of the other levels, but also influence our
> leaders and spokesmen. (Dittmann, 1979, p. 196)

The first part of this section presents some central ideological and
value issues that have important implications for American families. The
second part addresses societal institutions that are organized around
major cultural values. Following that, we discuss some of the implications of the United States' pluralistic culture for family-related social
policies and also the relationship of some current family-related social
policies to our ideology of pluralism.

Ideological Systems and Family-Related Values

Some cultural values pertain directly to the family. One of the important ideological issues for any culture, for example, is the fundamental
relationship between the individual family and the larger society. Are
families the creation of the state or is the state the creation of families?
People who assume that the answer is self-evident—in either direction—may not be sensitive to the assumptions they carry with them.
Like the fish who was asked to describe water and could not because he
had nothing with which to compare it, these people need to look at the
alternatives.

The Soviet Union viewed families as entities defined by the state and designed to serve the needs of the state (Makarenko, 1954). Children in a Soviet family were held in trust for society, and parenthood was the job of correctly preparing citizens who would serve the state. The Soviet government sought to dictate expected socialization and childrearing practices in the form of a "regime" for child rearing (Bronfenbrenner, 1970). China similarly translates its concern for children and their families into totalitarian control of social relations (Kessen, 1975). In contrast, contemporary American ideology holds that power and control reside initially with individuals, and hence with families, and that families create the state's authority so it may employ collective resources to achieve goals that families desire but cannot achieve by acting individually. However, this was not always so.

In colonial America—Puritan New England to be specific—quite another view held sway. Puritans believed that parents held children in trust for God (Demos, 1986). Thus religious officials (as God's representatives on Earth) made policy for families regarding the treatment of children. In contemporary America there are still groups that maintain allegiance to this theological view (and thus may come into conflict with constitutional doctrines about the separation of church and state, privacy and freedom of choice, etc.).

Another of our culture's strong family-first values holds that the family is a private matter and not an appropriate arena for public intervention, unless the circumstances are so critical that they warrant violating the privacy norm. On the one hand, this firm belief in family privacy offers important protection for families and is consonant with the idea that the state is responsible to families rather than the other way around. On the other hand, as we have seen in earlier chapters, absolute allegiance to privacy as a value may keep damaging conditions like domestic violence from being identified in some families. Furthermore, delaying intervention until a serious disruption occurs reduces significantly both the range of feasible options and the chances of their being effective.

Returning to the statement by Laura Dittmann, we find yet another set of beliefs with important implications for families. If one assumes that hard work produces success and those who fail are weak or otherwise undeserving, it then follows that being poor or troubled means being inadequate, and that a family's problems reflect that family's deficiencies—"us" vs. "them." The assumption that troubled families are inadequate often accompanies the assumption that troubled families are not able to make good choices for themselves. We see this attitude frequently in policies that take the right of choice-making away from a family and give it to some "wise" outsider, such as a social caseworker or family court investigator.

This is also a major component in "blaming the victim" (Ryan, 1976). It is regrettable that somehow determining that those suffering misfortune are in a way deserving of their lot cleanses the collective conscience of a sense of responsibility—"they" not "we" are to blame. As we shall see later, this orientation ignores important risk factors such as poverty, homelessness, hunger, and racism, factors that can impede the normal development of children and disturb family well being. William Blake (1757 to 1827) put it in poetry thus:

Every morn and every night
Some are born to sweet delight
Some are born to endless night.

In addition to cultural values *about* the family, there are cultural beliefs transmitted *through* the family. We expect families to instill in their offspring fundamental values concerning religion, education, citizenship, personal conduct, and much more. As we pointed out in Chapter 4, some people say that the role of families in some of these areas is decreasing, that it is being usurped by other systems in society. Others say that families are being overloaded with responsibilities that other social systems have cast off as our society has unraveled. Unfortunately, both groups may be correct. Society is placing increasing demands on families at the very time that formerly supportive social systems may be weakening or receding.

There also are many cultural values pertaining to nonfamily issues that have repercussions for families. Significant among these is the American commitment to the individual. This commitment undergirds our many safeguards on individual rights and liberties but often leads to an inappropriate individualistic focus that at times operates at the expense of families. Attending only to the child with a disability and not to the entire family, for example, leads to policies that encourage institutionalization rather than home care with appropriate supports for the family. Focusing on just the juvenile offender results in intervention strategies almost certain to ignore the family crisis that may have precipitated the offense.

When dysfunctional families are divided up among agencies (e.g., adults handled by the Department of Mental Health and children are handled by the Children and Youth Service Agency), already frail families are further fractured. This is particularly true in the handling of child maltreatment and the roles and responsibilities of law enforcement and child protective agencies.

A final and related ideological issue relevant to American families is the accommodation of interdependence in a society that values independence. Extension of this insistence on independence from the individual level to the family sphere has produced the image of the family as a self-sustaining unit that is expected to take care of itself and succeed or fail on its own. This expectation of self-sufficiency, like other macrosystem values we have discussed, becomes evident in social policy and practice. The goal of independence, however, ignores the many direct and essential ties between the family and its social ecology. These ties affect the family's supplies of economic and social resources and the range of options available in the environment. They thereby affect the family's ability to attain self-sufficiency and to carry out its other tasks effectively. The *goal* of independence, in other words, ignores the *fact* of interdependence—the mutual dependency of American families and the social systems of their environment.

Notions of appropriate interdependence, a hallmark of many early American communities, have yielded to an ethic of fierce individualism that is also social Darwinism (survival of the fittest families). Both individualism and interdependence have their place in a well-balanced society. Neither should be seen as exclusive of the other.

A cross-cultural perspective shows us that some cultures have positive conceptions of interdependence and place high value on people's reliance on one another. In Japan, for example, a major goal of psychotherapy is to restore the positive experience of interdependence. Other cultures, such as in Denmark (Wagner, 1978) and Sweden (Myrdal, 1968), have established family policies that explicitly recognize the notion of group interdependence. They emphasize the concept that "we're all in this together," while we seem to say "every man (woman and child) for himself!" Again, a balance must be struck. Societies emphasizing interdependence are not without failure and those characterized as individualist do have successful outcomes.

Cultural Norms and Institutional Systems

The values and ideologies of the macrosystem translate into cultural norms and institutions that make the abstract concrete. A social "institution" is a system of roles and practices structured in accordance with a cluster of related values. In fact, a good way to identify or discover what is valued by a culture is to examine its institutions and what is considered normal behavior. A social institution includes mechanisms for regulating behavior with the intention of assuring that roles and practices in the society continue to adhere to fundamental cultural values (Kenkel, 1960). Institutions, thus, are built on organizing ideologies, the normative behavior prescribed by such ideologies, and regulatory mechanisms for producing compliance. These mechanisms are developed and maintained in various ways (e.g., legislation vs. tradition, fiat vs. consensus). In most cultures, value clusters related to government, law, education, the family, and other social matters are institutionalized through norms and sanctions and are important macrosystem influences in the ecology of human development. These cultural institutions set the boundaries and rules within which many specific exosystems operate. In a pluralistic society such as our own, there is a general consensus within which divergent groups can pursue their goals.

The institution of "the family" in the United States is like other institutions. There is diversity within consensus. At its core is a cluster of shared values about what families should and should not be and do, and norms about expected roles and actions that are derived from those values. Mechanisms for ensuring that actual practice corresponds to societal values and norms include family law and the family court system, and the informal but potent influence of social pressure exerted by neighbors, kin, and friends. Underlying values, prescribed norms, and regulating mechanisms pertaining to "the family" all have undergone gradual adjustments to adapt to changing historical, economic, and social circumstances. For example, divorce is no longer a source of social stigma in this country—for most subgroups, at least—as it once was. Active parenting is becoming an expected part of fatherhood as well as motherhood.

Other changes affecting norms about families include redefinition of the role of employment outside the home for mothers of young children (from stigma toward acceptance), adult children living with their parents (at least partially in response to diminished economic prospects for the younger generation relative to their parents), and greater willingness of teenagers to have children without marriage (often a multigenerational pattern). All these changes in the family as an institution may have effects on children and their development—the direction of which is not always self-evident. Public policy is often struggling to keep up with these changes. Laws governing child custody are changing to reflect shared parental responsibility and involvement, with more tolerance for joint custody. Tougher child support enforcement can result in somewhat more responsibility among absent fathers in taking care of their offspring financially (Dixon & Duggan, 1985).

As we saw in Chapter 4, it is important to distinguish between the family institution, which is an abstraction, and any particular family or collection of families, which is not an abstraction at all but a group of very real people. While the institution may be quite influential in shaping the actions of individual families, the collective decisions of individual families, in turn, shape the characteristics of the family institution. "The American family" is getting smaller, for instance, because thousands of individual couples have opted for a family size that is, on the average, smaller than the average family size chosen by their parents. And as they have smaller families they shift the norms, making big families less "normal" and one-child families less "deviant." Social change proceeds through the collective actions of individuals, even when it is in response to macrosystem forces such as technological change. Family norms are bound up in personal choice and belief *and* public language and policy. Even those whose behavior is at odds with general norms may subscribe to them, and thus to the macrosystem of family (Blake, 1979). Those who do not marry may still believe in marriage; those who have no children may still believe in the value of parenthood. This probably exerts a stabilizing effect, providing a focal point around which social change proceeds as a negotiated settlement between what people believe and what they do.

Of course, it also may produce feelings of guilt, sadness, and anger among individuals caught between belief and action—e.g., the woman who believes mothers should stay home with their infants and yet is out in the work force while her baby is in day care, the father who believes men should be breadwinners and yet is a "house husband," the homosexual who values the heterosexual orientation, the unmarried mother who believes in marriage, etc.

As patterns of behavior change, we see more clearly the judgments contained in common language. In 1960, for example, the term "illegitimate child" was acceptable in mainstream professional discussions (cf. Kenkel, 1960, p. 192). Now, most responsible professionals reject that term—arguing instead that all children are "legitimate," regardless of the marital status of the parents who conceive and bear them.

There are, then, two active sides to the interaction between families and the family institution, each influencing the other. Which side of the interaction is given primacy is in itself an important ideological issue for any society. It determines, for instance, how people evaluate a particular family being different from the culture's norm. If priority is given to the institution, if adherence is valued over individualism, or if the family is the creation of the state, then the family will be labeled "deviant," and social mechanisms will work to eliminate the aberration. On the other hand, if primacy is given to the individual family, if we value family autonomy over social uniformity, and if the state is the creation of the family, then we will see the family as "variant"—different, but not necessarily less accepted—and social mechanisms will adapt to the family rather than requiring that the family adapt to them. This is a fundamental aspect of pluralism. It is never easy to understand the ultimate consequences for children. How do we calculate the net effect of accepting divorce, for example? Does less stigma counterbalance the quite real risk that comes with the single parent status?

Pluralism in the Macrosystem: Toward an Appreciation of Cultural Diversity

Discussions of "the family institution" often give the impression that there is a single set of culturally endorsed norms regulating family form and function in this country. Many cultures, such as the Japanese, where people are generally homogeneous with respect to ethnic background, religion, social history, and cultural heritage, and also those cultures with totalitarian forms of government, do tend to have monolithic family institutions. America, however, is a culture of cultures, and little is more characteristic of Americans than their diversity.

Saul Alinsky, who described himself as an American Radical, opened his book *Reveille for Radicals* with a powerful description of the diversity of Americans. He described their geography as being "from Back Bay Boston to the Bottoms of Kansas City . . . to the sharecroppers of Arkansas," their religion as including "followers of all the major religions on the face of the earth," their origins as being "the people of the world. They have come from all corners of the earth." "The people of America are . . . creating a new bridge of mankind *in between* the past of narrow nationalistic chauvinism and the horizon of a new mankind—a people of the world. Their face is the face of the future" (Alinsky, 1969, p. 7). The decades since Alinsky wrote these words have brought still further diversification of America—with the predominant European and African groups being segmented with an enormous influx of Asian and Hispanic populations.

That our people come from so many places means that there is literally a world of variation in the values and norms active in the American culture. And probably nowhere is that accepted variation of beliefs and practices, that American pluralism, reflected more clearly or more significantly than in the families of America. "The American family" is, in fact, a collection of families that are as remarkable for their diversity as they are for the intensity of the loyalty they inspire. To evaluate all families against the unitary norms of any one culture is both to miss the richness and strength represented in this variety and to expect individual families to adapt their own lives to patterns that may not be adaptive for them—that is, to give the institution primacy over the individuality of families.

Our cultural respect for pluralism in family life is highly compatible with other fundamental values in our culture, such as independence, freedom of choice, and assured rights for minorities. "The concept of pluralism suggests that people know what they want and what they need. It contrasts with the principle that someone else knows best" (Demone, 1978, p. 17). "Pluralism rests on the conservative ideal of toleration, of a policy of live and let live, that may come to characterize the pluralistic society in which no group is powerful enough to prevail" (Livingston & Thompson, 1971, pp. 126–127).

Pluralism in the American family institution is a fact, and respect for pluralism is an American value—only at the extremes is it an issue. Pluralism, in other words, is a macrosystem characteristic in the ecology of human development in this country. For our children, it is a characteristic that offers opportunity. It means that society should protect them and their parents from being labeled "deviant" or "bad" because of cultural differences. It offers those who provide child and family services an opportunity to build on unique cultural strengths for more effective service delivery. And, it provides our children with the chance to encounter and develop an appreciation for the diversity and adaptability that characterize the human condition.

Unfortunately, when the values of our culture's macrosystem are translated into the practices of various exosystems, this respect for cultural pluralism sometimes gets lost. Policies, regulations, court decisions, and other exosystem actions are based on various assumptions about how families "ought" to be. If these assumptions are unitary ("families should be *this* way") rather than pluralistic ("families can be *many* ways"), then the effect of these policies and other exosystem decisions will probably be not to help families but to punish diversity. And *that* is un-American.

Social Policies and Children

The previous section looked at the ideological and institutional roots of social policies related to children and at the implications of these macrosystem factors for the way our culture regards its families. If the macrosystem furnishes the ideological roots of policy, the exosystems bring policies into being. We are concerned with social policies because they affect the quality of the child's social ecology in important ways and influence the ability of those who care for children to meet the children's essential developmental needs. This means first and foremost an interest in promoting family well-being as the best way to nurture children.

The Issue Is Children

It is a common assumption that the arena of child-related social policies is limited to policies dealing directly with children and their families. The ecological framework used throughout this text, however, reminds us that children are affected by a large number of forces in their environments. Considering the direct ways in which social policies affect children and their families is a start, but it is not enough. We also must consider the impact of policy on schools, on neighborhoods, on other of the child's microsystems, on important mesosystems that incorporate those microsystems, and on exosystems that the child never encounters directly but that have weighty influence on the child's growth and development.

When guided by an ecological perspective, we are aware of the importance of considering not only the effects of social policies targeted directly at children (e.g., immunization laws) but also the indirect effects that ripple out from efforts aimed at targets other than children and families, such as highway systems, farm subsidies, and milk price supports. We must also be sure to deliberately include children and families in our considerations of complex, and seemingly overwhelming issues, such as substance abuse (cf. Bresnahan, Brooks, & Zuckerman, 1991, for a discussion of the effects of cocaine use during pregnancy).We see that social policies affecting children encompass an enormous range of social and economic issues. These forces do much to maximize or undermine the sociocultural opportunities available to children and to minimize or compound sociocultural risks to child development.

Our ecological perspective thus sends us in many directions to search for sources and impacts of government- and private-sector policies. The focus of our concern, however, is children and how social policies of all types are cognizant of and respond to their essential needs. Throughout this book we have discussed children's needs for physical, emotional, and social nurturance assured by enduring, positive, and reciprocal relationships with a developmentally appropriate number of adults in different roles. These needs are either met or not met in the microsystems of childhood. If the composition and activities of a child's microsystems are characterized by pro-child qualities, then opportunities for optimal growth and development are present. If microsystems are socially or economically impoverished so that these needs cannot be met adequately, then the child is at risk and development is threatened—and the community beyond the family must be prepared to intervene, to compensate, to ameliorate. But it must do all this in a way that maximizes the child's chances for permanent support. This means—in most cases—in a way that preserves the child's family.

The single most important microenvironment for most children is their immediate families. If the policies that guide actions by both public and private endeavors are to be truly and actively pro-child, then policy makers must consider carefully the potential effects of their decisions on the parents' ability to provide for their children's physical needs and to maintain the enduring, supportive relationships that are necessary for emotional and social well-being. There are other important microsystems for children, of course, such as the school and the neighborhood. To foster an environment that is rich in support for child development, policies should positively affect the stability, social density, adult–child ratio, and other child-related attributes of these social systems, to be sure. But families come first.

Public and private sector social policies are important to children, not only because they affect children's microsystems, but also because they affect the mesosystems or linkages between those microsystems as well. It is important to a child's development that mesosystems be characterized by multiple, diverse, and stable connections, and by complementary values. Policies that support strong mesosystems with these characteristics represent opportunities for children. Those that weaken connections between microsystems place children at risk.

Having summarized those attributes of a child's micro- and mesosystems that pro-child policies must consider and protect, we turn now to the exosystems in the child's environment. These are the agencies, organizations, mediating structures, and settings affecting the family's social environment. Our discussion considers three subgroups of policy decision makers: governmental, legal/judicial, and private sector. Although we address them separately, we do not mean to imply that they should function in isolation from each other. Indeed, a coordination among these exosystems is essential if we are to meet children's needs.

Governmental Exosystems

Let us begin this discussion with a surprise quiz. How many of these alphabet agencies can you identify: HHS, NIH, ACYF, NIMH, OSAP, NICHD, DHHS, AFDC, GAO, CRS, OMB, HSMHA, ADAMHA, OCD, HRA, FDA, and PHS? And the list could go on. All of these are acronyms for some of the hundreds of federal agencies that have some programmatic concern for children and families. Not mentioned, but very influential, are governmental bodies at the state, county, city, and other levels. Within the federal alphabet avalanche, in 1978 at least 34 federal programs administered by six different federal agencies were directly involved in child welfare and foster care services (Children's Defense Fund, 1978). In 1988, 46 programs in 11 agencies could be linked to activities monitoring, subsidizing, providing food for, or offering child care services for families (U.S. General Accounting Office, 1989).

The federal bureaucracy is constantly being expanded, restructured, and redirected through both legislative enactments and executive branch orders in ways that daze all but the most alert and determined insiders. This is one reason why private organizations concerned with children often band together to hire Washington-based representatives to keep track of the interests and issues. It is also why the field relies so heavily on the Children's Defense Fund to keep an eye on legislation and executive actions that translate into influence on children.

Usually we think of legislators as the creators of governmental policy and public administrators as the implementers of those policies. Much legislation, however, is written with a "broad brush," and in developing and implementing regulations and protocols, the program administrators in the bureaucracy become powerful policymakers in their own right. In fact, what child educators and the service program industry cannot accomplish at the Congressional level is often targeted at the level of bureaucrats who implement policy and devise specific programs.

The federal government now is involved in every social welfare category, and all levels of government are involved in a staggering array of social programs (Lynn, 1980). We can trace the impetus for our present reliance (some would say *over*reliance) on the federal government at least back to 1935 and the creation of the Social Security Act. This "safety net," devised in reaction to the Great Depression of the 1930s, evolved to the point where "by 1978, states and localities were eligible for approximately 270 different human service grants" (Light, 1972, p. 2).

The 1970s took the Social Security System to the brink of fiscal disaster as the system was broadened to include a very wide range of safety net programs without commensurate increases in its fiscal foundation. Although some stability has been brought to Social Security through Congressional attention, better agency management, and higher Social Security taxes, the long-term fiscal health of this program is still in question. What was originally intended to be a short-term answer to the particular problems of the Depression of the 1930s became a central and permanent tool in national efforts to address the unmet needs of children. Important policy decisions regarding how to best care for those most vulnerable among us will continue to dominate the political scene in the 1990s and beyond. That much is clear.

Several approaches have been taken with the aim of assisting families more effectively by shifting the focus from federal to local initiatives. These include decentralizing community services, fostering the development of informal helping networks, promoting volunteer efforts and private sector initiatives, and (most importantly) encouraging coordination of these separate, but related, resources.

Community-based agencies and organizations have the potential to form an important mesosystem support network. This was a theme in Chapter 9, and here we recover some of this ground, but with a different slant. Community service agencies have traditionally dealt with individual family problems in a discrete, case-by-case manner focused on intrafamilial troubles—an approach that has not kept up with family needs. The ever-rising caseloads of most agencies are testimony to this failure. The traditional approach is too narrow and neglects the importance of extended family, community, and neighborhood supports. An increase in services based "close to home" can contribute much to the child's ecological niche. The quality of mesosystem connections is enhanced by congruence between the value systems of helper and helpee. Being closer to problems can help attune workers to ethnic and other indigenous values (although in some cases it can itself be a problem, as "indigenous" staff cannot overcome their own issues—issues that they share with "clients"—and thus are unable to deal with them, relegating them to "domains of silence" (cf. Musick & Stott, 1990). Coordinating service agencies at the local level can add important new linkages to the child's mesosystems if these issues can be overcome.

The child's ecology improves still further by the inclusion of diverse connections through informal networks. New models for service delivery rely more on approaches that attempt to harness informal community strengths on behalf of families (Garbarino, Stocking, & Associates, 1980; Whittaker, Garbarino, & Associates, 1983). Although it is a far cry from model to program, the promise is there. Self-help groups (e.g., Parents Anonymous) are good examples of the power of supportive groups, in this instance with an emphasis on the professional helper (Lieber & Baker, 1977). We are reminded of the ways in which other groups in our nation's history have dealt with the problems of oppressive environments.

In discussing "Ethnic Enterprise in America," Light (1972) detailed the occurrence of informal welfare systems among immigrant Chinese and Japanese peoples. For example, these groups developed systems "rotating credit associations" to help finance new business enterprises for group members who could not get regular bank loans. Other immigrant groups have had similar support systems that included finance and job hunting assistance, English classes, and other means of fostering a feeling of community belonging and support. We can build on these traditions in programs for promoting family and community well-being in today's social scene.

As we have noted repeatedly, schools provide another microsystem for the child, and the school–home mesosystem is a very important influence on development (Garbarino, 1981b). Here we observe that neighborhood schools have long been the traditional means of meeting the educational needs of children in American communities. They naturally lend themselves to school–home and school–neighborhood mesosystems. Thus, policies that undermine neighborhood schools can have a negative effect on these mesosystems, whatever else they may accomplish. For example, busing to achieve racial integration of schools may have this as one of its liabilities, whatever its benefits in other areas. A more active effort to promote residential integration—at the neighborhood level—makes more ecological sense.

Local boards that govern schools must be careful to support the school–home and school–neighborhood mesosystem. Involving parents in school programs, providing home visits by school personnel, and increasing recognition of the rights of parents in matters related to the education of their children can enhance the school–home relationship. The school–neighborhood mesosystem can be strengthened in many ways also. Schools can allow local volunteer groups to use their educational facilities. These groups are often thwarted in their attempts to organize and contribute, simply because they have few resources. Schools can involve students and staff in neighborhood-related projects to the mutual benefit of all, and otherwise improve a waning public image that many schools are experiencing. Schools are perhaps the most pervasive institutional outposts in contact with America's children and we should utilize this valuable resource.

Local governments figure prominently in discussions of decentralized services and informal supports. This will continue to be volatile as states and localities engage in new forms of budget battling under the federal block grant programs in which federally collected dollars go directly to the states for disbursement. Presently, in the face of economic downturns and many a state's penchant for balancing deficit-ridden budgets by skimming inordinate proportions of block grant monies truly intended for localities, many cities, towns, and neighborhoods will be required to fight even harder than before to maintain acceptable levels of funding. Human services, one of the hardest hit categories, have struggled to devise alternative, cost-effective approaches.

The Legal/Judicial System

Besides the legislative and administrative branches of government described above, there is the judicial branch, the legal or court system. Judicial decisions can have both direct and indirect effects on families. A court decision to remove a child from his or her home because of abuse or neglect, for instance, affects one particular family, whereas judicial mandates about family life in general affect the institution of the family. Both sometimes result from the same "landmark" or "precedent-setting" case. "The judicial decision to intrude into a family, in the main, rests on legal standards formulated by a legislature and interpreted by courts. From a governmental perspective, state intervention is meant to be a response to parental failure" (Katz, 1971, p. 56). The American macrosystem has evolved into one in which the judiciary is the arbitrator in most domains of family and community life.

The issue of child custody is a good case in point because it is an example that can relate our earlier discussions about ideology and values to an actual practice situation, the removal of children from their homes (as we discussed it in Chapter 9). Goldstein, Freud, and Solnit (1973, 1979) have been among the leaders in redefining the issues involved in child custody. They base their arguments on what they call the "least detrimental alternative" model. Essentially, they argue that a family's "integrity" should be safeguarded at all costs by raising the threshold for state-sponsored intervention to the highest possible level.

It is essential that we continue to develop more and better strategies to support families and prevent their demise. If your only "tool" is removal, then every "problem family" is a broken one. We believe that more early preventive action by the community can forestall the need for judicially driven intervention later. If a strong family privacy/autonomy model inhibits this preventive relationship, then the model is part of the problem not the solution, as Goldstein, Freud, and Solnit maintain. None of this is easy, as the frustrating history of foster care and adoption policy initiatives makes amply clear (Children's Defense Fund, 1981).

A major problem with their model is that it precludes early interventive or preventive involvement with families to avoid family breakup. The least detrimental alternative model results in intervention being legitimized only at the point of quite serious family trouble (Garbarino et al., 1982). As Maybanks and Bryce (1979) pointed out, "The distinctive skills in child welfare are those developed in the placement of children, and the distinctive body of knowledge is that pertaining to separation of the child from his family" (p. 17). This is clearly not enough! A child's welfare is best served, however, by strengthening the most important microsystem in the child's life, not by removing the child from it. Thus, the skills and systems most needed are those that help families deal effectively with problems underlying abuse or neglect, such as inadequate income, substance abuse, medical problems, stress, lack of social supports, and lack of effective child rearing and discipline skills.

The emphasis on case review included in the Adoption Assistance and Child Welfare Act of 1980 has received empirical justification. A 1985–1986 study of factors affecting how quickly children in foster care were reunified with their families found a very strong positive relationship between the amount of time between case reviews and how long the child was in foster care (Hubbell et al., 1986). The act appears initially to have prompted a reduction in the number of children in out-of-home placements across the country. From a 1977 high of over one-half million children, the number of children in foster care declined to a 1983 low of 269,000.

Since then, the curve has turned upward: 276,000 in 1985 and 340,300 in 1988 (Family Impact Seminar, 1990). Experts discussing the steep and continuing rise (Family Impact Seminar, 1990) cite several causes, including "lack of federal leadership and guidance" (p. iii), "fragmentation of the child welfare system, which is not really a 'system' in any state" (p. iii), and "too many wrangles between mental health, child protective services, special education, juvenile justice, and foster care workers about who is responsible for what pieces of the treatment that the child and family will get" (p. iv)—in other words, failure and confusion in the exosystems affecting children and their families.

The Private Sector

Much of our discussion has centered on issues in public policy—that is, policy in the form of enforceable legal mandate. But the private sector is an extremely important source of social policy as well. The previously mentioned impact of business's "move to move up" policy, along with our generally transient society, has done much to disrupt naturally occurring forms of support networks in neighborhoods. People often do not settle down in the place where they grew up or elsewhere near to their family. And the "next best thing to being there" (the telephone company's cheerful ad for its long-distance service) is still *not* being there. These problems can be compounded by economic policies that seek to induce, even coerce, movement away from old established neighborhoods, (e.g., in failing Northeastern industrial centers) to provide a workforce for rapidly developing areas of our nation in the Sun Belt. Such policies are not intended to break up networks of kin and kith. Rather they are based on hopes for revitalizing the economy and corporate needs. But such approaches have not given adequate consideration to the quite predictable impact of these policies on extended support networks of families and to the potential consequences for children and the quality of social life in the affected areas.

The private sector (business and industry) affects families in many ways. Individual companies directly affect the lives of their employees and employees' families through hiring, promotion, and relocation practices, maternity/paternity and sick leave policies, fringe benefit packages (health, life, and disability insurance, retirement plans, flexible spending accounts for dependent care, etc.), employee assistance programs, and other company practices.

Employers can support families by making family-oriented choices in these areas. They can, for example, plan initiatives to humanize the work situation, such as reducing mandatory overtime that causes parental fatigue, thereby returning a more satisfied parent to a child's microsystem. They can provide training to sensitize managers to the role of family concerns in employee productivity and to increase managers' skills in dealing with family-related issues. They can provide family-relevant information—on insurance options, quality child care, child-rearing issues, family budgeting, dealing with grief, and many other topics—in employee lounges, on employee bulletin boards, in paycheck envelopes, and through the personnel office.

Private sector companies affect a wide network of families by affecting the community's economy and other quality-of-life factors through operational practices, such as buying locally, recycling, providing adequate parking, and assuring noise and pollution control. Also affecting families and children are businesses' philanthropic activities, such as supporting local civic and social causes, participating in adopt-a-school and similar programs, and encouraging volunteerism among employees. Private concerns can be more aware of the parental responsibilities of employees and consider family-related needs in fringe benefits and company activities (e.g., child care vouchers as a fringe benefit, and parental leave programs).

Another way in which the private sector can make contributions to the well-being of families is to become active in supporting community-based family prrograms. Landrum Bolling, Chairman of the Council on Foundations, has written that

> The strengthening of private initiatives to serve human needs ought to be *one* national objective around which all political factions could unite [to] support those voluntary, nonprofit, nongovernmental institutions, agencies, and programs that care for the needy, promote community well-being, and enrich all our lives. (1980, p. 1)

But we must use caution here, lest we be drawn into an approach that makes unrealistic assumptions about the ability and willingness of the private sector to replace the public sector in child welfare.

The key to a positive role for the private sector is Alfred Claassen's (1980) depiction of social problems as "investment opportunities." That is, "capital disposed in a specified fashion over a given period of time will effect a greater contribution to the value of the net output of a set of social actors than will its employment in any known alternative pattern" (p. 529).

Private sector investment in the well-being of children and families may appear at first glance to be motivated by altruism, but increasingly, business leaders are viewing it as enlightened self-interest. For example, in calling for business involvement in educational reform, a committee of business executives noted:

> If present trends continue without corrective action, American business will confront a severe employment crisis. This scarcity of well educated and well qualified people in the work force will seriously damage this country's competitive position in an increasingly challenging global marketplace. . . . Our industries will be unable to grow and compete because an expanding educational underclass will be unable to meet the demand [of jobs resulting from new technologies]. (Committee for Economic Development, Research and Policy Committee, 1987, pp. 4–5)

An example of such private sector action is an insurance company's investment in a community-based program to prevent juvenile delinquency. There are obvious benefits to the community from a successful program of this sort. Beyond these, the company could accrue considerable benefit by a reduction in delinquent acts and a consequent reduction in insurance claims. It would seem that private sector investment in healthy families and safe communities can complement the free enterprise concern for profit when there is a strong macrosystem blueprint for corporate social responsibility (cf. Garbarino & Crouter, 1982).

Moreover, the private not-for-profit sector must be included in any comprehensive child and family services policy. Issues ranging from education to family counseling, homelessness to hunger, are being addressed by countless charitable, civil, and religious organizations.

For example, one response to inadequacies in public food-stamp programs has been local food banks that aid people in need of food by providing emergency supplies. Food banks are often housed in church basements and are informal, volunteer-staffed programs relying on private donations. Food banks are now found in most communities. Many are associated with religious organizations. Indeed, the religious community has long been a quiet giant in the family support field. However, due mostly to government avoidance of this fact, church groups are an underdeveloped resource in translating family policy into practice.

Indeed, some recent examples demonstrate that government sometimes is biased against churches in the human service field. Concern for separation of church and state and the narrow interests of some religious groups works against the fair distribution of government resources to all families. An obvious example of this lies in federal day care proposals that explicitly exclude church-based programs from eligibility for day care subsidies. It is out of touch with the realities of day care provision at the local level to view eliminating these service providers as appropriate, but it is a reality.

An Integrated Approach

Until now our discussion has taken us *from* various policy sources *to* their respective costs or benefits for children and families. However, as policy practitioners, we may be more interested in how to identify an appropriate source of policy after being confronted with a particular problem. Here we see the point about multiple influences shaping a specific issue being well illustrated.

Consider the problem of "latchkey children" who get themselves ready for school in the morning and/or return to empty homes after school or are at home in the evening, on weekends, or on school holidays because their adult caretakers are still at work. With increasing numbers of single-parent households and economic conditions requiring both parents in two-parent families to work, more and more children are in this situation. At the same time, many households lack extended networks of family and highly involved neighbors to watch out for children who are on their own. Alternative policies, initiated by both the public and private sectors, could and should come to the aid of children and their caretakers. Government can support parents remaining at home to do the important job of childrearing and support the enforcement of child-support payments. The public sector can supply supports and incentives (e.g., tax write-offs) for before- and after-school care programs. Businesses can institute assorted alternative scheduling programs for employees (e.g., flextime, job sharing, and support care for school-aged children in group settings and family day care homes). Voluntary and religious organizations can staff before- and after-school co-ops and telephone helplines for children at home alone. This should help ensure the consistent care and supervision of school-aged children, and support for child care could function in a similar manner for very young children.

The coordination of policy decisions is important for at least two reasons. First, policies frequently work against one another or have unintended negative consequences. Second, there is rarely a single clear solution to problems that trouble children and their families. Each level of policy intervention contributes to the overall goal of providing the care that children require. In the latchkey example, some potential solutions would enable increases in the amount of time that children and parents spend together. This would enhance the opportunity for reciprocal parent–child relationships. Other approaches focus more on supplying sufficient other adults to care for the children while parents are absent, thereby, increasing the quality and density of a child's network. Still others are primarily concerned with relieving the financial burdens that can drain an otherwise enthusiastic parent. All of these contribute to a positive approach to supporting children by supporting their caregivers. Indeed, it is becoming an adage in the child and family services field that to support children, we must be willing to support their parents (Emlen, 1977).

Social Policy and Family Support: It Is Everybody's Business

In the first two sections of this chapter, we have considered some macrosystem and exosystem effects on social policies that affect children and their families. There is another level at which social policies are influenced, and that is the individual level. A personal commitment to supporting families and caring about children in everyday life can be expressed in both professional and personal efforts. Of course, this starts with one's own children and family and extends to all those with whom one has contact and relationships (e.g., co-workers, neighbors, and church members). It may extend to taking personal action to prevent child abuse by supporting high-risk parents one knows who are under specially stressful circumstances—as survey research conducted by the National Committee for Prevention of Child Abuse suggests significant numbers of American adults do. A personal commitment goes beyond attention to specific children and families, but also extends to a "political" concern for their networks. A personal commitment to the quality of life of our children may include, therefore, efforts to influence social policies in pro-child directions. Everyone can do something, whether it be voting for pro-child and family candidates or joining a child-oriented political action committee (such as KidsPAC) to influence legislation.

One issue mentioned at the outset of this chapter was the translation of romanticized notions of family into vigorous and concrete activities on behalf of children and their families. How do you turn emotion into action? This is a recurrent focus of all policy practitioners. For example, in an effort to prevent child abuse, many organizations focused attention on heightening public awareness during the 1980s. The result, according to pollster Lou Harris, is that there was a phenomenal rise in those identifying child abuse as a major problem during those years (from about 10% to about 90%). However, we began the 1990s with the National Advisory Committee on Child Abuse and Neglect concluding that because of deteriorating social and economic conditions for families we faced a spreading epidemic of child maltreatment.

More broadly, in 1991 the National Commission on Children concluded that the general status and well-being of children in American society continue to deteriorate, linked in large measure to the growing economic disparities (with the poor getting poorer and the rich getting richer) and the rising tide of violence, abandonment, and exploitation associated with the drug culture. We are not suggesting that human services professionals cast aside their chosen professions to become full-time political activists. Rather, we are recognizing that the roots of environmental risks to children often lie in social policies, and meeting the developmental needs of children may require policy-level adjustments in priorities and practices. In this respect, there is ample opportunity for all of us to make a difference in the lives of children and their families. We must reduce the demand for remedial services *and* increase the supply (Goffin & Lombardi, 1988).

Children need concerned adults to become their advocates on both a personal and a political level. As Steiner and Milius (1976) pointed out, children neither vote, contribute to candidates, nor lobby. "As political actors, children are useless and dependent. If children are to be either advantaged or simply protected, other groups must speak on their behalf" (p. 143). These groups are made up of committed individuals, and the level of intervention is not always the Congress of the United States. Demonstrating concern for children can involve helping an abused teenager find appropriate services or working on behalf of a needed school bond issue, as well as expressing approval for a proposed piece of legislation.

In both our professional and our personal lives, we should be alert to policies and practices that weaken supports for families and increase risks to children, and we should act as agents of change in those situations. Harold Demone (1978) described the change-agent role in human services reform as "part art form, part science, part experience, and part luck" (p. 8). He describes several types of "change agentry," of which three are most important to us here: the *lobbyist,* the *advocate,* and the *citizen participant.*

Lobbying is simply the act of letting one's views be known to elected representatives charged with policy decision making. As Demone put it:

Fundamentally, the goal of the game is to enhance one's interest and failing that, to protect that interest. The interest may be personal, organizational, or an extended network. It may be self-centered or humanitarian, special interest or public interest. Often one lobbyist's special interest is another's public interest, and vice versa. Although one can lobby all sorts of organizations, it is commonly perceived as an activity directed at a public official or body. (p. 17)

Related to the more formalized, rule- or law-governed lobbying tactic is the role of the advocate. "Advocacy has classical origins as an essential component of the practice of law. Similarly, the physician advocate speaks for his patient. Social workers have traditionally intervened on behalf of their clients, as architects do for their clients. Most, perhaps all, client-serving professions would define representation of their clients as a time-honored task" (Demone, 1978, p. 31).

Jane Knitzer favors the adoption of an advocacy role for professionals:

The term advocacy has become an integral part of the vocabulary of social-change agents. Advocacy refers to interventions designed to reduce or eliminate barriers within institutions or systems that result in the inequitable treatment of individuals or classes of individuals, the denial of needed services and resources, or the undermining of the individual's capacity for healthy development and self-determination. The target for change in advocacy is not the individual, but the policies and practices of the institution with which individuals must daily interact—the schools, the courts, the welfare bureaucracies, the hospitals; the local, state, and federal laws that shape so much of what happens in these institutions; the political decision-making process at all levels of government by which priorities and fiscal policies are determined; the administrative regulations that interpret laws and political mandates; and the practices and ideologies of professionals that get in the way of responsive help, particularly to those of a different culture or ethnic background. (1980, p. 293)

The purposes and levels of advocacy and lobbying are similar. The distinction is usually thought of in terms of structure. That is, lobbying activity is regulated by law, whereas advocacy is not so structured. Also, lobbying is typically a class-action event (i.e., directing change for a group), while advocacy can be either class- or case-action directed (Knitzer, 1980). A good example of case advocacy is the "guardian ad litem,"—a volunteer individual who may be appointed by the court in child abuse and neglect cases (see Fraser, 1977). In effect, the guardian ad litem offers independent representation for the abused or neglected child to advocate for his or her rights and best interest in court battles.

The last change-agent role—the citizen participant—is perhaps the most direct. Rather than working to influence policymakers, citizen participants become policymakers themselves, representing the needs of their own neighborhoods and communities on boards, commissions, and advisory councils of all types. Under the leadership of former HEW Secretary David Mathews, for example, the Department of Health, Education and Welfare (now Health and Human Services) set a goal of increasing public interaction and citizen involvement in its activities. At the peak of this effort, approximately 90 HEW programs called for citizen participation (Demone, 1978). Head Start continues this tradition. At the local level, citizen participation can be an important force for change in human services agencies and hospitals, schools, zoning commissions, economic development departments, transportation authorities, and numerous other community policy bodies. Such grass-roots participation is a most effective means for people to get the services they need. It is the cornerstone of the family policy for the Good Society.

RESEARCH CAPSULE

One of the foundations of social policy is information (others include political influence, self-interest, ideology, economic conditions, the mass media's interpretation of historical events). Social indicators are statistical statements about conditions. The Center for the Study of Social Policy (1250 I Street, Suite 503 NW, Washington, D.C. 20005) has mounted a major project designed to identify, develop, and communicate social indicators of childhood well-being in the United States. Such social indicators have included health measures (e.g., percent born with no early prenatal care, infant mortality rate, and percent low birthweight babies), economic measures (e.g., percent living in poverty), and measures of education and intellectual competence (e.g., academic achievement and IQ).

However, in choosing social indicators, it is necessary to explore the conceptual issues involved (Garbarino, 1991). These conceptual issues include

- The role of "well-being" in contrast to risk and illness in the assessment of childhood.
- The role of context in defining the significance of indicators. (How do demographic and economic changes affect the significance of indicators?)
- The relative importance of child indicators and family indicators. (How do we balance the fact that family level factors are quite powerful with the fact that the variability of childhood experience for siblings within the same family is significant?)
- Balancing the need for simplicity and complexity in the selection and construction of indicators. (How do we deal with the fact that simple measures communicate to a broader audience than complex measures, but that simple measures are liable to distort reality and be unable to capture subtleties?)
- Finding an appropriate way to combine indicators of input with indicators of output. (Is it enough to measure the "raw materials" that families and schools start with? Or should we include measures of how well children are doing once they leave childhood?)
- Clarifying the cultural and value foundations for setting standards and selecting goals. (Can we assume that all the various ethnic groups within

our society have common goals for their children? If not, who should decide when there are competing definitions of "childhood well being?")

Thus, the prospect of constructing a set of social indicators of child well being is challenging. The information must not only be timely, but be comprehensible to the naive user, and offer a path to action.

PRACTICE CAPSULE

During the 1970s, the Columbia University School of Social Work conducted a cross-national study of social services in Canada, France, Israel, Poland, the United Kingdom, the United States, West Germany, and Yugoslavia. The purposes of the study were not only to compare the various social service systems, but also to analyze ways in which political, economic, social, and cultural factors in each nation influenced those systems and their service-delivery mechanisms. One facet of the study focused on service provisions for early identification and intervention into child abuse and neglect. Thus, this study provided an excellent examination of *how* social policy affects professional practice.

One finding of the study was that different nations had different perceptions of how large the child maltreatment problem was and whether it was a distinct problem or part of a broader set of child development issues. Poland, for instance, reported the incidence of child abuse to be small, while in Yugoslavia it was viewed as part of the general problem of "predelinquency." Other nations saw the problem as being greater. Canada, the United Kingdom, and the United States were making efforts to define and distinguish among types and levels of abuse and neglect, whereas France, Israel, and West Germany were reluctant to distinguish abuse as a focus of concern separate from the problem of child maltreatment.

The United States, at the time of the study, was beginning to develop case identification strategies that often called for additions to existing social service mechanisms. In France, Israel, Poland, and the United Kingdom, on the other hand, case identification was being incorporated into existing universal maternal and child health programs that see all children from infancy on. Whether the nation's program included visiting health workers, as in the United Kingdom, or a network of low-cost clinics, as in Israel, these countries already had mechanisms for encountering all children at regular intervals. Case finding thus entailed alerting existing systems and personnel to look for signs of maltreatment or for situations that put children at risk for abuse or neglect, rather than initiating new systems for this purpose. Thus, a nation's need for a specific child-abuse identification policy differed significantly on the basis of the broader state of family policy. This tells us to keep the total policy context in mind whenever we consider specific policies.

FOR FURTHER READING

Advisory Committee on Child Development. (1976). *Toward a national policy for children and families*. Washington, D.C.: National Academy of Sciences, 133 pages.

Data on families and children are reviewed with particular attention to economic resources, health care, child care and special services, government programs, and modes of service delivery. Future research recommendations emphasize naturalistic studies, program evaluation, impact analysis, and the development of social indicators on children—all important methods for policy interventionists.

Berger, P. L., & Neuhaus, R. J. (1977). *To empower people: The role of mediating structures in public policy.* Washington, D.C.: American Enterprise Institute for Public Policy Research, 45 pp.

This is a short, concise, and handy document. The authors have an easily read style. Issues in the welfare state are discussed in terms of institutions that mediate between individuals and the society at large (i.e., family, neighborhood, church, and voluntary associations). It emphasizes pluralism, people's strengths, and alternative policy strategies.

Gaylin, W., Glasser, I., Marcus, S., & Rothman, D. (1978). *Doing good: The limits of benevolence.* New York: Pantheon, 171 pp.

This thought-provoking set of essays examines both the appropriateness and the effectiveness of paternalism as a model for the relationship between society and its dependent members. The final essay offers an agenda for social policy based on an amended model.

Kamerman, S. B., & Kahn, A. J. (Eds.) (1978). *Family policy: Government and families in fourteen countries.* New York: Columbia University Press, 522 pp.

Policies and practices of various European nations relative to children, the elderly, women, and families are described by the contributors to this volume. It provides an interesting contrast to United States policies and programs. Content and style vary among contributors.

Keniston, K. (1977). The Carnegie Council on Children. *All our children: The American family under pressure.* New York: Harcourt, Brace Jovanovich, 255 pp.

The Council investigates from a broad perspective the changing social contexts within which American families live. A great volume of data is harnessed to demonstrate the pressures of contemporary family life, and recommendations for remedy are made. These solutions are not limited to the typical services, which are also discussed, but include radical suggestions such as guaranteed income levels, changes in laws related to children and families, and other interventions aimed at altering societal institutions.

Miller, G. (Ed.) (1989). *Giving children a chance.* Washington, D.C.: Center for National Policy Press.

This collection brings together a policy agenda for children. George Miller chaired the U.S. Congress's Joint Committee on Children, Youth and Families. Chapters were contributed by leading researchers and advocates. Together they present a good outline of the knowledge base and its policy implications.

Rice, R. M. (1977). *American family policy: Content and context.* New York: Family Service Association of America, 159 pp.

This readable book has become a primer in family policy discussions. After documenting many of the ways in which families are vulnerable to societal pressures, Rice reviews several approaches to development of a family policy for the U.S. and outlines overarching values that should be supported by such a policy.

Steiner, G. Y., & Milius, P. H. (1976). *The children's cause.* Washington, D.C.: The Brookings Institution, 265 pp.

Tracing the history of children's defense movements, the authors illustrate the politicization and institutionalization of child development policy. Values are investigated, specific agencies are described from inception to demise, and the influence of the political environment is discussed. The text also reviews policy strategies, discussing dilemmas in certain types of programming and the politics of comprehensive policymaking.

QUESTIONS FOR THOUGHT

1. Although respect for diversity in family forms is an American value, many policies and practices reflect an assumption that families consist of a husband who is employed, a wife who stays home, children, and no others. What are some of the consequences (positive and/or negative) of these policies and practices for other family forms (e.g., two-earner, single-parent, childless, three generation)? Consider, for instance, tax policies, family health insurance coverage and benefits, and social security provisions.

2. The apartment is dirty, the kids are dirty, and they obviously do not get enough to eat, but their mother never leaves them unattended, and there is much affection among them. Should the state intervene on behalf of these children? If so, what form should the intervention take? What values and assumptions about children, families, and the role of the state are reflected in your answers?

3. What recent economic or employment trend, legislative enactment, court ruling, business or consumer protection decision, or other social policy action can you think of that will affect children and families? Was the intention of the policy to influence family life? How does it influence family life? How does it influence families? Are the results likely to be beneficial or harmful?

4. Conflicts often arise in policy decisions (e.g., between needs of children and needs of parents, between costs and allocations, and between the promise of a policy and its practical implication). Identify the probable origins of these conflicts. Explain how this identification can aid in resolving these problems.

5. How is a policy different from a practice? Is there overlap? What are the problems of a patchwork approach to policy? What are some barriers to a comprehensive approach?

6. Traditional approaches to family troubles emphasize remedial, individual interventions. List alternatives that the human ecological model might suggest as legitimate types of intervention. (See Chapter 9.) Now, what would a policy practitioner do to influence decisions that would encourage and support these innovations?

7. In Norway and Sweden, fathers are offered paid paternity leaves following the birth of each child. Should paternity leaves be offered in the United States? Why or why not? If paternity leaves were available to American men, what do you think is the likelihood that men would use them? Should we focus attention on better *maternal* leave policies instead?

8. Looking back over the past few months, what opportunities for child advocacy have you missed? Seized?

11

In Conclusion: The Issue Is Human Quality

James Garbarino and Anne C. Garbarino

The fundamental thing is for both decision makers and ordinary people to understand that the human lot cannot be trusted essentially to technologies, structures, legislations, and treaties—however indispensable this societal patrimony and its updating and revamping indeed are. There cannot be any salvation, unless people themselves change their values, mores, and behavior for the better—The question is, then, one of human quality, and how this can be improved. . . . This is the human revolution, which is more urgent than anything else if we are to control the other revolutions of our time and steer mankind towards a viable future.

(Peccei, 1977, p. xi)

Children always offer an opportunity for making the future better. Our physical resources may diminish, but our human ones will not. The quality of life for the next generation could be better than it was for past ones. To make the human quality of our children's lives better, we must understand children's needs and how to enhance elements in their lives to lead to a richer, more varied, more satisfying growing up both for them and their parents. This is what we will discover in "The Issue Is Human Quality."

Childhood as the Eternal Frontier

The frontier has been an important part of the American character and history. It stands for openness, independence, and equality among people. It also served as an important safety valve for defusing conflict in the established, populated areas of the East. The United States' Census Bureau declared the American Frontier closed in 1890 (Turner 1965/1897). And according to Turner, with its closing came a change in America, and the special American character was in jeopardy. Of course what was "opening the frontier" to generations of European immigrants meant invasion and genocide for native peoples—"the American Indians." In North, Central, and South America "invaders" from Europe displaced, enslaved, killed the natives—wantonly and with disregard for their culture, indeed for their very humanity. Millions perished in this holocaust that began in the fifteenth century and continues to this very day in some countries—particularly in Brazil and Guatemala.

1992 was the 500th anniversary of the voyage of Christopher Columbus to "the New World." This event is no longer called the *Discovery* but rather the *Encounter*, to signify that it was not the finding of a hitherto unknown place, but rather the beginning of a relationship between one set of peoples (who had "discovered" America thousands of years earlier) and another (who sought new lands and peoples to dominate and exploit for their own ends). So the frontier, like most human phenomena, has a dark side too. Couple that with the role of slavery in the history of our society, and we can come to the issue of human quality with our eyes open.

Yet the frontier image is a powerful one. There is psychological and sociological truth in Turner's analysis, whatever its historical flaws and limitations. We are, in the 1990s, also at the end of a frontier. Just as the opportunities for western expansion were drying up at the turn of the last century, we now find the frontier of cheap energy and unlimited, petroleum-based industrial growth similarly "closing" (Garbarino, 1992). With the increasing emphasis on "the limits to growth" (e.g., Council on Environmental Quality, 1981), we need to find where our next frontier lies.

Here, as was the case with literal frontier, there is a dark side too. We need only look to the legacy of toxic pollution, the extinction of animal and plant species, the great disparities of wealth, and the general ugliness of much modern life.

So, where can we go to find open spaces to test and offer us the scope we need for our fullest human development without creating more death and destruction? The exploration of outer space is a challenge open to only a few. The challenges of our material world—ecological, agricultural and economic—are mainly to conserve. That is good, but we still need frontiers. The personal and social frontiers, however, will always offer challenges. Personal, spiritual, and social challenges come together in raising children. The opportunity is open to almost all, and it offers the awesome and wonderful task of breaking new ground, making the future. Childhood and childrearing are the new frontier, to find new ways to become human without the dark side.

Although they are not "unknown territory," children always offer an opportunity to make the future better. They allow parents to reaffirm and rejuvenate their basic commitments to love, life, work, and play. Children allow them to say to the human race that they think well enough of the world and of people to bring new people into it, or to foster those already here. However, each new generation brings with it a challenge: How will the adults of their world make things "better for my kid than they were for me?" An impulse to better the human condition, although it is now tempered and toned down from bouncing nineteenth-century optimism, is still a part of the human character. How shall we improve the quality of life for our children? Where do we stand now, and what can be done for the future? To answer these questions, we should look anew at children, their characteristics and needs, and at the conditions of childhood.

When it comes to human resources, the most important basic measure is the welfare of children. A society that does not do well by its children abandons the quality of its future. Mary Ellen Burris, writing in 1979, presented a disturbing picture based on public opinion surveys that offered a snapshot of the dark side of the new America:

> A happy marriage, an interesting job, and a job that contributes to the welfare of society—each of these factors *decreased* in the percentage of people naming them as ingredients of the good life. In contrast, these things *increased* in importance: a color TV, a lot of money, really nice clothes, a second color TV. And consider this: in late 1975, more people named children as an ingredient in the good life than a car; now it's just the reverse. (*Behavior Today*, June 4, 1979)

Is this the beginning of an ugly future in which we turn our backs on children in favor of material comforts? Is the new frontier to be as destructive of our basic values as the destruction of the Native American population? If so, we lose our souls. For the best quality of life, we must focus our attention on the well-being of children. In the long run, color TVs, cars, and nice clothes are a losing proposition when contrasted with children on *both* practical and moral grounds.

Why care for children in the first place? Because they are the future. The continuing of this good earth and whatever is good on it depends on them. If children are to have first claim as our new frontier, then parents and the conditions of parenthood are of crucial importance. The condition of families is our first topic.

We begin with families because it is foolhardy to think of children apart from the conditions of life for their parents and guardians. Hansel and Gretel were left in the woods as they were because their family was starving and could not feed them. Scientists as well as story tellers affirm this. Arthur Emlen, an ally of children, put it: "If you care for children, then care for parents" (Emlen, 1977). "Parents" should be broadened, of course, to include all the caregivers: grandparents, foster parents, child-care workers, etc.

Children reflect the quality of life for the adults in the society, for better or for worse. Child abuse reflects the worse. Commenting on domestic violence in the animal world, Desmond Morris (1970) observes that adults typically respond to stress and pressure by taking out their frustrations on children:

> The viciousness with which children . . . are subjected to persecution is a measure of the weight of dominant pressures imposed on their persecutors. (Morris, 1970)

Complementing this observation is Rock's report (1978) that gorilla mothers who are socially impoverished (isolated from their peers) are prone to mistreat their infants. When they are restored to the simian community, however, these mothers perform adequately. Social impoverishment is equally destructive to human childrearing. Domestic violence among humans is also an indication of excessive stresses and strains (Straus et al., 1980). Abuse and neglect are associated with the family's isolation from friends, neighbors, and helpers (Garbarino, 1977a,b). Parents need love and support in order to be loving and supporting to their children. Their ability to be good parents is not solely their own doing—their society has a great say in what stresses and supports they will encounter.

For the thesis presented by Burris—that valuing things is taking the place of valuing children—there is the antithesis presented by public opinion polls that continue to show family life at the top of people's lists of what is important. Based on a survey of adults in the United States conducted at the same time as Burris did hers, Harris (1978) concludes that, "Clearly, the most satisfying part of life to many Americans today is family life. A substantial 92 percent of the public say this is very important to them. And 67 percent say they are very satisfied with the way their family life is going." Apparently, despite flirtations with materialism, most of us recognize that more luxury items are "the unreal objects of this world," as one Eastern philosopher puts it. The challenge in designing a better world for the future is to support and build on the truth that children are of paramount importance, not obscure it by over-emphasizing and falsifying people's basic material needs.

There is a cultural struggle here. The things of real value that we have, and thus can offer to our children, are our time, our interest, and our attention—that is, our love and care. However, it must be a value of society as well as of the individual parent for that person to do the job well. We need to look at the adult's larger context—the society—for a moment.

Society and the Good Life

Searching for the meaning of the "Good Life" has been *the* traditional philosophical issue. Although largely abandoned by contemporary philosophy, the search for the Good Life has been taken up by some within the social sciences. In its "soft" side, under the guidance of the gentle theorists Maslow and Rogers, modern psychology has sought to provide psychological answers to the eternal question: What is the good life? The *psychology* of self-actualization is an *ethic* of existential meaningfulness. There is, however, even within the "hard" side of psychology, a recognition of the centrality of this most qualitative of issues. "Quality of life" is an important research issue in its own right. To ask, What is the good life? is to pose the fundamental issue of psychological quality. It is to ask, What brings meaning to human experience? It is to ask, What makes reality a positive experience? Once this question is posed, it opens a whole new vista, or rather reopens it.

The issue of quality in a psychological context has new implications in the modern era. In the past, considerations of quality were intrinsically elitist. The material conditions of life did not permit a widespread concern with the quality of life. The promise (and premise) of the modern era has been its tantalizing prospect of making available adequate material conditions to permit quality of life to become a concern for the masses. Indeed, the whole body of utopian writing dating from the eighteenth century is built on the premise that technological improvements permit the dispersion of human quality (Garbarino & Garbarino, 1978). The trick is to build a society that can offer "the good life" in the long run and to do so without slavery, genocide, and exploitation. We call this "the sustainable society," and it requires technology to serve human needs in a humane way, without creating subordinate classes of people.

It is ironic that the same technology that offered the promise of the good life for all is now seen as the principal threat to that life in the future by making us hostages to an energy-intensive, unsustainable economy (Garbarino, 1988). Universal dispersion of the benefits of technology was (and still is) presumed to be the shortest route to widespread qualitative improvement in the human condition. This ideology permeated even to the creation of statistical indicators for measuring the day-to-day life and future of societies. As Campbell (1976) has noted, as early as 1798, Sir John Sinclair described statistics in the following language when he introduced them in his *Statistical Account of Scotland*: "The idea I annex to the term (statistics) is an inquiry into the state of the country for the purpose of ascertaining the quantum of happiness." Some statistics are "transparent" in the sense that they tell us something important about the quantum of happiness. For example, census data tell us something important when we learn that life expectancy is decreasing for African-Americans and is increasing for Caucasians—69 vs. 76 years in 1988—and the gap is widening.

As is often the case, the fullest picture of reality comes not from social science, but from fiction, where the rough edges of incomplete factual information can be smoothed by the visionary imagination. Some of the best thoughts on the sustainable society in which quality predominates over quantitative concerns come from the utopian novelists. Austin Tappan Wright's *Islandia* (1958/1942) presents such a totally sustainable society, one in which the pursuit of human quality is totally preeminent over concerns with materialist quantity. The productive and social unit in Islandia is the small family farm, handed down through generations. Family members make extended visits to other farms and meet annually for their only political event, a congress of landowners. Islandians have no contact with other countries and little "modern technology." They are educated in one-room schoolhouses and have one university. Individual work pace and family integrity are valued over speed and production. Formal social services are nonexistent. Informal helping networks provide routine help to individuals and families faced with acute problems. *Islandia* presents an alternative to all the superficial trappings of what we consider modern society. But, it allows for universal dispersion of quality through social organization and enough material technology to permit the dignity of economic adequacy to all. The two characters in the excerpt below are discussing how Islandia would change were it to become "modern" in the sense of the term understood by John, the contemporary American.

DORN: Why should I change?
JOHN: Progress!
DORN: Speed, is that progress? Anyhow, why progress? Why not enjoy what one has? Men have never exhausted present pleasures.

JOHN: With us, progress means giving pleasures to those who haven't got them.

DORN: But doesn't progress create the very situation it seeks to cure—always changing the social adjustment so that someone is squeezed out? Decide on an indispensable minimum. See that everyone gets that, and until everyone has it, don't let anyone have any more. Don't let anyone ever have any more until they have cultivated fully what they have.

JOHN: To be unhappy is a sign we aren't stagnating.

DORN: Nor are we. "Happy" wasn't the right word. We are quite as unhappy as you are. Things are too beautiful; those we love die; it hurts to grow old or be sick. Progress won't change any of these things, except that medicine will mitigate the last. We cultivate medicine, and we are quite as far along as you are there. Railroads and all that merely stir up a puddle, putting nothing new in and taking nothing out. (Wright, 1942, pp. 84–85)

The essential issues of human experience are direct, simple, universal, and unchanging: the parents' mating, childbearing, and childrearing, is repeated by the children's puberty, adulthood, and once again mating. Wright's utopian *Islandia* envisions a society in which technology is *selected* to permit a style of life in which those fundamental human concerns are the principal agenda for the human community, unencumbered by false issues of social change and social development. Wright's vision of "what matters" for quality in human life is paralleled in the "scientific study of human experience." Psychology merges with ethics in this utopian vision.

In a paper entitled "Subjective Measures of Well-Being" (1976), Campbell reviewed the limitations of modern, objective measures of human society. He noted their fundamental falseness because they cannot attend to the subjective experience of reality, the ultimate criterion for judging meaning. Campbell built on the findings from national surveys, showing that during the period between 1957 and 1972, when most of the economic and social indicators were moving rapidly upward, the proportion of the American population who described themselves as "very happy" declined steadily, and that this decline was most apparent among the part of the population that was most affluent. Affluence alone is not enough. It must be accompanied by social meaning. When people living in those states (primarily in the Southeast) that have the lowest "objective quality of life" (measured by socioeconomic development) were asked about the subjective quality of their life, they reported more positive experiences than did their counterparts in the more affluent "developed" states. We should be wary of simple economic solutions to human problems. Campbell concludes that we need indicators of personal well-being to complement conventional social indicators. On the negative side, James Gilligan (1991) has argued persuasively that shame (built on negative comparisons by and with others) is one of the principal causes of violence and social nihilism. We need social indicators of shame and self-esteem.

These subjective measures would, in large part, tell us how things stand between children and their parents. Rather than being the simple accumulation of characteristics, human development is the process by which an individual constructs a picture of the world and acquires the tools to live in and with that picture. It is all about identity, personal and social. Bronfenbrenner (1979) defines development as

> the person's evolving conception of the ecological environment, and his relation to it, as well as the person's growing capacity to discover, sustain, or alter its properties. (p. 9)

This concept of development will figure prominently in efforts to understand how the future of a sustainable society depends on the quality of life it offers to children. *Although children develop abstractions, they do not develop in response to abstractions.* They are a genuine reflection of the actual quality of life as it is directly experienced. Compared to adults, children are much less liable to delusion, to being drawn away from the basics of life quality. But just what are "the basics," the fundamental determinants of quality for the subjective human organism? Campbell concludes that the basics are "the presence or absence of those various forms of interpersonal exchange that provide psychological support to people" (Campbell, 1976, p. 122).

Those interpersonal supports are just the things that provide a positive influence on human development, as Bronfenbrenner defines the term. They both enlarge the capacity of the developing human to utilize the environment and provide the raw material that humans need to fashion a satisfying existence. The need for interpersonal support is the fundamental human need; satisfaction of that need is the foundation of social quality. Campbell was concerned with this fundamental need in adults, but when we consider the world of children, we recognize that the same interpersonal factors dominate.

For the child to flourish, the parent must have access to the social riches of family or family surrogates, kin and kith. Just as child and family are inseparable, both in interests and in functions, so family and community are wedded by a functional connection. Unless a society assures that parents have the means to rear children, it will be faced with an unfortunate mixture of unhappy parents and inadequately prepared children. Both are a direct threat to the goal of quality in the human experience.

It is reassuring to know that the fundamental needs of children and adults are relatively simple and basically unchanging. It is a challenge to meet both those needs simultaneously. To do so for the whole population—resulting in a quantum leap in happiness—is still further a challenge to the skill of society's social engineers, managers, politicians, and individual citizens. The task is not an easy one, and it demands a more precise examination of the conditions favoring an intensive social investment by parents in children without psychological bankruptcy to those adults. To that task our attention next turns.

Poverty and Affluence

Although the economic needs of children are actually quite modest, we know that poverty is bad for children and adults alike. Severe economic stress is a fact of life for at least 20% of American children and their parents. We know poverty is bad for children because it undermines their health and well-being (National Academy of Sciences, 1976), unless they have compensatory social resources. It subjects them to damaging stresses, both directly by placing them in threatening situations and indirectly by undermining the ability of their parents to give what children rightfully deserve—finely attuned and affectionate responsiveness. Severe economic deprivation robs families of the social necessities of life; it leads to social impoverishment. Social impoverishment is the principal direct threat to human development. A socially rich child is better off developmentally than a socially impoverished one, even if the latter is materially wealthy.

The promise of modernity is to release families from the burden of poverty. The reality of poverty as a destructive social and psychological force is undeniable. Margaret Sanger, a leader in the American family planning movement, gave this account of her work with mothers living on the Lower East Side of Manhattan during the early 1900s:

> Each time I returned to this district, which was becoming a recurrent nightmare, I used to hear that Mrs. Cohen "had been carried to a hospital, but had never come back," or that Mrs. Kelly "had sent the children to a neighbor and had put her head into the gas oven." Day after day such tales were poured into my ears—a baby born dead, great relief—the death of an older child, sorrow but again relief of a sort—the story told a thousand times of death from abortion, children going into institutions. I shudder with horror as I listened to the details and studied the reasons back of them—destitution linked with excessive childbearing. The waste of life seemed senseless. One by one worried, sad, pensive and aging faces marshalled themselves before me in my dreams, sometimes appealingly, sometimes accusingly. (Sanger, 1938, p. 89)

When life is so impoverished that children are a burden, they tend to impoverish further rather than to enrich the quality of life. In our efforts to design a sustainable society centering on the labor-intensive nature of childrearing, we must avoid naive sentimentality about "the good old days." This parallels issues in the economic and technological spheres (Schumacher, 1973). Childrearing is fundamentally a labor-intensive rather than a capital-intensive enterprise. That is, it requires a person's time even more than money. Therein lies the challenge and the hope for a sustainable society.

Just how labor-intensive *must* childrearing be? This is an important issue. Can we substitute money for time and still get well-developed children? Children learn the world they experience and then seek to live in that world. A sustainable society must be composed of people who have constructed an internal reality based on "human" rather than material values. If material investment is substituted for psychological and social investment in the rearing of children, the only outcome can be a materialism incompatible with a sustainable society. The essence of development is the child's conception of the world and his or her ability to "discover, sustain, or alter its properties" (Bronfenbrenner, 1979, p. 9).

A sustainable society requires people who will direct their developing competence toward cultivating renewable, nonpolluting resources. Chief among these "clean" resources is social intercourse. Campbell found that social interchange, set in the context of enduring relationships, is the primary reliable source of meaning and satisfaction in the human experience. In the 1990s we are witnessing a national rebirth in story-telling—certainly reflecting a yearning for "authentic" social experience. This bodes well for designing a sustainable society. Such a society is compatible with "human nature," if that society is built on enterprises that generate and sustain a comfortable social web, surrounding, dignifying, and supporting the individual human being and giving dignity to simplicity. Children and childrearing must stand at the heart of such a web. They are the most reliable "occasion" for knitting people together in mutually satisfying, socially productive work and developmentally enhancing play. They are the perfect vehicle for organizing a sustainable society. What we need to do (and it is no small task) is to work out the implications of this principle for every aspect of our economic, political, and social life.

The temptation to use material investment as a substitute for psychological investment is real. The Soviet Union tried creating boarding schools to provide "disadvantaged" children with high-quality, professional child care. It abandoned this compensatory intervention program when they discovered that "you can't pay a woman to do what a mother will do for free" (Bronfenbrenner, 1979). We would add that the same is true of fathers—they are not for sale. Material investment seems an easy way out of making the necessary labor-intensive investment, but it is ineffective at best and developmentally damaging at worst. Surveys in the 1950s showed that high on the list of reasons given for purchasing a television was "to bring the family back together" (Garbarino, 1975b). The actual result, of course, was physical togetherness but psychological apartness, parallel rather than interactive social experience.

A reservoir of support for childrearing and family life exists, but its potential effects are often blunted by the tantalizing proposition that parents can have their cake and eat it too, invest in their children and do their own thing as well. Unless their "thing" is childrearing or they find someone else whose "thing" it is (the English nanny and Chinese granny come to mind), children may suffer a lack of attention and involvement with others. To do this thing well, parents need a social environment that cares for them as they care for their children, that values parenthood concretely. The issue is not simply working mothers or day care, but a social environment that supports parents—fathers and mothers—in meeting all their parental, occupational, and spiritual needs. It is the processes of caring that count: the structures affect only the odds for or against caring.

In discussing material versus social/psychological investment in childrearing, we must return to the concept of support systems raised in earlier chapters. Support systems provide *both* nurturance and feedback. They provide the individual with warmth and security in addition to guidance and direction. The protective function is particularly important for effective parenthood and nontraumatic childhood.

Support systems are the staff of life in childrearing. Indeed, the principal factor mediating between the parent and child relationship and the larger society is precisely the family's network of support systems. The richness, diversity, and strength of these support systems contribute to their effectiveness in providing nurturance and feedback to parent–child relationships. This richness is one of the principal environmental determinants of the child's developmental robustness. In this respect, the good life for families resembles the political good life for communities: Social pluralism both protects society from dangerous excesses and provides diverse and enriching experiences by combining consensus and diversity (Garbarino & Bronfenbrenner, 1976b).

Although most of the public debate concerning the fate of children centers around the "decline of the American family," the issue actually lies outside the family, in the family's relation to the community. Understanding this relationship is necessary for looking at the state and future of American families. The principal threat of the modern world to the psychological quality of life is the weakening of traditional sources of social pluralism. Social pluralism is a wide range of people and groups surrounding the family, which, although they may differ in some attitudes and values, share a basic commitment to the family in whatever form it takes. Without support systems, the parent–child relationship is thrown into jeopardy, and it is this jeopardy that is commonly referred to as "the decline of the American family." Lack of support systems is "social impoverishment."

Social impoverishment springs from a variety of factors. Among these are geographic mobility, instrumental interpersonal relationships, and the erosion of stable neighborhoods. Though it has its positive side (financial benefits in some cases), geographic mobility strains and often breaks the functional relationships that underlie support systems. Although modern communications permit support systems to function over long distances, as in the case of the weekly transcontinental phone call to grandparents, such geographically dispersed social networks cannot have the same day-to-day significance as more concentrated, localized ones. Perhaps equally threatening, however, is the fact that geographic mobility may produce an adaptive cultural response in which short-term, immediate relationships become desirable in place of the more long-term interpersonally invested relationships that require daily contact over an extended period. Geographic mobility may make it more difficult for children and parents to have a common history with those in their current support system and to have shared experiences that build trust, understanding, and the motivation needed to provide nurturance and feedback. Interpersonal relationships may become more instrumental. Such relationships are inconsistent with genuine support systems in which validating the intrinsic worth of the person is the essential element. The unraveling of community support systems—nurturance *and* feedback—is linked to a six-fold increase in depression among American adults (Seligman, 1989).

The notion of "designing a sustainable society" presupposes that we can make alternative arrangements even if we cannot recapture what was good about the past. The promise of modern life was to relieve the physical burdens of the past, and thus permit social enrichment to grow in the context of material adequacy. Will it? It all depends upon whether or not we can shape a cultural consensus on the new social frontier. Our goal in this book has been to help define that new social frontier in terms of childhood and meeting the needs of children. In that frontier, we will find the very social and cultural agenda that will also deliver *adults* from spiritual and material crisis.

It may seem to be a contradiction in terms, but we think there is a need for "applied utopian thinking" to meet the social challenges before us. We say this because so many of our problems seem to call forth extremes of thinking—either so concrete they never get beyond noses on faces, or so visionary they don't help people see how we might get from the proverbial here to there. We need a kind of middle range vision to guide us. As we have stated before in this book, we think children and child rearing *can* provide the necessary focus—if we are willing to see it.

Making the Social Investment in Children

Just where do we stand on the matter of psychosocial investment in children? What are the prospects for the future? The evidence is mixed and often ambiguous. The challenging intellectual task of sorting out this evidence is complicated by the fact that experts often go—and are driven—well beyond their data to reflect their hunches, their bias, their fears, and even their political aspirations. Issues of family and children were the leading edge for political ideologies and social activism in the 1970s and 1980s. This complicates the task before us because it demands that we separate enduring patterns of change and development from transitory politicized "events."

There is a deeply rooted tension—one might even say conflict—in American life about children. We hold ourselves up as a child-oriented society, but we consistently place ourselves at odds with the needs of children. We do so because of a kind of cultural poison (Zigler, 1976). As *Time* magazine put it "those who detect a pervasive, low-grade child aversion in the United States find it swarming in the air like pollen" (Morrow, 1979, p. 42). Politically, children are losers (Featherstone, 1979; Hewlett, 1991; Zigler, 1976). When the crunch comes in matters of budget and priorities, children lose out to the economic interests of adults and corporations. The issue is really one of investment: Where do we place that which we value? We think that several important points can be made on this score.

First, most Americans retain a fundamental and unwavering commitment to parenthood, despite the declining birth rate (Glick, 1979). In an extensive review of childlessness in the United States, Judith Blake (1979) reported the results of a nationwide survey of adults dealing with the advantages and disadvantages of childlessness. She found that adults will not be priced out of the parenthood market by the high economic costs of childbearing and child rearing, although they will decrease the number of children. People do value children for their intrinsic worth, and this affirmation is our bedrock for the future (Blake, 1979).

On balance, it seems clear that having and caring for children is a primary investment that is still being made and will continue to be made in the future. Smaller families are still families and tend to be good families at that (Lieberman, 1970). This fundamental commitment to having a child or children saves us from one side of the problem. It does not, however, guarantee the future. The quality of life (that is, the quality of children) in the future is by no means assured simply by the fact of their being born. The issue of enduring, appropriate, and necessary psychological and social investment remains. The fate of children born to young, poor, unmarried drug-addicted mothers is a definitive statement on that score.

The thrust toward self-gratification may be incompatible with parenthood. Some data we cited earlier (Chapter 3) suggest this is a real problem and bear repeating. A study by Bahr (1978) offers us a rare opportunity to compare adolescents' views of their parents in the same community over a 50-year span. It should come as no surprise that teenagers value fathers who spend time with them. Having enough time with one's father is a continuing and pervasive issue. In 1924, 64% of the females and 62% of the males felt that the most desirable attribute in the father is the fact that he spends time with his children. In 1977, these figures had risen to 71 and 64%, respectively. This change is small and reflects the unchanging nature of father–adolescent relations. What is of real interest, however, is a significant change occurring in how much adolescents value their mothers spending time with them.

In 1924, 34% of the boys and 41% of the girls placed a premium on having their mothers spend time with them. By 1977, the percentages had risen to 58 and 66%. This may reflect the gradual departure of mothers from the day-to-day lives of their adolescents over a 50-year period; a period that corresponds directly with the tremendous increase in mothers working outside the home. Mothers and fathers have become more alike in their day-to-day relations with children, we suspect. These data complement others collected by Bronfenbrenner (1979) and his colleagues that show a continuing decline in the amount of active time spent by parents with their children and link this decrease to a variety of disturbing trends, including impaired social functioning, alienation, and even profound unhappiness.

What makes people happy? For most adults, happiness ultimately lies in what Erikson (1963) called the issue of one's relation to the future, that of "generativity versus stagnation." Happiness lies in psychological and social investment in the future, for the quality of the future. Investment in children, either directly as a parent or indirectly as one who makes the world a better place for children, is important for happiness and shows a generally healthy world view. How well does our society do, and how well can it do in the future, in making this investment a productive one, a happy one? The answer will be found in the neighborhood and institutional lives of adults.

Neighborhoods and the Institutional Life of the Community

Whether or not the intrinsic value of children will triumph over their cost depends in some measure on how supportive the family's neighborhood is. The quality of neighborhoods as contexts for family life has become a significant issue for students of community and human development. Although attractive in principle, "neighborhood" has proven very difficult to define in operational, specific terms as we reported in Chapter 8. Perhaps one of the best statements of what a good neighborhood is comes from Kromkowski (1976), when he says that:

> A neighborhood's character is determined by a host of factors, but most significantly by the kinds of relationships that neighbors have with each other. . . . A healthy neighborhood has some sort of cultural and institutional network which manifests itself in pride in the neighborhood, care of homes, security for children, and respect for each other. (p. 228)

When stated this way, the significance of neighborhoods as support systems for families is clear and indisputable. A strong and supportive neighborhood can make the task of parenthood easier and more rewarding.

Economically and demographically, similar settings can present very different social environments, and the quality of life for parents and children can be likewise affected. Our studies (Garbarino & Sherman, 1980; Garbarino & Kostelny, 1992a), have highlighted how neighborhoods selected on the basis of their economic and demographic similarity can differ in their child maltreatment and infant mortality rates.

When these settings were examined, expert informants ranging from elementary school principals to mailcarriers saw low-risk areas as healthy neighborhoods and the high-risk areas as socially sick environments. Samples of families drawn from each neighborhood have been interviewed. The families identified very different patterns of stresses and supports, different patterns in the use and source of help, differences in the size and quality of family social networks, differences in the use of formal support systems, and differences in parental evaluation of the neighborhood as a setting in which to raise children. Also, parents in the high-risk neighborhoods report high levels of stress in their day-to-day lives, and a general pattern of social impoverishment.

High-risk neighborhoods are areas in which neighbors do not help each other, where there is suspicion about contact between parents and children, and in which the norms and behavior (including local politicians) increase family weakness. We do not know exactly how this applies to rural areas, but the available evidence suggests social impoverishment is a threat in the rural environments as well (Rosenberg & Repucci, 1981).

Creating and maintaining strong neighborhoods for families are principal challenges in designing a sustainable society. All the elements of quantitative growth work against neighborhoods. Mobility is a threat. Use of motorized transportation permits bedroom communities, undermines walking, and works against neighborhoods. Restrictive rezoning that produces residential ghettos works against neighborhoods because a functioning neighborhood requires a mix of commercial and residential activity. Within cities, strong neighborhoods resemble strong small towns (see Chapter 8). Will the seemingly inexorable trends toward the destruction of neighborhoods be permitted to continue? The answer will come in public decisions concerning rezoning and mass transportation. The quality of life for children is determined in large part by progress in the institutional (exosystem) life of the community.

The design and delivery of human services, the nature of adult work, and the structure and function of educational institutions all have a significant effect on the quality of life for children. Human services are delivered formally through a variety of public and semipublic institutions. How well can these formal support systems be integrated and balanced with the informal support systems, the "private enterprise system" of human services that offers most help on a day-to-day basis? As Chapter 9 showed, models for integrating formal and informal support systems are being developed, and in fact, are already in place in some communities (Garbarino, Stocking, & Associates, 1980).

In the world of work, the concern is whether the role of parent will be sufficiently recognized. The entrance of large numbers of mothers of young children into the workforce has made us keenly aware of the need to balance the relationship between work and home. The issue of working mothers has not been resolved satisfactorily—both their needs and the children's needs must be met. Providing adequate and developmentally enhancing day care for preschool children is an unsettled and highly charged issue. Our solutions to these dilemmas will have a bearing on the quality of life for children and, in fact, on the quality of children—their ability to be happy, productive adults—for life.

When the world of work forces an adult, male *or* female, to choose between being a good parent and a good worker, children suffer and ultimately, the future is impoverished. As we move toward designing a sustainable society, we must keep in mind the need to establish norms about the world of work that will reduce its intrusion into family life. As we saw in Chapter 2, a well-adjusted person is distinguished by the ability both to work and to love. A high-quality society will arrange itself so that people can do justice to both. We find a parallel process at work in the schools.

Children's primary "work" is play, but most of their formal work takes place in school. Research on school size suggests that large schools (enrollments greater than 600 in grades 9–12) tend to become psychologically unsustainable (Garbarino, 1980d). Large schools discourage participation, create elitism, encourage staff inflexibility, and most insidiously, alienate those students who are already academically marginal (Barker & Gump, 1964). By 1970, most youth in the United States were enrolled in big schools. Historical data on school size chronicle the decline of quality of life for children in this, their primary institutional setting. In this area perhaps more than any other, we have seen an unthinking policy of growth undermine and destroy socially desirable settings (small schools) in deference to goals of quantitative progress. The assumption that big schools mean power and opportunity directly parallels the notion that an unlimited policy of economic growth means progress. However, depersonalization and a reduction of social pluralism in the child's experience are alarming consequences of large schools. Bigger means, paradoxically, *less* social diversity for the individual student. Although school size nearly tripled from 1950 to 1970 (Garbarino, 1980d), the data suggest that a reverse of this trend is possible. Just as escalating energy costs have given pragmatic impetus to "walking neighborhoods," these same forces demonstrate the cost effectiveness of small schools. Such schools can now be technology intensive to permit a resource-ladened environment: both academically rich *and* character building (Garbarino, 1981b). Even where physically separate, small schools are not feasible, several small, complete schools can share the same facility.

Family, neighborhood, and the institutional life of the community are always in flux. Economic and demographic conditions may shift the direction of their influence, sometimes favoring supportive environments, sometimes undermining them, but the constant issue in all three areas is the stance taken by social policy.

A cross-national survey of public policy and public services for families concluded that the United States is relatively lax in providing for families and their support systems. The study conducted by Kahn and Kamerman (1975) found that in many respects: "The rhetoric in the United States proclaims the value and sanctity of children in family life; reality is something else. We provide nothing like the child-care services or cash benefits to protect child and family life that the European countries do." Former director of the Office of Child Development Edward Zigler (1976) echoed Kamerman and Kahn's judgment: "We think we care more than our actions would say." The scene in Washington seems to pit the "truly needy" vs. the "truly greedy," with powerful special interests winning out. This message from the mid-1970s rings true today.

Decisions in the future must take into account the needs of children (our future) and of their parents (our present). For example, can we give workers adequate time for family and still have profitable corporations? The answer, we believe, is "yes." It is the nature of ideology to permeate all aspects of everyone's daily life. Thus, whether or not we develop a suitable pro-child ideology will be revealed not in grand pronouncements or even in master legislation, but in the day-to-day decisions that affect and shape the lives of families. The central position of ideology returns us to the political debate about the future.

Children and the Social Policy Debate

To recapitulate, social impoverishment is the denuding of the individual's environment of those relationships that function as support systems and that provide nurturance and feedback. Growth defined by quantitative product only leads to social impoverishment. If we permit the social impoverishment of parents' lives, we undermine the quality of life for children and thus the quality of our future. An ideology of gross economic growth undermines children by contributing to social impoverishment. It does so by destroying the social integrity of neighborhoods, by increasing the demographic and social homogeneity of communities, by devaluing parenthood, by overemphasizing the importance of material productivity as a criterion for personal value, by increasing the instrumentality of social relations, by divorcing work and home, by promoting large schools, and by fostering values that emphasize material gratification over social responsibility. The growth policy debate must come to terms with the possibility that conventional thinking—the quantitative product orientation—is not socially sustainable.

It is a great temptation to propose a nostalgic, "good old days" solution, but this is useful only for comparison. What did families need in the old days that they still need now? Basic needs are the same. With our different world, how can we give them what they still need? As individual families struggle with this issue, institutions (schools, courts, businesses, labor unions, churches, etc.) can make a vital contribution; they will decide how successful most families will be. If institutions are dominated by a quantitative orientation to growth, then families will be swimming against a tide that, for most, will be irresistible. The future is a public policy issue. There are at least five areas in which productive action is possible. These topics reflect an intermingling of action and ideology, of cause and effect, of shaping events and shaping minds. To design a sustainable society we must make progress on each of the following fronts.

Family Impact Analysis

A scientific basis for evaluating the impact of change—particularly economic growth—on families is rudimentary. Investment in this area of research and development is a high priority item on the agenda in designing a sustainable society (Johnson, 1978). We need to make progress in moving toward a kind of "social currency" that can be used to compute the costs and benefits to families of various policies and decisions (Giarini, 1980; Garbarino, 1992).

For work to proceed on the family impact analysis concept in earnest we need to make progress in developing some sort of "social currency" with which to evaluate the wisdom and costs of alternative social arrangements. The "beauty" of economics is that it has an irrefutably important, dependent variable with palpable face validity: goods and services to which dollar values are readily attached. This elegantly simple conception of reality allows the advance of economic theory and research. It enhances the value of economic theory and research. Moreover, it permits economists to participate in the formulation and implementation of social policy.

The forecasting and prediction that economists offer are often misleading, if not simply wrong. More important than those errors, however, is the fact that we know when they are wrong and have a reasonably firm basis for evaluating the magnitude and consequences of those errors—in terms of wholesale and retail price indices, GNP, unemployment rates, inflation rates, and all the other dollar-based paraphernalia of economic analysis.

It is true that economists have many faulty assumptions about social reality. The concept of "rational economic Man," for example, argues that all human behavior is governed by conscious, rational weighing of advantage. It is furthermore true that most economists do not have an adequate concept of the "hidden costs" of technology and the modern, energy-intensive, petroleum-based economy (Schumacher, 1973; Commoner, 1971). All this and more is true.

Yet the strength of economics remains: It has a basic, dependent variable that provides coherence and a measure of conceptual order to its efforts. We find one of the best example of the value of dollars as an organizing principle in the set of "budgets" published by the Department of Labor. For an economic environment such as the typical urban or suburban area, these budgets indicate the dollars needed for a family to function at several standards of living—what are termed "poverty," "low," "middle," and "high" income levels. These budgets provide an anchor point for socioeconomic analyses of all types (e.g., Garbarino, 1975a, 1980d). Based on the availability of dollar resources to meet essential needs (food, clothing, housing, taxes) and make discretionary purchases (vacations, recreation, cultural resources), the standard budgets are a marvelous product of economic analysis, even if one disagrees with the specific dollar values at each level.

The budgets are important and insightful because they begin to recognize that the value of money is not primarily a matter of each additional dollar having the same impact as the previous one. That is, when using money as a factor in analyzing social phenomena, the key question is not simply, How much does one have?, but rather, What *kind* of life style can one purchase? The major phenomena are essentially qualitative. Is a family doomed to poverty? To struggle with no discretionary income? To a comfortable material existence? When applied to broader social analysis, the questions become these: What proportion of the population is comfortable? Are some groups confined to poverty while others are uniformly comfortable?

Simple analyses of average income do not answer these questions, for they do not address the essential issue of human behavior and development. The beauty of "dollars" as a unifying variable is that it can translate diverse items of interest (such as the multiple factors in the material conditions of life) into a single composite measure with validity and analytic power. The concept of dollars is, of course, limited in its application, since many vital social phenomena are not readily translatable. And that limitation brings us to the need for a social equivalent to "dollars."

Students of human development do not as yet have an equivalent to "dollars" as an organizing concept for research and theory. Research focuses on the documentation of statistically reliable differences. These differences are usually hard to relate to one another for purposes of combination or comparison. There is no underlying "currency" into which we can translate variables for purposes of integrating analyses. Does human development research and theory have a direct analog to GNP? to poverty? to price indices? to inflation rates? Is there a basis for the delineation of model social "budgets" to establish different standards of living in the noneconomic spheres?

The answer, of course, is no. But the need is quite real. One of the big tasks facing social science in the coming decades is to make progress on such a social currency. This will reform economics as well (Giarini, 1980). We believe the development of competence is a natural focus for such progress. A rich environment is one that succeeds in socializing competent children while maintaining a high quality environment.

Neighborhoods as Units for Analysis and Planning

Local governments and corporate leaders need to become aware of the importance of thinking of neighborhoods—not simply of individuals and communities—as units of analysis. Data collection policies of the U.S. Census Bureau have been changed to reflect this orientation, and in many ways adequate data are a precondition for intelligent policy. Growth policies must consider how they affect existing neighborhoods as well as how socially sustainable new residential developments will be (National Commission on Neighborhoods, 1979). Without such a conception at the heart of planning and zoning decisions, neighborhoods are doomed to be eroded and new "developments" will not be neighborhoods. Decisions about transportation subsidies and zoning regulations will have a large impact on the micro- and mesosystems of children.

Education of the Public

People should be educated about the importance of families in the social structure. The allure of materialism is great, but there are reservoirs of support for the primacy of family-related "payoffs" manifest in public opinion polls (cf. Harris, 1978). There is support for family life and there is recognition that family stability is a precondition for meaningful existence. We need public articulation of how personal and institutional decisions can tap these resources and respect the values they reflect. We need to resolve the conflict between home and work.

Linking Professionals and Natural Helping Networks

Natural helping networks provide effective "human services" as well as substantial psychic payoffs (see also Chapter 9). A socially sustainable society requires that we reduce the exclusiveness of professionalized institutions. Also, it requires that we not build up budgetary expectations that are a constant economic drain and a periodic political liability.

Instead, we should encourage greater sharing of helping functions with natural helping networks (Froland et al., 1979; Whittaker, Garbarino, & Associates, 1983) and demystify psychological services.

Age Integration

We need to decrease age segregation in our society. One goal is bringing adults into contact with youth in the context of purposeful, goal-directed activities and projects that encourage cooperation (Sherif, 1958). A second is to reward peer groups for pursuing prosocial goals. Coleman (1974) has noted our failure to make use of peer groups as a positive force in children's lives. Coleman's proposal for varsity academics is one way to approach this (Coleman, 1961). A third is to promote cross-age tutoring (Gartner, Kohler, & Riessman, 1971) and residential integration on the basis of age (VanVliet, 1985).

In Praise of Children

A sustainable society, one that is ecologically sound, should have children as its focal point. Children benefit from a "small is beautiful" philosophy. Producing smaller, rather than larger schools is one concrete step that can serve as a focal point for efforts to enhance the psychological and social circumstances of childhood, and thus generally enrich the quality of human life. Directing institutional practice and policy toward families is imperative. This includes everything from giving families priority in the logistics of travel to offering tax incentives for responsible parenthood. As we look for ways to shift recreational activities away from excessive energy/material consumption, children and their activities are appealing. Play is both developmentally important and socially enriching. Some have lost sight of this in their efforts to make children's play more professional, as in the proliferation of costly and equipment-dependent sports. Family hikes and other "primitive" activities provide ecologically sound and psychologically satisfying, as well as developmentally enhancing, alternatives to energy-consuming activities.

As pointed out earlier, since it is demonstrably true that the thing of greatest value we have to offer children is our time and interest, it is a pleasant coincidence that such an investment is also a precondition for an ecologically sound and sustainable future society. Will we come to terms with the eternal frontier, with childhood? Children tell us much about the adults who rear them. What story will we tell about ourselves through our children? Our faith in the species is reflected in our having them and in our treatment of them.

> The childhood shows the way
> as morning shows the day.
>
> John Milton, *Paradise Regained*

What will tomorrow bring?

PRACTICE CAPSULE

Kanter, R. M. (1977). *Work and family in the United States: A critical review and agenda for research and policy.* New York: Russell Sage Foundation.

In her 1977 volume, *Work and family in the United States*, Rosabeth Moss Kanter explored theoretical and practical issues in the interactions of family systems and the work world. She cited a number of factors that are eliciting adjustments in those relationships, including the women's movement, the increase of women in the paid-labor force, the increasing numbers of single-parent families, changes in expectations regarding life-styles, growing awareness of life-style options, and revaluing of family life by organizational professionals. In reviewing some of the research on family–work relationships, she noted findings linking the skill level of a person's job to health indices; continued employment and work satisfaction to high longevity; occupational level in an organization to type of stress experienced; socioeconomic status to type of mental illness experienced; and income and socioeconomic status to happiness.

In the conclusion of her book, Kanter outlined a number of social policy innovations to adjust the family–work place relationship more in favor of families. Her proposals for changes in the policies and practices of employers included:

1. Widespread adoption of flextime (flexible working hours) systems in which workers, within specified limits, set their own hours.
2. Organizational change and job redesign—for instance, to increase job control, expand sense of personal efficacy and discourage "workaholic" executives.
3. Joint family and work-group meetings and workshops in which families of co-workers raise, explore, and work to resolve common problems.
4. Bringing children (and perhaps spouses) to work for shared time with workers.
5. Leaves and sabbaticals, including maternity and paternity leave and other brief career interruptions.
6. Worker's compensation for families of work victims and for white-collar worker disabilities such as heart attacks.
7. "Family responsibility statements" in which organizations document their concern for families, perhaps including a review of the potential family impacts of organizational policies such as working hours, promotion practices, job control, and executive transfers.

FOR FURTHER READING

Bennett, J. W. (1967). *Hutterian Brethren: The agricultural economy and social organization of a communal people.* Stanford: Stanford University Press, 298 pp.
    A detailed account of a working alternative to the standard American one-family/one-home system.

Bronfenbrenner, U. (1970). *Two worlds of childhood: U.S. and U.S.S.R.* New York: Simon and Schuster, 1972; orig. Russell Sage Foundation, 190 pp. (Although this also appears after Chapter 2, it is worth mentioning again.)
    Bronfenbrenner is concerned that "we are experiencing a breakdown in the process of making human beings human" (xv). He contrasts life in the Soviet Union (a highly collectivist society) with life in the individualist United States. The books is a modern classic, particularly in light of recent events.

Carter, F. (1976). *The education of little tree.* Albuquerque, NM: University of New Mexico Press, reissued in 1991, 216 pp.
    This is a remarkable statement of what human quality means in the life of a child. The book is an autobiographical account of Forrest Carter's early life in the hills of Tennessee during the 1930s. Orphaned as a young boy, Carter was adopted by his grandparents. His grandfather was half Cherokee and his grandmother was full Cherokee. From them he receives love and is taught "The Way" of the Cherokees—Little Tree is Carter's Cherokee name.
    Intervention by "White Society" into their life provides an excellent case study of what a child needs to develop, how different cultures meet those needs, and how "unconventional" family forms can meet our criteria for "optimal development.

Coomer, J. (Ed.). (1980). *Quest for a sustainable society.* New York: Pergamon Press, 253 pp.
    This book contains the 1979 winners of the Mitchell Prize, awarded by the Woodlands Conference on Growth Policy. Each chapter describes strategies and tactics for building a more ecologically sane and sustainable society in which human quality is the primary motivation and rationale for institutional life.

Elgin, D. (1981). *Voluntary simplicity.* New York: William Morrow, 312 pp.
    The subtitle of this book is, "Toward a way of life that is outwardly simple, inwardly rich." Elgin suggests ways to simplify material needs while fulfilling emotional, psychological, and spiritual needs. Although not specifically a work on families, this book offers both theoretical and practical suggestions that would lead to a sounder environment for children and their care givers.

The family of man. (1955). New York: Museum of Modern Art, 192 pp.
    This classic photo essay expresses the basic human themes of Chapter 11 with unparalleled clarity. If a picture can be worth a thousand words, these 503 pictures are an eloquent feast.

Garbarino, J. (1981). *Successful schools and competent students.* Lexington, MA: Lexington Books, 170 pp.
    This book applies the human-quality theme developed in Chapter 11 to schools and schooling. It is a case study of how to analyze from an ecological perspective the workings and failings of one sector of the social environment.

Peccei, A. (1977). *The human quality.* New York: Pergamon Press, 214 pp.

Peccei asserts "the human lot cannot be trusted essentially to technologies" (xi); he helped found the Club of Rome on this basis, and gives several practical examples (businesses and international agreements) of how the emphasis on human quality works. The problem of growth is a concern of Peccei's and the Club's; he outlines values and goals for policymakers. Peccei describes "six missions for mankind"—ways to preserve the quality of life in the world community. Peccei is a self-described "revolutionary humanist," and his concerns are global.

Zablocki, B. (1971). *The joyful community: An account of the Bruderhof.* Baltimore: Penguin, 362 pp.

A utopian description rather than a theoretical piece, this book shows the successes (and failures) of child rearing and parenthood in an intentional community. The Bruderhof is the oldest collective in America.

QUESTIONS FOR THOUGHT

1. Read the sections of Plato's *Republic* and B. F. Skinner's *Walden Two* that deal with child rearing and education. Do they advocate the same methods? The same goals?

2. Is a child infinitely malleable? What are the constraints and the probabilities? Sociobiologists offer some ideas on this (see Caplan's edited collection, *The Sociobiology Debate*, New York: Harper & Row, 1978).

3. "The tragedy of life is that we need other people." Explore this statement.

4. What does "labor-intensive" mean? Create a childrearing scenario with this idea in mind.

5. Why are children important? Are they only important to their parents? How does the community define and exhibit its responsibility for children?

6. What elements in our society point toward a positive valuing of children? What ones to a negative valuing?

7. What are the essentials of happiness? (Bertrand Russell thought they were good health, good work, and good friends, in that order.) Where do children fit in?

Afterword: What Does It Mean To Be Human?

James Garbarino

We have come a long way in this text. We have wrestled with a broad range of issues in applied human development, and that is a major accomplishment. But we cannot end without posing one fundamental question that has lurked beneath the surface of our discussion, never fully surfacing: What does it mean to be fully human? We have left this question unspoken for two reasons. First, our primary task was to examine the nuts and bolts of applied human development: the role of the professional helper in the social environment of children and families. Second, this unspoken question goes beyond the conventional scope of professional development and social science research. These are reasons enough to put off this question, but they do not justify ending our discussion without raising it, and so we ask: *What does it mean to be fully human?* In this section, we will consider this most fundamental of questions for the student of behavior and development. In so doing, we will raise some philosophical and theological matters with which each of us should wrestle as we seek to recognize and fulfill our roles as professionals and our destinies as people.

Who Are We? How Do We Know? Should We Be So Sure?

Who are we? Where do we come from? How did we get here? Where are we going? These are the fundamental and eternal questions of human existence, yet we rarely find time for them in social service and social science discussions. Here we make the time.

Notice that these questions use the collective pronoun "we" instead of the singular "I." This may seem strange because as Americans we are

329

accustomed to thinking of ourselves first as individuals, and only sec-
ondarily as part of a group. But our individualistic emphasis may obscure some of the most important truths about human existence. To
understand individuals, we must understand the groups from which
they come. To know who we are as individuals, we must know where
we fit into the human community. This even applies to genetics, where
the sum of a group's genes (its gene pool) is its biological potential and
its legacy. To know where we are going, we must understand where our
people have been. We can understand individual characteristics only
when we can place those characteristics in the context of the larger
human community in which they develop.

When a baby is born there is a rush to see who it looks like. "Your
nose, but my eyes!" "Uncle George's chin!" "His brother's ears." Children are the currency of kinship. They are what bind the generations
together.

When we scrutinize old photos of ourselves, we look to find some
evidence of our current self in that younger stranger frozen in time.
Many adopted children search endlessly in their adult lives to discover
their "true roots," meaning their biological origins. When we see teenagers struggling with pimples, we remember. When we hear the old
people tell stories about the "way it was," we seek some way to connect
ourselves to that past. When a person struggles to avoid becoming what
her or his parents were, we can sympathize. Human life is as much the
past as it is the present and the future.

Who cannot be moved by the excitement of discovering one's ancestors? Who is not enriched by uncovering the connections of kinship?
After searching through old and faded archives in a small Scottish parish
church and tracking down the kindly rector, Anne Garbarino received a
suggestion that she search among the gravestones for a relative who had
been dead for some two hundred years. The search was rewarded. The
moment was magnificent. Equally so was the expression on her paternal
grandmother's face when she saw pictures of the gravestones and the
records from the parish church. This feeling of wholeness and connection with the past through one's family is central to the human experience.

When we see a young child struggling to master a skill we now possess, we are made aware of the enormous growth and change that takes
place in the everyday life of our fellow human beings. What parents do
not share the unbounded glee of their infant child's accomplishments!
Ah, to be able to turn over! To sit unaided! To crawl! To stand unassisted!
And, miracle of miracles, to walk! Then miracle beyond belief, to talk! We
all can appreciate these wonders, but the special bond between parent
and child goes further. To be a parent is to have a special feeling of

responsibility for a special being. The Russian novelist Leo Tolstoy captured the parental perspective in his epic *War and Peace*.

> The universal experience of the ages, showing that children grow from the cradle to manhood, did not exist for the Countess. The growth of her son had been for her at every stage as extraordinary as though millions and millions of men had not already developed in the same way. Just as twenty years before it had seemed unbelievable that the little creature lying under her heart would ever cry, nurse at the breast, or talk, so now she could not believe that this same little creature could be that strange brave officer, that paragon of sons and men, which, judging by his letter he now was. (Tolstoy, pp. 291–292)

The study of human development is literally a science of miracles. The baby is created out of near nothingness, built from minute specks of human matter. From two people comes the potential for a third. From a tiny creature—capable only of the most primitive functions—comes a person capable of language, love, thought, art, and science. From infant organism to cultured person, human development is a series of miracles, one after another.

And then there are the painful challenges arising from the growth process gone awry. The human condition also contains the potential for hate, disfigurement, violence, greed, and evil. We cannot ignore the stagnation of a biologically healthy brain by a harsh and depriving environment. We cannot avoid seeing the pain in broken relationships or in personal decline (e.g., despair, depression, frustration, violence) that replaces growth with deterioration in an uncaring environment (a sociocultural risk factor). What does it all mean?

What does it mean to be human? Ask a fish to describe water. Like the fish, we *experience* our existence, and are hard-pressed to know what that existence is like in contrast to other, alternative existences. But unlike the fish, *we* can try to answer the question. And try we must. For the human service professional, who must deal with the limits of humanness on a day-to-day basis, the question cannot long remain unasked, if not unanswered. The profoundly retarded, the senile, the psychotic, the terminally comatose, all these force us to ask, "What does it mean to be human?" For those of us who choose the role of professional helper, it certainly means to choose to do what we can do to make the world a better place for children and families. To do this, we must know what will not be accepted in the name of political expediency and economic self-interest. Writing in the fourth century B.C., the Chinese philosopher Mericius said it well when he said that people

> must be decided on what they will not do, and then they are able to act with vigor in what they ought to do. (Book IV, 2:8)

We must act on our beliefs and our feelings with compassion and with vigor.

> The only thing necessary for the triumph of evil is for good men to do nothing. (Edmund Burke)

To be fully human is to decide.

When does life begin? Is abortion "murder"—or perhaps "justifiable homicide," or is it an acceptable medical procedure on behalf of the mother? When does life end? Is it homicide to cease treating a permanently comatose accident victim, a terminally ill elder, a grotesquely deformed neonate? What does it mean to be a person? How can we decide the appropriate point at which individual interests should be subordinate to group interests, at which living should be subordinate to life? Can science tell us?

Consider the classic case of the Elephant Man, John Merrick. What does science contribute to our understanding of this character made famous by a film and a Broadway play? Merrick, living in the 1880s, in England, was the victim of a severe case of neurofibromatosis in which his entire body was misshapen and covered with large discolored tumors. That grotesque body hid his beautiful spirit and fine mind, and he had to struggle daily to achieve recognition of his very personhood. In analyzing Merrick and his life, Ashley Montague offered the following conclusion:

> Merrick bore with courage and dignity the hideous deformities and other ills with which he was afflicted. The nightmare existence he had led during the greater part of his life, he put behind him. He never complained or spoke unkindly of those who had maltreated him. His suffering, like a cleansing fire, seems to have brought him nearer to that human condition in which all the nonessentials of life having fallen away, only the essential goodness of man remained. (Montague, 1979, p. 78)

His physician and friend, John Treves, said of Merrick:

> As a specimen of humanity, Merrick was ignorable and repulsive; but the spirit of Merrick, if it could be seen in the form of the living, would assume the figure of an upstanding and heroic man, smooth browed and clean of limb, with eyes that flashed undaunted courage. (cited in Montague, 1979, p. 37)

What does it mean to be human? What does it take to be a person? Intelligence? Language? Soul? We can easily get out of our scientific depth here, but we cannot avoid at least asking. Research on primates and dolphins forces the issue. A monkey can now communicate with a person via sign language and symbolic computerized machinery. Dolphin language is being subjected to sophisticated analyses. Some say that if the intelligence of the planet's organisms was viewed as a landscape, we would readily acknowledge two peaks towering above the hills and plains below. On one would be the *Homo sapiens*; on the other, the dolphin. Likewise, recent developments in the study of language and thought among the apes lead Carl Sagan to ask how far chimpanzees will have to go in demonstrating their abilities to reason, feel, and communicate before we define killing one as murder, before missionaries will seek to convert them.

And, after visiting a lab in which chimps were kept imprisoned in their cages, Sagan wondered:

> If they are "only" animals, if they are beasts which abstract not, then my comparison is a piece of sentimental foolishness . . . but I think it is certainly worthwhile to raise the question: Why, exactly, all over the civilized world, in virtually every major city, are apes in prison? (Sagan, 1977, p. 120–121)

This is no new issue, of course. One of the first items on humankind's agenda has always been to ask, Who are we? and Where do we stand in the world? Classical philosophy arose in part as an attempt to wrestle with the very question before us: What does it mean to be human? We, of the late twentieth century, have a particularly hard time of it because science has debunked many of our most cherished myths. Darwin's theory of evolution put us into the animal lineup as what Desmond Morris so aptly called "the naked ape" (1972). Sigmund Freud undermined the very rationality to which we have appealed for a sense of superiority.

Science seems to put us in our place, and it is not surprising that many people feel uncomfortable, if not actually resentfully angry, about what that place appears to be. We are left to make a place for ourselves, to make peace with the world. It is fundamentally human to search for the Good. But to seek the Good as we do is to turn away from The Bad. And so, as professionals, as social scientists, and as people, we need to consider the perennial and inescapable problem of Good and Evil. We close our discussion with this issue and hope that raising it will be a stimulus to professional and personal growth and development.

Does evil exist? Certainly we would all agree that terrible things occur in our world. Can we infer the existence of evil from our observations of the day-to-day world, just as we infer the existence of gravity? Both are all but inescapable conclusions, so long as we do not torture common language to escape them. Although evil may be a theoretical or hypothetical idea, it is no less real for being such.

Developments in the emerging field of sociobiology even suggest genetic mechanisms for both good and evil, altruism and selfishness.
There are ample grounds for presuming the existence of evil in human
behavior. The practical corollary is that the harmful conditions in which
many people exist (sometimes just barely), are themselves evil. A visit to
the "killing fields" in Cambodia where children were slaughtered and
infants killed by smashing their heads against trees, and a look at the
"tower of skulls" there is sufficient evidence (Garbarino et al., 1991).

This concern about the nature of being human, and the conception of
good and evil, is alien to most of what we call social science. However,
there is a kind of shadow government, a counterforce to the dominant
view, that has questioned the moral limitations of social science since its
inception. This view is most naturally represented by those people who
seek to combine, in one person, the secular (nonreligious) rationality of
modern social analysis and the transcendent moral commitment of religion. Reinhold Niebuhr, twentieth-century American theologian and
social critic, was such a notable person. Niebuhr's injunction was to do
good with our eyes open.

> The children of light must be armed with the wisdom of the children of
> darkness but remain free from their malice. They must know the power of
> self-interest in human society without giving it moral justification. They
> must have this wisdom in order that they may beguile, deflect, harness,
> and restrain self-interest, individual and collective, for the sake of the
> community. (Niebuhr, 1960, p. 41)

Can we ignore good and evil in social policy and practice? Can we
ignore the conflicts inherent in setting priorities among values, in order-
ing our principles? Should the proper foundation for social policy and
practice include a set of principles designed to enhance good and suppress evil? As Niebuhr points out, our characteristic scientific philosophy results in an idealism that may not be suited to the real world.

> Whenever modern idealists are confronted with the divisive and corrosive
> effects of man's self-love, they look for some immediate cause of this
> perennial tendency, usually in some specific form of social organization.
> One school holds that men would be good if only political institutions
> would not corrupt them; another believes that they would be good if the
> prior evil of a faulty economic organization could be eliminated. Or an-
> other school thinks of this evil as no more than ignorance, and therefore
> waits for a more perfect educational process to redeem man from his
> partial and particular loyalties. But no school asks how it is that an essen-
> tially good man could have produced corrupting and tyrannical political
> organizations or exploiting economic organizations, or fanatical and super-
> stitious religious organizations. (Niebuhr, 1960, p. 17)

We face this problem as well when we attempt to deal with issues in human services. Where do social problems such as child abuse, rape, and economic exploitation come from? In what way are they a manifestation of evil? In what way are they a corruption of goodness? What are our prospects for dealing with them if we rely only on education and persuasion, while ignoring social control and conversion? Can we develop a legitimately scientific stance toward good and evil in the world?

How do we appreciate and respect our own identity while not denying or denigrating the worth of others? How do we embrace multiculturalism as a positive force? What *does* is mean to be human? What will we make of this opportunity that we all share to answer this question in the way we live our lives?

Bibliography

Aiello, J. R. (1985). Children, crowding, and control: Effects of environmental stress on social behavior. In J. F. Wohlwill & W. van Vliet (Eds.), *Habitats for children: The impact of density*. Hillsdale, NJ: Erlbaum.

Ainsworth, M. D. S. (1973). The development of infant-mother attachment. In B. M. Caldwell & H. N. Ricciuti (Eds.), *Review of child development research* (Vol. 3). Chicago: University of Chicago Press.

Albee, G. (1980). *Politics, power, prevention and social change*. In G. Gerbner, C. Ross, & E. Zigler (Eds.), *Child abuse: An agenda for action*. New York: Oxford University Press.

Albrecht, K. M. (Ed.). (1991). *Quality criteria for school-age child care programs*. Alexandria, VA: American Home Economics Association.

Albrecht, K. M., & Plantz, M. C. (1991). *Developmentally appropriate practice in school-age child care programs*. Alexandria, VA: American Home Economics Association.

Aldous, J., & Hill, R. (1969). Breaking the poverty cycle: Strategic points for intervention. *Social Work, 14*, 3–12.

Aldrich, R. (1979). The influences of man-built environment on children and youth. In W. Michelson, S. Levine, & E. Michelson (Eds.), *The child in the city*. Toronto: University of Toronto Press.

Alinsky, S. D. (1969). *Reveille for radicals*. New York: Vintage Books.

Almond, G., & Verba, S. (1965). *The civic culture: Political attitudes and democracy in five nations*. Princeton, NJ: Princeton University Press.

American Medical Association. (1977). *Statement on parent and newborn interaction*. Chicago, IL.

Anderson, R. E., & Carter, I. (1978). *Human behavior in the social environment: A social systems approach* (2nd ed.). New York: Aldine.

Anisfield, E., & Pincus, M. (1987). The postpartum support project: Serving young mothers and older women through home visiting. *Zero to Three, 8*, 13–15.

Aries, P. (1962). *Centuries of childhood*. London: Jonathan Cape.

Baer, M. T., Farnan, S., & Mauer, A. M. (1990). Children with special health care needs. In C. S. Sharbaugh (Ed.), *Background papers for call to action: Better nutrition for mothers, children, and families* (pp. 121–137). Washington, DC: National Center for Education in Maternal and Child Health.

Bahr, H. (1978). *Change in family life in Middletown: 1924–1977.* Paper presented at the Annual Meeting of the American Sociological Association, Chicago, IL, August.

Bahr, S. J. (1979). The effects of welfare on marital stability and remarriage. *Journal of Marriage and the Family, 41*(3), 553–560.

Baker, S., O'Neill, B., & Karpf, R. (1984). *The injury fact book.* Lexington, MA: Lexington Books.

Baldwin, W. H. (1976). Adolescent pregnancy and childbearing: Growing concern for Americans. *Population Bulletin, 31*(2), 305–322.

Baltes, P., & Danish, S. (1979). Intervention in life-span development and aging: Issues and concepts. In R. R. Turner & H. W. Reese (Eds.), *Life-span developmental psychology: Intervention.* New York: Academic Press.

Baltes, P. B., Reese, H. W., & Nesselroade, J. R. (1979). *Life-span developmental psychology.* Monterey, CA: Brooks/Cole.

Bane, M. J. (1976). *Here to stay: American families in the twentieth century.* New York: Basic Books.

Barash, D. P. (1977). *Sociobiology and behavior.* Elsevier: New York.

Barker, R., & Gump, P. (1964). *Big school, small school.* CA: Stanford University Press.

Barker, R. G., & Schoggen, P. (1973). *Qualities of community life: Methods of measuring environment and behavior applied to an American and an English town.* San Francisco: Jossey-Bass.

Bass, M., Kravath, R., & Glass, L. (1986). Death-scene investigations in sudden infant death. *New England Journal of Medicine, 315,* 100–128.

Bassuk, E., & Rosenberg, L. (1988). "Why does family homelessness occur?" *American Journal of Public Health, 78,* 7 (July): 783–788.

Bassuk, E. L., Rubin, L., & Lacriat, Al. (1986). Characteristics of sheltered homeless families. *American Journal of Public Health, 76,* 1097–1101.

Bates, J. E. (1980). The concept of difficult temperament. *Merrill-Palmer Quarterly, 26,* 299–319.

Bateson, G. (1972). *Steps to an ecology of mind.* New York: Chandler.

Bathurst, K., Gottfried, A. W., Guerin, D., & Hobson, L. L. (1988a, April). *Home environment and infant temperament: A longitudinal analysis.* Paper presented at the biennial International Conference on Infant Studies, Washington, DC.

Bathurst, K., Gottfried, A. W., Hobson, L. L., & Nordquist, G. (1988b, April). *Infant temperament as a predictor of adaptive behavior at 6 and 8 years of age.* Paper presented at the biennial International Conference on Infant Studies, Washington, DC.

Baumrind, D. (1979). A dialectical materialist's perspective on knowing social reality. *New Directions in Child Development, 2,* 61-82.

Baumrind, D. (1980). New directions in socialization research. *American Psychologist, 35,* 639–652.

Baumrind, D., & Block, A. E. (1967). Socialization practices associated with dimensions of competence in pre-school boys and girls. *Child Development, 38,* 291–327.

Bayley, N. (1969). *Bayley Scales of Infant Development: Manual.* New York: The Psychological Corporation.

Beckwith, L. (1976). Caregiver-infant interaction as a focus for therapeutic intervention with human infants. In Walsh, D. & Greenough, E. (Eds.), *Environments as therapy for brain dysfunction.* New York: Plenum.

Bell, R. Q. (1968). A reinterpretation of the direction of effects in studies of socialization. *Psychological Review, 75,* 81–95.

Bell, R. Q. (1974). Contributions of human infants to caregiving and social interaction. In M. Lewis & L. A. Rosenbaum (Eds.), *The effect of the infant on its caregiver.* New York: John Wiley.

Belsky, J. (1981). Early human experience: A family perspective. *Developmental Psychology, 17,* 3–23.

Belsky, J., & Benn, J. (1986). Beyond bonding: A family-centered approach to enhancing early parent-infant relations. *Proceedings of the Sixth Annual Vermont Conference for the Primary Prevention of Psychopathology.* Hanover, NH: New England Press.

Belsky, J., & Steinberg, L. (1978). The effects of day care: A critical review. *Child Development, 49,* 929–949.

Belsky, J., Lerner, R., & Spanier, G. (1984). *The child in the family.* New York: Random House.

Benedict, R. (1938). Continuities and discontinuities in cultural conditioning. *Psychiatry, 1,* 161–167.

Benn, J. (1987, April). *Being expectant is more than just being pregnant.* Poster session presented at the annual meeting of the Society for Research in Child Development, Baltimore.

Bergdorf, K. (1981). Recognition and reporting of child maltreatment: Findings from the National Study of the Incidence and Severity of Child Abuse and Neglect. Washington, DC: National Center on Child Abuse and Neglect.

Berger, P. L., & Neuhaus, R. J. (1977). *To empower the people: The role of mediating structures in public policy.* Washington, DC: American Enterprise Institute for Policy Research.

Bernard, J. (1981). The good-provider role. *American Psychologist, 36,* 1–13.

Berreuta-Clement, J. R., Schweinhart, L. J., Barnett, W. S., Epstein, A. S., & Weikart, D. P. (1984). *Changed lives: The effects of the Perry Preschool Program on youths through age 19.* Monographs of the High/Scope Educational Research Foundation, 8, Ypsilanti, MI: High/Scope Press.

Berry, W. (1977). *The unsettling of America.* San Francisco: Sierra Club.

Bettelheim, B. (1980). Untying the family. In E. Douvan, H. Weingarten, & J. Scheiber (Eds.), *American families.* Dubuque, IA: Kendall and Hunt.

Bing, E. (1975). Lamaze childbirth among the Amish people. *Birth and the Family Journal, 2,* 39–42.

Blake, J. (1979). Is zero preferred? American attitudes toward childlessness in the 1970s. *Journal of Marriage and the Family, 41,* 245-265.

Block, C. R., & Block, R. L. (1975). The effect of support of the husband and obstetrician on pain perception and control in childbirth. *Birth and the Family Journal, 2,* 43–47.

Block, C. R., Norr, K. L., Meyering, S., Norr, J. L., & Charles, A. G. (1981). Husband gatekeeping in childbirth. *Family Relations, 30,* 197–204.

Bloom, B. (1975). Changing patterns of psychiatric care. New York: Human Science Press.

Boger, R., & Kurnetz, R. (1985). Perinatal positive parenting: Hospital-based support for first-time parents. *Pediatric Basics, 41,* 4–15.

Bogue, D., & Bogue, E. (1976). *Essays in human ecology.* Chicago: University of Chicago.

Bolling, L. R. (1980). For the strengthening of private and volunteer services. *Foundation News, 21*(6), 1.

Bolton, F. G., Jr. (1980). *The pregnant adolescent: Problems of premature parenthood.* Beverly Hills, CA: Sage Publications.

Booth, A. (1983). Quality of children's family interaction in relation to residential type and household crowding. In J. F. Wohlwill & W. van Vliet (Eds.), (1983). *Habitats for children: The impact of density.* New York: Academic Press.

Brackbill, Y. (1958). Extinction of the smiling response in infants as a function of reinforcement schedule. *Child Development, 86,* 3–80.

Brackbill, Y. (1979). Obstetrical medication study. *Science, 205,* 447–448.

Bradley, R. H., Caldwell, B. M., & Rock, S. L. (1988). Home environment and school performance: A ten-year follow-up and examination of three models of environmental action. *Child Development, 59,* 852–867.

Brazelton, T. B. (1973). Brazelton Neonatal Behavioral Assessment Scale. Clinics in Developmental Medicine, No. 50. Philadelphia: Lippincott.

Brazelton, T. B. (1981). Parental perceptions of infant manipulations: Effects on parents of inclusion in our research. In V. L. Smeriglio (Ed.), *Newborns and parents.* Hillsdale, NJ: Lawrence Erlbaum.

Brazelton, T. B. (1985). *Working and caring.* Reading, MA: Addison-Wesley.

Brazelton, T. B., Koslowski, B., & Main, M. (1974). The origins of reciprocity: The early mother-infant interaction. In M. Lewis & L. A. Rosenblum (Eds.). *The effects of the infant on its caregiver.* New York: John Wiley.

Bredekamp, S. (Ed.). (1987a). *Accreditation criteria and procedures.* Washington, DC: National Association for the Education of Young Children.

Bredekamp, S. (Ed.). (1987b). *Developmentally appropriate practice in early childhood programs servicing children from birth through age 8.* Washington, DC: National Association for the Education of Young Children.

Bredekamp, S. (1987). *Guidelines for developmentally appropriate practices for young children 0–8.* Washington, DC: National Association for the Education of Young Children.

Bredekamp, S., & Shepard, L. (1989). How to best protect children from inappropriate school expectations, practices, and policies. *Young Children, 44*(3), 14–24.

Bresnahan, K., Brooks, C., & Zuckerman, B. (1991). Prenatal cocaine use: Impact on mothers and infants. *Pediatric Nursing, 17,* 2 (March–April).

Brim, O. G. (1975). Macro-structural influences on child development and the need for childhood social indicators. *American Journal of Orthopsychiatry, 45,* 516–524.

Brim, O. G., Jr., & Kagan, J. (Eds.) (1980). *Constancy and change in human development.* Cambridge, MA: Harvard University Press.

Bromwich, R., Khokha, E., Burge, D., Baxter, E., Kass, W. and Fust, S. (1981). Apparent behavior progression, In Weissbourd, B. and Musick, J. (Eds.). *Infants: Their Social Environment*, pp. 95–110. Washington, D.C.: National Association for the Education of Young Children.

Bronfenbrenner, U. (1970). *Two worlds of childhood.* New York: Russell Sage Foundation.

Bronfenbrenner, U. (1974). Developmental research, public policy, and the ecology of childhood. *Child Development, 45,* 1–5.

Bronfenbrenner, U. (1975). The origins of alienation. In U. Bronfenbrenner & M. Mahoney (Eds.), *Influences on human development.* Hinsdale, IL: Dryden Press.

Bronfenbrenner, U. (1979). *The ecology of human development: Experiments by nature and design.* Cambridge, MA: Harvard University Press.

Bronfenbrenner, U. (1986). Ecology of the Family as a context for human development: Research perspectives. *Developmental Psychology, 22*(6), 723–742.

Bronfenbrenner, U., & Crouter, A. (1982). Work and family through time and space. In S. B. Kamerman & C. D. Hayes (Eds.). *Families that work: Children in a changing environment of work, family, and community.* National Academy of Sciences.

Bronfenbrenner, U., & Crouter, A. C. (1983). The evolution of environmental models in developmental research. In P. Mussen (Ed.), *The handbook of child psychology,* pp. 357–414. New York: John Wiley & Sons.

Bronfenbrenner, U., & Mahoney, M. (1975). The structure and verification of hypotheses. In U. Bronfenbrenner & M. Mahoney (Eds.). *Influences on human development.* Hinsdale, IL: Dryden Press.

Bronowski, J. (1965). *Science and human values.* New York: Harper & Row.

Bruner, J. S. (1960). *The process of education.* Cambridge, MA: Harvard University Press.

Bule, J. (1988). "Me" decades generate depression. *American Psychological Association Monitor, 19*(10), 18.

Burgess, R. L. (1980). Relationships in marriage and the family. In S. Duck & R. Gilmour (Eds.), *Personal relationships.* London: Academic Press.

Burgess, R. L., & Conger, R. (1978). Family interaction patterns in abusive, neglectful and normal families. *Child Development, 49,* 163–173.

Burgess, R. L., Garbarino, J., & Gilstrap, B. (1983). Violence to the family. In E. Callahan & K. McCluskey (Eds.), *Life-span developmental psychology: Non-normative life events.* New York: Academic Press.

Burgess, R. L., Anderson, E. A., & Schellenbach, C. J. (1980). A social interactional approach to the study of abusive families. In J. P. Vincent (Ed.), *Advances in family intervention, assessment and theory* (Vol. 2). Greenwich, CT: JAI Press.

Burris, M. E. (1979). Food marketing institute: State of the industry. Presentation made in American Marketing Institute Conference, Dallas, Texas, May 7, 1979. *Behavior Today* (June 4, 1979).

Buss, A. H., & Plomin, R. (1975). *A temperament view of personality development.* New York: Wiley Interscience.

Butnarescu, G. F., Tillotson, D. M., & Villarreal, P. P. (1980). *Perinatal nursing* (Vol. 2). *Reproductive Risk.* New York: John Wiley.

Caine, L. (1974). *Widow: The personal crisis of a widow in America.* New York: William Morrow.

Cairns, E. (1987). *Caught in crossfire: Children and the northern Ireland conflict.* Syracuse University Press: Syracuse, NY.

Campbell, A. (1976). Subjective measures of well being. *American Psychologist, 31,* 117–124.

Campbell, A., Converse, P. E., & Rodgers, W. (1976). *The quality of American life: Perceptions, evaluations and satisfactions.* New York: Russell Sage Foundation.

Campbell, D. T. (1975). On the conflicts between biological and social evolution and between psychology and moral tradition. *American Psychologist, 30,* 1103–1126.

Caplan, G. (1974). *Support systems and community mental health.* New York: Behavioral Publications.

Carlsson-Paige, N., & Levin, D. (1990). *Who's calling the shots?* Philadelphia: New Society Publishers.

Chasnoff, I., et al. (1985). Cocaine use in pregnancy. *New England Journal of Medicine* (313), 666–669.

Cherlin, A. (1981). *Marriage, divorce, remarriage. Changing patterns in the postwar United States.* Cambridge, MA: Harvard University Press.

Chess, S., & Thomas, A. (1984). Origins of behavior disorders. In S. Chess & A. Thomas (Eds.), *Origins and evolution of behavior disorders: From infancy to early adult life.* New York: Brunner/Mazel.

Children's Defense Fund. (1974). *Children out of school in America.* Washington, DC: Washington Research Project, Inc.

Children's Defense Fund. (1978). *Children without homes: An examination of public responsibility to children in out-of-home care.* Washington, DC: Children's Defense Fund.

Children's Defense Fund. (1981). *CDF Reports, 3,* No. 9, September, 1 ff.

Children's Defense Fund (1980). New York City Agency keeps families together. Washington, D.C.: *Children's Defense Fund Reports, 2*(6), 6–7.

Chilman, C. S. (1973). Public social policy and families in the 70's. *Social Casework, 54,* 575–585.

Chilman, C. S. (1980). *Adolescent sexuality in a changing American society: Social and psychological perspectives.* Washington, DC: Department of Health, Education, and Welfare.

Chodorow, N. (1978). *The reproduction of mothering: Psychoanalysis and the sociology of gender.* Berkeley, CA: University of California Press.

Cisneros, S. (1988). My name. In *The House on Mango Street.* Houston: Arte Publico Press.

Claassen, A. (1980). The policy perspective: Social problems as investment opportunities. *Social Problems, 27*(5), 526–539.

Clark, A. L. (1979). Historical perspectives. In A. L. Clark & D. D. Affonso (Eds.), *Childbearing: A nursing perspective* (2nd ed.). Philadelphia: F. A. Davis Co.

Clausen, J. A. (1966). Family structure, socialization, and personality. In L. W. Hoffman & M. L. Hoffman (Eds.), *Review of child development research* (Vol. 2). New York: Russell Sage.

Clemente, F., & Sauer, W. J. (1976). Life satisfaction in the United States. *Social Forces, 54*, 621–631.

Cleveland, H., & Wilson, T. (1978). *Human growth: An essay on growth, values, and the quality of life.* Aspen, CO: Institute for Humanistic Studies.

Cohen, N. W. (1983). *Silent knife: Vaginal birth after caesarean and caesarean prevention.* Framingham, MA: C/Sec Association.

Coleman, J. S. (1961). *The adolescent society: The social life of the teenager and its impact on education.* Glencoe, IL: Free Press.

Coleman, J. S. (1966). *Equality of educational opportunity.* Washington, DC: U.S. Government Printing Office.

Coleman, J. S. (1974). *Youth: Transition to adulthood.* Chicago, IL: University of Chicago Press.

Coleman, M. (1991). Planning for the changing nature of family life in schools for young children. *Young Children, 46*(4), 15–20.

Coles, R. (1978). *Children of crisis: Privileged ones.* Boston: Little, Brown.

Colletta, N. (1981, April). *The influence of support systems on the maternal behavior of young mothers.* Paper presented at the biennial meeting of the Society for Research in Child Development, Boston.

Collins, A. (1979). The establishment and maintenance of a family day care network. In S. Maybanks & M. Bryce (Eds.), *Home-based services for children and families: Policy, practice, and research.* Springfield, IL: C. C Thomas.

Collins, A. H. (1980). Helping neighbors intervene in cases of maltreatment. In J. Garbarino, S. H. Stocking, & Associates, *Protecting children from abuse and neglect.* San Francisco: Jossey-Bass.

Collins, A., & Pancoast, D. (1976). *National helping networks.* Washington, DC: National Association of Social Workers.

Collins, A., & Watson, E. (1976). *Family day care.* Boston: Beacon Press.

Colman, R. A. D., & Colman, L. L. (1971). *Pregnancy: The psychological experience.* New York: Herder & Herder.

Comer, J. P. (1988). *Maggie's American dream: The life and times of a black family.* New York: Penguin.

Committee for Economic Development, Research and Policy Committee. (1987). *Children in need: Investment strategies for the educationally disadvantaged.* New York: Committee for Economic Development.

Commoner, B. (1971). *The closing circle: Nature, man and technology.* New York: Alfred P. Knopf.

Cooper, B., & Gath, D. (1977). Psychiatric illness, maladjustment, and juvenile delinquency: An ecological study in a London borough. *Psychological Medicine, 7*, 465–474.

Coopersmith, S. (1967). *The antecedents of self-esteem.* San Francisco: Freeman

Cosaro, W. & Eder, D. (1990). Children's peer cultures. *Annual Review of Sociology, 16*, 197–220.

Council on Environmental Quality. (1981). *Global Future: Time to Act.* Washington, DC: U.S. Department of State.

Crnic, K. A., & Greenberg, M. T. (1990). Minor parenting stresses with young children. *Child Development, 61,* 1628–1637.

Cross, T. L., Bazron, B. J., Dennis, K. W., & Isaacs, M. R. (1989). *Towards a culturally competent system of care.* Washington, DC: Georgetown University Child Development Center.

de'Anda, D. (1984). Bicultural socialization: Factors affecting the minority experience. *Social Work 20,* 101–107.

Daly, H. E. (1973). *Toward a steady-state economy.* San Francisco: W. H. Freeman.

Danish, S., Smyer, M., & Nowak, C. (1980). Developmental intervention: Enhancing life-event processes. In P. B. Baltes & O. G. Brim, Jr. (Eds), *Life-span development and behavior* (Vol. 3). New York: Academic Press.

Danziger, S. (1979a). The medical context of childbearing: A study of social control in doctor-patient interaction. *Social Science and Medicine.*

Danziger, S. (1979b). On doctor watching: Fieldwork in medical settings. *Urban Life, 7*(4).

Degler, C. N. (1980). *At odds.* London: Oxford University Press.

deLone, R. (1979). *Small futures: Children, inequality, and the limits of liberal reform.* New York: Harcourt, Brace Jovanovich.

Demone, H. W. (1978). *Stimulating human services reform.* Washington, DC: U.S. Government Printing Office, DHEW Publication No. OS-76-130, 1978. (Also, *Human Services Monograph Series,* No. 8, June).

Demos, J. (1986). *Past, present and personal: The family and the life course in American history.* New York: Oxford University Press.

Derryberry, D., & Rothbart, M. K. (1984). Emotion, attention, and temperament. In C. E. Izard, J. Kagan, & R. Zajonc (Eds.), *Emotion, cognition, and behavior* (pp. 132–166). New York: Cambridge University Press.

Devereux, E. (1977). *A critique of ecological psychology.* Paper presented at the Conference on Research Perspectives in the Ecology of Human Development, Cornell University, Ithaca, NY: August.

DeVos, G. (1973). *Socialization for achievement.* Berkeley: University of California Press.

Dittmann, L. (1979). Affecting social policy in community and nation. *Childhood Education,* February/March, 194–199.

Doering, S. G., & Entwisle, D. R. (1975). Preparation during pregnancy and ability to cope with labor and delivery. *American Journal of Orthopsychiatry, 45*(5), 825–837.

Douvan, E., & Adelson, J. (1966). *The adolescent experience.* New York: John Wiley.

Dreeben, R. (1968). *On what is learned in school.* Reading, MA: Addison-Wesley.

Dunu, M. (1979). The Lower East Side Family Union: Assuring community services for minority families. In S. Maybanks & M. Bryce (Eds.), *Home-based services for children and families: Policy, practice, and research.* Springfield, IL: C. C. Thomas.

Duvall, E. M. (1975). *Family development.* Philadelphia: J. B. Lippincott.

Eckardt, M. J., Haford, T. C., Kaelber, C. T., Parker, E. S., Rosenthal, L. S., et al. (1981). Health hazards associated with alcohol consumption. *Journal of the American Medical Association 246*(6), 648–666.

Eells, L. (1981). The good life: Smaller is better. *Nebraska Annual Social Indicators Survey* (NASIS-80 #11).

Elder, G. H. (1974). *Children of the great depression*. Chicago: University of Chicago Press.

Elder, G. H. (1980). Adolescence in historical perspective. In J. Adelson (Ed.), *Handbook of Adolescent Psychology* (pp. 3–46). New York: John Wiley.

Elder, G. H., & Rockwell, R. (1977). *The life course and human development: An ecological perspective*. Unpublished paper. Boys Town, NE: Boys Town Center for the Study of Youth Development.

Elkind, D. (1985). *The hurried child*. Reading, MA: Addison-Wesley.

El Sherif, C., McGrath, G., & Smyrski, J. T. (1979). Coaching the coach. *Journal of Obstetrical and Gynecological Nursing*. March–April, 87–89.

Emlen, A. (1977). *If you care about children, then care about parents*. Address to the Tennessee Association for Young Children, Nashville, TN, November.

Erickson, M. F., Sroufe, L. A., & Egeland, B. (1985). The relationship between quality of attachment and behavior problems in preschool in a high-risk sample. *Monographs of the Society for Research in Child Development*, 50(1–2, Serial no. 209).

Erikson, E. (1963). *Childhood and society* (2nd ed.). New York: Norton.

Erikson, E. (1968). *Identity: Youth and crisis*. New York: Norton.

Erikson, K. T. (1976). *Everything in its path: Destruction of community in the Buffalo Creek flood*. New York: Simon and Schuster.

Eron, L. D. (1980). Prescription for reduction of aggression. *American Psychologist*, 35, 244–252.

Family Impact Seminar. (1990). *The crisis in foster care: New directions for the 1990s*. Washington, DC: Family Impact Seminar, American Association for Marriage and Family Therapy.

Featherstone, J. (1979). Family matters. *Harvard Educational Review*, 49, 20–56.

Fein, R. A. (1976). Men's entrance to parenthood. *The Family Coordinator*, 25, 341-348.

Feiring, C., & Lewis, M. (1978). The child as a member of the family system. *Behavioral Science*, 23, 225–233.

Fine, G. (1986). The dirty play of little boys. *Society*, 24, 63–67.

Finkelhor, D. (1979). *Sexually victimized children*. New York: The Free Press.

Fleischman, A. R. (1986). The immediate impact of the birth of a low birth weight infant on the family. *Zero to Three*, 6, 1–5.

Ford, D. (1974). Mental health and human development: An analysis of a dilemma. In D. Harshbarger & R. Maley (Eds.), *Behavior analysis and systems analysis: An integrative approach to mental health programs*. Kalamazoo, MI: Behaviordelia.

Foss, B. M. (Ed.). (1965). *Determination of infant behavior*. London: Methuen.

Fraiberg, S. (1968). Parallel and divergent patterns in blind and sighted infants. *Psychoanalytic Study of the Child*, 23, 264–299.

Fraiberg, S. (1973). Blind infants and their mothers: An examination of the sign system. In M. Lewis & L. Rosenblum (Eds.), *Origins of behavior* (Vol. 1). New York: John Wiley.

Fraiberg, S., Adelson, E., & Shapiro, V. (1975). Ghosts in the nursery. *Journal of the American Academy of Child Psychiatry, 14*(3), 387–421.

Fraser, B. G. (1976–77). Independent representation for the abused and neglected child: The guardian ad litem. *California Western Law Review, 13*(1), 16–45.

Frazier, D., & De Blassie, R. (1982). Comparison of self-concept in Mexican American and non-Mexican American late adolescents. *Adolescence, 17*, 327–334.

Freedman, D. (1974). *Human infancy: An evolutionary perspective.* Hillsdale, NJ: Lawrence Erlbaum.

Freeman, R. (1990). Intrapartal fetal monitoring: A disappointing story. *New England Journal of Medicine, 322*, 624–626.

Freud, A., & Dann, S. (1951). An experiment in group upbringing. In *The psychoanalytic study of the child* (Vol. 6, pp. 127–168). New York: International Universities.

Friedman, R. (1976). Child abuse: A review of the psychosocial research. In Herner & Co. (Eds.), *Four perspectives on the states of child abuse and neglect research.* Washington, DC: National Center on Child Abuse and Neglect.

Froland, C., Pancoast, D., Chapman, N., & Kimboko, P. (1979). Networking: What's it all about. *Caring, 5*(3), 1–10.

Furby, L. (1978). Sharing: Decisions and moral judgments about letting others use one's possessions. *Psychological Reports, 43*, 595–609.

Furstenberg, F. (1976). *Unplanned parenthood: The social consequences of teenage childbearing.* New York: The Free Press.

Furstenberg, F. et al. (1991).

Galinsky, E. (1987). *The six stages of parenthood.* Reading, MA: Addison-Wesley.

Galle, O., Gove, W., & McPherson, J. (1972). Population density and pathology: What are the relationships for man? *Science, 176*, 23–30.

Gannett, E. (1989). *City initiatives in school-age child care.* Wellesley, MA: School-Age Child Care Project, Wellesley College Center for Research on Women.

Garbarino, J. (1968). *Religion and democracy.* Unpublished thesis, St. Lawrence University, Canton, NY.

Garbarino, J. (1975a). The meaning and implications of school success. *The Educational Forum, 40*, 157–168.

Garbarino, J. (1975b). A note on television viewing. In U. Bronfenbrenner & M. Mahoney (Eds.), *Influences on human development.* Hinsdale, IL: Dryden Press.

Garbarino, J. (1976). A preliminary study of some ecological correlates of child abuse: The impact of socioeconomic stress on mothers. *Child Development, 47*, 178–185.

Garbarino, J. (1977a). The human ecology of child maltreatment. A conceptual model for research. *Journal of Marriage and the Family, 39*, 721–736.

Garbarino, J. (1977b). The price of privacy: An analysis of the social dynamics of child abuse. *Child Welfare, 56*, 565–575.

Garbarino, J. (1980a). Changing hospital childbirth practices: A developmental perspective on prevention of child maltreatment. *American Journal of Orthopsychiatry, 50*, 588–597.

Garbarino, J. (1980b). Some thoughts on school size and its effects on adolescent development. *Journal of Youth and Adolescence, 9,* 19–31.

Garbarino, J. (1981a). *The child as an organism: Implications for family structure.* Paper presented to the International Symposium on "The Child and the City." International Pediatric Society and the Japanese National Institute for Research Advancement, Tokyo, Japan, March 26.

Garbarino, J. (1981b). *Successful schools and competent students.* Lexington, MA: Lexington Books.

Garbarino, J. (1981c). The issue is human quality: In praise of children. In J. Coomer (Ed.), *The quest for a sustainable society.* New York: Pergamon Press.

Garbarino, J. (1985a). *Adolescent development: An ecological perspective.* Columbus: Charles E. Merrill.

Garbarino, J. (1985b). Habitats for children: An ecological perspective. In J. F. Wohlwill & W. van Vliet (Eds.), *Habitats for children: The impact of density.* Hillsdale, NJ: Lawrence Erlbaum.

Garbarino, J. (1988). Preventing childhood injury: Developmental and mental health issues. *American Journal of Orthopsychiatry, 58*(1).

Garbarino, J. (1991). *Conceptual issues in the search for social indicators of child well-being.* Paper prepared for the Center for the Study of Social Policy, Washington, DC. (March).

Garbarino, J. (1992). *Toward a sustainable society: An economic, social and environmental agenda for our children's future.* Chicago, IL: The Noble Press.

Garbarino, J., & Bronfenbrenner, U. (1976a). *Research on parent-child relations and social policy: Who needs whom?* Paper presented at the Symposium on Parent-Child Relations: Theoretical, Methodological and Practical Implications. University of Trier, Trier, West Germany, May.

Garbarino, J., & Bronfenbrenner, U. (1976b). The socialization of moral judgment and behavior in cross-cultural perspective. In T. Lickona (Ed.), *Moral development and behavior.* New York: Holt, Rinehart & Winston.

Garbarino, J., & Crouter, A. C. (1978). Defining the community context of parent-child relations. *Child Development, 49,* 604–616.

Garbarino, J., & Crouter, A. (1982). *Corporate self-reliance and the sustainable society.* Mitchell Prize, Woodlands Conference on Growth Policy Essay Competition.

Garbarino, J., & Ebata, A. (1983). The significance of ethnic and cultural differences in child maltreatment. *Journal of Marriage and the Family,* November, 773–783.

Garbarino, J., & Garbarino, A. (1978). *Where are the children in Utopia?* Paper presented at the Second National Conference on International Communities, Omaha, NE, October 17.

Garbarino, J., Gaboury, M. T., Long, F., Grandjean, P., & Asp, E. (1982). Who owns the children: An ecological perspective on public policy affecting children. *Child and Youth Services Review, 5*(1/2), (Spring/Summer), 41–61.

Garbarino, J., & Gilliam, G. (1980). *Understanding abusive families.* Lexington, MA: Lexington Books.

Garbarino, J., Guttman, E., & Selley, J. (1986). *The psychologically battered child:*

Strategies for identification, assessment, and intervention. San Francisco: Jossey-Bass.

Garbarino, J., & Jacobson, N. (1978). Youth-helping-youth as a resource in meeting the problem of child maltreatment, *Child Welfare, 57,* 505–512.

Garbarino, J., & Kostelny, K. (1992a). Child maltreatment as a community problem. *International Journal of Child Abuse and Neglect,* 16(4).

Garbarino, J., & Kostelny, K. (1992b). Neighborhood and community influences on parenting. In T. Luster & L. Okagaki (Eds.). *Parenting: An Ecological Perspective.*

Garbarino, J., Kostelny, K., & Dubrow, N. (1991). *No place to be a child: Growing up in a war zone.* Lexington, MA: Lexington Books.

Garbarino, J., & Plantz, M. C. (1980). *Urban environments and urban children.* ERIC/CUE Urban Diversity Series, #69. New York: ERIC Clearinghouse on Urban Education.

Garbarino, J., Schellenbach, C., Sebes, J., & Associates. (1986). *Troubled youth, troubled families: Understanding families at-risk for adolescent maltreatment.* New York: Aldine de Gruyter.

Garbarino, J., & Sherman, D. (1980). High-risk neighborhoods and high-risk families: The human ecology of child maltreatment. *Child Development, 51,* 188–198.

Garbarino, J., Stocking, S. H., & Associates. (1980). *Protecting children from abuse and neglect: Developing and maintaining effective support systems for families.* San Francisco: Jossey Bass.

Gardner, H. (1978). *Developmental psychology: An introduction.* Boston: Little, Brown.

Garmezy, N., & Rutter, M. (Eds.). (1983). *Stress, coping and development in children.* New York: McGraw-Hill.

Gartner, A., Kohler, M., and Riessman, F. (1971). *Children Teach Children.* New York: Harper & Row.

Gaudin, J., & Polansky, N. (1985). Social distancing of the neglectful family: Sex, race, and social class influences. *Social Service Review, 58,* 245–253.

Gay, K. (1987). The Rainbow Effect: Interracial Families. New York: Franklin Watts.

Gearing, J. (1978). Facilitating the birth process and father-child bonding. *The Counseling Psychologist,* 7(4), 53–56.

Germain, C. (1978). Space: An ecological variable in social work practice. *Social Casework, 59,* 515–522.

Getzels, J. W. (1974). Socialization and education: A note on discontinuities. *Teacher's College Record, 76,* 218–225.

Giarini, O. (1980). *Dialogue on wealth and welfare.* New York: Pergamon Press.

Gibbs, J. (1989). American adolescents. In J. Gibbs & L. Huang (Eds.), *Children of color: Psychological interventions with minority youth.* San Francisco: Jossey-Bass.

Gibbs, J., & Huang, L. (Eds.). (1989). *Children of color: Psychological interventions with minority youth.* San Francisco: Jossey-Bass.

Gilligan, C. (1982). *In a different voice.* Cambridge, MA: Harvard University Press.

Gilligan, J. (1991). *Shame and humiliation: The emotions of individual and collective violence.* Paper presented at the May 23, 1991 Erikson Lectures, Harvard University, Cambridge, MA.

Ginsberg, H., & Opper, S. (1969). *Piaget's theory of intellectual development.* Englewood Cliffs, NJ: Prentice-Hall.

Glick, P. (1979). *The future of the American family.* Washington, DC: U.S. Government Printing Office.

Gloger-Tippelt, G. (1984). A process model of the pregnancy course. *Human Development.*

Goffin, S. G., & Lombardi, J. L. (1988). *Speaking out: Early childhood advocacy.* Washington, DC: National Association for the Education of Young Children.

Gold, M. (1963). *Status forces in delinquent boys.* Ann Arbor, MI: University of Michigan.

Goldberg, S. (1977). Social competence in infancy: A model of parent-infant interaction. *Merrill-Palmer Quarterly, 23,* 164–177.

Goldberg, S. (1979). Premature birth: Consequences for the parent-infant relationships. *American Scientist, 67,* 214–219.

Goldsmith, H. H. (1983). Genetic influences on personality from infancy to adulthood. *Child Development, 54,* 331–355.

Goldsmith, H. H., Buss, A. H., Plomin, R., Rothbart, M. K., Thomas, A., Chess, S., Hinde, R. A., & McCall, R. B. (1987). Roundtable: What is temperament: Four approaches. *Child Development, 58,* 505–529.

Goldsmith, H. H., & Campos, J. J. (1986). Fundamental issues in the study of early temperament: The Denver Twin Development Study. In M. E. Lamb & A. Brown (Eds.), *Advances in developmental psychology* (pp. 231–283). Hillsdale, NJ: Lawrence Erlbaum.

Goldstein, J. (1986). *Aggression and crimes of violence.* New York: Oxford University Press.

Goldstein, J., Freud, A., & Solnit, A. J. (1973). *Beyond the best interests of the child.* New York: The Free Press.

Goldstein, J., Freud, A., & Solnit, A. J. (1979). *Before the best interests of the child.* New York: The Free Press.

Gottesman, I. I. (1963). Genetic aspects of intelligent behavior. In N. Ellis (Ed.), *Handbook of mental deficiency: Psychological theory and research.* New York: McGraw-Hill.

Gottlieb, B. (1980). The role of individual and social support in preventing child maltreatment. In J. Garbarino, S. H. Stocking, & Associates, *Protecting children from abuse and neglect.* San Francisco: Jossey-Bass.

Gottlieb, B. H., & Pancer, S. M. (1988). Social networks and the transition to parenthood. In G. Y. Michaels & W. A. Goldberg (Eds.), *The transition to parenthood.* Cambridge, England: Cambridge University Press.

Gray, E., & Cosgrove, J. (1985). Ethnocentric perception of childrearing practices in protective services. *Child Abuse and Neglect, 9,* 389–396.

Gray, J., Cutler, C., Dean, J., & Kempe, C. (1977). Prediction and prevention of child abuse and neglect. *Child Abuse and Neglect, 1,* 45–58.

Greenberg, M. T., & Crnic, K. A. (1988). Longitudinal predictors of developmental status and social interaction in premature and fullterm infants at age two. *Child Development, 59,* 554–570.

Greenberg, M., & Morris, N. (1974). Engrossment: The newborn's impact upon the father. *American Journal of Orthopsychiatry, 44,* 520–531.

Greenberg, M., Rosenberg, I., & Lind, J. (1973). First mothers rooming-in with their newborns: Its impact upon the mother. *American Journal of Orthopsychiatry, 43*(5), 783–789.

Greenberg, P. (1989). Parents as partners in young children's development and education: A new American fad? Why does it matter? *Young Children, 44*(4), 61–74.

Greer, C. (1972). *The great school legend.* New York: Viking Press.

Grossman, F. K., Winickoff, S. A., & Eichler, L. S. (1980). *Psychological sequelae of caesarean delivery.* Paper presented at the International Conference on Infant Studies, New Haven, CT, April.

Gruber, A. R. (1978). *Children in foster care: Destitute, neglected, betrayed.* New York: Human Services Press.

Gump, P., & Adelberg, B. (1978). Urbanism from the perspective of ecological psychologists. *Environmental and Behavior, 10,* 171–191.

Gurry, D. L. (1977). Child abuse: Thoughts on doctors, nurses and prevention. *Child Abuse and Neglect, 1,* 435–443.

Gutierrez, J., & Sameroff, A. (1990). Determinants of complexity in Mexican-American and Anglo-American mothers' conceptions of child development. *Child Development, 61,* 384–394.

Gwinn, M., Pappaioanou, M., George, J. R., Hannon, W. H., Wasser, S. C., Redus, M. A., et al. (1991). Prevalence of HIV Infection in childbearing women in the United States. *Journal of the American Medical Association, 265*(13), 1704–1708.

Haapala, D., & Kinney, J. (1979). Homebuilders' approach to the training of in-home therapists. In S. Maybanks & M. Bryce (Eds.), *Home-based services for children and families: Policy, practice, and research.* Springfield, IL: C. C Thomas.

Hagberg, B. (1975). Pre-, peri-, and postnatal prevention of major neuropediatric handicaps. *Neuropaediatrie, 6,* 331–338. Cited in Kopp, C., & Krakow, J. (1983). The developmentalist and the study of biological risk: A view of the past with an eye toward the future. *Child Development, 54,* 1086–1108.

Hagestad, G. O. (1981a). Personal communication.

Hagestad, G. O. (1981b). Problems and promises in the social psychology of intergenerational relations. In R. Fogel, E. Hatfield, S. Kiesler, & J. March (Eds.), *Stability and change in the family.* New York: Academic Press.

Haire, D. (1973). The cultural warping of childbirth. *Environmental Child Health, 19,* 171–191.

Hale-Benson, J. (1982). *Black children: Their roots, culture, and learning styles* (rev. ed.). Baltimore, MD: Johns Hopkins University Press.

Hales, D. J., Lozoff, B., Sosa, R., & Kennell, J. H. (1977). Defining the limits of the maternal sensitive period. *Developmental Medicine and Child Neurology, 19,* 454–461.

Halpern, R. (1987). Major social and demographic trends affecting young families: Implications for early childhood care and education. *Young Children, 42*(6), 34–44.

Halpern, R. (1991). Supportive services for families in poverty: Dilemmas of reforms. *Social Science Review, 65*(3).

Harris, L. (1978). Importance and satisfaction with factors in life. *The Harris Survey,* November 23.

Harrison, A. O., Wilson, M. N., Oine, C. J., Chan, S. Q., & Buriel, R. (1990). Family ecologies of ethnic minority children. *Child Development, 61,* 347–362.

Hartman, A. (1990). Children in a careless society. *Social Work, 35,* 483–484.

Hartup, W. W. (1978). Perspectives on child and family interaction: Past, present, and future. In R. M. Lerner & G. B. Spanier (Eds.), *Child influences on marital and family interaction.* New York: Academic Press.

Harvey, M. (1977). Home births. *Boston Sunday Globe* (New England magazine), October 16, 10–60.

Havighurst, R. J. (1962). *Growing up in River City.* New York: John Wiley.

Hawley, A. (1950). *Human ecology: A theory of community structure.* New York: Ronald Press.

Heath, S. B. (1983). *Ways with words: Language, life and work in communities.* Cambridge, England: Cambridge University Press.

Helfer, R. E. (1980). Developmental deficits which limit interpersonal skill. In C. H. Kempe & R. E. Helfer (Eds.), *The battered child.* Chicago: University of Chicago Press.

Heller, P. L., & Quesada, G. (1977). Rural familism: An interregional analysis. *Rural Sociology, 42,* 220–240.

Hempel, C. G. (1966). *Philosophy of natural science.* Englewood Cliffs, NJ: Prentice-Hall.

Hennepin County. (1979). *Family study project.* Unpublished program materials. Minneapolis, MN.

Henry, J. (1973). *Pathways to madness.* New York: Random House.

Hermes, P. H. (1981). WD medical update: Crib death. *Woman's Day,* February 10, 14–16.

Hersh, S., & Levin, K. (1978). How love begins between parent and child. *Children Today, 1*(2), 2–6, 47.

Hetherington, E. M. (1988). Family relations six years after divorce. In E. M. Hetherington & R. D. Parke (Eds.) *Contemporary readings in child psychology.* New York: McGraw-Hill.

Hetherington, E. M. (1989). Coping with family transitions: Winners, losers, and survivors. *Child Development, 60,* 1–14.

Hetherington, E. M., Cox, M., & Cox, R. (1978). The aftermath of divorce. In J. H. Stevens, Jr. & M. Matthews (Eds.), *Mother-child father-child relationships.* Washington, DC: National Association for the Education of Young Children.

Hetherington, E. M., & Parke, R. D. (1979). *Child psychology: A contemporary viewpoint* (2nd ed.). New York: McGraw-Hill.

Hewlett, S. A. (1991). *When the bough breaks: The cost of neglecting our children.* New York: Basic Books.

Hillery, G. A., Jr. (1955). Definitions of community: Areas of agreement. *Rural Sociology, 20,* 111–123.

Hock, E., & DeMeis, D. K. (1990). Depression in mothers of infants: The role of maternal employment. *Developmental Psychology, 26*(2), 285–291.

Hofferth, L. (1989). What is demand for and supply of child care in the United States? *Young Children 44,*(5), 28–33.

Holt, L. H. (1988). Medical perspectives on pregnancy and birth: Biological risks and technological advances. In G. Y. Michaels & W. Goldberg, (Eds.), *The transition to parenthood.* Cambridge, England: Cambridge University Press.

Honig, A. (1986). Stress and coping in children (part 1). *Young Children, 41*(4), 50–63.

House, J. S. (1981). *Work stress and social support.* Reading, MA: Addison-Wesley.

Houston, J. (1973). *Farewell to Manzanar: A true story of Japanese American experience during and after World War II internment.* Boston: Houghton Mifflin.

Howard, A., & Scott, R. (1980). The study of minority groups in complex societies. *Handbook of cross-cultural human development.*

Howells, J. G. (1972). Childbirth is a family experience. In J. G. Howells (Ed.), *Modern perspectives in psychoobstetrics.* New York: Brunner/Mazel.

Howes, C. (1988). Infant day care. *Young Children, 44*(6), 24–27.

Huang, L. (1989). Southeast Asian refugee children and adolescents. In J. Gibbs & L. Huang (Eds.). *Children of color: Psychological interventions with minority youth.* San Francisco: Jossey-Bass.

Hubbell, R., Hirsch, G., Barrett, B., Condelli, L., & Plantz, M. (1986). *Evaluation of reunification for minority children* (Contract No. 105-84-1803). Washington, DC: Administration for Children, Youth and Families.

Huessy, H. R. (1972). Tactics and targets in the rural setting. In S. E. Golann & C. Eisdorfer (Eds.), *Handbook of community mental health.* New York: Appleton-Century-Crofts.

Hughey, M., McElin, T., Young, F., & Young, T. (1978). Maternal and fetal outcomes of Lamaze-prepared patients. *Obstetrics and Gynecology, 51,* 643–647.

Hutt, C. (1972). Sex differences in human development. *Human Development, 15,* 153–170.

Iber, F. L. (1980). Fetal alcohol syndrome. *Nutrition Today,* September/October, 4–11.

Inclan, J. (1985). Variations in value orientations in mental health work with Puerto Ricans. *Psychotherapy, 22*(2S), 324–334.

Jacobs, J. (1961). *The death and life of great American cities.* New York: Random House.

Janson, C. G. (1980). Factorial social ecology: An attempt at summary and evaluation. *Annual Review of Sociology, 6,* 433–456.

Jencks, C. (1972). *Inequality: A reassessment of the effect of family and schooling in America.* New York: Basic Books.

Jenkins, S. (1981). *The ethnic dilemma in social services.* New York: Free Press.

Johnson, S. (1978). Interim report of the family impact seminar. Washington, DC: George Washington University.

Jones, M. C. (1965). Psychological correlates of somatic development. *Child Development, 36,* 899–911.

Josselson, R. (1980). Ego development in adolescence. In J. Adelson (Ed.), *Handbook of adolescent psychology.* New York: John Wiley.

Kadushin, A. (1978). Child welfare strategy in the coming years: An overview. In *Child welfare strategy in the coming years.* USDHEW 78-30158.

Kadushin, A. (1980). *Child welfare services.* New York: Macmillan.

Kadushin, A., & Martin, J. A. (1981). *Child abuse: An interactional event.* New York: Columbia University Press.

Kahn, A. (1976). Service delivery at the neighborhood level: Experience, theory, and fads. *Social Service Review, 50,* 23–56.

Kahn, A., & Kamerman, S. (1975). *Not for the poor alone: European social services.* Philadelphia: Temple University Press.

Kalter, H., & Warkany, J. (1983). Congenital malformations: Etiological factors and their role in prevention. *New England Journal of Medicine, 308*(8), 424–431.

Kamerman, S. B. (1975). Eight countries: Cross-national perspectives on child abuse and neglect. *Children Today, 4*(3), 34–37.

Kamerman, S. B., & Kahn, A. J. (1976). *Social services in the United States: Policies and programs.* Philadelphia: Temple University Press.

Kamerman, S. B., Kahn, A. J., & Kingston, P. (1983). *Maternity policies and working women.* New York: Columbia University Press.

Kanter, R. M. (1977). *Work and family in the United States: A critical review and agenda for research and policy.* New York: Russell Sage Foundation.

Kantor, D., & Lehr, W. (1975). *Inside the family.* San Francisco: Jossey-Bass.

Katz, S. (1971). *When parents fail: The law's response to family breakdown.* Boston: Beacon Press.

Keller, S. (1968). *The urban neighborhood: A sociological perspective.* New York: Random House.

Keller, S. (1971). Does the family have a future? *Journal of Comparative Family Studies, 2,* 1–14.

Kelly, J. (1981). The last days of Poletown. *Time, 117,* 29.

Kempe, R. S., & Kempe, C. H. (1978). *Child abuse.* Cambridge, MA: Harvard University Press.

Kemple, K. M. (1991). Preschool children's peer acceptance and social interaction. *Young Children, 46*(5), 47–54.

Keniston, K. (1972). Youth: A new stage of life. In T. J. Cottle (Ed.), *The Prospect of Youth.* Boston: Little, Brown.

Keniston, K. (1977). *All our children: The American family under pressure.* New York: Harcourt, Brace Jovanovich.

Kenkel, W. F. (1960). *The family in perspective.* New York: Appleton-Century-Crofts.

Kennell, J. H., Jerauld, R., Wolfe, H., Chesler, D., Kreger, N. C., McAlpine, W., Steffa, M., & Klaus, M. H. (1974). Maternal behavior one year after early and extended post-partum contact. *Developmental Medicine and Child Neurology, 16,* 172–179.

Kennell, J., Voos, D., & Klaus, M. (1976). Parent-infant bonding. In R. Helfer & C. H. Kempe (Eds.), *Child abuse and neglect: The family and the community.* Cambridge, MA: Ballinger.

Kessen, W. (Ed.). (1975). *Childhood in China.* New Haven, CT: Yale University Press.

Kessner, D. M., Singer, J., Kalk, C. E., & Schlesinger, E. R. (1973). *Infant death: An analysis by maternal risk and health care.* Washington: Institute of Medicine.

Kinney, J., Haapala, D., & Booth, C. (1991). *Keeping families together.* New York: Aldine de Gruyter.

Klaus, M., Jerauld, K., Kreger, N., McAlpine, W., Steffa, M., & Kennell, J., Jr. (1972). Maternal attachment—importance of the first postpartum days. *New England Journal of Medicine, 286,* 460–463.

Klaus, M., & Kennell, J. (1976). *Maternal-infant bonding.* St. Louis, MO: C. V. Mosby.

Klerman, L. V. (1986). Teenage pregnancy. In M. W. Yogman & T. B. Brazelton (Eds.), *In support of families* (pp. 211–223). Cambridge, MA: Harvard University Press.

Klugman, E., & Benn, J. (1987). The elementary school principal's role in integrating early childhood perspectives. *School Administrators Association of New York State Journal,* 5–20.

Knitzer, J. (1980). Advocacy and community psychology. In M. S. Gibbs, J. R. Lachenmeyer, & J. Sigal (Eds.), *Community psychology: Theoretical and empirical approaches.* New York: Garner Press.

Kogan, L., Smith, J., & Jenkins, S. (1977). Ecological validity of indicator data as predictors of survey findings. *Journal of Social Service Research, 1,* 117–132.

Kohn, M. L. (1977). *Class and conformity: A study in values* (2nd ed.). Chicago: University of Chicago Press.

Konner, M. J. (1976). Relations among infants and juveniles in comparative perspective. In M. Lewis & L. Rosenblum (Eds.), *Friendship and peer relations.* New York: John Wiley.

Kopp, C., & Krakow, J. (1983). The developmentalist and the study of biological risk: A view of the past with an eye toward the future. *Child Development, 54,* 1086–1108.

Kopp, C. B. & Parmelee, A. H. (1979). Prenatal and perinatal influences on infant behavior. In J. D. Osofsky (Ed.), *Handbook of infancy.* New York: John Wiley.

Korbin, J. (1977). *Changing family roles and structures: Impact on child abuse and neglect?—A cross-cultural perspective.* Paper presented at the Second Annual National Conference on Child Abuse and Neglect, Houston, April.

Korbin, J. (Ed.). (1981). *Child abuse and neglect: Cross-cultural perspectives.* Berkeley: University of California Press.

Korbin, J. (1982). Very few cases: Child abuse in the People's Republic of China. In J. Korbin (Ed.), *Cross cultural perspectives on child abuse.* Berkeley: University of California Press.

Kotlowitz, A. (1991). *There are no children here. The story of two boys growing up in the other America.* New York: Doubleday.

Kowinski, W. (1980). Suburbia: End of the golden age. *New York Times Magazine.* March 16, 16ff.

Kozol, J. (1988). *Rachel and her children.* New York: Crown.

Kromkowski, J. (1976). *Neighborhood deterioration and juvenile crime.* (U.S. Department of Commerce, National Technical Information Service, PB-260 473), The South Bend Urban Observatory, Indiana, August.

LaFromboise, J. & Low, K. (1989). American Indian children and adolescents. In J. Gibbs & L. Huang (Eds.), *Children of color: Psychological interventions with minority youth.* San Francisco: Jossey-Bass.

Lally, J. R., Mangione, P. L., Honig, A. S., & Wittner, D. S. (1988). More pride, less delinquency: Findings from the ten-year follow-up study of the Syracuse University Family Developmental Research Program. *Zero to Three,* 13–19.

Lamb, M. E. (1976). *The role of the father in child development.* New York: John Wiley.

Lamb, M. E. (1977a). The role of the father: An overview. In M. E. Lamb (Ed.), *The role of the father in child development.* New York: John Wiley.

Lamb, M. E. (1977b). Father-infant and mother-infant interaction in the first year of life. *Child Development, 48,* 167–181.

Lamb, M. E. (1978). Infant social cognition and "second order" effects. *Infant Behavior and Development, 1*(1), 1–10.

Lander, B. (1954). *Towards an understanding of juvenile delinquency: A study of 8,464 cases of juvenile delinquency in Baltimore.* New York: Columbia University Press.

Lasch, C. (1978). *The culture of narcissism: American life in an age of diminishing expectations.* New York: Norton.

Lazar, I., Darlington, R., Murray, H., Royce, J., & Snipper, A. (1982). Lasting effects of early education. *Monographs of the Society for Research in Child Development* 47(1–2, Serial No. 194).

Leboyer, F. (1975). *Birth without violence.* New York: Alfred A. Knopf.

Lee, E. (1987). *Assessment and treatment of Southeast Asian-American survivors of mass violence.* Paper presented at the third annual meeting of the Society for Traumatic Stress Studies, Baltimore, October.

Leidermann, P. H., & Seashore, M. J. (1975). *Mother-infant neonatal separation: Some delayed consequences.* Ciba Foundation Symposium 33, Parent-Infant Interaction, Amsterdam, ASP, 213–239.

Lerner, J. V., & Lerner, R. M. (1983). Temperament and adaptation across life: Theoretical and empirical issues. In P. B. Baltes & O. G. Brim (Eds.), *Lifespan development and behavior* (Vol 5, pp. 197–231). New York: Academic Press.

LeShan, E. (1967). *The conspiracy against childhood.* New York: Atheneum.

Levine, J. (1976). *Day care and the public schools.* Newton, MA: Education Development Center.

Levine, M., & Levine, A. (1970). *A social history of helping services: Clinic, court, school and community.* New York: Appleton-Century-Crofts.

Lewin, T. (1988, March 20). Fewer teen mothers but more are unmarried. *The New York Times,* p. 6.

Lewis, D. (1975). The black family: socialization and sex roles. *Phylon, 36,* 221–237.

Lewis, J. M., Beavers, W. R., Gossett, J. T., & Phillips, V. A. (1976). *No single thread: Psychological health in family systems*. New York: Brunner/Mazel.

Lewis, M., & Weinraub, M. (1976). The father's role in the child's social network. In M. E. Lamb (Ed.), *The role of the father in child development*. New York: John Wiley.

Lieber, L., & Baker, J. (1977). Parents anonymous and self-help treatment for child abusing parents: A review and an evaluation. *Child Abuse and Neglect, 1*, 133–148.

Lieberman, E. J. (1970). Reserving a womb: Case for the small family. *American Journal of Public Health, 60*, 87–92.

Liebert, R. M., Neal, J. M., & Davidson, E. S. (1973). *The early window: Effects of TV on children and youth*. New York: Pergamon Press.

Lifschitz, et al. (1986). *Pediatric Research, 20*, 206A.

Light, I. N. (1972). *Ethnic enterprise in America: Business and welfare among Chinese, Japanese and Blacks*. Berkeley, CA: University of California Press.

Lightfoot, S. (1978). *Worlds apart: Relationships between families and schools*. New York: Basic.

Lin, K., Masuda, M., & Tazuma, L. (1982). Adaptation problems of Vietnamese refugees: Part III. Case studies in Clinic and field: Adaptive and maladaptive. *Psychiatric Journal of the University of Ottawa, 7*(3), 173–183.

Livingston, J. C., & Thompson, R. G. (1971). *The consent of the governed*. New York: Macmillan.

Lösel, F., & Bliesner, T. (1990). Resilience in adolescence: A study on the generalizability of protective factors. In K. Hurrelmann and F. Lösel (Eds.), *Health Hazards in Adolescence*. Berlin: Walter de Gruyter.

Lynn, L. (1980). *The state and human services: Organizational change in a political context*. Cambridge, MA: M.I.T. Press.

Maccoby, E. (Ed.). (1966). *The development of sex differences*. Stanford, CA: Stanford University Press.

Maccoby, E., & Jacklin, C. (1974). *The psychology of sex differences*. Stanford, CA: Stanford University Press.

Maccoby, E., & Jacklin, C. (1980). Sex differences in aggression: A rejoinder and reprise. *Child Development, 51*, 964–980.

Maccoby, E., Johnson, J. P., & Church, R. M. (1958). Community integration and the social control of juvenile delinquency. *Journal of Social Issues, 14*, 38–51.

MacFarlane, A. (1977). *The psychology of childbirth*. Cambridge, MA: Harvard University Press.

MacIntyre, S. (1977). The management of childbirth: A review of sociological research issues. *Social Science and Medicine, 11*, 477–484.

Makarenko, A. S. (1954). *A book for parents*. Moscow, USSR: Foreign Languages Publishing House (American edition).

Mangurten, H. H., Slade, C., & Fitzsimons (1979). Parent-parent support in the care of high-risk newborns. *JOGN Nursing*, 275–277.

Marcia, J. (1980). Identity of adolescence. In J. Adelson (Ed.), *Handbook of adolescent psychology* (pp. 159–187). New York: John Wiley.

Margolis, L., & Runyan, C. (1983). Accidental policy: An analysis of the problem of unintended injuries of childhood. *American Journal of Orthopsychiatry, 53,* 629–644.

Mass, A. (1986). Psychological effects of the camps on Japanese Americans. In R. Daniels, S. C. Taylor, & H. H. L. Kitano (Eds.), *From relocation to redress.* Salt Lake City: University of Utah Press.

Matas, L., Arend, R. A., & Sroufe, L. A. (1978). Continuity of adaptation in the second year: The relationship between quality of attachment and later competence. *Child Development, 49,* 547–556.

Maybanks, S., & Bryce, M. (1979). *Home-based services to children and families: Policy, practice, research.* Springfield, IL: C. C Thomas.

Maziade, M., Cote, R., Boudreault, M., Thivierge, J., & Boutine, P. (1986). Family correlates of temperament continuity and change across middle childhood. *American Journal of Orthopsychiatry, 56*(2), 195–203.

McBride, S., & Belsky, J. (1985, April). *Maternal work plans, actual employment, and infant temperament.* Poster presented at the biennial meeting of the Society for Research in Child Development, Toronto.

McClelland, D. C. (1973). Testing for competence rather than for "intelligence." *American Psychologist, 28,* 1–14.

McClelland, D. C. (1975). *Power: The inner experience.* New York: Irvington.

McGoldrick, M., Pearce, J. K., & Giordano, J. (Eds.). (1982). *Ethnicity and family therapy.* New York: Guilford Press.

McLane, J., & McNamee (1990). *Early literacy.* Cambridge, MA: Harvard University Press.

Mead, G. H. (1934). *Mind, self and society.* Chicago: University of Chicago Press.

Mead, M. (1935). *Sex and temperament in three savage tribes.* New York: William Morrow.

Mead, M. (1955). *Cultural patterns and technical change.* New York: New American Library.

Mead, M. (1966). Neighbourhoods and human needs. *Ekistics, 21,* 124–126.

Mead, M., & Heyman, K. (1965). *Family.* New York: Macmillan.

Mendelberg, H. (1986). Identity conflict in Mexican-American adolescents. *Adolescence, 21*(81), 215–224.

Michelson, W., & Roberts, E. (1979). Children and the urban physical environment. In W. Michelson, S. Levine, & A. Spina (Eds.), *The child in the city.* Toronto: University of Toronto Press.

Miller, A. (1987). *Maternal health and infant survival: An analysis of medical and social services to pregnant women, newborns, and their families in ten European countries.* Washington, DC: National Center for Clinical Infant Programs.

Miller, G. (Ed.) (1989). *Giving children a chance. The case for more effective national policies.* Washington, DC: Center for National Policy Press.

Mills, C. W. (1975). *The sociological imagination.* New York: Oxford University Press.

Mindel, C. & Habenstein, R. (1976). *Ethnic Families in America.* New York: Elsevier.

Money, J., & Ehrhardt, A. (1972). *Man and woman, boy and girl.* Baltimore: Johns Hopkins University Press.

Montague, A. (1979). *The elephant man: A study in human dignity.* New York: E. P. Dutton.

Moos, R. (1979). *Evaluating educational environments: Procedures, measures, findings and policy implications.* San Francisco: Jossey-Bass.

Moroney, R. (1976). *The family and the state: Considerations for social policy.* New York: Longmans.

Moroney, R. (1980). *Families, social services, and social policy: The issue of shared responsibility.* Washington, DC: Government Printing Office, DHHS Publication No. ADM 80-846.

Morris, D. (1970). *The human zoo.* New York: Dell.

Morris, D. (1972). *The naked ape.* New York: Dell.

Morrow, L. (1979). Wondering if children are really necessary. *Time,* March 5, p. 42ff.

Moritsugu, J., & Sue, S. (1983). Minority stress as a stressor. In R. Felner, L. Jason, J. Moritsugu, & S. Farber (Eds.), *Preventive psychology: Theory, research and practice.* Elmsford, NY: Pergamon Press.

Munroe, R. L., & Munroe,, R. H. (1975). *Cross-cultural human development.* Monterey, CA: Brooks/Cole.

Musick, J. (1990). Adolescents and mothers: The being and the doing. *Zero to Three, 11,* 21–28.

Musick, J. and Stott, F. (1990). Paraprofessionals, parenting, and child development: Understanding the problems and seeking solutions. In *Handbook of Early Childhood Intervention.* Meisels, S. and Shonkoff, J. (Eds.). New York: Cambridge University Press.

Myrdal, A. (1968). *Nation and family: The Swedish experiment in democratic family and population policy.* Cambridge, MA: M.I.T. Press.

Nann, B. (1982). Settlement programs for immigrant women and families. In R. Nann (Ed.), *Uprooting and surviving.* Dordrecht, Holland: Reidel.

National Academy of Sciences. (1976). *Toward a national policy for children and families.* Washington, DC: U.S. Government Printing Office.

National Association for the Education of Young Children. (1990). NAEYC position statement on school readiness. *Young Children, 46*(1), 21–23.

National Association of Attorneys General. (1976). *Legal issues in foster care.* Raleigh, NC: Committee on the Office of Attorneys General.

National Commission on Children. (1991). *Beyond rhetoric: A new American agenda for children and families.* Washington, DC: U.S. Government Printing Office.

National Commission on Neighborhoods. (1979). *Final report of the commission.* Washington, DC: U.S. Government Printing Office.

Needleman, H. L. (1991). Lead exposure: The commonest environmental disease of childhood. *Zero to Three, 11*(5), 1–6.

Newman, D., & Associates. (1979). Cross-cultural psychology's challenges to our ideas of children and development. *American Psychologist, 34,* 827–833.

Newton, N. (1979). Cross-cultural perspectives. In A. L. Clark & D. D. Affonso (Eds.), *Childbearing: A nursing perspective* (2nd ed.). Philadelphia: F. A. Davis.

Niebuhr, R. (1960). *The children of light and the children of darkness.* New York: Charles Scribner's Sons.

Nielsen Media Research (1990). Report on Television.

Norwood, C. (1980). *At highest risk: Environmental hazards to young and unborn children*. New York: McGraw-Hill.

Nuttal, R. (1980). *Coping with catastrophe: Family adjustments to natural disasters*. Paper presented at Groves Conference on Marriage and the Family, Gatlinburg, TN, May 31.

Oakley, A. (1979). A case of maternity: Paradigms of women as maternity cases. *Signs: Journal of Women in Culture and Society, 4,* 607–631.

O'Connor, S., Vietze, P., Hopkins, J., & Altemeir, W. (1977). Postpartum extended maternal-infant conflict: Subsequent mothering and child health. *Sociological Pediatric Research* (Abstract).

Ogburn, W. F. (1922). *Social change*. New York: B. W. Huebsch.

O'Hara, R. (1962). The roots of career. *Elementary Journal, 62,* 277–280.

Olds, D. (1980a). *Selected prenatal outcomes in the pilot study of the Prenatal-Early Infancy Project*. Paper presented at the annual meeting of the American Public Health Association, Detroit, October.

Olds, D. (1980b). Improving formal services for mothers and children. In J. Garbarino, S. H. Stocking, & Associates, *Protecting children from abuse and neglect*. San Francisco: Jossey-Bass.

Olds, D., et al. (1986). Preventing child abuse and neglect: A randomized trial of nurse home visitation. *Pediatrics, 78*(1), 65–78.

Ooms, T. (1979). *Teenage pregnancy and family impact: New perspectives on policy. Preliminary Report*. Family Impact Seminar. The George Washington University, Institute for Educational Leadership, June.

O'Reilly, J. P., Tokuno, K. A., & Ebata, A. T. (1986). Cultural differences between Americans of Japanese and European ancestry in parental valuing and social competence. *Journal of Comparative Family Studies, 17,* 87–97.

Osofsky, J. D., Osofsky, H. J., & Diamond, M. O. (1988). The transition to parenthood: Special tasks and risk factors for adolescent parents. In G. Y. Michaels & W. A. Goldberg (Eds.), *The transition to parenthood* (pp. 209–232). Cambridge, England: The Cambridge University Press.

Otto, S. E. (1978). ICEA: The challenges of childbirth education . . . yesterday, now and tomorrow. *Mother's Manual*, January–February, 36–38.

Ou, Y. S., & MacAdoo, H. (1980). *Ethnic identity and self-esteem in Chinese children*. Unpublished report submitted to NIMH Center for Minority Group Mental Health Programs. Columbia, MD: Columbia Research Systems.

Pancoast, D. L. (1980). Finding and enlisting neighbors to support families. In J. Garbarino, S. H. Stocking, & Associates, *Protecting children from abuse and neglect: Developing and maintaining effective support systems for families*. San Francisco: Jossey-Bass.

Parke, R. (1974). Father-infant interaction. In M. H. Klaus, T. Leger, & M. A. Trause (Eds.), *Maternal attachment and mothering disorders: A round table*.

Parke, R. D. (1979). Perspectives on father-infant interaction. In J. D. Osofsky (Ed.), *Handbook of infant development*. New York: John Wiley.

Parke, R., & Collmer, C. W. (1975). Child abuse: An interdisciplinary analysis. In E. M. Hetherington (Ed.), *Review of child development research* (Vol. 5). Chicago: University of Chicago Press.

Parke, R. D., & O'Leary, S. E. (1975). Father-mother-infant interaction in the newborn period: Some findings, some observations and some unresolved issues. In K. Riegel & J. Meacham (Eds.), *The developing individual in a changing world* (Vol. 2). *Social and environmental issues*. The Hague: Mouton.

Parke, R. D., & Sawin, D. B. (1976). The father's role in infancy: A reevaluation. *The Family Coordinator, 25,* 365–371.

Parsons, T. (1949). The kinship system of the contemporary United States. In T. Parsons, *Essays in Sociological Theory.* New York: The Free Press.

Parsons, T., & Bales, R. (1955). *Family, socialization and interaction process.* New York: The Free Press.

Parsons, T., Bales, R., & Shils, E. (1955). *Working papers in the theory of action.* Glencoe, IL: Free Press.

Patterson, G. R. (1979). A performance theory for coercive family interaction. In R. B. Cairns (Ed.), *The analysis of social interactions: Methods, issues, and illustrations.* Hillsdale, NJ: Lawrence Erlbaum.

Peccei, A. (1977). *The human quality.* Oxford, England: Pergamon Press.

Pedersen, F. A., & Robson, K. S. (1969). Father participation in infancy. *American Journal of Orthopsychiatry,* 466–472.

Pedersen, F., Zaslow, M., Cain, R., & Anderson, B. (1980). *Caesarean childbirth: The importance of a family perspective.* Paper presented at the International Conference on Infant Studies, New Haven, CT, April.

Perry, T. (1988). Personal communication.

Peters, D. L. (1980). Social science and social policy and the care of young children. *Journal of Applied Developmental Psychology, 1,* 7–27.

Peters, D. L., & Benn, J. L. (1980). Day care: Support for the family. *Dimensions, 9,* 78–82.

Peterson, G. H., Mehl, L. E., & Leiderman, P. H. (1979). The role of some birth-related variables in father attachment. *American Journal of Orthopsychiatry, 49,* 330–337.

Photiadis, J. D. (1970). Rural southern Appalachia and mass society. In J. D. Photiadis & H. K. Schwarzweller (Eds.), *Change in rural Appalachia: Implications for action programs.* Philadelphia: University of Pennsylvania Press.

Piaget, J. (1952). *The origins of intelligence in children.* Trans. M. Cook. New York: International Universities Press.

Polansky, N. (1976). Analysis of research on child neglect: The social work viewpoint. In Herner & Company (Eds.), *Four perspectives on the status of child abuse and neglect research.* Washington, DC: National Center on Child Abuse and Neglect.

Phillips, D. (1987). Socialization of perceived academic competence among highly competent children. *Child Development 58,*(5), 1308–1320.

Powell, G. J. (1985). Self-concepts among Afro-American students in racially isolated minority schools: Some regional differences. *Journal of the American Academy of Child Psychiatry, 24,* 142–149.

Powell, G. J., & Fuller, M. (1970). Self-concept and school desegregation. *American Journal of Orthopsychiatry, 40,* 303–304.

Powers, J. (1989, December 3). Too much, too soon. *The Boston Glove Magazine, 22,* 55–62.

Price, D. (1991). A true understanding of children's culture can enhance adult interventions. *Child and Adolescent Behavior Letter, 7*(8), 1–3, August.

Pritchard, J. A., MacDonald, P. C., & Gant, N. F. (1985). *William's Obstetrics* (17th ed.). Norwalk, CT: Appleton-Century-Crofts.

Proceedings of the Conference on the Care of Dependent Children. (1909). Washington, DC, January 25–26, pp. 17–18.

Rabkin, J. (1979). Ethnic density and psychiatric hospitalization: Hazards of minority status. *American Journal of Psychiatry, 136*, 1562–1566.

Ramirez, M., & Castaneda, A. (1974). *Cultural democracy, biocognitive development, and education.* New York: Academic Press.

Rebelsky, F., & Hanks, C. (1971). Fathers' verbal interaction with infants in the first three months of life. *Child Development, 24*, 63–68.

Reed, R. (1988). Education and achievement of young black males. In J. T. Gibbs (Ed.), *Young, black, and male in America: An endangered species.* Dover, MA: Auburn House.

Reiss, I. (1980). *Family systems in America* (3rd ed.). New York: Holt, Rinehart & Winston.

Ricciuti, H. (1974). Fear and development of social attachments in the first three years of life. In N. Lewis & L. A. Rosenblum (Eds.), *The origins of human behavior: Fear.* New York: John Wiley.

Ricciuti, H. (1977). Effects of infant day care experience on behavior and development: Research and implications for social policy. In *Policy issues in day care: Summaries of 21 papers.* Washington, DC: Office of the Secretary for Planning and Evaluation.

Robinson, D. (1991). Save our babies. *Parade,* June 30, 8–9.

Robinson, N. M., Robinson, H. B., Darling, M. A., & Holm, G. (1979). *A world of children: Daycare and preschool institutions.* Monterey, CA: Brooks/Cole.

Rock, M. (1978). Gorilla mothers need some help from their friends. *Smithsonian, 9*(4), 58–63.

Rockwell, R. (1978). Personal communication.

Rodes, T., & Moore, J. (1975). *National child care consumer study: American consumer attitudes and opinions on child care.* Arlington, VA: Kappa Systems.

Rogers, E. M., & Shoemaker, F. F. (1971). *Communication of innovations: A cross-cultural approach.* New York: The Free Press.

Rohner, R. (1975). *They love me, they love me not.* New Haven, CT: Human Relations Area Files Press.

Rohner, R., & Nielsen, C. (1978). *Parental acceptance and rejection: A review of research and theory.* New Haven, CT: Human Relations Area Files Press.

Rollins, B., & Cannon, K. (1974). Marital satisfaction over the family life cycle: A reevaluation. *Journal of Marriage and the Family, 36*, 271–282.

Rollins, B., & Feldman, H. (1970). Marital satisfaction over the family life cycle. *Journal of Marriage and the Family, 32*, 20–28.

Rooks, J. P., Wetherby, N. L., Ernst, E. K. M., Stapleton, S., Rosen, D., & Rosenberg, A. (1989). Outcomes of care in birth centers: The National Birth Care Center Study. *New England Journal of Medicine, 32*, 1804–1811.

Rosen, M. G. (chairman) (1980). Cesarean childbirth. *National Institute of Health Consensus Development Conference Summary, 3*(6).

Rosenberg, B., & Sutton-Smith, B. (1972). *Sex and identity.* New York: Holt, Rinehart & Winston.

Rosenberg, M. (1965). *Society and the adolescent self-image.* Princeton, NJ: Princeton University Press.

Rosenberg, M. S., & Reppucci, D. (1981). Child abuse: A review with special focus on an ecological approach in rural communities. In T. Melton (Ed.), *Rural Psychology,*

Rosenberg, M., & Simmons, R. (1971). *Black and white self-esteem: The urban school child.* Rose Monograph Series. Washington, DC: American Sociological Association.

Rossi, A. (1968). Transition to parenthood. *Journal of Marriage and the Family,* 26–39.

Rotenberg, M. (1977). Alienating-individualism and reciprocal-individualism: A cross-cultural conceptualization. *Journal of Humanistic Psychology,* 17, 3–17.

Rutter, M. (1979). Maternal deprivation, 1972–1978: New findings, new concepts, new approaches. *Child Development,* 50, 283–305.

Rutter, M. (1988). Temperament: Concepts, issues, and problems. In E. M. Hetherington & R. D. Parke (Eds.), *Contemporary readings in child psychology* (3rd ed.).

Ryan, W. (1976). *Blaming the victim.* New York: Vintage Press.

Sagan, C. (1977). *The dragons of Eden: Speculations of the evolution of human intelligence.* New York: Random House.

Sale, K. (1980). *Human scale.* New York: Coward, McCann, & Geoghegan.

Sameroff, A. J. (1983). Parental views of child development. In R. A. Hoekelman (Ed.), *A round table on minimizing high-risk parenting.* Media, PA: Harwal.

Sameroff, A. J., & Chandler, M. J. (1975). Reproductive risk and the continuum of care-taking casualty. In F. Horowitz, M. Hetherington, S. Scarr-Salapatek, & G. Siegel (Eds.), *Review of Child Development Research* (Vol. 4). Chicago: University of Chicago Press.

Sameroff, A., & Fiese, B. (1990). Transactional regulation and early intervention. In S. Meisels & J. Shonkoff (Eds.), *Handbook of Early Childhood Intervention.* New York: Cambridge University Press.

Sameroff, A., Seifer, R., Barocas, R., Zax, M., & Greenspan, S. (1987). Intelligent quotient scores of 4-year-old children: Social-environment risk factors. *Pediatrics* 79(3), 343–350.

San Francisco Chronicle. (1987). Asian immigrants say schoolmates harass them, March 28.

Sanger, M. (1938). *Margaret Sanger: An autobiography.* New York: W. W. Norton.

Satir, V. (1972). *Peoplemaking.* Palo Alto, CA: Science & Behavior Books.

Sattin, D., & Miller, J. (1971). The ecology of child abuse. *American Journal of Orthopsychiatry,* 41, 675–678.

Sawin, D. B., & Parke, R. D. (1979). Fathers' affectionate stimulation and caregiving behaviors with newborn infants. *The Family Coordinator,* 28(4), 509–513.

Schorr, A. (1979). The child and the community. In W. Michelson, S. Levine, & E. Michelson (Eds.), *The child in the city.* Toronto: University of Toronto Press.

Schorr, L. (1988). *Within our reach: Breaking the cycle of disadvantage.* New York: Doubleday.

Schumacher, E. R. (1973). *Small is beautiful: Economics as if people mattered.* New York: Harper & Row.

Schwartzweller, H. K. (1970). Social change and the individual in rural Appalachia. In J. D. Photiadis & H. K. Schwarzweller (Eds.), *Change in rural Appalachia: Implications for action programs.* Philadelphia: University of Pennsylvania Press.

Seashore, M. J. (1981). Mother-infant separation: Outcome assessment. In V. L. Smeriglio (Ed.), *Newborns and parents: Parent-infant contact and newborn sensory stimulation.* Hillsdale, NJ: Lawrence Erlbaum.

Segal, J., & Yahraes, H. (1978). *A child's journey.* New York: McGraw-Hill.

Seligson, M., & Fink, D. B. (1989). *No time to waste: An action agenda for school-age child care.* Wellesley, MA: School-Age Child Care project, Wellesley College Center for Research on Women.

Shanock, R. S. (1990). Parenthood: A process marking identity and intimacy capacities. *Zero to Three, 11,* 1–9.

Shaw, C. R., & McKay, H. D. (1942). *Juvenile delinquency and urban areas.* Chicago: University of Chicago Press.

Shaw, C. R., Zorbaugh, F. M., McKay, H. D., & Cottrell, L. S., Jr. (1929). *Delinquency areas.* Chicago: University of Chicago Press.

Shelton, L. G., & Gladstone, T. (1979). *Childbearing in adolescence.* Paper presented at the American Orthopsychiatric Association, Washington, DC, April.

Sherif, M. (1958). Superordinate goals in the reduction of intergroup conflict. *American Journal of Sociology, 63,* 349–356.

Shevky, E., & Bell, W. (1955). *Social area analysis.* Stanford: Stanford University Press.

Shirer, W. L. (1960). *The rise and fall of the third reich: A history of Nazi Germany.* New York: Simon & Schuster.

Short, J. F., Jr. (1966). Juvenile delinquency: The sociocultural context. In L. W. Hoffman & M. L. Hoffman (Eds.), *Review of child development research* (Vol. 2). New York: Russell Sage Foundation.

Shreve, A. (1988). Fast-lane kids. *The New York Times Magazine, 50,* 54–58.

Shy, K. K., Luthy, D. A., Bennett, F. C., Whitfield, M., & Larson, E. R. (1990). Effects of electronic fetal-heart-rate monitoring, as compared with periodic auscultation, on the neurologic development of preterm infants. *New England Journal of Medicine, 322,* 588–593.

Sibbison, V. (1972). *The influence of maternal role perception of attitudes toward and utilization of early child care services.* The Pennsylvania State University: Center for Human Services Development, PDCSP Tech, Report 10.

Sidel, R. (1986). *Women and children last: The plight of poor women in affluent America.* Viking Publication.

Slater, P. E. (1961). Toward a dualistic theory of identification. *Merrill-Palmer Quarterly, 7,* 113–126.

Slater, P. E. (1970). *The pursuit of loneliness: American culture at the breaking point.* Boston: Beacon Press.

Slaughter-Defoe, D., Nakagawa, K., Takanishi, R., & Johnson, D. (1990). Toward cultural ecological perspectives on schooling and achievement in African- and Asian-American cultures. *Child Development, 61,* 363–383.

Sluzki, C. (1979). Migration and family conflict. *Family Process, 18*(4), 379–390.

Smith, C. J. (1976). Residential neighborhoods as humane environments. *Environment and Planning, 8,* 311–326.

Snyder, D. J. (1979). The high-risk mother viewed in relation to a holistic model of the childbearing experience. *Journal of Obstetrical and Gynelogical Nursing,* May–June, 164–170.

Soares, A. T., & Soares, L. M. (1971). Comparative differences in the self-perceptions of disadvantaged and advantaged students. *Journal of School Psychology, 9,* 424–429.

Solnit, A. J., & Provence, S. (1979). Vulnerability and risk in early childhood. In J. D. Osofsky (Ed.), *Handbook of infant development.* New York: John Wiley.

Sosa, R., Keena, J., Klaus, M., Robertson, S. and Urrutia, J. (1980). The effect of a supportive companion on perinatal problems, length of labor and mother–infant interaction. *New England Journal of Medicine, 303*(11), 597–600.

Spanier, G. B. (1980). The family: Alive but not well. *Wilson Quarterly.* Washington: Smithsonian Institute.

Spanier, G. B., & Anderson, E. A. (1979). The impact of the legal system on adjustment to marital separation. *Journal of Marriage and the Family, 41,* 605–613.

Spanier, G. B., Lewis, R. A., & Cole, C. L. (1975). Marital adjustment over the family life cycle: The issue of curvilinearity. *Journal of Marriage and the Family, 37.*

Spencer, M., & Markstrom-Adams, C. (1990). Identity processes among racial and ethnic minority children in America. *Child Development, 61,* 290–310.

Spitz, R. A. (1945). Hospitalism: An inquiry into the genesis of psychiatric conditions in early childhood. In A. Freud et al. (Eds.), *The psychoanalytic study of the child* (Vol. 1). New York: International Universities Press.

Sroufe, A. (1983). Infant-caregiver attachment and patterns of adaptation in preschool: The roots of maladaptation and competence. In M. Perlmutter (Ed.), *Minnesota symposium in child psychology* (Vol. 16, pp. 41–81). Hillsdale, NJ: Lawrence Erlbaum.

Staulcup, H. J. (1980). *Primary prevention in social welfare: Practice, education, and research.* Unpublished manuscript, National Committee for Prevention of Child Abuse.

Steinberg, L. (1985). Stability (and instability) of type A behavior from childhood to young adulthood. *Developmental Psychology, 21*(6).

Steinberg, L., Catalano, R., & Dooley, D. (1981). Economic antecedents of child abuse and neglect. *Child Development, 52,* 975–985.

Steinberg, L. D., & Hill, J. P. (1978). Patterns of family interaction as a function of age, the onset of puberty, and formal thinking. *Developmental Psychology, 14,* 683–684.

Steiner, G. Y., & Milius, P. H. (1976). *The children's cause.* Washington, DC: The Brookings Institution.

Stern, D. (1971). A micro-analysis of mother-infant interaction. *Journal of the American Academy of Child Psychiatry, 10,* 501–517.

Stern, D. (1973). Mother and infant at play: The dyadic interaction involving facial, vocal, and gaze behaviors. In M. Lewis & L. Rosenblum (Eds.), *Origins of Behavior* (Vol. 1). New York: John Wiley.

Sternberg, R. (1985). *Beyond IQ: A triarchic theory of human intelligence.* New York: Cambridge University Press.

Stevens, J. H., Jr. (1988). Social support, focus of control, and parenting in three low-income groups of mothers: Black teenagers, black adults, and white adults. *Child Development, 59,* 635-642.

Stevenson, D., & Baker, D. P. (1987). The family-school relation and the child's school performance. *Child Development, 58,* 1348–1357.

Stevenson, H. W., & Lee, S. (1990). Contexts of achievement. *Monographs of the Society for Research in Child Development* Serial 221, 55(1–2).

Stinnett, N., Chesser, B., & DeFrain, J. (1979). *Building family strengths: Blueprints for action.* Lincoln, NE: University of Nebraska Press.

Straus, M., & Gelles, R. (1990). *Physical violence in American families: Risk factors and adaptations to violence in 8,145 families.* New Brunswick, NJ: Tranaction Publ.

Straus, M., Gelles, R., & Steinmetz, S. (1980). *Behind closed doors.* New York: Doubleday.

Sue, D. W. (1981). *Counseling the culturally different.* New York: John Wiley.

Szapocznik, J., & Kurtines, W. (1980). Acculturation, biculturalism and adjustment among Cuban Americans. In A. M. Padilla (Ed.), *Acculturation: Theory, models and some new findings.* Boulder, CO: Westview.

Tajfel, H. (1978). *Differentiation between social groups: Studies in the social psychology of intergroup relations.* London: Academic Press.

Tannen, D. (1990). *You just don't understand: Women and men in conversation.* New York: Morrow.

Terkel, S. (1963). *Hard times.* New York: Parthenon.

Texas Department of Community Affairs. (1978). *78 things you need to know about Texas children: Still the darker side of childhood.*

The Boston Globe. (1990, December 4). The lead-poisoning peril.

Theodorson, G. A. (1961). *Studies in human ecology.* Evanston, IL: Harper & Row.

Thomas, A., & Chess, S. (1977). *Temperament and development.* New York: Brunner/Mazel.

Thomas, A., Chess, S., & Birch, H. (1968). *Temperament and behavior disorders in children.* New York: New York University Press.

Thomas, W. I., & Thomas, D. S. (1928). *The child in America.* New York: Alfred P. Knopf.

Tietjen, A. (1980). Formal and informal support systems: A cross-cultural perspective. In J. Garbarino, S. H. Stocking, & Associates, *Protecting children from abuse and neglect.* San Francisco: Jossey-Bass.

Toennies, F. (1957). *Community and society* (Trans. Charles Loomis.) East Lansing, MI: Michigan State University Press.

Toffel, S. M., Placek, P., Molen, M., & Kosary, C. L. (1991). 1989 U.S. Cesarean section rates steadies—VBAC rate rises to nearly one in five. *Birth, 18*(2), 73–76.

Toffler, A. (1970)). *Future shock.* New York: Bantam Books.

Tolstoy, L. (1949). *War and Peace.* London: John C. Winston Co., orig. 1865–1869.

Toufexis, A. (1990, October 8). Struggling for sanity. *Time, 136*(15), 47–48.

Trivers, R. L. (1974). Parent-offspring conflict. *American Zoologist, 14,* 249–264.

Tucker, M. J. (1974). The child as beginning and end: Fifteenth and sixteenth century English childhood. In L. de Mause, *The history of childhood.* New York: The Psychohistory Press.

Tulkin, S. R. (1972). An analysis of the concept of cultural deprivation. *Developmental Psychology, 6,* 326–339.

Turner, F. J. (1965). *The frontier in American history.* New York: Holt, Rinehart & Winston, orign. 1897.

Udry, J. R. (1974). *The social context of marriage* (2nd ed.). Philadelphia: J. B. Lippincott.

Unco. (1975). *National child care consumer study.* Washington, DC: U.S. Department of Health, Education, and Welfare.

Unger, D. G., & Powell, D. R. (1980). Supporting families under stress: The role of social networks. *Family Relations, 29,* 566–574.

Unger, D. G., & Wandersman, L. P. (1988). The relation of family and partner support to the adjustment of adolescent mothers. *Child Development, 59,* 1056–1060.

Urban, H., & Vondracek, F. (1977). Delivery of human intervention services: Past, present, and future. In S. R. Goldberg and F. Deutsch (Eds.), *Life-span individual and family development.* Monterey, CA: Brooks/Cole.

U.S. Bureau of Labor Statistics. (1980). *State, county, and selected city employment and unemployment: January–December, 1979.* Washington, DC: U.S. Bureau of Labor Statistics, April.

U.S. Bureau of the Census. (1976). *Daytime care of children,* Current Population Reports, Population Characteristics Series P-20, No. 298. Washington, DC: U.S. Bureau of the Census, October.

U.S. Bureau of the Census. (1979). *Divorce, child custody and child support,* by R. Sanders & G. B. Spanier, Current Population Reports Series P-23, No. 84. Washington, DC: U.S. Bureau of the Census.

U.S. Bureau of the Census. (1980a). *Current population reports: Population characteristics.* Washington, DC: U.S. Bureau of the Census.

U.S. Bureau of the Census. (1980b). *Current population reports: American family and living arrangements.* Washington, DC: U.S. Bureau of the Census.

U.S. Bureau of the Census. (1981). *1980 census of population and housing.* Advance Reports, Florida (PHC80-V-11), Rhode Island (PHC80-V-41). Washington, DC: U.S. Bureau of the Census.

U.S. Bureau of the Census. (1983a). *1980 Census of Population: General population characteristics, United States Summary.* Washington, DC: U.S. Government Printing Office.

U.S. Bureau of the Census. (1983b). *1980 Census of Population: General social and economic characteristics, United States summary.* Washington, DC: U.S. Government Printing Office.

U.S. Bureau of the Census. (1985). *Persons of Spanish origin in the United States: March 1985* (Advance Report). Current Population Reports, Population Characteristics, Series, P-20, No. 403. Washington, DC: U.S. Government Printing Office.

U.S. Bureau of the Census. (1986). *Statistical Abstract of the United States, 1987.* (107th ed.). Washington, DC: U.S. Government Printing Office.

U.S. Bureau of the Census. (1987). *Statistical Abstract of the United States, 1988.* (108th ed.). Washington, DC: U.S. Department of Commerce.

U.S. Bureau of the Census. (1990). *Who's minding the kids? Child care arrangements: 1986–87.* Current Population Reports, Series, P-70, No. 20. Washington, DC: U.S. Government Printing Office.

U.S. Department of Health and Human Services. (1987). *Refugee resettlement program: Report to the congress.* Washington, DC: U.S. Department of Health and Human Services.

U.S. Department of Health and Human Services (1990). *Healthy people 2000: National health promotion and disease prevention objectives.* Washington, DC: U.S. Government Printing Office.

U.S. Department of Health and Human Services, National Center for Health Statistics (1991). Births, marriages, divorces, and deaths for 1990. *Monthly Vital Statistics Report, 39*(12), 1.

U.S. General Accounting Office. (1989). *Child care: Government funding, sources, coordination, and service availability.* Washington, DC: U.S. General Accounting Office.

van den Berghe, P. (1979). *Human family systems: an evolutionary view.* New York: Elsevier.

Vanes, J. C., & Brown, J. E. (1974). The rural-urban variable once more: Some individual level observations. *Rural Sociology, 39*, 373–391.

van Vliet, W. (1985). The role of housing type, household density, and neighborhood density in peer interaction and social adjustment. In J. F. Wohlwill & W. van Vliet (Eds.), *Habitats for children: The impact of density.* Hillsdale, NJ: Lawrence Erlbaum.

Vygotsky, L. S. (1962). *Thought and language.* Cambridge, MA: M.I.T. Press.

Wachs, T. D., Uzgiris, I. C., & Hunt, J. McV. (1971). Cognitive development in infants of different age levels and from different environmental backgrounds: An exploratory investigation. *Merrill-Palmer Quarterly, 17*, 283–317.

Wagner, M. (1978). *Denmark's national family guidance program: A preventive mental health program for children and families.* Washington, DC: U.S. Government Printing Office, DHEW Publication No. ADM 77-512.

Wald, M. S. (1980). Thinking about public policy toward abuse and neglect of children: A review of *Before the best interests of the child. Michigan Law Review, 78*(5), 645–693.

Waldman, S. (1991, July 15). Lead and your kids. *Newsweek*, 42–48.

Wallerstein, J. S. (1983). Children of divorce: Stress and developmental tasks. In N. Garmezy & M. Rutter (Eds.), *Stress, coping, and development of children.* New York: McGraw-Hill.

Warren, D., & Warren, R. (1977). *The neighborhood organizer's handbook.* Notre Dame, IN: University of Notre Dame Press.

Warren, R. L. (1973). *The community in America* (2nd ed.). Chicago: Rand-McNally.

Warren, S. (1968). *The relocation of Ozawkie, Kansas.* Unpublished manuscript, University of Kansas.

Weatherly, D. (1963). Self-perceived rate of physical maturation and personality in late adolescence. *Child Development, 35,* 1197–1210.

Weinraub, M., Jaeger, E., & Hoffman, L. (1988). Predicting infant outcomes in families of employed and nonemployed mothers. *Early Childhood Research Quarterly, 3,* 361–378.

Weisner, T. S., & Gallimore, R. (1977). My brother's keeper: Child and sibling caretaking. *Current Anthropology, 18,* 169–190.

Weissbourd, B. & Grimm, C. (1981). Family focus: Supporting families in the community. *Children Today, 10*(2), 1–11.

Weissman, M., & Paykel, E. (1974). *The depressed woman.* Chicago: University of Chicago Press.

Werner, E. E. (1988a). Resilient children. In E. M. Hetherington & R. D. Parke, (Eds.), *Contemporary readings in child psychology* (3rd ed., pp. 51–57). New York: McGraw-Hill.

Werner, E. E. (1988b). Individual differences, universal needs: A 30-year study of resilient high risk infants. *Zero to Three, 8*(4), 1–5.

Werner, E., & Smith, R. S. (1982). *Vulnerable but invincible: A longitudinal study of resilient children and youth.* New York: McGraw-Hill.

Wertz, R., & Wertz, D. (1977). *Lying in: A history of childbirth in America.* New York: The Free Press.

West, B. (1983). The new arrivals from Southeast Asia: Getting to know them. *Childhood Education,* Nov–Dec, *60*(2), 84–89.

White, R. (1959). Motivation reconsidered: The concept of competence. *Psychological Review, 66,* 297–333.

Whittaker, J., Garbarino, J., & Associates. (1983). *Social support networks on informal helping in the human services.* Hawthorne, NY: Aldine de Gruyter.

Whitman, B. Y., Accardo, P., Boyert, M., & Kendagor, R. (1990). Homelessness and cognitive performance in children. *Social Work, 35,* 516–519.

Williams, D., & Westmeyer, J. (1983). Psychiatric problems among adolescent southeast Asian refugees: A descriptive study. *Journal of Nervous and Mental Disease, 1983,* 171.

Wilson, W. (1987). *The truly disadvantaged: The inner city, the underclass, and public policy.* Chicago: University of Chicago Press.

Wiltse, K. T. (1978). Current issues and new directions in foster care: In *Child welfare strategy in the coming years.* Washington, DC: DHEW Publ. No. (OHDS) 78-30158.

Wohlwill, J. F. (1983). Residential density as a variable in child-development research. In J. Wohlwill & W. van Vliet (Eds.), *Habitats for children: The impact of density.* New York: Academic Press.

World Health Organization (1986). *Environmental criteria 59, principles for evaluating health risks from chemicals during infancy and early childhood: The need for a special approach.* Geneva: World Health Organization.

Wright, A. T. (1958). *Islandia.* New York: Holt, Rinehart & Winston; orig. 1942.

Wynne, E. (1975). *Privacy and socialization to adulthood.* Paper presented at the meeting of the American Educational Research Association, Washington, DC, March.

Wynne, E. (1976). Adolescent alienation and social policy. *Teachers College Record, 78,* 33–39.

Wynne, E. A. (1977). *Growing up suburban.* Austin: University of Texas Press.

Yang, R. K. (1981). Maternal attitudes during pregnancy and medication during labor and delivery: Methodological considerations. In V. L. Smeriglio (Ed.), *Newborns and parents.* Hillsdale, NJ: Lawrence Erlbaum.

Young, K. T. (1990). American conceptions of infant development from 1955 to 1984: What the experts are telling parents. *Child Development, 61,* 17–28.

Zajonc, R. B., & Markus, G. B. (1975). Birth order and intellectual development. *Psychological Review, 82,* 74–78.

Zigler, E. (1976). The unmet needs of America's children. *Children Today,* May-June, 39–42.

Zigler, E. (1986). The "gourmet baby" and the "little wildflower." *Zero to Three, 7*(2), 8–12.

Zigler, E., & Lang, M. E. (1990). *Child care choices: Balancing the needs of children, family and society.* New York: The Free Press.

Zill, N. (1991, Winter). U.S. children and their families: Current conditions and recent trends, 1989. *SRCD Newsletter,* 1–3.

Zimmerman, C. C. (1947). *Family and civilization.* New York: Harper & Row.

Zuckerman, B. (1986). *Maternal health habits study.* Unpublished manuscript. Boston City Hospital, Boston, MA.

Zuspan, R. P., Quilligan, E. J., Iams, J. D., & Geijn, H. P. (1979). HICHD consensus development task force report: Predictions of intrapartum fetal distress—the role of electronic fetal monitoring. *The Journal of Pediatrics, 95,* 1026–1030.

Author Index

Subject Index

Academics (*See* School)
Acceptance, 158
Accidents, childhood, 237, 262–266
Acculturation, 193–196
Acculturation gap, 195
Acquaintance process, 150–151
Acquired immunodeficiency syndrome (AIDS), 108
ACT (Action for Children's Television), 170
Act for Better Child Care, 163
Action for Children's Television (ACT), 170
Activist approach to human services, 251–252
Adaptability, 12, 63, 118
Adolescence, 107, 186–187 (*See also* Teenage parenthood; Teenage pregnancy)
Adoption Assistance and Child Welfare Act of 1980, 292
Advocacy, 261, 297, 298
AFDC (Aid to Families with Dependent Children), 220
Affluence, 309, 311–315
African Americans, 50, 104, 181–182, 183, 193 (*See also* Ethnicity)
"Age and stage" approach of child development, 102
Age-graded events, 117
Age integration, 324
Agent Orange, 110
Age segregation, 324
AIDS (acquired immunodeficiency syndrome), 108
Aid to Dependent Children (*See* Aid to Families with Dependent Children)
Aid to Families with Dependent Children (AFDC), 220, 245
Alcohol, 110
Alienation, 57
American Indians, 183, 184, 192–193 (*See also* Ethnicity)
Amniocentesis, 105–106

Anglo Americans, 183, 192, 197 (*See also* Ethnicity)
Anticoagulants, 109
Anticonvulsants, 109
Antidepressants, 109
Apathy-futility syndrome, 43
Asian Americans, 182 (*See also* Ethnicity)
Assault, 263, 265
Atomistic family, 76–77
Attachment, 114–115, 157–158
Attacks by strangers, 265
Authoritarian style of child rearing, 41–42, 159

Balanced power, 40–42
Bayley Scales of Infant Development, 102
Belgium, 163
Benedictin, 109
Berlin Wall, dismantling of, 27
Beyond IQ (Sternberg), 2
Birth control, 93–94
Birthing rooms, 135
"Blaming the victim," 280
Bonding, 137–139, 157
Boundaries, family, 81

Caffeine, 109, 110
California Achievement Test, 68
Caregiver, 265 (*See also* Parents)
CDF (Children's Defense Fund), 266–268
Center for the Study of Social Policy, 299–300
Cesarean delivery, 135, 144–145, 146
Cesarean-Support, Education, and Concern (C-SEC), 135
Charity, 242, 244–245
Chemical agents, 109–110
Child abuse, 67–68, 82–83, 153, 250 (*See also* Maltreatment; Violence)
Childbearing, 133–177
in Colonial period, 143–144

378